K

CHANGING REGULATORY INSTITUTIONS IN BRITAIN AND NORTH AMERICA

The world of regulatory institutions has been in a state of flux for the last two decades, and valuable lessons can be learned from a comparative focus on the nature and causes of institutional change and reform in the regulatory agencies and institutions of the United States, Canada, and Great Britain.

The contributing authors, mainly political scientists and legal scholars but also practising regulators, make the case for a much broader conceptual view of regulation, arguing that it is increasingly necessary for key regulatory interests – business and consumers – to understand regulation in terms of an interplay among four regimes: sectoral, framework, intra-cabinet, and international. They also explore inter-regime regulatory institutional relations through case studies to demonstrate how regulatory institutions respond to competing regulatory requirements and to tensions between sectoral utility regulators and competition and environmental regulators.

Other key comparisons among the three nations are drawn out through an examination of the independence and autonomy of regulators, implementation, economic governance, and different paths towards reform. The essential contrast studied shows that institutional change in the United Kingdom has been explicitly structural, and that a new 'regulatory state' has been more openly and fully rediscovered in that country, whereas change within federal structures such as the United States and Canada has tended to remain more intra-governmental.

The book seeks to provide students with a work that focuses on the political and institutional dimensions of regulation, to complement existing studies from the economic and legal perspective.

G. BRUCE DOERN is a professor of public administration at Carleton University, and Joint Chair in Public Policy in the Politics Department at Exeter University.

STEPHEN WILKS is a professor of politics at Exeter University.

OKANAGAN UNIVERSITY COLLEGE
LIBRARY
BRITISH COLUMBIA

EDITED BY G. BRUCE DOERN AND STEPHEN WILKS

Changing Regulatory Institutions in Britain and North America

UNIVERSITY OF TORONTO PRESS
Toronto Buffalo London

© University of Toronto Press Incorporated 1998
Toronto Buffalo London
Printed in Canada

ISBN 0-8020-4260-0 (cloth)
ISBN 0-8020-8100-2 (paper)

Printed on acid-free paper

Canadian Cataloguing in Publication Data

Main entry under title:

Changing regulatory institutions in Britain and North America

Includes bibliographical references.
ISBN 0-8020-4260-0 (bound)   ISBN 0-8020-8100-2 (pbk.)

1. Administrative agencies – Great Britain. 2. Administrative agencies – Canada. 3. Administrative agencies – United States. I. Doern, G. Bruce, 1942– . II. Wilks, Stephen.

HD3612.C42 1998   352.8   C98-931455-3

University of Toronto Press acknowledges the financial assistance to its publishing program of the Canada Council for the Arts and the Ontario Arts Council.

Contents

Preface

The examination of regulatory institutions is, in many ways, a new realm in the study of public policy and political economy in Britain and Europe. On the other side of the Atlantic, regulation has been a long-established feature of the intellectual landscape. Our purpose in this book is to lessen the distance between the old and new worlds of regulatory institutional analysis. Appropriately enough, the project emerges from a collaboration between a Canadian and a British political scientist, first in a joint project on comparative competition policy and later as colleagues at the University of Exeter and at Carleton University in Ottawa.

In conceiving this project, we were keen to undertake a conceptually grounded comparison, but also to anchor it in current empirical research and to expose material to the discerning eyes and minds of practising regulators. Accordingly, the majority of the chapters draw on current empirical work by leading specialists in their fields, and four of the chapters are written either by current regulatory practitioners (Booker and Locke) or by experts who are currently both practitioners and academics (Vass and Hill). Initial drafts of the chapters were presented at an international conference at the University of Exeter in April 1996. We were fortunate in securing the involvement of leading practitioners, including Tom Bass (Civil Aviation Authority), Chris Shapcott (National Audit Office), David Fisher (Monopolies and Mergers Commission), and Andrew Miller (Office of Telecommunications) in Britain; and Steve Harris (OECD), Val Traversy (Canadian Competition Bureau), and Allan Darling and David Colville (Canadian Radio-television and Telecommunications Commission) in Canada. Several prominent academics specializing in the field also acted as commentators, including Colin Scott (London School of Economics), Piotr Jasinski (University of Oxford), and Roland Sturm (University of Erlangen, Nuremberg). We are grateful to all these participants, who should be assured that their comments were well taken. Indeed, the debate on specific papers and on the general analytical questions and trends allowed us to revise the papers and also provided material for the cross-cutting chapters. The dialogue continued after the conference as papers were revised, and some of the chapters are able to take the debate up to Labour's victory in the British general election of May 1997 and to developments early in 1998. The Labour government's changes to the utility regulators directly were quite modest.

The maintenance of the status quo must, however, be seen in the context of a further, more recent development in the shape of a radical reconstruction of UK competition policy. A new competition bill, the most radical reform in forty years, was introduced immediately by Labour, based on earlier plans by the outgoing Conservative government, and became law in the autumn of 1998. It aligns UK law with European practice as seen in articles 85 and 86 of the Rome Treaty and subsequent case law. The UK will retain its existing agencies, including the Monopolies and Mergers Commision, which will be renamed and expanded into a new Competition Commission. The UK will also retain the complex and scale-monopoly provisions of the Fair Trading Act and the prevailing system of merger control, which will give it possibly the strongest antitrust regime in the world.

For the regulated utilities the startling element is the continuation of concurrent competition-law powers in the hands of the utility regulators as regards their industries. This means that the regulators (which will now be composed as executive boards of three members) will be able to apply prohibitions on European lines and impose substantial fines that can be appealed to the Competition Commission. At the same time, they will retain the power to refer mergers and price disputes to the commission. The utility companies have expressed concern about this substantial extension of competition powers, the impact of which will become clear only from 1999 onwards, as the regulators begin to apply them.

In revising the papers and developing the final book, we have been especially conscious of the need to relate this work to two kinds of readers. One is the general student of the politics of regulation who is seeking a reasonably orderly understanding of how regulatory institutions have changed in the three countries and of the nature of their key political features; the other is our fellow academics and practitioners in regulatory institutions, for whom we think the book can offer some new ways of visualizing the regulatory state of the late 1990s. The academic and practitioner readership for this book will tend to be centred in political science, public administration, and law, but we have also drawn where appropriate on the literature in economics and on the role that economists play in the design of regulatory institutions. We trust that both economists and students of business studies will find this volume a helpful complement to the more abstract regulatory theorizing or evaluation of business strategy.

As the title indicates, the book is grounded in the study of the 'institutions' of regulation in the United Kingdom, Canada, and the United States. Institutional approaches have become more influential in recent years, and in this context represent an important starting point in political science and public administration. But to be adequate, any study of regulation must be multidisciplinary. We have noted the importance of economics, and we are also fortunate to be able to include a legal approach, from Cosmo Graham, and one that stresses accountancy, from Peter Vass. In terms of the different countries under discussion, we have a good balance, with six British and six North American authors (three Canadian, three from the United States). While the majority of the authors have concentrated on economic regulation, we have also paid attention to the importance of 'horizontal' multi-industry regulation and of social and especially environmental regulation.

This enterprise would have been impossible without the generous financial assistance of several bodies, and we would like to thank the Economic and Social Research Council, the Social Sciences and Humanities Research Council of Canada, the Canadian Bureau of Competition Policy, Industry Canada, the Canadian Radio-television and Telecommunications Commission, and the Centre for the Study of Regulated Industries in London, who jointly sponsored the conference.

The other joint sponsors were the School of Public Administration at Carleton University and the Politics Department of the University of Exeter. We are extremely appreciative of the support of Darlene Zeleney and Virgil Duff at the University of Toronto Press. We also wish to thank *Canadian Public Administration* for permission to adapt an earlier journal article as major sections of Chapter 15.

It is not customary to dedicate edited volumes, but we would like to express our thanks to Joan and Philippa, whose patience and support really did make all the difference.

B.D. and S.W.
Ottawa, May 1998

CHANGING REGULATORY INSTITUTIONS IN BRITAIN AND NORTH AMERICA

1

Introduction

G. BRUCE DOERN AND STEPHEN WILKS

It is a timely point in history to undertake a conceptual and practical comparison of British and North American[1] regulatory institutions. In an era in which the United States has abolished the Interstate Commerce Commission, the first of its historic independent regulatory commissions, and in which the UK's newly created utility regulators are a significant political issue, a comparison can be helpful and instructive. Canadian regulatory change is also under way, with radical changes occurring in the transportation and telecommunications sectors, but with institutional reconfiguration being propelled equally by technological change, by the realities of budgetary cutbacks and the search for new compliance approaches, and by the imperatives of trade agreements such as the North American Free Trade Agreement (NAFTA).

Comparison in the regulatory fields between North America and the UK has clearly taken place, but has been rather sparsely represented in the academic literature. The more significant studies have included comparisons of environmental regulators in the United States and the United Kingdom (Vogel 1986); considerations of the relevance of North American 'capture theory' to other political and legal cultures (Hancher and Moran 1989); basic comparisons in selected sectors that have experienced recent privatization and deregulation initiatives (Richardson 1990; Hood 1994; Ayres and Braithwaite 1992); and a general sharing of approaches, especially among economists, on public utility regulation (Beesley 1994; 1995; Veljanovski 1991, 1993; Bishop, Kay, and Mayer 1995). Indeed, in the last of these realms of comparison, the designers of the UK approach to regulating the privatized utilities drew strong lessons from the weaknesses of the North American 'rate-of-return' approach and fashioned the 'price-capping' alternative used by regulators such as the Office of Telecommunications (OFTEL) (Bishop, Kay, and Mayer 1995; Crandall and Waverman 1995; Vass 1995).

A logical opening question is why the comparison should be limited to or focused on these three countries? In the case of the UK, is Europe not a more important comparative reference point? With respect to the first question, we concluded that the important shared features of Anglo–North American capitalism and the similarity of so many legal and political traditions made this a natural comparison. Canada and the UK share parliamentary forms of government, and Canada and the United States not only have in common federal systems of government and a similar regulatory history, but also share a very integrated North American economy. Our interest in paths to reform and learning also anchored the focus, because there is evidence of intellectual exchange and contact among practitioners in the three countries. As for the second question, although there is little doubt that Europe is institutionally more important for the UK than it has ever been before, a fact that is evident from the discussion in several of the chapters in this book, there is still a tendency in both Europe and the UK to avoid emulating each others' regulatory institutions (Majone 1996).

This book's contribution to the literature on national and comparative regulatory institutions is fourfold. First, it makes the case for a much broader conceptual definition of regulation, in part because regulatory institutional analysis requires it. Second, it argues the increasing necessity of viewing a nation's regulatory institutions as the result of an interplay among four regulatory regimes: sectoral, framework, management (for regulation within the state), and international. Third, it argues that, to understand contemporary regulatory institutional realities, we must broaden the way we view key regulatory interests, particularly those of business and consumers. Similarly, a broader view must be taken of the ideas that underpin the positions of these interests and the often particular or detailed reform ideas that have been articulated in recent years in the British and North American contexts. This is especially the case for such core interests as business and consumers, where more complex subsets of interests and ideas compete for political attention and influence. Fourth, by exploring inter-regime regulatory institutional relations through case studies, the book draws out more concretely how regulatory institutions respond to competing requirements.

These four focal points are the subject of this introductory chapter. In our concluding chapter we extend the analysis to a more particular examination of comparative regulatory reform by examining institutional issues such as the independence and autonomy of regulators, regulatory implementation, economic governance, and comparative paths to reform.

Broadening the Concept of Regulation and Regulatory Institutions

Almost inevitably one needs a broadened conceptual view of regulation and

TABLE 1.1 Definitions of regulation

- 'Governing' in an overall sense (including constitutions, statutes, regimes)
- A separate policy instrument distinct from taxation, spending, persuasion, and direct service provision
- Delegated legislation and related statutory instruments (orders, rules, guidelines, codes, or standards)
- An *output* of the state as opposed to an *outcome* or an implemented activity

regulatory institutions to analyse successfully the regulatory institutions of Britain and North America in the late 1990s. As Table 1.1 suggests, regulation can be defined in at least four ways, with many authors who specialize in the subject easily and necessarily slipping from one to the other. Often, this tendency results not from a lack of analytical rigour, but from the fact that regulation is a complex and densely interwoven activity (Baldwin and McCrudden 1987; Doern 1978; Meier 1985).

Regulation in its broadest definitional sense is often equated with *governing*, and in this sense it is broadly an amalgam of ways in which public purposes are authoritatively decided on and implemented. Accordingly, it is linked to democratic values and processes of a most profound and fundamental kind (Pildes and Sunstein 1995). This broad view extends the definition of regulation to statute law and beyond that to constitutional provisions, such as the division of powers between levels of government in a federal constitution and the rules on the separation of powers between executive bodies, legislatures, and the courts.

Regulation is also defined as a particular and separate *policy instrument*, where it is distinguished from other instruments such as exhortation, spending, taxation, or the direct delivery of services (Linder and Peters 1989; Hood 1986; Trebilcock et al. 1982). Regulation is, in this instrumental sense, a rule of behaviour backed by the sanctions of the state. This definition may narrow the analytical terrain, but it does not solve the practical analytical problems that arise when real situations are studied or when regulators talk about what they are actually doing (Byatt 1995; Wilson 1980; Doern 1978; Ratushny 1987).

Finally, regulation is often defined to encompass only *delegated legislation*, or rules that are made pursuant to powers granted in a parent statute (Ogus 1994; Law Reform Commission 1986). This more limited view of regulation as delegated legislation or as 'the regs' may or may not include such other rule-like creations as the promulgation of guidelines, codes, rules of procedure, and voluntary codes (Grabosky 1995).

In all three of these notions of regulation there is a sense in which it is seen as

TABLE 1.2 Conceptual views of institutions

- As an entrenched set of values and rules structured through an organization and constrained internally and externally
- As historical constructs
- As systems of veto points and constrained realms of power
- As systems of individual preferences and incentives

an *output* of government or of the state. These definitions do not necessarily allow us to deal with the *outcomes* or impact of regulation. The world that is the product of regulatory implementation, compliance, enforcement, non-compliance, symbolic regulation, and other outcomes is an even denser and more complex one (Grabosky 1995; Sparrow 1994).

These varied and broadened definitions of regulation are a central part of institutional analysis because they indicate in and of themselves how difficult it is to tell whether regulation is contracting, expanding, or being reconfigured. Does one count only 'the regs,' or should statutes be considered as well? How can one regulatory output be weighed relative to others? Should compliance costs be the norm and be set against the benefits that are actually achieved? (If so, the range of costs calculated can vary enormously.) These are among the analytical problems raised in dealing with the underlying tendency in political debate to refer to the last two decades as an era of 'deregulation' despite the fact that studies show that regulation has in fact increased (Mihlar 1996; *Economist* 1996).

A compelling reason for the need for definitional breadth is the importance of recognizing that these boundary problems exist within countries but that they are even more endemic in cross-country and cross-regional comparison. Different national legal traditions and systems of law are of no small import (Susskind and McMahon 1985; Baldwin 1995a). Moreover, both regulatory analysts and practitioners always face the practical problem of their own more limited knowledge of the second, third, or fourth countries they are trying to compare or interact with. It is also important to recognize that there does not exist an analytical quick fix for the boundary issues. No regulatory analyst can solve the dilemma in any fully convincing sense (Vogel 1996).

The definitional boundaries are also an important starting point because they are inherent in dealing with how we conceptualize regulatory institutions. Table 1.2 suggests a few of the possibilities.

Regulatory institutions are institutions that regulate, but in which of the above senses do they do so? How institutions are analytically visualized is also important, and this book is very much centred on an institutionalist focus. As a political institution, a regulatory body can be thought of as an entrenched set of values or rules, and hence it is structured by the external and internal constraints of the organization or body involved (March and Olsen 1989; Ostrom 1990). But institutions are also historical constructs. Early formative choices have a pervasive influence over later decisions. Regulatory bodies can and do change but not without overcoming these internal features, which may be seen as valuable by some interests and as sources of inertia by others (Weaver and Rockman 1993; March and Olsen 1989). Even structuralist conceptualizations of regulatory institutions exist that highlight more fundamental veto points or constraints on how subsets of public policy are made or are allowed to be made (Searing 1991).

While the focus of the book is on a broad understanding of institutions that is centred in political science and public administration and in the applied world of regulatory practitioners, we also have a dual interest in how economists view regulatory institutions. First, economists are of interest as members of a cognate academic discipline that views institutions differently and with a particular aim towards achieving efficient economic outcomes. Second, economists have quite explicitly influenced the design and reform of regulatory institutions because they have been open advocates of change. This is the case in areas such as rate-of-return versus price-cap approaches, the institutionalized use of cost-benefit analysis in regulatory analysis processes within the state, the insistence on comparative competition 'league tables,' where more than one supplier is available, and the preferred use of 'performance' rather than 'design' approaches in health,safety, and environmental regulation (Jacobs 1995; Doern 1990).

Institutional analysis by economists has tended to focus on institutions as aggregates of individual preferences. Hence the reform of regulators and regulations is seen to turn on either getting rid of unproductive rules or on redesigning them with the appropriate new mix of incentives that will produce more efficient outcomes (Ogus 1994). A holistic notion of institutions as prior or larger sets of beliefs or views of the public interest tends to be eschewed; indeed, it is a suspect concept among mainstream economists.

There are, however, more recent strands of institutional analysis by economists that are broader and more in line with how political scientists and many practitioners have always seen institutions, including regulatory institutions (North 1990; de la Mothe and Paquet 1996). In short, they focus on a more historical evolutionary form of economics, analyse systems of trust and cooperation, and seek to locate the core structure of regulatory incentives in larger sets of often crucial kinds of 'institutional endowment and regulatory governance' (Levy and Spiller 1996).

Four Regulatory Regimes and National Regulatory Institutional Portraits

The second focal point in the book is our view that national regulatory institutions must be increasingly examined in the context of an interplay among four regimes. Chapter 2 examines these four regimes: Regime I, the immediate regime of the sectoral (utility or monopoly) regulator; Regime II, the horizontal framework regulatory regime (including mechanisms for dealing with competition, environment, social or health and safety, intellectual-property, and consumer-protection issues); Regime III, the overall governmental-executive regime for managing regulation within the state, including regulatory priority setting; and Regime IV, the international regime, embracing global, regional, and bilateral approaches based on rules or on de facto co-decision making by national or international bodies. A regime is understood for analytical purposes to be an interacting set of organizations, statutes, ideas, interests, or processes. The first test for the existence of a regime is the presence of some inner core of shared norms, features, or characteristics that warrant such a designation for analytical and practical purposes.

The subsequent portraits of national institutional regulatory change in chapters 3, 4, and 5 can be located within this broad framework. Thus the chapters by Peters, Hogwood, and Schultz and Doern supply the foundational national institutional portraits for the United States, Britain, and Canada, respectively. However, in each case the chapters cover only part of the full panoply of the national institutional mix. Thus they must be looked at with regard not only to what they include but also to what they exclude.

Looking at the United States, Peters sees a broad and arguably irreversible trend towards deregulation. He portrays a general 'deinstitutionalization' of older Progressive and Depression era assumptions about regulation, and their replacement (i.e., in a process of 'institutionalization') by ideas, analysis, and decision-making processes that tend to question regulation and to promote deregulation. In other words, deregulation has not just *occurred*, it has been pervasively institutionalized in the decision-making approaches of all three branches of the U.S. government and in the approaches of major interest groups (McGarity 1991). There may well be some areas of regulation where this institutionalizing trend does not apply as readily, but the overall trend is seen by Peters as having been clearly established.

Peters also argues that the United States has witnessed only limited structural change but has internalized major changes within institutions, not only in the realm of ideas sceptical of regulation but also in such changes as the greater use of non-career appointments to regulatory bodies and the institutionalization of the economics and law establishments into public organizations.

In addition to an ideology favouring deregulation, Peters draws attention to two other ideas that have gained curency; that of 'empowering' citizens as consumers, especially regarding their own decisions about risk, and that of 'regulatory takings.' The former is also linked to pressures for more compliance-oriented cooperative approaches to implementing federal regulations (Michael 1996). The latter is centred on the 'takings clause' of the Fifth Amendment of the U.S. Constitution, which states that private property shall not be taken for public use without just compensation (Fischel 1995; Tiefer 1996). In recent years the U.S. Supreme Court, in the area of local land-use restrictions, has increased the rights of property holders. The same has not been the case for those affected by federal regulatory agency actions. Pressure in the Republican-controlled Congress has reached the point where legislation has been introduced for a takings bill that would not only require more federal compensation for the negative impacts of regulation, but also provide for the compensation being taken directly out of the budget of the regulatory agency rather than out of the larger governmental budget (Tiefer 1996).

The chapter by Schultz and Doern on Canadian regulatory institutions focuses more on three key national *sectoral* or Regime I regulators in the transportation, energy, and broadcasting-telecommunications fields. The chapter demonstrates that in the early part of the twentieth century Canadian and U.S. sectoral regulatory institutions were quite similar in being conceived for minimalist 'policing' purposes. It shows how this was followed, from the 1930s to about the end of the 1960s, by a significant Canadian departure. During this phase the core Canadian sectoral regulators became virtual 'governments in miniature,' in that the regulatory institutions were given broad ranges of functions, powers, and policy instruments that went well beyond narrowly defined regulation. They possessed a mix of functions that included regulation-making, licensing, adjudicative, quasi-judicial, subsidy-spending, policy-making, and policy advisory and monitoring roles. Over this period as a whole they were cast in various ways as planning and nation-building structures overseeing sectoral markets that typically included one major crown corporation (or state enterprise) and other private-sector firms. The regulatory bodies were also multi-member commissions to ensure reasonable forms of regional and other representation in their deliberations and decisions.

This basic Canadian portrait goes on to show how an institutional transformation in the last two decades has occurred. There has been a significant diminution of the status of governments in miniature, especially for the transportation and energy regulators but less so for the telecommunications regulator. The causes of this overall transformation in the 1980s and 1990s cannot be attributed simply to a U.S.-style liberalized deregulation impulse. It was also the result of institutional factors, namely the actions of the Canadian Cabinet, which wanted to reclaim policy-making powers as a matter of both principle and power (Doern et al. 1998).

The portrait by Hogwood of the regulatory institutions in the UK is bound to be quite different from that for the North American countries. The key difference is that although Britain has been transformed by a pro-market and neo-Conservative ideology, centred initially on privatization initiatives, it also had vastly to increase regulation, and even quite literally to discover or rediscover a full-blown 'regulatory state.' While Hogwood's chapter focuses on the 'new regulatory state' of Thatcher and Major, which consists, in essence, of the sectoral utility regulators established in the last decade, he wisely does so in the larger context of an analysis of the myriad administrative forms in which regulators have been cast for decades. British authors have long recognized, of course, that the state rules, governs, and regulates, but this has not been seen in the context of a 'regulatory state' in same way as in the United States and Canada (Baldwin 1995b). The basic nature of British law and institutions also favoured an informal constitution, considerable ministerial discretion, and broad statutory drafting, and it left much less room for formally identified delegated legislation and statutory instruments (Ogus 1994).

This account also illustrates two other key features of macro-regulatory institutional change in the UK. First, the set of utility regulators was, from the outset, given mixed sectoral and competition framework regulatory roles. For the North American sectoral regulators, created much earlier, this mixed framework only recently has become an imperfectly acquired habit. For the UK regulators, it was a matter of design from the very beginning. Second, unlike Canada and the United States, there has indeed been overt structural change in the UK. New regulators and regulatory bodies appeared and became nationally known to a remarkable degree. Moreover, Britain favoured the particular institutional mode of the single regulator, a statutory person, instead of the collective commission-style institutions found in the sectoral regulators of the United States and Canada (Department of Trade and Industry 1998; European Public Policy Forum 1996; National Audit Office 1996).

However, Hogwood goes on to show that the need for an expanded regulatory state in the UK goes well beyond the new utility sector regulators. To a far greater degree than either the United States or Canada, the UK has also recast its entire structure of executive government through the 'Next Steps' executive agency reforms, through the adoption of the Citizen's Charter, and through the adoption of quasi-markets in the delivery of social services. These initiatives seek to separate policy from delivery and, importantly, funders from providers. Precisely because they are *quasi*-markets and not full markets, they require major new areas where the state regulates the state as well as private suppliers or services (Walsh 1995; Hood and Scott 1996). And all of this is occurring and is being *seen* to occur at the national level in a unitary state.

Thus it cannot be said that the UK has entered a deregulatory phase in any overall North American sense of that concept. To this purely domestic picture, one must add the looming reality of European and European Union influences (Begg 1996; Majone 1996). Any institutional portrait for the UK must also include the mixed domestic and European regulatory realms of social and environmental regulation. The 1996–7 debacle over bovine spongiform encephalopathy (BSE) in cattle and the related issues of regulating the health and safety of food brought to the forefront strong support for strengthened social regulation and the need for the regulator to be independent of the agriculture department. It thus raised the issue of the extent to which the Conservative government of John Major had given preferred treatment to the interests of agricultural producers over those of consumers.

Influences on Reform: Interests and Ideas

The third aim of the book, reflected mainly in chapters 6 through 10, is to draw out several recent influences on regulatory reform through both an analysis of key interests – party politics, business, and consumers – and an examination of more specific ideas.

Party Politics

In one sense the superstructure of interests is centred in partisan politics and party representation. In the recent UK setting, the partisan forces are important because the array of utility regulators was created in the wake of a massive privatization program that was intended not only to increase the role of markets but also to establish a Thatcherite share-owning society (Veljanovski 1991, 1993). Thus, despite the provisions in UK regulatory laws that sought to balance the interests of producers and consumers, the political impetus was clearly towards making the great partisan project succeed. The structure of power therefore strongly tilted the set of regulatory institutions in a pro-business direction (Ernst 1994). This in turn produced a partial partisan counter-reaction from the Labour Party, largely against the alleged excessive returns to producers, especially executives of the privatized utilities. There is no intention in the Blair Labour government to renationalize the utilities but there is a political concern that the scales need to be rebalanced in favour of consumers. Indeed, the Labour government's discussion paper on the utility regulators was titled *A Fair Deal for Consumers* (Department of Trade and Industry 1998).

This rebalancing has centred on the Labour government's plan to impose a windfall tax on the privatized utilities, a plan ostensibly linked to raising money for job creation and training in a time of tight fiscal constraint. The tax was imposed and it raised £5.2 million, with the bulk borne by the water and electricity companies. However, the Labour government's discussion paper proposals on regulatory institutions are quite mild (Department of Trade and Industry 1998). These proposals include ideas to supplement the one-person regulator system adopted in the UK with either a statutory advisory group or a small executive board or commission. Other reforms relate broadly to enhancing transparency and increasing ministerial guidance in limited spheres of regulation. Thus, except for the windfall tax, the utility regulatory institutions have actually received a considerable level of support from the main political parties.

In all of the above, it is worthwhile remembering that the Thatcherite privatizations in fact only brought the size of the UK nationalized state down closer to the level that the two North American countries were *already* at. This is even true of Canada, which had a larger state-owned sector than the United States but a much smaller one than the UK (Tupper and Doern 1988; Richardson 1990). And, of course, the United States and Canada had long before created their sectoral utility regulators (Bernstein 1955; Doern 1978; Eisner 1993).

Accordingly, in the United States and Canada the degree of partisan controversy is much less evident and is not focused on one large structural creation as in the UK. There are some partisan differences to be sure. The Clinton Democrats have made a political issue over environmental regulation, accusing the Republican-led Congress of rolling back previous environmental gains (Campbell and Rockman 1996). The Democrats have also made the regulation of the tobacco industry a partisan matter. But this partisanship must be seen against a backdrop of basically bi-partisan support for efforts to tame the *federal* regulatory state as a whole.

In Canada the Mulroney Conservative government from 1984 to 1993 was undoubtedly a more ardent deregulator and reformer than the then Liberal Party opposition, but since taking power in 1993 the Chrétien Liberal government has adopted as its own most of the Conservative regulatory reform agenda (Doern et al. 1998).

Business Interests

It is impossible to assess, in a single edited volume, the influence of business interests in the regulatory process in three countries, and across several regulatory sectors. However, some important issues and changes can be examined. The chapter by Wilks focuses on some aspects of the nature of the regulated corporation, and several other chapters raise issues about business interests and their strategies towards different kinds of regulation and regulators.

The chapter by Wilks examines utility regulation in the UK through a focus on the creature being regulated, the large company, and its varied relationships with the regulator and with financial markets and institutions. Wilks explores a number of issues of accountability when the basis of accountability is extended beyond that of fundamental regulator–firm relations to the realm of corporate governance, including corporate social responsibility, with essential services being delivered through the regulated firm. He stresses the particular and disproportionate influence of financial markets in this larger view of regulatory regimes, and advocates the need for a reform agenda that rebalances interests to reflect the very real consumer and social aspects of utility regulation as a whole. Through particular reference to electricity regulation, Wilks also shows how regulators increasingly find themselves dealing with a rapidly changing set of targets as companies merge or are taken over by other utilities. In addition, the chapter explores the many bases on which companies might cooperate with the regulator and the related ways in which the regulator needs and is dependent on the firms.

Perhaps because of the overt nature of institutional change in the regulated utility sector in the UK, it is the country that most exhibits a debate about business interests and power. While, as we have seen, some of this debate centres on real and alleged business greed, in the whole utility sector the role of business interests is often very subtle and complex, and of course it varies by sector and by the degree of evolution since privatization (e.g., telecommunication companies versus railways).

The system of periodic price reviews and the concentration of action on amending the licences of regulated firms rather than on general regulation making also ensure a focus on the regulated firms. The politics of business thus varies enormously across the utility sectors of the UK, if only because of the underlying structure of markets and the different degrees of competition arranged at the moment of privatization. For the Office of Telecommunications (OFTEL), and the telecommunications sector, the dominant political reality is the market dominance of British Telecom (BT). But in other product and service markets in the telecommunications sector, the regulator must deal with, and listen to, a wide variety of new firms that seem to appear almost daily.

The contrast in the UK between the regulatory politics of the business of the water and the telecommunications sectors is in some respects stark. The Office of Water Services (OFWAT) has to deal with thirty-one water companies and ten sewage disposers, and hence there has been a more explicit reliance on the concept of 'comparative competition,' centred on the use of league tables and other yardsticks. Moreover, OFWAT's institutional logic is driven by a regulatory formula that contains not only RPI-X (price index minus an efficiency requirement) but also a +K or +Q factor that stands for the cost of quality of the water supplied, which is, hence, an environmental regulatory component. The relationship of firms with OFWAT is intensive, and centres partly on the submission of strategic business plans (Byatt 1995, 23) and detailed information. The regulatory system has been referred to as 'mandatory schizophrenia' by the director of the lobby group for the water companies, the Water Services Association (Langdon 1995, 41), with the water companies seen as service providers but also contractees for environmental regulations set largely outside OFWAT.

Obviously, the business politics of regulation is partly sectoral politics. But an overall trend across the three countries is that business politics is far more complex than in earlier decades, and that business interests seek out varied regulatory and political arenas (e.g., competition versus sectoral regulators, the Cabinet, the courts, and legislatures) both to liberalize markets and to seek new kinds of protection, subtle or otherwise. Another change is simply that there are more firms and generally more competition in the three economies as a whole, including the greatly increased presence of foreign-owned firms in national markets that are applying pressure on national regulators. This broader dynamic resonates in all regulated sectors. In addition, the policy communities in regulated sectors contain better organized interests and often powerful individual firms that are the *users* of regulated services. Thus, for example, the banks are major telecommunications users. Transportation regulation and deregulation in North America has been profoundly influenced by well organized user-group lobbies.

A further factor of importance is that big-business lobbies in general have focused key parts of their 'regulatory' fire at the international level and have led the way in advocating free-trade agreements, whose regulatory and deregulatory predispositions then feed their way back into domestic change. And finally, the small-business lobby, an especially active force in Canada and the United States, has worked hard and often successfully to have deregulation cast as the elimination of red tape and the paper burden of government. This lobbying is partly a direct one by small-business assciations but, as the chapter by Hill shows, it is also carried out for them by industry and trade departments, which are among the chief internal advocates of regulatory reform based on assessing regulation through requirements for competiveness analysis and 'flexibility' criteria. The small-business lobby is thus an important special source of change, arguing for better overall ways of managing, reducing, and refining the regulatory state as a whole.

Consumer Interests

Like business interests, consumer interests also need to be modelled in a broader way. Stephen Locke's chapter is insightful in this regard, and, though focused on UK consumer interests, has wider comparative relevance. Tracing the arrival of the late-1960s consumer-policy era, Locke describes the national and international emergence of core consumer principles such as choice, information provision, safety, and the right to be heard that found expression in consumer-protection laws and regulations. He also illustrates the more recent broadening of consumer-related policies, regulations, and guidelines as revealed through competition policy, international trade, citizen–consumer interests in public-service delivery (e.g., the Citizen's Charter), and, not least in the UK case, the new utility regulatory regime where consumer interests related to principles of access and universal service are crucial.

All of this leads Locke to conclude that there is an ever broadening and more complex set of consumer interests and thus potentially more conflict among various classes of consumers not only in general markets but also in regulated utility markets. Thus there are trade-offs and conflicts between the economic interests of consumers and their interest in safety, between general consumers and subsets of consumers (low income, aged, vulnerable, regional, isolated), and between current and future consumers. The encouragement of quasi-markets and the viewing of citizens as public-service 'customers' does not solve the main issues, where citizens are more citizens than consumers and have views about the efficacy of regulations in areas as diverse as gun control, abortion, and environmental pollution (Eisner, Worsham, and Ringquist 1996; Hood 1986).

When applied to UK utility regulators, Locke sees a mixed result for consumer interests and their involvement. In an overall sense he agrees that there is more choice and lower prices in several sectors. In other respects he sees considerable variation in the degree to which the regulators embrace and seek out consumer views as a counterweight to business power. First, statutory consumer-related goals and mandates vary considerably among the utility regulators. Second, some regulators such as OFTEL have gone out of their way to engage and institutionalize consumer interests, while others are far less aggressive. Third, some issues that regulators face (e.g., OFWAT and water quality) are simply not resolvable through consumer-interest involvement as such because they involve citizen and other forms of political representation.

A North American observer of the utility regime in the UK is struck by the array of specific consumer-centred institutions appended to it (National Audit Office 1996; Ogden and Anderson 1995; Devon County Council and Department of Trading Standards and Consumer Protection 1996). These include various national and regional committees, some of which are appointed by the regulator rather than by the minister (European Public Policy Forum 1997; National Audit Office 1996). The Consumers Association, the UK's private-sector consumer interest group, also seems more robust than its North American counterparts, while the state-funded National Consumer's Council manages to maintain considerable independence.

A key question here is whether this institutional apparatus is a sign of weakness or strength. On the one hand, it might be argued that if underlying UK markets were more competitive, the presence of consumers would be felt simply in their capacity to buy, sell, and make choices. It would not have to be made evident through institutional voice. On the other hand, consumer interests may be more buoyantly visible in the UK in part because the single-regulator model causes regulators to reach out to consumer groups to garner increased legitimacy and support for their own roles. OFTEL may be an example of this, not only because its defined statutory powers are somewhat vague but also because it operates in the one realm where markets are changing so fast that the regulator simply must keep talking to, and consulting with, various consumers.

The North American consumer-interest equation for regulatory institutions has some differences. In Canada the main national consumer association that used to be the main champion before Canadian utility regulators has never been weaker (Schultz 1998). Some of the decline has been caused by festering conflicts among classes of consumers and by reductions in direct state funding of national consumer groups in regulatory interventions. But its overall weakness may also be due to the fact that larger pro-consumer institutional changes have occurred, thus diversifying the voices of consumers in important ways. These changes include the greater voice of business user groups and the free-trade agreements of the last decade (FTA and NAFTA), but also specific areas of deregulation (Hadfield, Howse, and Trebilcock 1996). The advent of the Internet, e-mail, and faxes has also increased the capacity of subsets of consumers to mobilize without the need for comprehensive consumer associations.

In North America special reference must also be made to consumer roles related to the handling of consumer grievances against utility regulators and regulated firms and service providers or both. Some of this is activity is still directly handled by sectoral regulators, but there has been a trend towards having more of it carried out by industry associations and coalitions of interest groups through devices such as voluntary codes (Cohen and Webb 1998). Budget cuts and requirements for user-fee funding of regulatory activities have also promoted this development.

The situation regarding consumers in the United States is of an institutional magnitude far greater than in the United Kingdom or Canada. Not only has the United States simply had a more market-oriented competitive economy, it has also had over the decades far stronger competition laws that are themselves, in a very real sense, core pro-consumer institutions (Eisner 1991; McChesney and Shuggart 1995; Doern and Wilks 1996). But above all, the United States has far greater institutional bases for private legal action, aided by provisions for treble damages and class actions. It also possesses a larger and more aggressive legal profession.

The Influence of Ideas and Reforms

A different set of influences and ideas on reform is examined in Margaret Hill's analysis in Chapter 8, which compares British and North American regulation in the context of policy learning. Set against the undoubted fact that UK regulatory institutions are partly different from their North American counterparts, the chapter looks both at academic and theoretical traditions and at practitioner concerns and exchange in the overall Anglo–North American setting. In assessing academic theory, she finds common ground in the use of private-interest theories of regulation and, more recently, agency theory in regulatory analysis. However, she sees much less use of theories of policy-instrument choice, with the latter scarcely even seen in UK analyses. This difference is perhaps also reflected in the far greater attention among practitioners in the United States and Canada to the problems of how to manage regulation as a whole in executive government. The North American penchant for devising different cross-governmental processes and criteria for assessing regulation (competitiveness, flexibility, and incentives, but also charters of rights) is far less evident in the UK, though by no means totally absent (Jacobs 1995). These issues will be examined further in the conclusions to the book.

In a different way, Francis in Chapter 9 emphasizes other combinations of interests and ideas as being influential, especially in social regulation. He examines key examples of resurgent regulation in the United States and, importantly, attributes it to two overall causes that focus not on regulatory bodies as such but instead on interests and the marshalling power of interacting ideas and on the preference for state-level action rather than federal action. With regard to interests, Francis sees the coalitions that form around social regulation as being significantly separate from, and broader than, those that might favour sectoral deregulation and competition. With respect to ideas, Francis sees a staying power arising out of the *combinations* of ideas that are mobilized, including appeals to fairness, environmental integrity, local control, and, yes, 'the public interest.'

The analysis by Vass in Chapter 10 discusses some aspects of analytical and technical reform in the UK utility regulators. He is basically laudatory about the central features of the utility sector. It is seen by him as having been designed to be a partially converged system of sectoral monopoly and competition regulation. Vass sees room for reforms centred on the idea of greater transparency in the system as a whole and on some greater technical improvements such as in assessing the cost of capital across sectors by the various regulators. He also sees a form of ultimate political litmus test in his view that the Labour Party, despite its criticisms, will only change the system marginally.

Sectoral versus Framework Regulators: Converging and Colliding Regimes

The final focal point in the book flows from our earlier identification of the four regimes of regulation. It suggests the growing importance of understanding particular inter-regime relationships and dynamics. Chapters 11 to 15 provide case studies and analyses of some of these relationships. Given the suggested framework of four regimes, many permutations and combinations of relationships are possible. The focus in the final part of the book tends to be on the relations between sectoral and framework regulators, but other dynamics also emerge in the individual case studies in the water environmental fields and in telecommunications and competition regulation.

Underpinning the analysis is an examination in Chapter 11 of the development in the United Kingdom, Canada, and the United States of some basic institutional mechanisms for managing relations among regulatory regimes, especially sectoral versus framework regulatory regimes. The four mechanisms are: (1) advocacy and representation rights of the competition regulator in the proceedings of the sectoral regulator; (2) 'regulated conduct' defence doctrines and concepts of regulatory forbearance; (3) mechanisms of appeal by firms from the sectoral regulator's decisions to competition regulators; and (4) private legal action. While these imply that the mechanisms are the creations of the state, the analysis also shows that the issue of who or which institutions get to manage or control the changing relationships is intensely political and increasingly complex. In an era of change, especially in some sectors, private interests in particular are less and less likely to cede these vital tasks to the state alone.

In his analysis in Chapter 12 of OFWAT and environmental regulation, Booker brings a practitioner's perspective to the close interactions involved in inter-regime relations. He traces the four regimes as they impinge on OFWAT, but the focus of his chapter is on the concrete example of the 'Cost of Quality' environmental case study. The regulation of water companies quickly converged on how to deal with, and factor in, the environmental costs (and benefits) of water quality. The process centred on a quite elaborate quadripartite machinery of discussion and negotiation involving OFWAT, the then existing National Rivers Authority, the Department of the Environment, and the companies. Also looming in the background were EU directives on water and pollution.

Booker sees the cost of quality regulatory process as having crucial features of transparency, which forced the debate and inter-regime trade-offs into a public domain more successfully than in earlier pre-OFWAT eras. However, he also sees the process as having features that were necessarily private and behind-the-scenes to protect aspects of commercial privilege, including the need by firms to attract capital. Booker reserves his greatest criticism of the larger inter-regime process to its European and EU aspects. It remains too random and disconnected to the basic regulatory cycle in the UK, and, moreover, EU regulatory processes are less informed by requirements to use cost-benefit analysis in deciding on regulatory standards and quality.

Hoberg's analysis in Chapter 13 of U.S. and Canadian environmental regulation also sees the relative staying power of environmental regulation. Hoberg observes differences between the two countries arising out of normal features of their respective Cabinet versus Congressional systems of government, but he also stresses the common development in both countries regarding the structure of interest involvement in the regulatory process. Over the last fifteen years, regulation has moved from being a bipartite process between business and environmental regulators to a multi-partite process involving environmental non-governmental organizations in more complex stakeholder relationships of power.

If regimes are converging in these larger North American environmental settings, Hoberg sees this trend occurring especially at the level of implementation and compliance. More economically sensitive approaches to compliance are viewed as emerging, but they are always tenaciously and suspiciously watched by environmental and social groups and policy communities.

The nature of the inter-regime dynamics clearly changes in the chapters on OFTEL by Graham and on the Canadian Radio-television and Telecommunications Commission (CRTC) by Doern. OFTEL is examined as a mixed sectoral and competition regulator; however, the crucial sectoral difference is that the sector is characterized by arguably the most dynamic competitive changes in terms of technological and product development. But at the same time, the crucial regulatory relationship is with BT. Graham traces the internal tensions in the political economy of OFTEL and in its links with other regulatory bodies, including the Monopolies and Mergers Commission but also the Department of

Trade and Industry where many of the key trade-offs still ultimately reside, especially in terms of the transition politics between the telephone and cable companies. Graham also questions whether the trend will be towards an expanded role for general competition regulators. Rather, there are strengths in having the sectoral regulator as the competition regulator who knows the sector and has the expertise to deal with it. He is also far more inclined than other recent commentators on the UK telecommunications regulatory system to characterize OFTEL as a social regulator and to pay full attention to the universal-service aspects of its mandate.

Doern's analysis of the CRTC focuses first on the broad mandate of the Canadian regulator. Unlike OFTEL, it is both a broadcasting and telecommunications regulator, and hence the underlying tensions in the technological conversion of the two industries are more intensely located within the CRTC but not exclusively so. Two parent ministries also tussle over the spoils of jurisdiction and rapid change. The CRTC is evolving towards a more mixed sectoral and competition regulatory role, but this has clearly not been a feature designed from the outset. Moreover, the CRTC has a range of powers that goes well beyond an ability to amend licences.

The CRTC's collective commission form of organization and its acquired and largely positive reputation as a forum for hearings and public debate also mean that it is continually brought into many related aspects of social regulation and of the content of broadcasting. At the same time, however, Doern casts the CRTC as having to regulate 'on the run,' beset by new competitive forces and more complex interests, and having to work out new accommodations both with Canadian competition regulators and with rapidly changing international and U.S. developments.

Conclusions

This chapter has highlighted the four main conceptual focal points of the book. First, comparative regulatory analysis across the Anglo–North American divide requires a broadened definitional base that closely approximates the changing situations that regulators actually must deal with in complex political-economic settings. Second, national regulatory institutions must increasingly be viewed in the context of an interplay between four regulatory regimes: sectoral, framework, intra-cabinet and executive within the state, and international. Third, influences on comparative reform must be cast in a broadened view of how key interests, particularly those of business and consumers, are visualized and how reform ideas are brought to the field of regulation. Fourth, it is increasingly necessary to examine specific mechanisms for handling relationships between regimes, particularly between sectoral and framework regulatory regimes.

Because of these focal points, we stress the need to be cautious about how regulation is fundamentally viewed in the different political and legal settings. This is perhaps especially necessary in a situation like that in the UK, which is more openly and fully discovering or, more accurately, rediscovering a regulatory state despite decades of regulation in many fields. In comparing across the three countries, we argue for greater breadth in how regulatory institutions are initially mapped. This has prompted our identification of four regulatory regimes, both to understand them separately and then, almost immediately, to see where they are converging and colliding with each other.

With respect to change in the three countries, perhaps the dominant one is in the UK regulatory institutional setting, where it has been very explicitly structural, with new institutions actually created, but where it still functions in the larger historical ambit of traditional British institutions. In both Canada and the United States, with their utility sectors having evolved over a longer period and functioning in a federal state, change has been more intra-institutional and with less overt structural change.

When the influences of interests and ideas on reform are brought in, the main conclusion is that the nature of interests among business and consumers is vastly more complex and varied in the fast-changing global economy of the late 1990s than it was in earlier economic and regulatory eras. Consumer interests break down into more subsets of interests, and, equally, the business politics of regulation in the three countries exhibit more differentiated interests and strategies among regulated utility and user firms, small businesses and big businesses, and the far greater number of foreign firms operating in domestic markets.

There are further important aspects of regulatory institutional comparison and analysis that we take up in the concluding chapter. These include issues of regulatory independence, implementation, economic governance, and the general nature of paths to reform.

NOTE

1 A North American focus should include Mexico, especially under NAFTA. An examination of Mexican regulatory institutions, however, is not a part of this book.

REFERENCES

Ayres, Ian, and John Braithwaite. 1992. *Responsive Regulation: Transcending the Deregulation Debate*. Oxford: Oxford University Press.

Baldwin, Robert B., ed. 1995a. *Regulation in Question: The Growing Agenda.* London: Law Department, London School of Economics and Political Science.
– 1995b. *Rules and Government.* Oxford: Clarendon Press.
Baldwin, R., and C. McCrudden. 1987. *Regulation and Public Law.* London: Wiedenfeld and Nicolson.
Beesely, M.E., ed. 1994. *Regulating Utilities: The Way Forward.* London: Institute of Economic Affairs.
– ed. 1995. *Utility Regulation: Challenge and Response.* London: Institute of Economic Affairs.
Begg, Iain. 1996. 'Regulation in the European Union.' *Journal of European Public Policy* 3, no. 4: pp. 525–35.
Bernstein, Marver. 1955. *Regulating Business by Independent Commission.* Princeton: Princeton University Press.
Bishop, Mathew, John Kay, and Colin Mayer, eds. 1995. *The Regulatory Challenge.* Oxford: Oxford University Press.
Byatt, Ian. 1995. 'The Importance of Process in Economic Regulation.' In *The Water Industry: Looking Forward from the Periodic Review.* London: Centre for the Study of Regulated Industries.
Campbell, Colin, and Bert A. Rockman, eds. 1996. *The Clinton Presidency: First Appraisals.* Chatham: Chatham House.
Cohen, D., and K. Webb, eds. 1998. *The Role of Voluntary Codes.* Ottawa: Government of Canada.
Corry, Dan. 1995. *Profiting from the Utilities.* London: Institute for Policy Research.
Crandall, R.W., and L. Waverman. 1995. *Talk Is Cheap: The Promise of Reguatory Reform in North American Telecommunications.* Washington: The Brookings Institution.
de la Mothe, John, and Gilles Paquet, eds. 1996. *Evolutionary Economics and the New International Political Economy.* London: Pinter.
Department of Trade and Industry. 1998. *A Fair Deal for Consumers.* Cmnd 3898. London: HMSO.
Devon County Council and Department of Trading Standards and Consumer Protection. 1996. *Off Who? What? Where? A Review of the Utility Regulators' Role in Protecting the Interests of Consumers.* Exeter: Devon County Council.
Doern, G. Bruce, ed. 1978. *The Regulatory Process in Canada.* Toronto: Macmillan of Canada.
– ed. 1990. *Getting It Green* Toronto: C.D. Howe Institute.
– 1995. *Fairer Play: Canadian Competition Policy Institutions in a Global Market.* Toronto: C.D. Howe Institute.
Doern, G. Bruce, M. Hill, M. Prince, and R. Schultz, eds. 1998. *Changing the Rules: Canadian Regulatory Regimes and Institutions.* Toronto: University of Toronto Press, chap. 1.

Doern, G. Bruce, and Stephen Wilks, eds. 1996. *National Competition Policy Institutions in a Global Market.* Oxford: Clarendon Press.

Economist. 'Over-Regulating America.' 27 July 1996, 19–21.

Eisner, M.A. 1991. *Antitrust and the Triumph of Economics.* Chapel Hill: University of North Carolina Press.

– 1993. *Regulatory Politics in Transition.* Baltimore: The Johns Hopkins University Press.

Eisner, M.A., Jeff Worsham, and Evan Ringquist. 1996. 'Crossing the Organizational Void: The Limits of Agency Theory in the Analysis of Regulatory Control.' *Governance* 9, no. 4 (October): 407–28.

Ernst, John. 1994. *Whose Utility? The Social Impact of Public Utility Privatization and Regulation in Britain.* Buckingham: Open University Press.

European Public Policy Forum. 1996. *The Report of the Commission on the Regulation of Privatised Utilities.* London: The Hansard Society for Parliamentary Government.

Fischel, William A. 1995. *Regulatory Takings.* Cambridge: Harvard University Press.

Grabosky, Peter N. 1995. 'Using Non-governmental Resources to Foster Compliance.' *Governance* 8, no. 4: 527–50.

Hadfield, Gillian, Robert Howse, and Michael Trebilcock. 1996. 'Rethinking Consumer Protection Policy.' Paper presented to the University of Toronto Roundtable on New Approaches to Consumer Law, 28 August, at University of Toronto.

Hahn, Robert W., and John A. Bird. 1991. 'The Costs and Benefits of Regulation: Review and Synthesis.' *Yale Journal of Regulation* 8, no. 1 (winter 1991): 233–78.

Hancher, Leigh, and Michael Moran, eds. 1989. *Capitalism, Culture and Regulation.* Oxford: Clarendon Press, 1–10, 271–300.

Hood, Christopher. 1986. *Administrative Analysis.* London: Harvester Wheatsheaf, chap. 3.

– 1994. *Explaining Policy Reversals.* Buckingham: Open University Press, chap. 2.

Hood, Christopher, and Colin Scott. 1996. 'Bureaucratic Regulation and New Public Management in the United Kingdom: Mirror-Image Developments.' *Journal of Law and Society* 23, no. 3 (September): 321–45.

Jacobs, S.H. 1995. 'Regulatory Cooperation for an Interdependent World: Issues for Government.' In OECD, *Regulatory Cooperation for an Interdependent World,* 1–17. Paris: OECD.

Langdon, Janet. 1995. 'The Water Industry: 1995–2000.' In *The Water Industry: Looking Forward from the Periodic Review,* 41–56. London: Centre for the Study of Regulated Industries.

Law Reform Commission. 1986. *Policy Implementation, Compliance and Administrative Law.* Ottawa: Law Reform Commission of Canada.

Levy, Brian, and Pablo T. Spiller, eds. 1996. *Regulations, Institutions, and Commitment: Comparative Studies of Telecommunications.* Cambridge: Cambridge University Press.

Linder, Stephen, and Guy Peters. 1989. 'Instruments of Government: Perceptions and Contexts.' *Journal of Public Policy* Vol. 9, no. 1: 35–58.

Majone, G., ed. 1996. *Regulating Europe*. London: Routledge.

March, J.G., and J.P. Olsen. 1989. *Rediscovering Institutions*. New York: Free Press.

McChesney, Fred S., and William F. Shuggart II, eds. 1995. *The Causes and Consequences of Antitrust: The Public-Choice Perspective*. Chicago: University of Chicago Press.

McGarity, Thomas O. 1991. *Reinventing Rationality: The Role of Regulatory Analysis in the Federal Bureaucracy*. Cambridge: Harvard University Press.

Meier, K.J. 1985. *Regulation: Politics, Bureaucracy, Economics*. New York: St Martins.

Michael, Douglas C. 1996. 'Cooperative Implementation of Federal Regulations.' *Yale Journal on Regulation* 13, no. 2 (summer): 535–602.

Mihlar, Fazil. 1996. *Regulatory Overkill: The Cost of Regulation in Canada*. Vancouver: The Fraser Institute.

National Audit Office. 1996. *The Work of the Directors General of Telecommunications, Gas Supply, Water Services, and Electricity Supply*. Session 1995–6. House of Commons, 645. London: HMSO.

North, D.C. 1990. *Institutions, Institutional Change and Economic Performance*. Cambridge: Cambridge University Press.

Ogden, Stuart, and Fiona Anderson. 1995. 'Representing Customer's Interests: The Case of the Privatized Water Industry in England and Wales,' *Public Administration* 73 (winter): 535–61.

Ogus, Anthony I. 1994. *Regulation: Legal Form and Economic Theory* Oxford: Clarendon.

Ostrom, E. 1990. 'Rational Choice Theory and Institutional Analysis: Toward Complementarity.' *American Political Science Review* 85: 237–43.

Pildes, R., and C. Sunstein. 1995. 'Reinventing the Regulatory State.' *University of Chicago Law Journal* 62, no. 1: 1–129.

Ratushny, Ed. 1987. 'What Are Administrative Tribunals? The Pursuit of Uniformity in Diversity.' *Canadian Public Administration* 30, no. 1: 1–13.

Richardson, Jeremy, ed. 1990. *Privatization and Deregulation in Canada and Britain*. Aldershot: Dartmouth.

Schultz, Richard. 1998. 'Winning and Losing: The Consumers Association of Canada and the Telecommunications Regulatory System.' In *Canadian Regulatory Institutions: Globalization, Choices and Change,* edited by G. Bruce Doern, M. Hill, M. Prince, and R. Schultz. Toronto: University of Toronto Press.

Searing, D.D. 1991. 'Roles, Rules and Rationality in the New Institutionalism.' *American Political Science Review* 85: 1239–60.

Sparrow, Malcolm K. 1994. *Imposing Duties: Government's Changing Approach to Compliance*. London: Praeger.

Susskind, L., and Gerald McMahon. 1985. 'The Theory and Practice of Negotiated Rulemaking.' *Yale Journal on Regulation* 3: 133–65.

Tiefer, Charles. 1996. 'Controlling Federal Agencies by Claims on Their Appropriations? The Takings Bill and the Power of the Purse.' *Yale Journal on Regulation* 13, no. 2 (summer): 501–34.

Trebilcock, Michael, R. Prichard, D. Hartle, and D. Dewees. 1982. *The Choice of Governing Instruments*. Ottawa: Minister of Supply and Services.

Tupper, Allan, and Bruce Doern, eds. 1988. *Privatization, Public Policy and Public Corporations in Canada*. Montreal: Institute for Research on Public Policy.

Vass, Peter, ed. 1995. *Regulated Industries 1995*. London: Centre For the Study of Regulated Industries.

Veljanovski, Cento. 1991. *Regulators and the Market: An Assessment of the Growth of Regulation in the UK*. London: Institute of Economic Affairs.

– 1993. *The Future of Industry Regulation in the UK*. London: European Policy Forum, 1993.

Vogel, David. 1986. *National Styles of Regulation: Environmental Policy in Great Britain and the United States*. Ithaca: Cornell University Press.

– 1995. *Trading Up: Consumer and Environmental Regulation in a Global Economy*. Cambridge: Harvard University Press.

Vogel, Steven K. 1996. *Freer Markets, More Rules: Regulatory Reform in Advanced Industrial Countries*. Ithaca: Cornell University Press.

Walsh, Kieron. 1995. *Public Services and Market Mechanisms: Competition, Contracting and the New Public Management*. London: MacMillan Press.

Weaver, R.K., and B.A. Rockman, eds. 1993. *Do Institutions Matter?* Washington: The Brookings Institution.

Wilson, James Q., ed. 1980. *The Politics of Regulation*. New York: Basic Books, 357–94.

PART ONE
NATIONAL REGULATORY INSTITUTIONAL CHANGE

2

The Interplay among Regimes: Mapping Regulatory Institutions in the United Kingdom, the United States, and Canada

G. BRUCE DOERN

Building on the overall comparative issues introduced in Chapter 1, this chapter focuses on a key analytical task if new ground is to be broken in Anglo–North American regulatory analysis, which is to develop a framework that can help map the modern nature of regulatory institutions. A basic map requires both a broadening of the conceptual scope of study and also, in some respects, a narrowing in order to re-till some of the old analytical soil. The broadening and the narrowing tasks are equally central to the realities faced by regulators and the regulated. The need to look 'up and out' and also 'down and in' essentially yields the framework that is profiled in Table 2.1 and in the organizational structure of the chapter. This dual examination suggests that national regulatory institutions in the United Kingdom, the United States, and Canada involve the existence of, and an increasing interplay among, four regulatory regimes. It also suggests that an understanding of particular regulatory bodies requires a more detailed analysis of particular organizational features and capacities.

This chapter is organized into three sections. The first looks at the four regulatory regimes. It also deals with some of the interplay among these regimes, where both convergence and collisions are in evidence. The second section then looks 'down and in,' with the focus more on the regulatory body (single statutory official, collective commission, or ministerially headed department), including its de jure and de facto mix of functions and the technical-political nature of its compliance roles and approaches. Conclusions follow, in the third section.

The Four Regulatory Regimes: Core Features and Interplay

The first part of the framework is premised on the view that a true or comprehensive mapping of the regulatory institutions of the United Kingdom, the

TABLE 2.1 Mapping regulatory institutions in the 1990s: The framework at a glance

The four regimes
- Regime I: The sectoral regime
- Regime II: The horizontal framework regulatory regime
- Regime III: The governmental executive regime for managing regulation
- Regime IV: The international regime

The regulatory body as an organization
- The mix of governing functions
- Regulatory modes: single regulator versus commissions
- Regulatory leadership, risk taking, and discretion
- Budgets and personnel: internal capacity
- Compliance approaches and shared public–private capacities

United States, and Canada in the late 1990s must be centred on the existence of four regulatory regimes. A regime is understood for analytical purposes to be an interacting set of organizations, statutes, ideas, interests, and processes.[1] In other words, the first test for the presence of a regime is some inner core of norms, features, and characteristics that warrant such a designation for analytical purposes. The four regimes are: Regime I, the sectoral regime; Regime II, the horizontal framework regulatory regime; Regime III, the overall governmental executive regime for making and managing regulation; and Regime IV, the international regime, embracing global, regional, and bilateral rules-based approaches or de facto co-decision-making by national or international bodies.

Each regime is profiled first in terms of its core features, but we are ultimately interested as well in the interplay among them. A desire for symmetry may suggest that they should be pictured as concentric circles extending outward from Regime I to Regime IV, but analytically it is probably more sensible to see them as interlocking circles. This is because the relative presence of the regimes varies across policy areas (e.g., energy, telecommunications, or transport), across countries, and across time. Despite this fluidity, comparative regulatory analysis of regulatory institutions as a whole must encompass some appreciation of at least these four regimes.

Regime I: The Sectoral Regime

Regime I centres on the vertical industrial sectors, historically sectors with the characteristics of natural monopoly regulation. Thus in the telecommunications sector of the three countries, there are regulatory bodies such as the Office of Telecommunications (OFTEL) in the UK, the Federal Communications Commission (FCC) in the United States, and the Canadian Radio-television and

Telecommunications CRTC. These bodies are immediately embedded in a regime of ideas and applied working concepts (such as rate-of-return and price-capping approaches, and universal service) and many day-to-day players in both rule-making and implementation (Doern 1995; Eisner 1993). The players include the interests being regulated (e.g., interest groups, firms, citizens, communities) and a set of regulatory rent-seekers and defenders of ideas that includes key professions (e.g., law, accounting, and financial experts), but also media critics and observers in the general or financial press.

Most important for our purposes, Regime I also includes one or more parent departments of government headed by Cabinet ministers (elected or appointed). For example, in the case of the UK, several of the regulators, while independent, are within the ambit of one department, the Department of Trade and Industry. Their precise roles and influences are difficult to determine in operational matters, but these were undoubtedly crucial in the bargains that shaped the initial statutory and discretionary shape of the regulators established in the last several years. Canadian regulators typically have one primary parent minister, but they may also have reporting obligations to other secondary ministers and departments. These Regime I relationships include varied kinds of powers, such as the power of the Cabinet or the parent minister to order the regulator to do certain things and the right of aggrieved interests to appeal to the Cabinet some of the decisions of the regulatory body.

Regime I forces attention on some of the most obvious matters of institutional comparison, such as which aspects of a policy field or industry are actually within the mandate of the regulatory body. In Canada and the United States, the telecommunications regulatory body regulates both radio and television broadcasting and telecommunications. In the UK there are separate regulators for broadcasting and telecommunications. Canadian and U.S. energy regulators tend to include all energy forms except nuclear in one federal agency, whereas in the UK the Office of Electricity Regulation (OFFER) and the Office of Gas Supply (OFGAS) split key parts of the energy regulatory portfolio, electricity and gas respectively.

Regime II: The Horizontal Framework Regulatory Regime

Regime II refers to a set of regulators whose mandates are horizontal or framework oriented. Therefore, its core logic, in principle at least, is that the regulatory mandates are intended to cut across economic sectors and not discriminate between sectors. As we will see, these realms are rarely as pure as the description suggests. There is little doubt, however, that Regime II is of growing importance and is certainly a crucial part of most countries' regulatory institutions.

Competition law and environmental regulation are arguably the most important recent manifestations of Regime II, but there are other areas that many would include, such as tax laws and rules, trade and investment, consumer safety, intellectual property, and banking and financial probity (Harris and Milkis 1989; Francis 1993; and Doern and Wilks 1996). Both the competition and the environmental regulatory realms have crossed paths with sectoral regulatory realms, often conflictually and sometimes cooperatively (Vass 1994).

Competition regulators have often been restrained by statutory provisions that have exempted sectors from their jurisdiction. But a decade or more of privatization and deregulation has made more compelling the case that competition law should take precedence over sectoral regulators, who may have only limited pro-competitive instincts or mandates (Doern and Wilks 1996; Veljanovski 1991). On the other hand, competition regulatory policy itself varies across the three countries in terms of its relative emphasis on such criteria as consumer welfare, industrial efficiency, and integration within economic blocs, as well as in terms of the functional areas of law that are included in these categories, such as mergers, abuse of dominant position, and predatory pricing. Moreover, the particular tools and time frames for competition regulators in making decisions might be quite inappropriate for the technical and political-economic realities of sectors such as energy or telecommunications.

Environmental regulators have been similarly restrained in the past and have often crossed swords with their sectoral brethren (and aligned interests). But the gradual articulation of sustainable development mandates in many governments has meant that the horizontal reach of green regulators is expanding, albeit in numerous particular forms and degrees, in the three countries (Doern and Conway 1995; Gray 1995; Weale 1992; Hoberg 1993). Environmental regulation is also tied to the view that technology-forcing approaches linked to tough regulations may be a positive 'industrial policy' for a country's emerging green industries.

Regime II's influence on a particular regulatory body and its sector will vary depending on the particular kinds of horizontal regulation that are especially germane. For example, U.S. transportation deregulation became linked with the bankruptcy laws, which allowed airlines to restructure in varied unexpected ways. At present, telecommunications regulation is crossing paths in vital ways with intellectual property regulation regarding both patents and copyright (U.S. Information Infrastructure Task Force 1995). In the UK, environmental regulation has its most obvious impact with the water regulator, the Office of Water Services (OFWAT).

The interplay between Regime I and Regime II can also be seen in more particular approaches for managing relations between sectoral and framework regulators such as competition regulators. Three approaches (examined further in Chapter 9) are: (1) advocacy and representation rights of the competition regulator in the proceedings of the sectoral regulator; (2) mechanisms of appeal by firms of the sectoral regulator's decisions to competition regulators; and (3) private legal action.

The first institutional approach is one that provides opportunities for the competition regulator to appear before sectoral regulators and advocate or raise concerns about competition in a given sector, either in general or, possibly, on a case under consideration. Canada is the main jurisdiction to adopt this approach. Over the years, this advocacy role has been carried out many dozens of times in transportation, energy, and telecommunications. Recently the range of sectors being examined has extended to agriculture, sports, the professions, and banking (Monteiro 1993).

The second approach is one that enables appeals of sectoral regulators' decisions to be made to competition regulators. The best example here is found in the role of the UK's Monopolies and Mergers Commission (MMC) in relation to public utility regulators (MMC 1994; Liesner 1995; Odgers 1995). The main responsibility for regulating the utilities lies with the regulators, such as OFTEL, OFWAT, and OFGAS (Vass 1994; Beesley 1995), but the various legislative acts for each sector also provide for a role for the MMC, in effect when there is a disagreement between the regulator and the regulated utility firm. The 'utility reference' provisions vary across the utility sectors. The MMC process on licence modifications is triggered when the regulator and the utility cannot agree on a licence modification or the outcome of a price review. It is then the regulator who takes the issue to the MMC. After a hearing that can take about six months, the MMC must report to the regulator 'whether any of the matters referred operate, or may be expected to operate, against the public interest' (Liesner 1995, p.3).

In the first two approaches sketched above, it is largely the state or its regulatory players that are the exercisers of decision making and discretion in managing the inter-regulatory regime relations. Private pressure points exist, but not wide realms of real private action. It is in the United States that the third approach most exemplifies one in which a wide realm of genuine private action is available as a way to deal with relations between the sectoral and competition regulators (White 1988; Eisner 1991; Peters 1996). For every action pursued by American competition regulators, there are ten pursued by private firms and citizens. Under section 4 of the Clayton Act, 'any person who shall be injured in his business or property by reason of anything forbidden in the antitrust laws may sue therefor.' The law also provides for treble damages plus costs, including legal fees. The opportunity to obtain treble damages is intended to be an incentive to plaintiffs to identify uncompetitive acts and to take the time and risk involved in bringing a case to court. Class-action suits can also be brought by otherwise dispersed and risk-averse consumers.

The main U.S. antitrust authorities, the Antitrust Division of the Department of Justice and the Federal Trade Commission, as well as the fifty state governments, cannot prevent and in many respects have little to do with private antitrust cases (Peters 1996). Firms found guilty in government-led cases can subsequently be sued privately. Private cases are brought through the general U.S. court system. Because private cases are motivated by self-interest, the public interest in promoting competition could lie with either the plaintiff or the defendant depending on the case. Many commentators point out that the purpose of such private-action enforcement mechanisms is to support competition not the competitor, but many decisions do not enhance competition.

Regime III: The Government Executive Regime for Managing Regulation

Regime III embraces the players and processes that exist in an even broader cross-governmental sense, particularly within the executive levels of the three national governments and also often extending to Parliament and Congress. This is frequently the least appreciated regime in conventional regulatory literature, perhaps because it is so easy, at first glance, to think of regulation only in terms of well-known regulatory bodies.

Nonetheless, the core logic of Regime III is simple and compelling. Regulation, along with taxation and spending, is one the three main instruments of governing (Doern and Phidd 1992). In thinking about spending in government, one instantly recognizes that there is a central budgetary process. The same is true for regulation, save for at least one crucial difference. The government's regulatory choices are not as readily converted into the common denominator of money or cash. This is because most of the costs of regulation show up in private budgets. The government's annual volume of regulatory choices is not as easily aggregated as spending. But individual regulations typically do go through some process of vetting, and hence this is a regime whose presence must be understood.

Regime III forces an understanding of how the regulatory function is managed within the executive or even within the state as a whole, including the courts (Stanbury 1992; McGarity 1991; Martin 1995; Jacobs 1992). In the first instance, this leads to a focus on so-called delegated legislation, or the 'regs,' that can be made under the authority granted by hundreds of parent statutes. Every government has some kind of process for 'managing' regulation but the visibility, complexity, and effectiveness of such processes vary widely. In the

United States and Canada there are quite explicit and increasingly transparent processes for proposing, analysing, scrutinizing, reforming, and eliminating regulations. The values or criteria that are brought to bear by such processes can include: cost-benefit, risk-benefit, and cost-effectiveness tests; legal tests such as adherence to charters of rights and freedoms; and constitutional tests for the level of government that is entitled to regulate a particular field or subject matter. The UK has its own version of Regime III, but it is less explicit and less frequently written about (Baldwin and McCrudden 1987; Cane 1992; Ogus 1994).

Alas, a discussion of Regime III cannot be left just to the notion of how delegated regulation is managed. The larger reality is that real regulation – in the sense of rules of behaviour backed up by the sanctions of the state – occurs in various enabling *statutes* as well. Hence, the processes for making law are themselves also a part of Regime III. Laws may or may not be subject to the same kinds of vetting that 'the regs' are typically subject to. Yet it is obvious that a crucial aspect of understanding how a regulatory body functions lies in the initial political-economic accommodations reached among ministers, officials, and interests when a body is established or when its mandate is subsequently changed.

Regime III also embraces a world where many regulatory (not to mention other) priorities are competing for attention among ministers and officials. Thus, understanding Regime III is important for a further reason. The inability to change a regulatory agency or its mandate or behaviour is a function of what else is on the government's list of priorities. It is also a function of other aspects of the inner executive government-wide processes, namely those that allocate budgets and personnel to the regulators in competition with all other bureaucracies in the public sector.

Last but not least, in recent years Regime III can be seen to include periodic initiatives in which all government departments are expected to look at their regulations in terms of competitiveness or in search of regulatory flexibility and the possibility of a greater use of alternative or complementary approaches such as voluntary codes (Grabosky 1995). Many of these initiatives were begun by industry departments including the Department of Trade and Industry in the UK, Industry Canada, and the U.S. Department of Commerce. Often the result of pressure from the small-business lobby in particular, these initiatives became, in various iterations, general government policy and hence a part of the already crowded multi-criteria-based central regulatory vetting process.

Regime IV: The International Regime

Regime IV can, in one sense, be seen as a virtual commonplace reflection of contemporary globalization and of the internationalization of most areas of public policy, including regulation (Coleman and Underhill 1995; Doern, Pal, and Tomlin 1996). Regulators are increasingly constrained by, or must interact with, a potential array of international agencies (regulatory and otherwise) and national regulatory counterpart bodies in other countries; international (rather than just national) agglomerations and coalitions of interest groups; and the existence of international rule-based dispute settlement processes or prescribed cross-boundary consultation processes (Taylor and Groom 1988; Trebilcock and Howse 1995).

However, the core feature of the international regulatory regime is that international regulation has not, for the most part, been 'authoritative,' in the sense that there is no world government to supply compliance through direct enforcement. The international system has typically had to rely especially on persuasion and diplomacy, both soft instruments of governing. Thus many policy fields are influenced by obligations, but these not usually backed by the same array of mechanisms for ensuring compliance as exists in domestic regulation.

This does not mean that particular regulators have not had to face the realities of international bodies or other countries' regulators. For example, Canadian and U.S. energy regulators in the oil, gas, and hydroelectric sectors have for decades had to deal with the co-decision-making powers of each set of national regulators before projects and sales can proceed, be expanded, or indeed be contracted in emergency situations (Doern and Toner 1985). However, in the telecommunications sector there was for a long period a mutual recognition of each other's national monopoly arrangements. This has obviously changed in the past decade, and hence Regime IV for the telecommunications sector in North America and elsewhere is more clearly a globalization-influenced process (Lee 1996; Drake 1994).

In the late 1990s, Regime IV must in particular be tied to the Uruguay Round agreement of the General Agreement on Tariffs and Trade (GATT) and to the establishment of a strengthened and broadened World Trade Organization (WTO). On a regional basis, Regime IV is also tied to the rules and decision processes of the EU and NAFTA. Not only are fundamental trade rules crossing borders and affecting practices in various 'domestic' regulatory realms, but it is also around the WTO that new 'crosswalk' institutions are being negotiated between such heretofore separate international realms as competition, environment, intellectual property, and investment (Trebilcock and Howse 1995; Wiener 1995; and Lanjouw 1995). In the EU and NAFTA contexts, the degrees of harmonization and integration vary both sectorally and horizontally, and thus crosswalks take many forms.

Many of these realms involve processes and changes whereby largely national fields of regulation such as environment and competition are seeking to become working international systems. For competition policy, these changes range from the quite limited progress towards the international harmonization of antitrust laws at the world level to quite extensive integration at the level of the EU (Doern and Wilks 1996). For environmental regulation, internationalization has taken the form of many bi-national cross-border agreements and some regional institutional experiments such as the NAFTA environmental commissions. At the global level there are fewer accomplishments, but there are nonetheless the very important protocols on particular pollutants (Vogel 1995; Doern 1995).

When dealing with Regime IV, it is vital in the institutional mapping process to know concretely whether a particular international regime has 'rule-based' dispute-settlement mechanisms at hand or whether it remains a looser set of arrangements with more subtle influences. Again, this is because there does not exist a world government as such; instead, there is an array of relationships in general and functional areas of international relations centred on diplomacy and persuasion.

A final glimpse into the interplay among the regimes can be seen by considering briefly an overall process of learning between regimes III and IV. As we have seen, Regime III refers to the overall process for managing regulation within the executive. While many vetting criteria have been used in these processes, there is a sense in which they have always been seen as domestic criteria. To put it more specifically, overall regulatory managers typically have had little to do with their own countries' foreign affairs departments. And, because of the historical characteristics of Regime IV, foreign policy departments have not seen themselves as being in the regulatory business. Now they do, and now they must. Thus governments that are signatories to the Uruguay agreement and to other regional pacts must be capable of knowing and assessing whether they are complying not only with particular provisions but also with whole systems of laws and regulations.

These capsule portraits of the four regimes and of some of the interplay between them are intended as an initial guide to an appropriate mapping of the regulatory institutions of the three countries in the 1990s. An approach that ignores the four-fold presence of these regimes would be quite inadequate to the task of regulatory analysis either for scholars of regulation or for regulatory practitioners.

Regulatory Bodies as Organizations: Old and New Realities

However important to the macro-mapping exercise the four regimes may be, they are an insufficient basis for examining the details of regulatory bodies. Here, as indicated, we must look 'down and in' at regulatory bodies and do so with a focus on the organizations as such. However, in the 1990s this is an analytical task that involves looking at both old and new realities. Three old realities are profiled below: the mix of governing functions actually assigned to, or carried out, by regulators; the modes of organization, especially the single regulator versus regulation by commission; and the nature of regulatory leadership or discretion that flows from the first two points or that is injected by the strategizing and risk taking of the incumbent leader of the agency. The two newer realities examined below – budgets and personnel (including actual technical capacities and information), and compliance approaches – may not appear to be new when one simply lists them, but in fact they constitute new or greatly changed regulatory realities because of the concerted search in recent years for reinvented government, because of the presence of severe budget cutbacks, and because of the search for newer methods of compliance to implement regulatory norms and provisions (Sparrow 1994; Grabosky 1995).

The task of looking concretely at regulatory agencies also involves, in some specific sense, a need to cease thinking of regulators and regulatory bodies in academic, hermetically sealed analytical categories. Regulators become more than wielders of political power, where the worry is about whether they are being captured or not, or become more than players in allocative economic activity, where textbook formulas can be tested as in some surrogate microeconomics laboratory. Regulators exist also to deliver directly or indirectly actual services, such as the appropriate kinds of electrical energy or natural gas, a modern mix of telecommunications services, and a functioning and safe transportation system.

Regulatory Bodies and the Mix of Governing Functions

The old realities that must be considered analytically and in practice include some that are too easily given short shrift or that fall into the crevices between academic disciplines. By far the most important of these is to identify the *de jure* and de facto mix of governing functions carried out by the regulator (Doern 1978; Linder and Peters 1989; Law Reform Commission 1986; Ayres and Braithwaite 1992). These functions can include: regulation making (in the sense of delegated legislation); rule making (e.g., about the agency's own procedures or hearings); quasi-judicial decisions, where norms and processes akin to court procedures must be adhered to; quasi-political allocative tasks, where licences or approvals are determined or negotiated; the complementary administration of spending grants or subsidies; policy advisory functions, either de facto or mandated by law; and broad leadership, educational, or exhortative tasks, where the regulator is expected to lead, guide, and persuade (Law Reform Commission 1986). Scholars have also attempted to group these functions in more compact ways by analysing, for example, the 'planning, promoting, and policing' functions of regulators (Schultz and Alexandroff 1985).

It is in a discussion of the mix of functions that one must also look for what a regulatory body's 'standard operating procedures' are, to use Graham Allison's concept (Allison 1971). In other words, one must ask whether there are one or two particular dominant dynamics or central working concepts that are endemic to the particular body and area of regulation. For example, this is where 'rate-of-return,' 'price-capping,' and 'auction-based' systems can be examined in utility or sectoral regulation, or where 'best-practicable technology,' 'risk-benefit,' and 'science-based' regulatory approaches can be looked at in horizontal health and safety and social regulation.

There is a significant economic literature on each of these approaches. For example, rate-of-return regulation involves the regulator limiting the overall earnings of a firm by specifying a rate of return on investment, usually capital investment. As mentioned earlier, this approach has garnered considerable criticism in that it can encourage inefficiency because attention is not focused on input costs. Indeed, the system encourages inflated costs that regulators have difficulty policing (Crandall and Waverman 1995).

Price capping is seen as a more incentive-based approach that partly overcomes the rigidities of rate-of-return approaches. Under it, the regulator establishes price ceilings for a specified period for the services of a multi-service industry (Crandall and Waverman 1995). Services are first divided into regulated and unregulated categories. The regulated services are then divided into individual categories based on criteria such as relatedness and degree of competition. The regulated firm is then given considerable freedom to price services within individual categories, subject to an overall cap or to a maximum annual increase on the average price of the services in the category. A final feature of price capping is that any increase is limited to the rate of increase in the designated level of inflation, less a specified annual productivity adjustment factor.

There is no doubt that these approaches are important to the basic internal dynamics of some regulatory bodies and that they are typically the analytical preserve of economists. But they are equally and quintessentially political in their make-up, in that they are basically different ways of structuring rules versus discretion and hence represent the politics of certainty versus uncertainty. In short, they are centred in the arrangement of a mix of governing functions.

Literally dozens of studies from the legal, political, and even economic disciplines point to the crucial nature of the mix of functions when regulatory and other organizations are looked at closely and seriously (Eisner 1991; Hood 1986). There is, however, often only limited agreement as to how one can precisely distinguish, say, a quasi-judicial decision from a quasi-political or administrative decision (Hood 1986; Ratushny 1987; Trebilcock 1991). Since few if any regulators are uni-functional and therefore engage *only* in narrowly defined regulation, it follows that regulators are more than just rule makers. They are also unelected politicians and administrators engaged in numerous acts of discretion and political choice, whether cast under the concept of rate of return, price capping, or other nominal approach to regulation.

Regulatory Modes: Single Regulator versus Commissions

The choice of the particular mode of regulation is intricately tied to negotiations over exactly which of the mix of functions a regulator might have. But often the choice of mode is polarized into one between single regulators (statutory persons) and collective multi-member commissions. The recently established UK regulatory system is noteworthy when compared to what prevails in North America. In the UK single statutory regulators have been the norm. Both Canada and the United States have had a historical preference for commission forms (Doern 1978; Economic Council of Canada 1979 1981; Meier 1985), but this is true only in the so-called public utility sectors. When one thinks of regulation more broadly, the situation in the three countries is not as clear-cut. Statutory persons as regulators are present in North America in some areas of business framework law and regulation (competition, bankruptcy, and intellectual property), and commission forms have certainly been present in the UK in the areas of local government and planning law. In addition, of course, there are many areas in all three countries where ministerially headed departments are the regulators (this is, in effect, a third but frequently used mode).

Important democratic and political issues are raised by these choices of mode (Hill 1994). For example, if a wide mix of functions is conferred on a single person, accountability is in one sense clearer but potential opposition to such concentrated power in an unelected official is also greater or more likely. The single person regulator can literally be policy maker, regulator, judge, and jury (Doern 1995).

If the commission mode is chosen, accountability may be less clear because it is more divided, but also power is distributed among commission members. Commission forms were in the past undoubtedly more prevalent in North America, in part because of the continental sweep of Canada and the United States and in part because of the need for representation to be built into the institutions either from regions or from diverse interest groups. But commissions also face their own decisions on how to arrange the mix of functions given to them. They are under pressure to separate, in a transparent way, the rule-making from quasi-adjudicative powers they may carry out. Commission forms also raise practical issues of the mix of members, who may be full-time or part-time. These choices in turn are bound up in controversy over whether appointments are based on political patronage or whether members have genuine expertise in the area concerned.

Regulatory Leadership, Risk Taking, and Discretion

It is next to impossible to examine regulatory leaders (whether statutory persons or heads of commissions or departments) without reference to the first two items discussed above. The regulator as individual is not a free agent. He or she is embedded in a state of permanent institutionalized tension with the regulated industry, the government, and consumers or other broad socio-economic interests. Regulators may seek the quiet life of regulatory normality, but this is a state of affairs that rarely lasts for long (Trebilcock 1991). The price-capping approach in the UK is particularly instructive in this regard in that the multi-year time frame for the capping system as a whole was intended to produce a climate of predictability for investment and planning purposes. But when regulated utility firms got too rich or paid their chief executive officers unseemly high stipends and benefits, consumers and politicians complained bitterly and demanded that prices be changed or rolled back. Regulated firms also found their circumstances changing raidly, and hence they often sought changes sooner than they had previously thought would be needed in the pricing agreement period.

In these and other settings there is clearly some room for the regulatory leader to be innovative and to be engaged in risk taking, discretion, and hence power. Analysing the prior predilections of appointees in terms of either their substantive views about the field or their attitudes towards risk taking or risk aversion can be useful, but is undoubtedly more art than science. The U.S. system in this regard is known for its open scrutiny by Congress of many regulatory appointees, whereas Canada and the UK have far fewer and more closed processes for appointing such officials and for scrutinizing them once in office.

Beyond these levels of studying or thinking about the leadership variable in the behaviour of agencies, there are other features of leadership that undoubtedly ring true for regulatory staff members. Staff members may quickly come to know the areas in which the agency head is broadly interested and those where there is no interest whatsoever. But even this kind of internal calculus can be overturned by the simple fact that most regulators are also driven by their caseloads and by the overall rhythm of demand-driven decision making.

Budgets and Personnel: Internal Agency Capacity

Internal agency capacity, or the ability of an agency to carry out tasks (the full mix of functions), is partly but crucially a function of budgets and personnel. In the case of staffing, real capacity in turn depends also on the availability of appropriate technical and other knowledge and the ability to attract people and maintain up-to-date competencies. A comparison of the staffing and budgets of sectoral regulators across countries and on a decade-by-decade basis (which this chapter does not attempt) would have to take into account the different mix of functions, and hence would require a great deal of subtlety in interpretation. But while evidence on this plane of comparison is difficult and sketchy, several points can be made about the kind of conceptual and research questions it suggests in the three countries.

First, a crucial and long-known aspect of regulatory institutional behaviour is the importance of asymmetrical knowledge and information between the regulatory staff and the industries and communities being regulated (Bernstein 1955; Makkai and Braithwaite 1992; Harris 1995). This asymmetry almost always produces an enormous political advantage for those that are regulated. The regulator can simply never know as much as the regulated, and this becomes a crucial basis for possible capture. Information asymmetry can come in the form not just of technical superiority but also in a capacity to inundate the regulator with information if need be. For the regulator, the only counterweight to this kind of de facto power of knowledge may well be the agency's capacity to exercise discretion, and hence to wield the power inherent in the presence of such uncertainty. This the regulator has because of its legal ability to exercise the 'authority' of the state.

Thus choices of regulatory mode involve situations where ministers can confer on the regulator extensive authority but limited resources, more limited powers but quite extensive resources, or various combinations of the two. These combinations can be altered as time goes on, and thus represent an ability by cabinets to 'discipline' or 'enable' the regulator, depending on political judgments of the regulator's performance. For example, there are often serious constraints placed on regulators in their ability to launch legal action when this is needed. Regulators know that legal costs can be enormous, even in good budgetary times, and that on an annual basis a small handful of cases could potentially 'exhaust' their legal war chests.

With respect to budgets and staffing in the aggregate, it would appear that the recently established UK regulators were deliberately kept extremely small relative to their North American equivalents. The notion of them as 'offices' of regulation suggests that they were to have the quality of regulatory boutiques. However, the small size of their staffs and budgets was complemented by the considerable powers given their single-person regulatory heads. In North America there is evidence that some regulatory bodies are shrinking in budgets and staffs or, occasionally, disappearing altogether, such as the U.S. Interstate Commerce Commission. The key Canadian regulators have certainly shrunk in this sense relative to their heyday in the 1960s and 1970s, and tendencies in the United States are the same. This has been the result of both deregulation and some loss of functions, but also of budget cutbacks in the battle to reduce fiscal deficits.

A final budgetary development is that some regulatory bodies on both sides of the Atlantic have become fully or close to fully fee-dependent. They obtain all of their capital and operating revenues from the industries they regulate through fees or tolls, and thus make little or no claims on budgetary appropriations. U.S., Canadian, and UK energy regulators have all reached this state of affairs, as have intellectual property regulators in all three countries. This change in financing has also changed the relationship between the regulatory body and the industry in that there are far more frequent discussions regarding exactly how the regulatory body is being managed and how it is serving particular clients.

Compliance Approaches and Shared Public–Private Capacities

Last, but hardly least in this survey of agency capacities, is the issue of the actual broad compliance approaches and capacities that are applied to regulation. Compliance has always to some extent been a shared task between the regulator and various players in the private sector (Hood 1986; Law Reform Commission 1986). However, it has become all the more so in the climate of recent years with new realities spurred on not only by fiscal exigencies but also by the thinking represented by the 'new public management' and 'reinvented government,' and by the inherent density of the four interlocking macro-regimes sketched out in the first section of this chapter (Sparrow 1994; Grabosky 1995).

In this regard, compliance approaches are cast broadly as alternatives to direct enforcement or as having a far greater reliance on the softer instruments of government, such as the combined use of education, economic as opposed to criminal penalties, codes, and guidelines. Enforcement does not disappear entirely from this form of thinking and action, but it is considerably reduced.

Compliance is also seen as much more partnership-based, with various kinds of players involved with the primary regulator. Indeed, rarely in these situations is there only one regulator, since many or all of the four regimes may be involved to some degree.

The UK–North American comparative situations in this regard produce interesting practices and differences. Clearly, the U.S. regulatory system has long been characterized by far greater opportunities than in Canada or the UK for private legal action (Harris and Milkis 1989; Meier 1985). In several regulatory areas the role of the citizen or firm as enforcement initiator has been pivotal. The greater litigious nature of the U.S. political culture also means that regulatory implementation cannot shift as easily from an enforcement to a compliance focus. Whether in telecommunications, environmental, antitrust, or trade law, the U.S. system arms its citizens with the tools of regulatory battle. For this reason, the U.S. reformers who dislike the excesses of such approaches have advocated more 'negotiated' forms of regulation ('reg-neg'), but a long uphill battle will be required for success (Pildes and Sunstein 1995).

In the UK (and arguably to a somewhat lesser extent in Canada), critics and cynics in many regulatory arenas will argue that softer compliance is all that has ever been practised. Regulatory implementation is always, according to this view, some kind a accommodating agreement struck between regulator and regulated. This has especially been the argument in the horizontal areas of regulation (Regime II), such as environmental and competition, but in other areas as well (Vogel 1995; Gray 1995; Doern and Wilks 1996).

However, compliance equations and relations among interests are changing in ways that go beyond these standard differences in the political and legal cultures of the three countries. This can be seen in two further areas: in international pressure for the greater use of performance instead of design criteria in regulations and their implementation, and in new realities for the role of consumers in regulatory realms, nationally and internationally.

The pressure for regulation and implementation to be cast in performance terms and criteria rather than design criteria has been argued in each country for some time, but is increasing because of the presence of performance standards in trade agreements, including environmental–trade links and other issues of standard setting (Dewees 1983; Trebilcock and Howse 1995; and Vogel 1995). For example, environmental performance standards might specify a given criterion, such as a particular level of reduced pollution emission, and then leave it up to the polluter as to how it will go about achieving the result. In principle, this allows the polluter to take action with the least costly methods suitable to that firm's or industry's production and market situation. The alternative to this approach is to define standards not in terms of output but of how precisely they must be carried out. This specification of the means is in a design sense viewed as doomed to inefficiency and unfair enforcement because it imposes uniform solutions to many different kinds of production situations. In environmental and occupational health areas, this design approach is often revealed by regulatory requirements either for the best practicable or available technology or for more particular kinds of equipment (e.g., the installation of scrubbers). In recent years, the latter approach has come to be viewed as 'command and control' regulation, while the former is seen as an example of the more beneficial use of regulation based on economic incentives or market approaches.

With respect to consumers and compliance, the regulatory systems of the three countries have been influenced by a variety of changes that affect the way we view and map the larger compliance realm of regulatory institutions. First, the UK regulatory changes have introduced (albeit not in all sectors) some interesting innovations in consumer representation. In water regulation, OFWAT established ten statutory regional customer-service committees. A recent study on water companies has assessed these consumer-centred institutions in quite positive terms when compared to the previous opportunities for consumer input when they were a single nationalized industry (Ogden and Anderson 1995). But there are clearly other aspects of consumer politics in the UK (such as the salaries and perquisites of the executives of privatized utilities) that are not adequately accommodated by such institutional appendages (Corry 1995).

U.S. and Canadian consumer politics in both regulation making and compliance have also changed under the effects of both free-trade agreements and deregulation. First, free trade itself is a pro-consumer policy in two senses. Tariff reductions help reduce prices and increase choice across the economy, and thus change the markets of sectors still subject to regulation. Second, liberalized trade has brought forth theories of national competitiveness that focus on the importance of tough informed consumerism in all areas of the national market place (Porter 1990). In this sense consumerism, instead of continuing in its guise of vocal 'Naderism,' has become more generically mainstream. Third, regulatory compliance is no longer, if it ever was, a world only of the mass public or of the citizen consumer. The deregulation of industries, coupled with technological change, has brought out the role of businesses and their interest groups as intermediary consumer and user constituencies to an extent that was not the case before.

The above points by no means exhaust the compliance issues. Federal states such as the United States and Canada face important choices of how compliance should be managed where regulatory regimes and jurisdictions overlap.

The UK faces similar choices under the rubric of a search for principles of subsidiarity within the European Union.

Conclusions

The analysis of regulatory institutions in the United Kingdom, the United States, and Canada needs to be looked at in a broader fashion than has typically been the case. Accordingly, this chapter has suggested a framework that draws attention to regulatory institutions as an interacting set of four regimes. The core features of each regime have been examined to show that there is an inner characteristic or core logic that helps define it as a regime not only for analytical purposes but also for those officials and interests participating in and around it.

However, in the late 1990s our interest is also drawn to some of the key features of the interplay between the regimes. As in virtually any discussion of regimes or analyical sub-systems, the boundaries between the regimes can never be fully clear. Moreover, we have seen how different mechanisms have been utilized in the three countries for managing inter-regime relations in such areas as in the links between framework competition regulators and sectoral regulators. It is also evident that the relations between international regulatory regimes and the approaches inside the executive for managing the government's overall regulatory process are changing.

The chapter has also shown that regulatory institutions cannot be fully appreciated only through the macro-level set of regimes. Thus it has suggested a number of analytical aspects that are needed as one focuses on a particular regulatory body and that may be being compared across national boundaries. Such micro- and middle-level analysis crucially includes many familiar features of organizational analysis but, in the 1990s, it must also include the impact of budget cuts and the emergence of new compliance approaches in an era of real or alleged 'reinvented' government.

NOTE

1 Anyone using the concept of regimes must do so knowing that there are varying usages of the term (Doern 1995; Eisner 1993; Harris and Milkis 1989). In domestic regulatory areas it is often used as suggested in Regime I, where quite formal organizations are present. In international relations literature it is often used to convey softer arrangements and agreements where there often is no real organization at the centre. Economists will also often refer to regimes in regulation by referring to 'rate of return' or 'price-capping' as different regimes for public utility regulation. Despite these difficulties, the term has analytical value for the reasons set out further below.

REFERENCES

Allison, Graham. 1971. *Essence of Decision*. New York: Little, Brown.

Ayres, Ian, and John Braithwaite. 1992. *Responsive Regulation: Transcending the Deregulation Debate*. Oxford: Oxford University Press.

Baldwin, R., and C. McCrudden. 1987. *Regulation and Public Law*. London: Wiedenfeld and Nicolson.

Beesley, M.E., ed. 1995. *Utility Regulation: Challenge and Response*. London: Institute of Economic Affairs.

Bernstein, Marver. 1955. *Regulating Business by Independent Commission*. Princeton: University Press.

Cane, Peter. 1992. *An Introduction to Administrative Law*. 2nd ed. Oxford: Clarendon Press.

Coleman, W.D., and G. Underhill. 1995. 'Globalization, Regionalism, and the Regulation of Securities Markets.' *Journal of European Public Policy* 2, no. 3: 488–513.

Corry, Dan. 1995. *Profiting from the Utilities*. London: Institute for Policy Research.

Crandall, R.W., and L. Waverman. 1995. *Talk Is Cheap: The Promise of Regulatory Reform in North American Telecommunications*. Washington: The Brookings Institution.

Dewees, Donald, ed. 1983. *The Regulation of Quality*. Toronto: Butterworths, chap. 1.

Doern, G. Bruce, ed. 1978. *The Regulatory Process in Canada*. Toronto: Macmillan of Canada.

– 1995. *Fairer Play: Canadian Competition Policy Institutions in a Global Market*. Toronto: C.D. Howe Institute.

Doern, G. Bruce, and Tom Conway. 1995. *The Greening of Canada*. Toronto: University of Toronto Press.

Doern, G. Bruce, Les Pal, and Brian Tomlin, eds. 1996. *Border Crossings: The Internationalization of Canadian Public Policy*. Toronto: Oxford University Press Canada.

Doern, G. Bruce, and Richard W. Phidd. 1992. *Canadian Public Policy: Ideas, Structure, Process*. 2nd ed. Toronto: Nelson Canada chap. 7, 12.

Doern, G. Bruce, and Glen Toner. 1985. *The Politics of Energy*. Toronto: Methuen.

Doern, G. Bruce, and Stephen Wilks, eds. 1996. *Comparative Competition Policy: National Institutions in a Global Market*. Oxford: Clarendon Press.

Drake, W.J. 1994. 'Asymmetric Deregulation and the Transformation of the International Telecommunications Regime.' In *Asymmetric Deregulation: The Dynamics of Telecommunications Policy in Europe and the United States*, edited by E. Noam and G. Pogorel. Norwood, N.J.: Ablex Publishing.

Economic Council of Canada. 1979. *Responsible Regulation*. Ottawa: Economic Council of Canada.

– 1981. *Reforming Regulation.* Ottawa: Economic Council of Canada.

Eisner, M.A. 1991. *Antitrust and the Triumph of Economics.* Chapel Hill: University of North Carolina Press.

– 1993. 'Bureaucratic Professionalism and the Limits of the Political Control Thesis: The Case of the Federal Trade Commission.' *Governance* 6:127–53.

Francis, John. 1993. *The Politics of Regulation: A Comparative Perspective.* Cambridge, Mass.: Blackwell.

Grabosky, Peter N. 1995. 'Using Non-governmental Resources to Foster Compliance.' *Governance* 8:527–50.

Gray, Tim S. 1995. *UK Environmental Policy in the 1990s.* London: Macmillan.

Harris, R.A., and S.M. Milkis. 1989. *The Politics of Regulatory Change.* New York: Oxford University Press, chap. 3.

Harris, Stephen. 1995. 'The Political Economy of the Liberalization of Entry and Ownership in the Canadian Investment Dealer Industry.'

Hill, Margaret. 1994. 'The Choice of Mode for Regulation: A Case Study of the Canadian Pesticide Registration Review 1988–1992. Ph.D thesis, Department of Political Science, Carleton University, Ottawa, chap. 3.

Hoberg, George. 1993. *Pluralism by Design: Environmental Policy and the American Regulatory State.* New York: Praeger.

Hood, Christopher. 1986. *Administrative Analysis.* London: Harvester Wheatsheaf, chap. 3.

Jacobs, Scott. 1992. *Regulatory Management and Reform: Current Concerns in OECD Countries.* Paris: OECD.

Lanjouw. G.J. 1995. *International Trade Institutions.* London: Longman.

Law Reform Commission. 1986. *Policy Implementation, Compliance and Administrative Law.* Ottawa: Law Reform Commission of Canada.

Lee, Kelly. 1996. *Global Telecommunications Regulation: A Political Economy Perspective.* London: Pinter.

Liesner, Hans. 1995. 'The Role of the MMC in Utility Regulation.' In *British Utility Regulation: Principles, Experiences and Reform,* edited by Dieter Helm. Oxford: Oxera Press.

Linder, Stephen, and Guy Peters. 1989. 'Instruments of Government: Perceptions and Contexts.' *Journal of Public Policy* 9, no. 1:35–58.

Makkai, Toni, and John Braithwaite. 1992. 'In and Out of the Revolving Door: Making Sense of Regulatory Capture.' *Journal of Public Policy* 12, pt 1 (January–March): 61–78.

Martin, James K. 1995. 'Regulating the Regulators: The Canadian Approach to Implementing Government-wide Regulatory Reform Strategies.' Paper presented to the New South Wales Regulatory Review Conference, 20 June, at Sydney, Australia.

McGarity, Thomas O. 1991. *Reinventing Rationality: The Role of Regulatory Analysis in the Federal Bureaucracy*. Cambridge: Harvard University Press.

Meier, K.J. 1985. *Regulation: Politics, Bureaucracy, Economics*. New York: St. Martins.

Monopolies and Mergers Commission (MMC). 1994. *1994 Review*. London: HMSO.

Monteiro, Joseph. 1993. *Interventions by the Bureau of Competition Policy*. Ottawa: Bureau of Competition Policy, Industry Canada.

Odgers, Graeme. 1995. 'What is the Role of the MMC in the Utilities Sector?.' Paper presented to the Adam Smith Institute Conference on the Future of Utilities, 12 December, at London.

Ogden, Stuart, and Fiona Anderson. 1995. 'Representing Customer's Interests: The Case of the Privatized Water Industry in England and Wales.' *Public Administration* 73 (winter): 535–61.

Ogus, Anthony I. 1994. *Regulation: Legal Form and Economic Theory*. Oxford: Clarendon Press.

Peters, Guy. 1996. 'United States Competition Policy Insitutions: Structual Constraints and Opportunities.' In *Comparative Competition Policy: National Institutions in a Global Market*, edited by G. Bruce Doern and Stephen Wilks, 40–67. Oxford: Clarendon Press.

Pildes, R., and C. Sunstein. 1995. 'Reinventing the Regulatory State.' *University of Chicago Law Journal* 62, no. 1:1–129.

Porter, Michael. 1990. *The Competitive Advantage of Nations*. New York: Free Press.

Ratushny, Ed. 1987. 'What Are Administrative Tribunals? The Pursuit of Uniformity in Diversity.' *Canadian Public Administration*, 30, no. 1:1–13.

Schultz, Richard, and Alan Alexandroff. 1985. *Economic Regulation and the Federal System*. Toronto: University of Toronto Press.

Sparrow, Malcolm K. 1994. *Imposing Duties: Government's Changing Approach to Compliance*. London: Praeger.

Stanbury, William T. 1992. *Reforming the Federal Regulatory Process in Canada, 1971–1992*. Appendix to House of Commons, Standing Committee on Finance, Subcommittee on Regulations and Competitiveness. Issue no. 23. Supply and Services Canada, chap. 5.

Taylor, Paul, and A.J.R. Groom, eds. 1988. *International Institutions at Work*. London: Pinter.

Trebilcock, Michael. 1991. 'Requiem for Regulators: The Passing of a Counter-Culture?' *Yale Journal of Regulation* 8, no. 2 (summer):497–510.

Trebilcock, Michael, and Robert Howse. 1995. *The Regulation of International Trade*. London: Routledge.

U.S. Information Infrastructure Task Force. 1995. *Intellectual Property and the National Information Infrastructure*. Washington: Department of Commerce.

Vass, Peter, ed. 1994. *Regulating the Utilities: Accountability and Processes*. London: Centre for the Study of Regulated Industries.

Veljanovski, Cento. 1991. *Regulators and the Market: An Assessment of the Growth of Regulation in the UK*. London: Institute of Economic Affairs.

– 1993. *The Future of Industry Regulation in the UK*. London: European Policy Forum 1993.

Vogel, David. 1995. *Trading Up: Consumer and Environmental Regulation in a Global Economy*. Cambridge: Harvard University Press.

Weale, Albert. 1992. *The New Politics of Pollution*. Manchester: Manchester University Press.

White, L.J., ed. 1988. *Private Antitrust Litigation: New Evidence, New Learning*. Cambridge, Mass.: MIT Press.

Wiener, Jarrod. 1995. *Making Rules in the Uruguay Round of the GATT: A Study of International Leadership*. Aldershot: Dartmouth.

3

Institutionalization and Deinstitutionalization: Regulatory Institutions in American Government

B. GUY PETERS

Regulation and deregulation might not appear to be a likely locus for intense political debate. Much of the discussion of proposed regulations in the United States occurs in virtually incomprehensible statements in the *Federal Register*, and the results of the regulatory process are enshrined in the 'legalese' of the *Code of Federal Regulations*. Regulatory politics are, however, also described by some authors as 'class warfare' (Weaver 1978) and as attempts to create an impractical 'zero-risk' society (Schultze 1979). Critics of regulation have been able to create the image of meddling and inefficient government agencies imposing unreasonable costs on consumers (Weidenbaum and DeFina 1978; Warner 1992); one recent estimate places the costs of regulations per person higher than federal per capita taxation (*Economist* 1996). Advocates of regulation, on the other hand, point to the health risks and the predations of capitalism that come from an unregulated society.[1] In short, regulatory politics can be real, bare-knuckled politics, as well they might. Although performed through law rather than more overtly through taxing and spending, regulation involves moving around billions of dollars of costs and benefits within the U.S. economy.

In that highly politicized context, deregulation has become, during at least the past two decades, a dominant ideology for the public sector in the United States. There have been complaints from business about the negative impact of government regulations almost since their initial adoption, but only with the 1980s did deregulation become the dominant approach for policies affecting almost all dimensions of the social and economic systems. There is a now widespread political and economic assumption that many if not most existing regulatory interventions are inefficient and that they damage not only the businesses affected directly by the rules but also the public in general. The burden of proof, therefore, now falls squarely on anyone who wants to extend, or even maintain, regulations. There have been relatively few structural changes in the organizations responsible for regulation; what has changed most are the ideas utilized by those organizations when making decisions about policies.

The ideology of deregulation continues to be powerful in the United States, as evidenced in part by the adoption of a massive deregulation of the telecommunications industry in 1996. This legislation was passed enthusiastically by a Republican Congress and signed equally enthusiastically by a Democratic president, who forecast the dawning of a new age for American consumers of a variety of electronic services (Healey 1995). The Brookings Institution, usually thought of as a bastion of the traditional Democratic Party, actually argued that the telecommunications area was not being deregulated sufficiently (Crandall 1996). At about the same time that the telecommunications legislation was adopted in Congress, the Interstate Commerce Commission (ICC), the oldest of the independent regulatory commissions, was allowed to go out of business (a major structural change to be sure) with hardly a whimper of regret (Victor 1995), further evidence of the contemporary strength of the deregulation ideology.[2]

The strength of this deregulatory idea can also be observed in the variety of political and economic actors who support it. Support for various forms of deregulation has come from business interests, unions, Ralph Nader's consumers' groups (Pertschuk 1982), and even some neo-Marxists (Horowitz 1986), as well as from partisan politicians. For different reasons, but often in relation to the same industries, these disparate political and social forces have argued that the market, or perhaps other forms of collective social action, could solve problems more effectively than do command and control regulation. While some of the pressure for deregulation from consumers' groups arises from dissatisfaction with the ways in which regulation has been implemented in practice rather than with the policy instrument per se, it is important to note just how widely the perception of failure of regulation has spread.

It is also interesting to note the extent to which even those regulatory agencies that are maintaining their level of activity have begun to utilize market-type mechanisms for addressing the policy problems for which they are responsible. This change in focus can be seen most clearly in environmental policy, where command and control regulations are being replaced by such instruments as tradeable permits. Under these permits, industries have an allotment of pollution based on the volume of emissions they gave off at the beginning of the program. If an industry is able to reduce its emissions it can sell the difference in allowable emissions to other industries that want to enter the 'bubble' or expand their operations within it. This market device is assumed to produce greater efficiency than more conventional command and control regulatory methods.

The increasing institutionalization of the concept of deregulation represents the deinstitutionalization of the previously dominant idea of regulatory policy in the U.S. political economy. Unlike most European governments the U.S. federal government never owned a significant share of the economy, other than vast tracts of public land.[3] The dominant mode of economic intervention has been through regulations of various sorts, including regulatory tariffs, rate setting, and anti-monopoly laws. Regulation was a powerful idea politically during the late nineteenth and most of the twentieth centuries (McKraw 1981), but has been challenged and eventually superseded during the 1970s and 1980s. This replacement of the dominant idea about economic policy was a function in part of the numerous failings of regulation, but also a reflection of a change in the patterns of thought within the economics and law establishments that have become institutionalized in public organization (McGarity 1991).

The deregulation movement in the United States also reflects the institutionalization of ideas concerning the rights of individuals to make their own decisions about risks and to use information to make decisions on their own. This aspect of deregulation tends to apply more to social regulations that are designed to protect citizens from the risks and externalities of the market place. The idea of 'empowering' citizens as consumers has a great deal of resonance with many Americans, but paradoxically appears to depend on the implementation of other types of regulations. If consumers are to have a fair opportunity to make decisions about which risks to assume, then they will need access to reliable information, but that information may be made available only when there are adequate regulations.

Finally, the increasing deregulation in American government can be seen as institutionalizing the idea of 'regulatory takings.' This is the idea that the owners of private property have a presumption of an ability to utilize that property as they see fit (Epstein 1985). Therefore, denying the free use of those assets through such policies as regulations on the development of wetlands is unjustifiable in this conception of the relationship between state and economy. This doctrine is a logical extension of the Fifth Amendment protection against denial of life, liberty, and property without due process, and it is becoming increasingly used in the courts to justify decisions in favour of property and against the regulatory interventions of government, including the exercise of eminent domain (Wise and Emerson 1994).

Institutions and Regimes

The massive shift in ideologies of regulation and deregulation has been described as a change in 'regimes,' meaning, in this instance, a change in the ideas governing management of a policy issue and the broad institutions that support those ideas (Harris and Milkis 1989). This shift can also be seen as an institutional change within the framework of March and Olsen (1984, 1989). In this view, public organizations are best understood through the 'logic of appropriateness,' which provides them an internal compass and a set of general statements about what constitutes good public policy. Changing policy therefore implies changing the governing ideas for those policies. It is clear that in this case the appropriate strategy for government changed from regulation to allowing the market to function and to assuming that competition would be sufficient to solve almost any problems. Similarly, the 'takings' doctrine represents a definition of appropriate policy quite different from the one that had been dominant previously.

The deregulation process can also be seen as a function of the rule-based version of institutionalism usually associated with Elinor Ostrom (1990) and with rational-choice versions of institutional theory. The logic here is that institutions are defined by the rules they use to produce compliance by their own members and by the objects of the regulations. In the context of deregulation another set of rules becomes important. These are the rules that are being applied to justify eliminating regulations, for example cost-benefit analysis. The construction of these rule-based regimes is an attempt to eliminate discretion and may be seen as a political version of the courts' 'hard look' doctrine (see below).

An alternative economic view of the institutions of regulation would be through the lens of 'principal-agent models' (Horn 1995, 40–7). In this view many or most of the regulatory agencies in the United States probably have failed in exercising their duties to reflect the view of their 'principals' – Congress and to some extent the president. As we will be noting throughout, many of the complaints about regulation arise from the failure of agencies to carry out the perceived legislative intent of Congress. This can be through excessively lax regulation and regulatory capture, for example the ICC, or it can be through excessively activist interventions, largely on the part of social regulators such as the Environmental Protection Agency (EPA), the Occupational Safety and Health Administration (OSHA), and the Consumer Products Safety Commission (CPSC).

The final approach to institutions that is of relevance is 'historical institutionalism,' or the assumption that the decisions made at the initial stages of government's involvement in a policy will have a pervasive effect on subsequent developments (Thelen, Longstreth, and Steinmo 1992). This approach seems very good for explaining the continuation of regulation and the difficulty encountered in producing deregulation in some policy areas. It appears much less capable of explaining the fundamental shift in thinking on the subject of regulation as a whole. It may be possible to make the approach fit by arguing that the idea motivating much of the initial regulation movement was the creation or preservation of markets, and that deregulation merely presses that idea in a new and, at present more appropriate, direction.

Another aspect of the change in the ideas concerning regulations and of the manner in which they are treated institutionally is the increasing politicization of the regulatory process. We have already said that the regulatory arena is one in which intense political battles can take place. Since at least the period of President Ford, the White House has taken an increasing interest in regulation, and more particularly in deregulation. The presidential interest in regulatory agencies can be seen manifested in the increasing level of non-career appointments in these organizations as compared to agencies supplying different types of services (Ingraham, Thompson, and Eisenberg 1995; Light 1995). Of course, this strategy cannot be used for the independent regulatory agencies, but it has been for those regulatory organizations within the executive branch, especially social regulatory organizations such as the EPA; non-career appointments increased by over 60 per cent during the Reagan and Bush administrations.

Forms of Regulation and Deregulation

There is a widespread tendency for Americans to think about regulation, and therefore deregulation, as if it were a single phenomenon. This may be true at a very general level of analysis; all forms of regulation involve employing government legal powers to produce changes in the behaviour of economic and social actors (Kahn 1988). Despite the apparent similarities of all forms of deregulation, there are substantial differences in the politics and the economic impact of various forms of regulation. Further, there are important institutional differences in the manner in which the dissimilar versions of regulation are developed and implemented. Despite the important analytic and practical differences, the ideology of deregulation tends to be applied equally to all situations, and often appears inappropriate to the economic questions being confronted.[4]

Market Regulation

The form of regulation that appears most commonly in the regulation and deregulation literature is one that is directed (at least initially) at creating or maintaining markets. In the United States this form of regulation began with the creation of the ICC in 1887 and was followed by a number of other independent regulatory agencies designed to be outside the direct control of either the president or Congress. These included the Federal Trade Commission (FTC) (1914), the Federal Reserve Board (as a bank regulator in 1913), and the Federal Power Commission (1920). There was a second wave of creation of structures of this type during the New Deal, including independent organizations such as the Securities and Exchange Commission (1934), the Federal Maritime Commission (1930), and the National Labor Relations Board (1935).

Although in many ways similar to the earlier forms, the New Deal regulation added another institutional element. This factor was the closer connection of government and private-sector interests, termed 'associational regulation' by Eisner (1993). The importance of this institutional arrangement is that some of the frequently cited capture of regulators by the regulated interests was, if not intended by government, certainly facilitated by government policies at the time. While the first wave of regulation tended to regularize markets by legalistic interventions such as rate setting, part of the New Deal style was to regularize markets by strategies that approached the corporatism of European countries (Brand 1988). These regulatory interventions were characterized by strong market-entry and rate controls that tended to guarantee the positions of firms already in the market.

The politics of these first two collections of economic regulatory organizations have been the classic 'regulatory politics' described by James Q. Wilson (1980). Wilson argued that regulatory politics are characterized by concentrated benefits and diffused costs. A relatively small number of private-sector interests benefited from the control of markets created by the regulatory interventions despite the intention of at least the initial wave to disadvantage some firms. Although regulated firms may have had their rates and conditions of service controlled, they were protected from other market pressures, especially entry into the market by firms that might have wanted to offer equal or better services at the same or better prices.[5] On the other hand, the costs of the regulatory interventions tended to be diffused over the entire economy. That diffusion of costs came not only through the taxes necessary to fund the regulators, but more importantly through the increase in prices that came from restricted competition, especially the restriction on market entry by potential competitors. It was argued that the absence of effective competition stifled technological innovation, for example, in telephone service (Crandall 1992, 37). Further, some regulations imposed practices, such as 'dead-heading' by truckers, that had negative environmental and energy consequences as well as the negative economic consequences that it was argued were the product of almost all regulations.

Social and Framework Regulation

The third wave of regulatory interventions is commonly referred to as 'social regulation' (Harris and Milkis 1989). These interventions are characterized by rather different distributions of costs and benefits and different political histories than the market-based interventions. In some cases these are very old forms of health and safety legislation, although in the United States the level at which these were applied moved from the state and local level up to the federal level, for example, with the OSHA and the Mine Safety and Health Administration. There were, however, some important federal regulatory interventions of this sort before the 1970s, perhaps most notably the Food and Drug Administration (FDA) in 1931 (begun as the Food, Drug and Pesticides Administration in 1927) and a number of other organizations, arising first from the Humane Slaughter Act of 1906,[6] regulating and inspecting agricultural products.

Another notable form of social regulation is environmental protection, through, for example, the EPA and the Office of Surface Mine Enforcement among other federal organizations. The EPA was, somewhat unexpectedly, a creation of the Nixon administration, but it has been under attack from most Republicans since that time. Finally, the federal government has become increasingly involved in protecting consumers against fraud (FTC) and unsafe products (CPSC). These regulatory functions had long been performed by state and local governments, but the federal government has gradually assumed a larger and larger role, given that most of the products in question are in interstate commerce.

This second pattern of regulation is characterized to a greater extent than the first by diffuse benefits and concentrated costs. The entire society tends to benefit from the actions of these organizations, especially from interventions, such as those through environmental regulations, that create classic public goods. For the other forms of social regulation, the benefits are more likely to accrue to consumers and to workers, relatively broader sectors of society than the beneficiaries of classic economic regulation. The costs tend to be borne by relatively few people, such as the employees or stockholders of the corporations being regulated. The concentration of the costs may, however, be more perceived than real, given that the firms may be able to transfer the costs of regulations onto consumers, especially if all complementary products are regulated approximately equally.

Although often coming from a different era and reflecting a different set of values, framework economic regulations have some of the same characteristics as social regulations. By framework regulations we refer to regulations that apply across the whole economy as opposed to regulations that are industry or sector specific. An obvious example would be antitrust regulations that apply to all industries, except perhaps professional athletics. A variety of regulations, ranging from traditional weights and measures to intellectual property law, that are administered by federal and state governments provide the framework within which business is conducted. The distribution of costs and benefits of these regulatory programs is similar to that of social regulations, although the object of most framework regulations is the manipulation of economic variables rather than health or environmental issues.

Social regulation is also significantly different from economic regulation in its dependence on science and its emphasis on risk avoidance rather than clearly discernible injury (largely economic in nature), which is central to economic regulation. Many of the regulations issued by EPA and by OSHA deal with minute quantities of dangerous chemicals that are usually unseen and even unsmellable. This future orientation and emphasis on risk often makes them appear to be excessively cautious, and critics can poke fun at the perceived remoteness of the risks being regulated. Some early regulations have been argued to cost $132 million per life saved (Sunstein 1990, 239–40), while a more recent one may reach $6.3 trillion per life (Hahn 1996). The remoteness of the risks being controlled may devalue politically some of the activities of the social regulatory agencies, given that the positive outcomes – if they are successful, then people don't die or fall ill – are rarely attributed to regulations.

Although social regulatory agencies have been under little or no internal pressure to deregulate, there have certainly been external pressures. Some of these pressures come from industries that feel constrained by health, safety, and environmental regulations. Their arguments have found a receptive audience in the current Congress and with several recent presidents. There are also pressures to deregulate coming from client groups, an example being the victims of deadly and incurable diseases like AIDS. These groups demand that the FDA relax its traditionally strict rules on licensing new drugs, rules that have proven fortunate in the past (in the thalidomide case, for example).[7] Lobbying from AIDS activists and from victims of other diseases have led to the creation of a 'fast track' system of approval for certain categories of drugs (Foreman 1991) and some general reconsideration of the standards applied by the FDA.

For both the economic and social versions of regulation, perceptions of the distribution of costs and benefits may be as important as the reality. The importance of perceptions is highlighted by the fact that the initial intentions for what has come to be considered anti-competitive legislation were to enhance competition and create viable markets. The ICC was designed to create fairer rates for shippers confronting monopolistic railways, but it was soon transformed into an organization that restricted market entry and prevented competition within or across modes of transportation (Breyer 1982, 224–5). This change in the real and perceived effects of regulation has to some extent been a function of changes within the transportation sector, for example, the creation of several substitutes for rail transportation, as well as a change in thinking about the nature of regulatory actions.

Structurally too there are important differences among the types of regulatory agencies. The most significant is between organizations that exist within the executive branch and those that are independent of direct control from either Congress or the president. The latter organizational format began with the ICC 1887. The idea behind these organizations, growing out of the Progressive Movement, was that important economic regulatory policies could be developed and implemented most effectively and fairly if they were depoliticized.[8] Further, the collegial commission organizational format tends to diffuse authority and legally prevents either the regulator or the regulated from monopolizing control over regulations. In large part because of the absence of direct political connections, these organizations, it is argued, proved to be subject to capture by the very economic interests they were designed to regulate (Huntington 1987; but see McCubbins, Noll, and Weingast 1989). Having no other source of support, the organizations had to turn to the only groups in society that really cared about their activities – the regulated industries themselves.

A number of important regulatory organizations are embedded within the executive branch of government. The shift away from the independent regulatory commission as the preferred form of organization represented a change in fashion after the end of the Progressive and the New Deal eras, as well as a change in the nature of the activities being regulated. The shift also represented an increasing desire on the part of presidents to have control over as much of economic policy as possible. At least one of the executive branch organizations, the EPA, is a free-standing executive organization that does report direct to the president. The others are components of executive departments. As components of the executive branch, these organizations must, everything else being equal, be more responsive to political pressures than are the independent organizations. Despite that, some executive agencies, such as the FDA and OSHA, have been at the centre of political controversies and have often appeared out of touch with the significant political forces in the United States.[9]

Assisted Suicide: The Initial Roots of Deregulation

Dr Jack Kevorkian was recently acquitted of murder charges in the state of Michigan for assisting in the suicide of several terminally ill patients. To some extent, the movement towards deregulation in the United States – at least in the area of competitive regulation – shows some similarities to assisted suicide: agencies have wanted to deregulate and they have been assisted by powerful outside actors, such as presidents and senators. The lemming-like desire to eliminate the justification for their own existence is explained in part by the spread of the ideology of deregulation, in part by the undermining of some of the logic of regulation in industries such as telecommunications, and in part by the failures (political and economic) of many existing regulatory regimes.

It is also important to note here that regulatory institutions can produce deregulation by implementing the same procedures they have always used for producing regulation. For example, prior to its demise, the ICC significantly deregulated of trucking simply by granting a much higher percentage of requests for entry into routes and for new rate structures than it had in the past. It also greatly extended the areas around cities where the regulations did not have force, thus creating more and more deregulated hauls. In short, it used its powers to undermine what its predecessors in the organization had done and to create a much less regulated trucking industry (Moore 1986).

We also need to remember that not all the agencies that have deregulated their policy areas have jumped off the cliff; some have been pushed. Congress has been active in forcing the deregulation of specific policy areas, and the White House also has been active in pushing to eliminate regulations. Combined, they helped terminate the Civil Aeronautics Board and later the ICC. Congress has also tried to make termination and deregulation automatic if the regulator does not act affirmatively. So-called sunset laws have been popular at the state level (Kearney 1990; Mahtesian 1992), if not always successful, and they have been spreading to the federal level. For example, Congress inserted a sunset provision into the act creating the Federal Energy Administration in 1974. That agency was changed drastically as a result of the creation of the Department of Energy, but its functions have continued without the formal sunset review required.

Macro- and Micro-Institutional Questions

The transformation of the institutional configurations delivering regulations during the contemporary period of deregulation can be observed at both macro- and micro-institutional levels. That is, there have been significant changes in the three major branches of government and in their relationship to the regulatory agencies. Further, the regulatory organizations have themselves been changing significantly. The changes are evident in an empirical sense of institutionalism, in, for example, their formal structures, and it is perhaps even more true in the value-driven sense of institutionalism (March and Olsen 1989). In some cases these changes are extreme – an instance would be organizational termination – but in most the changes are substantially more subtle.

Macro-Institutionalism

The era of deregulation appears to have depreciated the power of the traditional three dominant branches of the U.S. government, but that appearance is somewhat deceiving. Much of the activity in deregulation – at least in the area of competitive regulation – has been conducted by the agencies themselves; the same legislative authority that enabled them to write secondary legislation also empowered them to eliminate those regulations. Despite that use of authority, the three major branches of government are still involved and, in some ways, have had their powers increased.

Although a good deal of the activity in deregulation has been initiated by the agencies themselves, there has also been a significant involvement from the three major branches of government. First, a succession of presidents from both the Democratic and Republican parties, going back at least to Gerald Ford, have advocated and promoted deregulation. This presidential advocacy has legitimated much of the activity of the administrative agencies, especially the activity with respect to the elimination of competitive regulation. The emphasis on the deregulation of competition was especially clear in the administrations of Republican presidents, some of whom developed institutions to facilitate the elimination of rules. But the enthusiasm for deregulation of Republican presidents has been almost matched by some Democrats, most notably Jimmy Carter (Derthick and Quirk 1985, 30–2).

In Congress there have been two somewhat contradictory reactions to the push for deregulation. On the one hand, a number of Congressmen, including very liberal ones such as Ted Kennedy, have been as anxious as their presidential counterparts to reduce the regulations that have constrained competition in some policy areas. Although a good deal of the action in deregulation has come from the agencies themselves, Congress has provided some guidance through such legislation as the Airline Deregulation Act of 1978 and the Motor Carriers Act of 1980. The net effect of these legislative efforts has been to reduce the impact of legislation over major segments of U.S. industry, especially transportation and telecommunications.

The second dimension of Congressional activity has been its use oversight powers to micro-manage agencies and their regulatory activities, especially the agencies directly within the executive branch (Gilmour and Halley 1994). Congress has found it advantageous to impose detailed controls over agencies and their rules, usually as a response to pressures coming from constituents. The use of legislative vetoes has been one of the manifestations of this control, even after their use was declared unconstitutional by the Supreme Court (*INS* v. *Chadha* 1983).[10] Legislative vetoes are rights retained by Congress or by committees of Congress to review the regulations issued by an agency and to revoke those they believe misinterpret the intentions of Congress.

The Republican 'Revolution' in 1994 reinvigorated another approach to oversight over regulations, namely regulatory analysis and the application of cost-benefit analysis to assess the utility of each regulation. This form of control over regulations was imposed initially during the Carter administration and then retained and somewhat expanded by subsequent Republican administrations. Regulatory analysis has played an increasingly significant role in the thinking about how to improve the performance of public-sector regulation, with the basic logic being that any regulation that does not have a positive balance of benefits and costs should be examined more closely and perhaps eliminated. In one of the most recent instance of such an examination Congress was the initiator of the analytic approach and attempted to include it as a part of its oversight operations.[11]

Third, the courts have also altered their own role in the regulatory process. In particular, they have altered the legal doctrines that they apply when considering regulatory and deregulatory activities. During the New Deal the courts developed a presumption that regulatory organizations had relatively broad grants of power to make secondary legislation, and so there had to be some compelling evidence for the courts to accept the argument that a regulation was *ultra vires*.[12] Although initially hostile to the idea, the courts became supportive of the capacity of government to regulate through administrative action.

The courts have, however, extended their consideration of rule making by agencies. This has come through two versions of the 'hard look' doctrine. The first of these was a substantive hard look, first propounded in 1970.[13] Increasingly, the courts have required agencies to demonstrate that the substance of the regulations they promulgated has a logical connection to their legislative mandate, that the agency has considered all relevant alternatives, and that a reasonable person (i.e., a judge) can understand the connection (Gormley 1989). Further, the courts have wanted to be sure that the procedures used to make the regulations are accessible and appropriate under the understanding of administrative law. Even regulations that appear to make good sense substantively may be voided by procedural problems (Needleman and Landrigan 1996).

Finally, in the United States the role of the states as regulators must be included as a part of any consideration of deregulation. The states engage in a great number of regulatory activities, ranging from simple weights and measures to very complex rate setting for public utilities. Further, the states often regulate on behalf of the federal government, seen, for example, in the requirement for state plans to implement federal clean air legislation and in the possible involvement of states in implementing occupational safety legislation. Indeed, one meaning of 'deregulation' has been that of transferring responsibility for issuing and implementing economic controls from the federal government to the states or even to local governments. It has been argued that federalism has become 'regulatory federalism' (Beam 1983; Reagan 1987, 187–207), with the federal government achieving its policy aims by regulating how the states implement programs. A number of the current battles in domestic policy in the United States centre around the degree to which regulatory federalism will be allowed to continue.

While the decentralization of power may produce more diverse regulations designed to meet the needs of the disparate parts of the country, it may in effect be an extension of regulation instead of a diminution.[14] Indeed, some states have adopted stronger regulatory statutes (Moore 1988) than has the federal government; emission control standards in California for automobiles have been much higher than the federal standards, and are now being extended across the country. On the other hand, however, there is a danger that decentralizing regulatory powers produces a 'race to the bottom,' with states vying with each another to have the least restrictive regulatory regimen and hence the most attractive environment for new businesses.

Within the sphere of state regulation itself there has been substantially less deregulation than at the federal level. This appears to be the case for several reasons. One is the political nature of the regulatory institutions at the state level (some with elected members), and their general unwillingness, unlike federal regulators, to commit suicide. Furthermore, many of the industries being regulated at the state level have not benefited from the technological changes that have affected many of the industries regulated federally. The tasks of providing electricity and natural gas to consumers still have most of the elements of natural monopolies, with the consequent advantage the firms have for maintaining a regulated market (Michaels 1992).[15] The states and the federal government also share responsibility for some regulatory areas, for example, unfair and deceptive advertising, and the federal government has been willing to give states the latitude to act first in some of these areas (Bloomquist 1990). Finally, there has been much less public or industry agitation in favour of deregulation than at the federal level. Indeed, there may exist a tacit bargain, with industries willing to exchange less intrusive state regulation for more stringent federal regulation.

The use of the states as agents for the federal government points to the reliance on private organizations for the enforcement of some programs. To some extent, self-enforcement has always been a part of regulation, given that governments do not have the staffs necessary to supervise continually all economic activities. Given staffing cuts in most regulatory organizations, the need for self-enforcement is increasing and will only continue to do so. Governments are also contracting out enforcement activities to a greater extent than in the past. Activities that, because of their legal nature, were once considered inherently governmental are now being handed over to the private sector for enforcement, raising important questions about the authoritative role of the public sector.

Micro-level Institutional Changes

As well as macro-level changes, there have been some important micro-level changes in regulatory bodies. If we look at some standard empirical indicators of these changes, we see relatively little variation for a number of the regulatory agencies. As Table 3.1 demonstrates, the levels of employment in these organizations have not varied as much as might have been expected given the increased emphasis on deregulation in U.S. policies. The evidence presented in the table illustrates that two social regulatory agencies, EPA and the Equal Employment Opportunities Commission, and a hybrid organization, the Nuclear Regulatory Commission, have fared somewhat better than have the more traditional economic regulatory organizations, the Federal Trade Commission and ICC. There has also been a great deal of stability in the structures of these organizations, with only relatively minor changes in their organization charts from the late 1970s and the 1990s (Figures 3.1 and 3.2).

Most of the changes that have occurred within regulatory organizations have to do with their reactions to the increasing demand for sophisticated economic analysis for justifying a regulation or deregulation, and to the adjustments arising from the greater internationalization of markets. The major regulatory organizations have always depended to some extent on economic analysis. The

TABLE 3.1 Employment in regulatory agencies (000s)

	1970	1975	1980	1985	1988	1990	1991	1992	1993
Environmental Protection Agency	n/a	10.7	14.7	13.8	15.3	17.1	18.2	18.2	18.4
Equal Employment Opportunities Commission	0.8	2.4	3.5	3.2	3.2	2.9	2.9	2.9	2.9
Federal Trade Commission	1.3	1.7	1.8	1.3	1.1	1.2	1.1	1.1	1.0
Nuclear Regulatory Commission	n/a	2.4	3.3	3.6	3.3	3.4	3.5	3.5	3.5
Interstate Commerce Commission	1.7	2.2	2.0	0.9	0.7	0.7	0.6	0.5	0.5

demand has grown greater, and economics rather than law tends to be the dominant language spoken in regulatory circles. Despite the history of regulation, especially in areas such as antitrust, there are increased demands for their economic justification coming from presidents, Congress, and even the public.

As noted above, one place where the idea of applying more economic analysis to regulatory activities has been prominent has been the White House and the Executive Office of the President. Most of the economic advice that presidents have received has been macroeconomic, and it came from the Council of Economic Advisors. Beginning at least with Gerald Ford, presidents have also begun to institutionalize micro-level analysis and to use that analysis to push deregulation.[16] President Ford began a limited program of regulatory analysis as a part of the attacks on inflation and the 'economic impact statements' of the Council on Wage and Price Stability (Miller 1977). President Carter later created a Regulatory Analysis and Review Group as an inter-agency organization charged with examining the economic impact of regulations, especially their contribution to inflation (still perceived as the major economic problem at the time).

Perhaps the clearest examples of the institutionalization of micro-level analysis of regulations came during the Reagan and Bush administrations. Very early in his administration President Reagan created the Task Force on Regulatory Relief, headed by then Vice-President Bush. It returned to some of the practices of the Carter administration in applying cost-benefit analysis and other forms of economic analysis to judge the efficacy of new or existing regulations. The assumption was that any proposed regulations unable to pass this test would not be implemented, and that over time existing regulations failing the test would be abolished.[17] Over time this task force became institutionalized within the

FIGURE 3.1 Environmental Protection Agency: Organizational charts

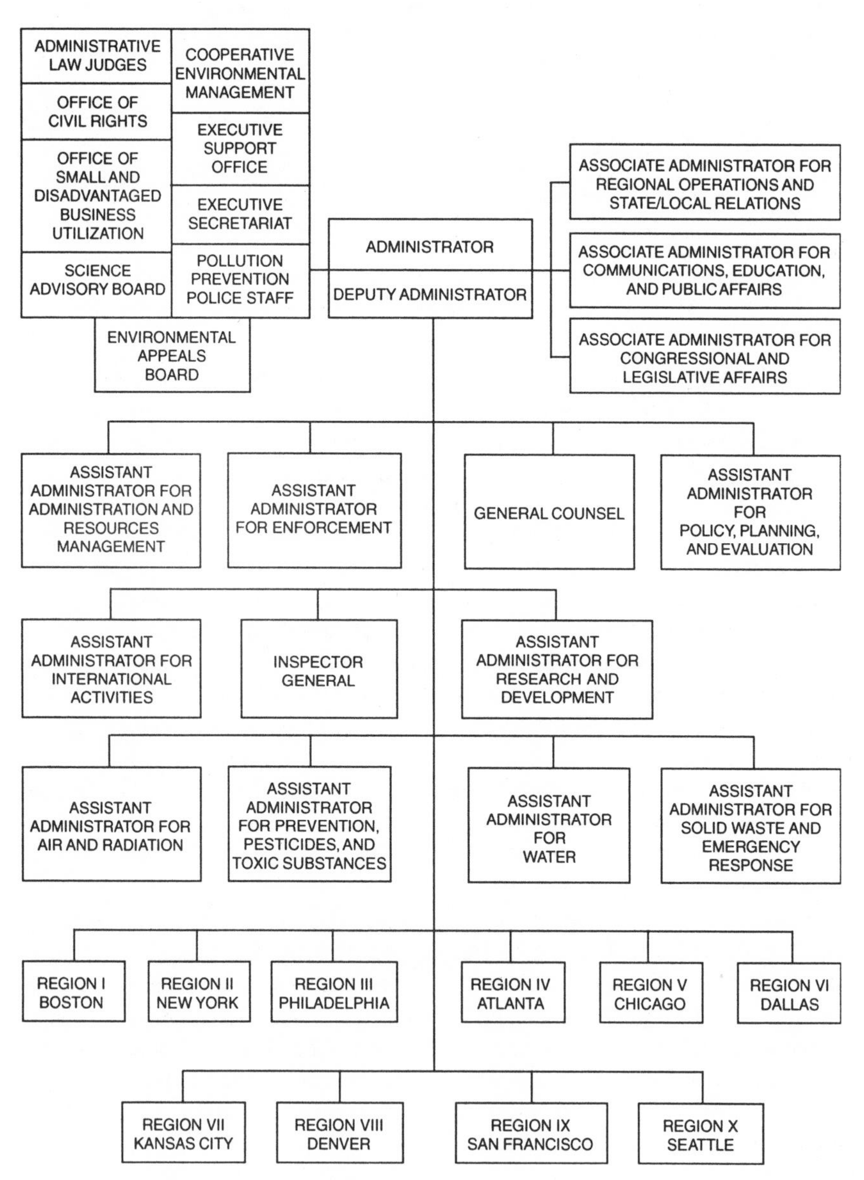

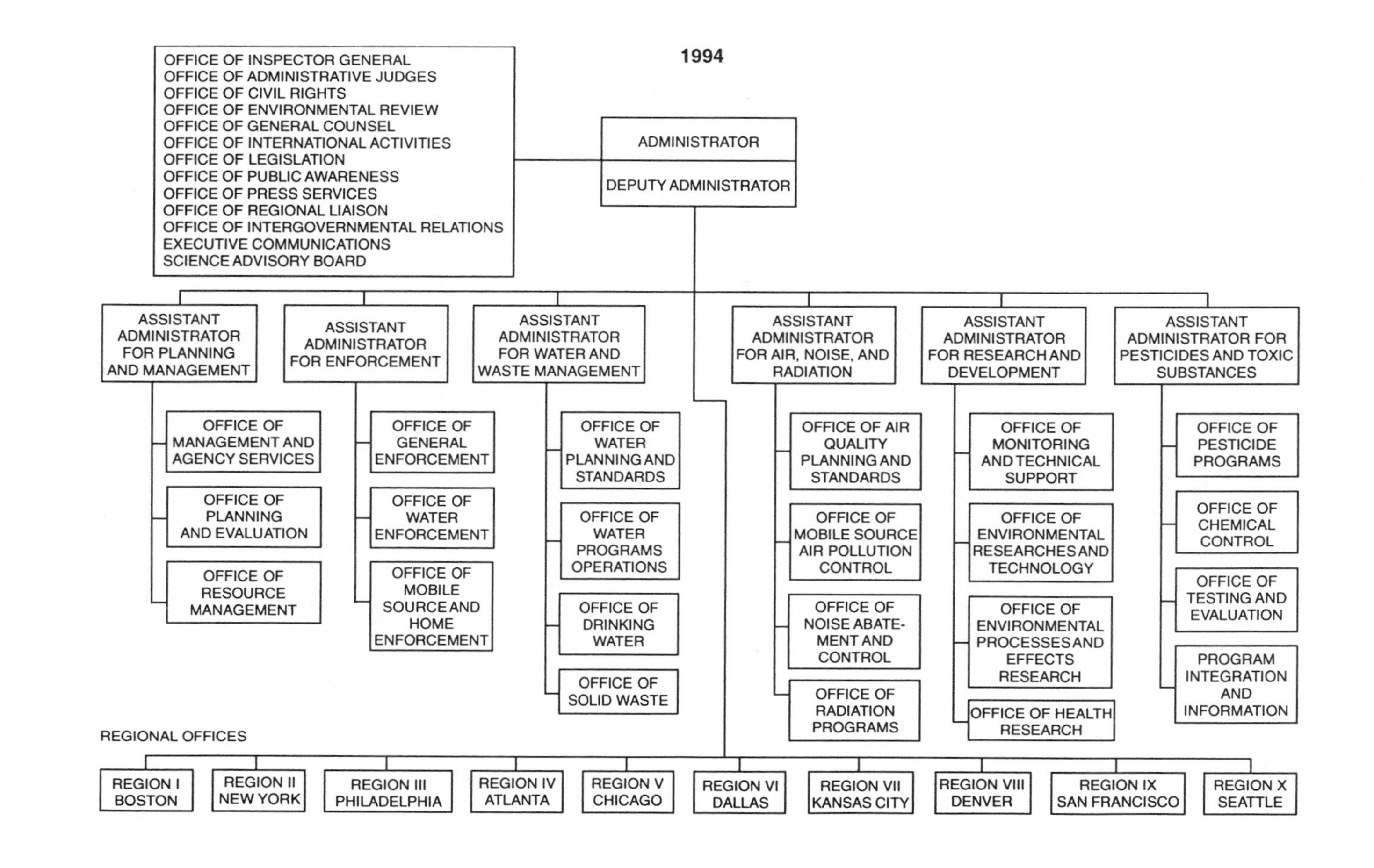
1994
OFFICE OF INSPECTOR GENERAL
OFFICE OF ADMINISTRATIVE JUDGES
OFFICE OF CIVIL RIGHTS
OFFICE OF ENVIRONMENTAL REVIEW
OFFICE OF GENERAL COUNSEL
OFFICE OF INTERNATIONAL ACTIVITIES
OFFICE OF LEGISLATION
OFFICE OF PUBLIC AWARENESS
OFFICE OF PRESS SERVICES
OFFICE OF REGIONAL LIAISON
OFFICE OF INTERGOVERNMENTAL RELATIONS
EXECUTIVE COMMUNICATIONS
SCIENCE ADVISORY BOARD
ADMINISTRATOR
DEPUTY ADMINISTRATOR
ASSISTANT ADMINISTRATOR FOR PLANNING AND MANAGEMENT
OFFICE OF MANAGEMENT AND AGENCY SERVICES
OFFICE OF PLANNING AND EVALUATION
OFFICE OF RESOURCE MANAGEMENT
ASSISTANT ADMINISTRATOR FOR ENFORCEMENT
OFFICE OF GENERAL ENFORCEMENT
OFFICE OF WATER ENFORCEMENT
OFFICE OF MOBILE SOURCE AND HOME ENFORCEMENT
ASSISTANT ADMINISTRATOR FOR WATER AND WASTE MANAGEMENT
OFFICE OF WATER PLANNING AND STANDARDS
OFFICE OF WATER PROGRAMS OPERATIONS
OFFICE OF DRINKING WATER
OFFICE OF SOLID WASTE
ASSISTANT ADMINISTRATOR FOR AIR, NOISE, AND RADIATION
OFFICE OF AIR QUALITY PLANNING AND STANDARDS
OFFICE OF MOBILE SOURCE AIR POLLUTION CONTROL
OFFICE OF NOISE ABATE-MENT AND CONTROL
OFFICE OF RADIATION PROGRAMS
ASSISTANT ADMINISTRATOR FOR RESEARCH AND DEVELOPMENT
OFFICE OF MONITORING AND TECHNICAL SUPPORT
OFFICE OF ENVIRONMENTAL RESEARCHES AND TECHNOLOGY
OFFICE OF ENVIRONMENTAL PROCESSES AND EFFECTS RESEARCH
OFFICE OF HEALTH RESEARCH
ASSISTANT ADMINISTRATOR FOR PESTICIDES AND TOXIC SUBSTANCES
OFFICE OF PESTICIDE PROGRAMS
OFFICE OF CHEMICAL CONTROL
OFFICE OF TESTING AND EVALUATION
PROGRAM INTEGRATION AND INFORMATION
REGIONAL OFFICES
REGION I BOSTON
REGION II NEW YORK
REGION III PHILADELPHIA
REGION IV ATLANTA
REGION V CHICAGO
REGION VI DALLAS
REGION VII KANSAS CITY
REGION VIII DENVER
REGION IX SAN FRANCISCO
REGION X SEATTLE

FIGURE 3.2 Federal Trade Commission: Organizational charts

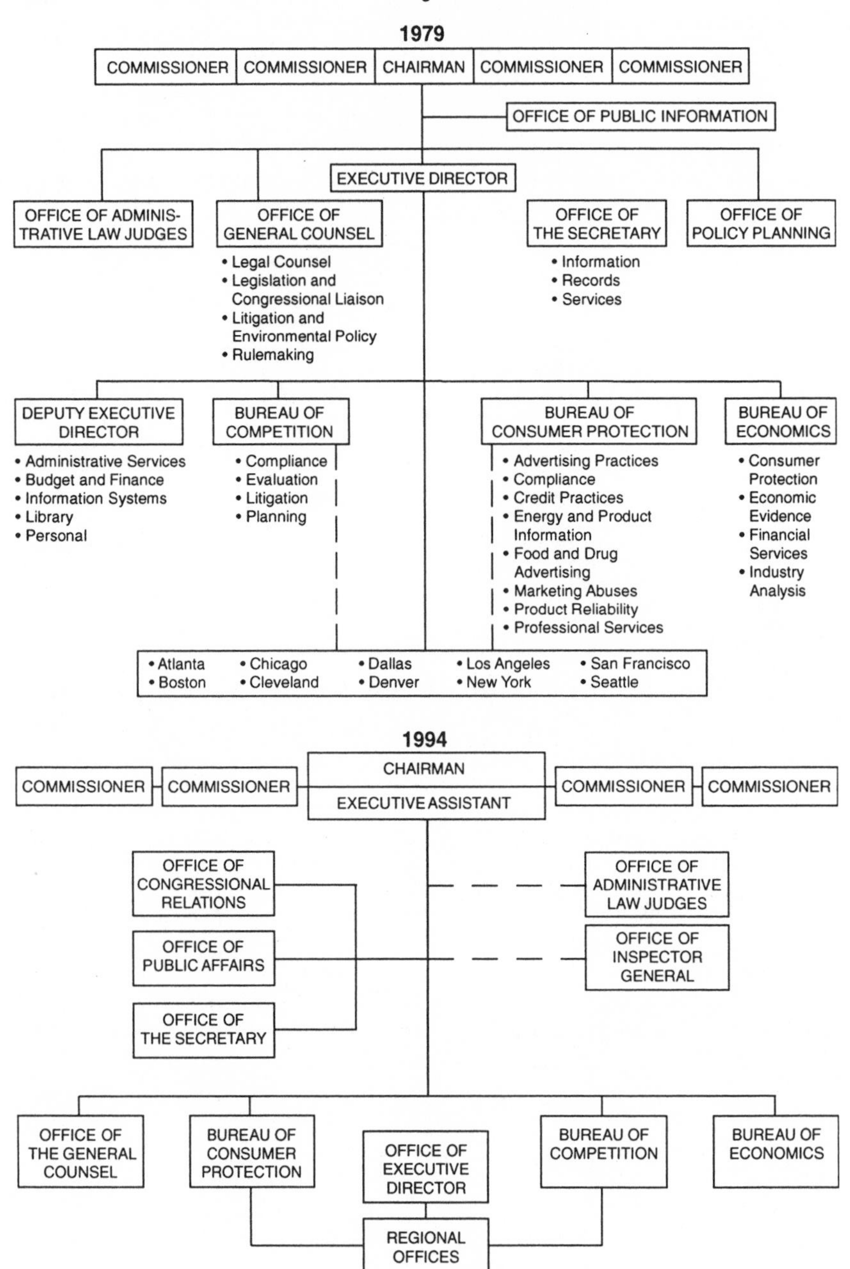

Office of Management and Budget (OMB) under the name of Office of Information and Regulatory Affairs, and it came to constitute what was called a 'regulatory KGB' (Kritz 1987) that thoroughly reviewed the attempts of agencies to impose new regulations.

The Bush administration linked the idea of deregulation with the then fashionable concept of 'competitiveness.' According to this argument, one of the reasons American industries were not more competitive in international markets was the costs imposed on them by environmental, health, and other forms of social regulation. Economic regulations were mentioned from time to time, but the real target of the Bush efforts was social regulation, especially in his ninety-day moratorium (Furlong 1995). The president created a Council on Competitiveness, headed by Dan Quayle, to investigate the impact of regulations on competitiveness and to make recommendations to him and to the regulatory agencies. Despite those actions, regulation made something of a comeback during the Bush administration (Rauch 1991).

The competitiveness and deregulation debate also became intertwined in foreign trade debates, especially in the ongoing discussion over the North American Free Trade Association (NAFTA). There was a great fear when NAFTA was adopted that the regulatory costs borne by American industries would place them at a disadvantage against Mexican industries and that there would be (in Ross Perot's term) a 'giant sucking sound' as jobs migrated south of the Rio Grande. This competitiveness debate continued to some extent even in the 1996 presidential campaign, as some candidates deplored the (alleged) loss of jobs as a result of free trade and the high costs of doing business in the United States because of regulations.

The Clinton administration has retained a regulatory analysis organization within the OMB. The pervasiveness of the deregulatory ideology can be seen in the perpetuation of this office and in the continuation of many of the ideas that dominated regulatory policies in the Reagan and Bush administrations. The Clinton administration lacks some of the deregulatory fervour of the previous administrations, and certainly it has not been moving sufficiently quickly on deregulation to satisfy Congressional Republicans (and some Democrats), who have proposed much more sweeping changes in both the substance of regulations and the manner in which regulations are reviewed. In particular, the Dole-Johnson bill would have allowed private firms to petition for relief from particular regulations and would have required courts to monitor the implementation of deregulation (Niskanen 1995).

Changes in the Structure of Industries

The spread of the idea of deregulation can be explained in part as the diffusion of an idea or ideology. It can also be explained by important changes in the structure of the industries being regulated. For example, the monopoly powers that justified the initial interventions by the ICC were undermined some time ago by the spread of truck and then air transport. Likewise, natural monopolies in some industries have been undermined, most notably in telecommunications, and market entry has become much easier. Regulation also depends on some stability in industries to be successful, and the increasing fluidity of markets and industries makes developing effective regulatory responses difficult. Finally, the international character of most important industries, especially areas such as financial services and banking, makes regulation more difficult and also tends to produce a national version of the 'race to the bottom' already mentioned for state governments. Countries may find it desirable to have minimal regulations in the hope of attracting capital, an example being the 'offshore' banking and insurance industries in the Cayman Islands.

The changing nature of the industries being regulated is to some extent mirrored in the changing nature of regulatory institutions. In the first place, there has been the creation of an International Trade Commission to attempt to monitor and regulate some aspects of the international trade of the United States.[18] Furthermore, many of the traditional regulatory organizations have created components within themselves that focus on international affairs and the impact of world markets on their regulation of American industry. Finally, the Office of the Special Trade Representative has become more central to American economic policy than the regulatory bodies, and political and economic attention has been transferred to it from the regulatory structures. In short, much old-fashioned regulation has simply become outmoded in the contemporary economy.

The increasing importance of financial and service industries in the American economy has required some rethinking of regulation of these activities. As noted already, the savings and loan fiasco has raised a number of questions about the efficacy of regulation in the financial area. Congress has also responded to the volatility and uncertainty of the burgeoning commodities market by creating the Commodities Futures Trading Commission in 1974 and subsequently renewing four times its regulatory authority. This was the only recent instance of Congress returning to the traditional multi-member independent commission structure for economic regulation.

Counter-trends

Although deregulation has been the dominant policy ideology, there have been some important counter-trends as well. These reactions tend to be the results of 'policy fiascos' in deregulation (Bovens and t'Hart 1996) that have affected certain industries. For example, regulators have been reluctant to go as far with banking deregulation as they might otherwise want to because of the massive losses to government and the public in the savings and loan bailout. The savings and loan disaster was seen by many people as a failure to regulate strictly enough, with unscrupulous actors in the industry able to evade the limited controls imposed on them (Tammen 1990). The role of the federal government as an insurer of bank deposits through the Federal Deposit Insurance Corporation tends to give it a greater stake in maintaining the health of this industry than might be true for others, although some advocates of deregulation still believe that this role works to the detriment of the industry (England 1992).

Public opinion about some issues is another barrier to pushing deregulation too far. Deregulating the environment may be a case in point. The attempts of the radical Republicans in Congress to eliminate or downplay environmental legislation such as the Endangered Species Act and the Wetlands Act have been met with substantial resistance, even from many fellow Republicans. There is some sense that the values of the environmental movement have become institutionalized in American politics at least as much as has the idea of deregulation. The Republicans have been able to cut the EPA's budget, and thereby weaken enforcement, but they have not been able to force legal deregulation in this area. Similarly, after the savings and loan failures the public has been extremely wary of further deregulation in financial services industries.

The public also appears willing to support the expansion of other forms of regulation, for example, on tobacco, that have a clear connection to health and safety values.[19] Some public opinion data suggest that the public is supportive of total bans on smoking in public places and on severe restrictions on sales of cigarettes to minors. A significant minority would support a total ban on cigarettes. There is also general public support for the idea behind the Americans with Disabilities Act, although there is some grumbling about specific regulations. In the case of regulation, it appears that the public is more discriminating than the experts, who seem determined to deregulate almost everything. The public appears to know what it wants and what it does not to be regulated.

As well as mass public opinion, the interests of powerful groups in society also continue to influence the shape, if not always the amount, of regulation. For example, it became clear in the early 1990s that the public wanted to have more detailed nutritional information on packaged foods. The question then became who would provide the regulations for implementing this new initiative. A battle developed between the FDA (representing health interests, consumer groups, etc.), which demanded extensive information on packages, and the Department of Agriculture (representing agri-business), which wanted to provide only minimal information. In the end the FDA won the battle, albeit with an amended program of labelling, but the victory represented the continuing, and perhaps growing, importance of some forms of consumer-oriented regulation. Other powerful interests, for example, the maritime industry, have been able to maintain their lucrative regulatory and subsidy protections (Derthick and Quirk 1985, 233–6).

Some analysts also argue that the era of deregulation is over and that there will necessarily be some return to regulation as a solution to problems in the economy. Cudahy (1993), for example, argues that much of the deregulation movement was premised on economic good times, and that in a period of less certain economic performance regulation becomes more desirable and necessary. There is, he argues, virtually a regulation cycle that mirrors the business cycle (see also Kahn 1988). Using the airline industry, which was the start of much of the contemporary interest in deregulation, Cudahy demonstrates that the market problems that regulation was intended to solve have re-emerged. The problems include predatory pricing, discriminatory fares, and the displacement of much of the cost of deregulation onto employees, passengers, and the society at large (see also Dempsey 1989). Also, some members of the labour movement have been attempting to impose regulations that would redress some of the perceived power imbalance in favour of business and that would reduce corporate downsizing (Estreicher 1995).

Are the Engines Reversible?

The institutions that once shaped regulatory interventions have, since the 1970s and 1980s, been taking the lead in fashioning deregulatory interventions. It appears that at least in this instance institutions could be made to reverse their policy direction and to apply the same vigour and the same instruments to produce very different policy solutions; the institutions and their policies are far from 'path dependent.' The question is whether another reversal could be made to happen. Although there may be little reason to deny that it is possible, a second reversal of policy direction by the same actors may not be probable.

Christopher Hood (1994) has examined the reversals of economic policy in industrialized democracies during the 1980s. He ascribes them to a number of different causes: interests, self-destruction, the environment of politics, and policy ideas. All of these factors played a role in the reversal of the regulatory policies already described. The interests supporting deregulation were crucial to the changes of the 1980s. Likewise, many regulatory programs appeared to have outlived their utility, especially given changes in technology. The environment of policy had also altered significantly, with a changing international economic environment making national regulation less effective. Finally, ideas were perhaps the crucial element in the changes of the 1980s, and they are crucial to subsequent difficulties in reversing policies.

This argument is based on the 'value-based institutionalism' of March and Olsen (1989) discussed above. Institutions reflect and incorporate important values as well as being manifestations of interests and power. The more fully an institution reflects its basis in ideas, the more difficult it will be to change that institution. By the beginning of the period of deregulation in the 1970s, most regulatory organizations – at least those concerned with economic regulation – in the U.S. government had lost whatever reformist zeal they may have had at their inception and were looking for ways to improve economic performance. Deregulation appeared to offer the solutions, and the organizations were willing to go along with, or even advocate, significant alterations of their role in the economy. Majone (1994) has argued that without the professionalization and commitment of the staffs of these regulatory organizations deregulation could not have been as successful, and this is what separated U.S. from European regulatory reform.

With the institutionalization of deregulation, some organizations are returning to being populated by 'true believers.' A coterie of free-market economists now tends to dominate thinking within the major regulatory agencies, and it continues to drive home its views on the negative consequences of federal regulations. In time, as Cudahy (1993) and others argue, these zealots may perceive that their pet solutions have failed and undertake some reregulation, but for the time being they remain solidly dedicated to the policy course on which they have been driving their organizations. Given their commitment to the market ideology, they are unlikely to be receptive to a shifting of the priorities of their organizations and to a resocialization to new values and new policy instruments. One alternative might to institutionalize other criteria, for example risk and scientific analysis, in the place of economic analysis (Bryner 1987). Thus, if significant reregulation is to occur there may need to be a new group of economists and lawyers to put it into effect.

The drive towards deregulation is also a function of the manner in which regulations have been enforced in the United States. A number of studies, both of the United States (Bardach and Kagan 1982) and comparative (Vogel 1986; Kelman 1981), have pointed out that the requirement of almost automatic fines for any firm found out of compliance with regulations actually tends to make the regulations less effective in achieving their aims. The regulatory process becomes 'cops and robbers' instead of a process of bargaining between the government and the regulated interests that is intended to produce greater compliance. In this bargaining model of regulatory enforcement, the aim is to allow any firm not in compliance to do so without fear of excessive punishment. This rule-dominated behaviour[20] is another implementation failure in regulation that tends to produce even greater pressures for deregulation.

Finally, there may be some pressures towards reregulation because of attacks on another institutional feature of American government that could be used as an alternative to regulation, especially social regulation. This alternative is the use of tort liability and private litigation to redress damages. In addition to the obvious problem that this form of protection may be more effective *ex post* than *ex ante*, the use of private litigation has also been argued as imposing, just like regulation, excessive costs on U.S. business. During the Bush administration, Dan Quayle led an attempt to minimize the exposure of business to product liability and environmental suits. Likewise, one proposed element of medical care reform in the United States was limiting malpractice awards. Neither of these efforts was successful, but combined with public disdain for attorneys they have helped to delegitimate private mechanisms that could substitute for, or augment, regulation.

Conclusions

This chapter has discussed the institutions of deregulation in the United States from two perspectives. One is the more formalistic sense of institutions, and consisted of looking at the types of structures involved in the process of making and implementing regulatory as well as deregulatory decisions. As we have demonstrated, there have been significant structural changes within the population of organizations and within individual organizations. These structural changes reflect the changes in policies advocated by presidents, Congress, and the leaders of the regulatory organizations themselves. The structural changes also create the conditions for continuing deregulation, and they constitute a challenge to any attempts to impose new regulations on the economy.

The second view of institutions is the more amorphous one of ideas and rules of behaviour. The formal structures of government are certainly important for explaining policy outcomes, but they may be only hollow vessels into which a variety of different ideas can be poured. Therefore, to understand what has happened with deregulation we must account for the acceptance of the ideas that motivate reformers of the policy process. These ideas have come from a revival of classical economics in that field of enquiry and the spread of policy analysis, as well as from the politicization of regulations by a variety of social groups, who consider themselves disadvantaged by the existing patterns of government regulation. Although in some ways vague, these ideas may be more important in explaining outcomes than are the formal structures of government. A formal structure can solidify the hold that an ideology or idea has on the public sector, but the idea itself may be what motivates the action.

One interesting aspect of the deregulation movement in the United States is its attempts to institutionalize new rules for making deregulatory, and regulatory, decisions. Whereas most regulatory decisions were adopted through following more or less legalistic norms, deregulation tends to impose rather clear economic guidelines for 'good' and 'bad' regulations. Of course, economic analysis was carried out by regulators before the recent spate of deregulation, especially in areas such as antitrust, but the deregulators appear to be making choices that depend more directly on the consequences of their economic analysis. It is easy to point to the possible weaknesses of so much reliance of that single methodology, but at least it does provide an unambiguous standard against which to compare government interventions.

Deregulation is now the conventional wisdom of American government. There are some policy areas in which this convention is still suspect, but even then some of the logic of deregulation, such as competition and market mechanisms, is accepted. Public institutions have adjusted their styles of policy making to reflect that change in policy ideologies, largely through the institutionalization of analysis and of judicial doctrines that 'de-privilege' regulations. Government is not going out of business, even in the United States, but it is clear that it has substantially diminished latitude to impose its will on the society.

NOTES

1 The Weidenbaum and De Fina figures of 1978 constitute the basis of their and other continuing analysis of regulatory costs. It is fair to say, however, that these cost estimates are not universally accepted as accurate.
2 The death of the ICC had been debated for some time. See Solomon (1986).
3 There are some important exceptions to this generalization, such as the Tennessee Valley Authority and communications facilities in Alaska. Also, the federal government is a major insurance provider for agriculture, higher education, and a variety of other policy areas.
4 The term ideology is used advisedly. The efficacy of deregulation has become an article of faith for many people in and out of government, and therefore the real consequences of the actions (other than raw economic efficiency) may be ignored.
5 This pattern can be seen clearly in the attempts of regulated industries such as trucking and airlines to stop deregulation (Noll 1983). Free enterprise was very much a threat to the way in which these firms had done business.
6 This act was closely associated with Upton Sinclair's novel *The Jungle*, published that same year, which details unsanitary (at best) conditions in the meat-packing industry.
7 The traditional FDA standard is that drugs be both safe and efficacious. Generally,

proving both of these conditions requires years of laboratory and clinical testing, more than many AIDS patients expected to have.

8 The Progressives sought to depoliticize and professionalize as much of government as possible. Woodrow Wilson's writings, among others, offers a good insight into the Progressives.

9 OSHA, for example, tends to be too intrusive for business interests during Republican administrations and to be insufficiently protective of workers during Democratic administrations.

10 In this case the court ruled on a specific Congressional control over an agency.

11 Any form of cost-benefit analysis begs a number of crucial questions, such as how to value non-tradeable commodities such as the human lives that may be saved by a regulation and the aesthetic value of the environment. This deficiency has not prevented rather simplistic ideas about improving regulation from being accepted.

12 Procedural due process appeared to be more important than substantive due process at this time. That is, regulations were more likely to be set aside if organizations had acted in an 'arbitrary and capricious' fashion (language from the Administrative Procedures Act of 1946) than if they were judged on the basis of their content.

13 *Greater Boston TV Corp.* v. *FCC*, 444 F2d 841 (1970).

14 This is especially true because the compliance costs for firms will be increased by having to meet the different requirements of a number of subnational governments.

15 Pennsylvania and other states are beginning to allow utilities to engage in modest forms of competition, albeit within the framework of continued rate-setting by a utilities commission.

16 President Nixon had earlier instituted a regulatory review procedure but it did not have as strong a microeconomic focus as the subsequent efforts. Further, it relied more on the reviews of other agencies rather than analytic efforts.

17 In this instance the word regulation referred to both regulations in the sense used here and in the sense of all secondary legislation.

18 This organization is the linear descendent of the Tariff Commission, but has a much broader range of activity, reflecting the increased importance of international trade.

19 There is now a move to regulate cigarettes as a medical device designed to deliver a drug (nicotine). The FDA may well go in that direction, and would have significant public support if it did so.

20 This is another institutionalist perspective, albeit one more associated with the rational choice perspective. See Ostrom (1990).

REFERENCES

Bardach, E., and R.A. Kagan. 1982. *Going by the Book: The Problem of Regulatory Unreasonableness*. Philadelphia: Temple University Press.

Beam, D. 1983. 'From Rule to Law: Exploring the Maze of Intergovernmental Regulation.' *Intergovernmental Perspective* 9 (spring): 7–22.

Bloomquist, R. 1990. 'FTC Mirrors Style of its New head.' *Governing* 3 (August): 19–22.

Bovens, M., and P. t'Hart. 1996. *Understanding Policy Fiascoes*. New Brunswick, N.J.: Transaction.

Brand, D.R. 1988. *Corporatism and the Rule of Law: A Study of The National Recovery Administration*. Ithaca, N.Y.: Cornell University Press.

Breyer, S. 1982. *Regulation and Its Reform*. Cambridge, Mass.: Harvard University Press.

Bryner, G.C. 1987. *Bureaucratic Discretion: Law and Policy in Federal Regulatory Agencies*. New York: Pergammon.

Crandall, R.W. 1992. 'Regulating Communications: Creating Monopoly while "Protecting" Us from It.' *Brookings Review* 10, no. 3: 34–9.

– 1996. 'Waves of the Future.' *Brookings Review* 14, no. 1: 26–9.

Cudahy, R.D. 1993. 'The Coming Demise of Deregulation.' *Yale Journal of Regulation* 10: 1–15.

Dempsey, P.S. 1989. *The Social and Economic Costs of Deregulation*. Washington: American Enterprise Institute.

Derthick, M., and P.J. Quirk. 1985. *The Politics of Deregulation*. Washington: The Brookings Institution.

Economist. 1996. 'Over-Regulating America.' 27 July: 17–19.

Eisner, M.A. 1993. *Regulatory Politics in Transition*. Baltimore: Johns Hopkins University Press.

England, C. 1992. 'Lessons from the Savings and Loan Debacle.' *Regulation* 15, no. 2:3–6.

Epstein, R.A. 1985. *Takings: Private Property and the Power of Eminent Domain*. Cambridge, Mass.: Harvard University Press.

Estreicher, S. 1995. 'The Dunlop Report and the Future of Labor Law Reform.' *Regulation* 18, no. 1: 28–34.

Foreman, C.H. 1991. 'The Fast Track: Federal Agencies and the Political Demand for AIDS Drugs.' *Brookings Review* 9: 30–7.

Furlong, S.R. 1995. 'The 1992 Regulatory Moratorium: Did It Make Any Difference?' *Public Administration Review* 55: 254–62.

Gilmour, R.S., and A.A. Halley. 1994. *Who Makes Public Policy?: The Struggle for Control between Congress and the Executive*. Chatham, N.J.: Chatham House.

Gormley, W.T. 1989. *Taming the Bureaucracy: Muscles, Prayers and Other Strategies*. Princeton, N.J.: Princeton University Press.

Hahn, R. 1996. *Risks, Costs and Lives Saved*. Oxford: Oxford University Press.

Harris, R.A., and S.M. Milkis. 1989. *The Politics of Regulatory Change*. New York: Oxford University Press.

Healey, J. 1995. 'Republican's Cable Plan Strikes a Nerve.' *Congressional Weekly Report* 53 (11 March) 749–51.

Hood, C. 1994. *Explaining Economic Policy Reversals*. Buckingham: Open University Press.

Horn, M.J. 1995. *The Political Economy of Public Administration: Institutional Choice in the Public Sector.* Cambridge: Cambridge University Press.

Horowitz, R.B. 1986. 'Understanding Deregulation.' *Theory and Society* 15: 139–74.

Huntington, S.P. 1987. 'The Marasmus of the ICC: The Commission, the Railroads and the Public Interest.' In *The Politics of American Economic Policy*, edited by P. Peretz. Armonk, N.Y.: M.E. Sharpe.

Ingraham, P.W., J.R. Thompson, and E.F. Eisenberg. 1995. 'Political Management Strategies and Political/Career Relationships: Where Are We Now in the Federal Government?' *Public Administration Review* 55: 263–72.

Kahn, A.E. 1988. *The Economics of Regulation: Principles and Institutions*. 2nd ed. Cambridge, Mass.: MIT Press.

Kearney, R.C. 1990. 'Sunset: A Survey and Analysis of State Experience.' *Public Administration Review* 50: 49–57.

Kelman, S. 1981. *Regulating America, Regulating Sweden: A Comparative Study of Health and Safety Policy.* Cambridge, Mass.: MIT Press.

Kritz, M. 1987. 'A Regulatory "KGB." ' *National Journal*, 30 May: 1404–6.

Light, P.R. 1995. *Thickening Government*. Washington: The Brookings Institution.

Mahtesian, C. 1992. 'Why the Sun Rarely Sets on State Bureaucracy.' *Governing* 5, no. 9: 24–5.

Majone, G. 1994. 'Paradoxes of Privatization and Deregulation.' *European Journal of Public Policy* 1: 53–70.

March, J.G., and J.P. Olsen. 1984. 'The New Institutionalism: Organizational Factors in Political Life.' *American Political Science Review* 78: 734–49.

– 1989. *Rediscovering Institutions*. New York: Basic Books.

McCubbins, M., R. Noll, and B. Weingast. 1989. 'Structure and Process, Politics and Policy: Administrative Arrangements and the Political Control of Agencies.' *Virginia Law Review* 75: 431–82.

McGarity, T.O. 1991. *Reinventing Rationality: The Role of Regulatory Analysis in the Federal Bureaucracy.* Cambridge: Cambridge University Press.

McKraw, T.K. 1981. *Regulation in Perspective: Historical Essays*. Cambridge, Mass.: Harvard University Press.

Michaels, R.J. 1992. 'Deregulating Electricity: What Stands in the Way.' *Regulation* 15, no. 2: 38–47.

Miller, J.C., III. 1977. 'Lessons of the Economic Impact Statement Program.' *Regulation* 1, no. 4: 16–18.

Moore, T.G. 1986. 'Rail and Trucking Deregulation.' In *Regulatory Reform: What Actually Happened?* edited by L.W. Weiss and M.W. Klass. Boston: Little, Brown.

Moore, W.J. 1988. 'Dear Feds–Help!' *National Journal* 20 (9 July): 1788–92.

Needleman, H., and P.J. Landrigan. 1996. 'Toxins at the Pump.' *New York Times*. 13 March.

Niskanen, W.A. 1995. 'Is Regulatory Reform Dead? Should Anyone Care?' *Regulation* 18, no. 3: 9–10.

Ostrom, E. 1990. 'Rational Choice Theory and Institutional Analysis: Toward Complementarity.' *American Political Science Review* 85: 237–43.

Pertschuk, M. 1982. *Revolt against Regulation: The Rise and Pause of the Consumer Movement*. Berkeley: University of California Press.

Rauch, J. 1991. 'The Regulatory President.' *National Journal* 23 (30 November): 2902–6.

Reagan, M.D. 1987. *Regulation: The Politics of Policy*. Boston: Little, Brown.

Schultze, C.L. 1979. 'Comments to Commonwealth Club of California, San Francisco.' Cited in S. Tolchin and M. Tolchin. *Dismantling America: The Rush to Deregulate*. Boston: Houghton Mifflin 1983.

Solomon, B. 1986. Is Death Really Knocking at the Door of the Interstate Commerce Commission? *National Journal* 18 (22 February): 51–2.

Sunstein, C.R. 1990. *After the Rights Revolution: Reconceiving the Regulatory State*. Cambridge, Mass.: Harvard University Press.

Tammen, M.S. 1990. 'The Savings and Loan Crisis: Which Train Derailed: Deregulation or Deposit Insurance?' *Journal of Law and Politics* 6: 311–42.

Thelen, K., T. Longstreth, and S. Steinmo. 1992. *Structuring Politics: Historical Institutionalism in Comparative Perspective*. Cambridge: Cambridge University Press.

Victor, K. 1995. 'Code Blue: Is the Nation's Oldest Independent Federal Regulatory Agency Headed for the Graveyard?' *National Journal* 13 August: 1909–12.

Vogel, D. 1986. *National Styles of Regulation: Environmental Policy in Great Britain and the United States*. Ithaca, N.Y.: Cornell University Press.

Warner, D. 1992. 'Regulation's Staggering Costs.' *Nation's Business* 80, no. 6: 50–3.

Weaver, P.H. 1978. 'Regulation, Social Policy and Class Conflict.' *Public Interest* 50: 45–63.

Weidenbaum, M., and R. DeFina. 1978. *The Cost of Federal Regulation of Economic Activity*. Washington: American Enterprise Institute.

Wilson. J.Q. 1980. *The Politics of Regulation*. New York: Basic Books.

Wise, C.R., and K. Emerson. 1994. 'Regulatory Takings: The Emerging Doctrine and the Implications for Public Administration.' *Administration and Society* 26: 305–36.

4

Regulatory Institutions in the United Kingdom: Increasing Regulation in the 'Shrinking State'

BRIAN W. HOGWOOD

Regulatory developments in Britain since 1979 have involved major institutional upheavals, reflecting both the consequences of the Conservative government's push to privatization and technical and economic developments in markets (Bishop, Kay, and Mayer 1995; European Policy Forum 1996). This chapter sets these dramatic developments in the context of the traditional style of regulation in Britain, and indicates the extent to which past models provided the basis for new institutions. The chapter focuses particularly on what form regulatory institutions took and why.[1]

The issue of why regulatory bodies are set up in one administrative form rather than another and what the consequence of this might be are largely neglected in the British literature. An exception is the Constitutional Reform Centre study (1991), though it too is rather confusing on the governmental status of regulatory bodies. Indeed, despite the fact that government regulation is almost by definition a matter of public administration, the organizational analysis of British regulatory arrangements has been relatively neglected. Hancher and Moran's analysis of regulatory space (1989), deals with the organization in the context of the large firm, but it does not examine the implications of the administrative type of regulatory body.

Regulatory Institutional Types

The basic task of setting out agency types in Britain and describing which bodies fall within which organizational form is a precondition to examining more analytical questions, such as how these different types of bodies interact and why they were set up in one form rather than another. The limited available literature on the administrative form that regulation takes tends to reduce the available forms to limited (and implicitly U.S.) typologies, which also assume a

Congressional-style legislature (Fiorina 1982; Horn 1995). Apart from the issue of networks of regulators, these simple typologies are inadequate as descriptions of the British case, excluding as they do self-regulation endorsed by the executive or legislature, as well as a wide range of variants of regulatory form that are considered sufficiently important to be the subject of policy choice or debate. The selection of regulatory form in Britain is largely a matter for the executive, and assessments of the reasons for choosing one form rather than another are unlikely to benefit from approaches concerned with the constituency interests of all individual members of Parliament.

Thus, in understanding the British system it is important to distinguish among broad categories:

- Regulation by government departments and by agencies within them directly accountable to ministers (e.g., 'Next Steps' agencies established from 1988), including possible direct involvement of ministers
- Regulation by civil-service–staffed regulators with separate statutory status
- Regulation by non-civil-service bodies in the public sector
- 'Self-regulation' by a range of non-governmental bodies, some with and some without a statutory remit

There is no standard British concept of British public law, and therefore no common framework for conceiving structures and their remit. Regulatory agencies in Britain have tended to be set up on an ad hoc basis (Constitutional Reform Centre 1991, 505). As Baldwin has noted, 'when designing and setting up regulatory agencies, the British way has been to muddle through in an ad hoc fashion without a great deal of regard for the suitability of the agency to the task set or the appropriateness of the system of accountability created' (Baldwin 1985, 263). This is not the same as stating that there are no common features between regulatory agencies: emulation, relying on previous examples (rather than a priori reasoning about the best solution or a common formal framework), leads to the echoing of features of agencies.

The remainder of the chapter looks at the evolution of the British regulatory style and the general framework of competition regulation before going on to examine developments since 1979 in privatization and regulation, regulation of the financial sector, and environmental regulation. Explanations for the selection of regulatory form are then considered.

A British Regulatory Style?

A number of studies have pointed to the importance in Britain of state-approved self-regulation by the industry or profession concerned (Baggott 1989; Vogel 1986). Even where there were formal regimes of regulation administered by government, there was close consultation with affected industries before legislation or regulations were drawn up (Vogel 1986). In administering regulation, the practice existed in many cases of relying on voluntary compliance and persuasion rather than on the full formal application of the relevant legislation. Peacock states that 'a framework of negotiated compliance, rather than strict enforcement of performance standards, is the dominant characteristic of regulatory policy' (Peacock 1984, 115). However, in recent years there has been a greater move to a formal enforcement role, even in cases such as pollution control where a previously less formal style was in operation.

Another important feature of the post-war regulatory arrangements concerned the nationalized industries, with blurred multiple relationships between departments and nationalized industries: government could be a customer, owner, and regulator of an industry. As we will seen later in the chapter, the removal of the ownership role through privatization did not mean that government could simply withdraw from involvement with the industry, but rather that it had to increase and formalize its regulatory relationship. In the case of regional water authorities between 1973 and 1989, these public corporations had a regulatory role, yet were themselves major actors in the activities they were supposed to regulate; again, the roles were separated following privatization.

The General Framework of Competition Regulation

Despite these remarks about informality and ambiguity in British regulation, Britain did develop a formal general framework for competition policy that is important for understanding the newer utility regulators (Wilks 1996). Developments since 1979 have involved additions being made to that framework, rather than replacing it or being organizationally consolidated with it. The major government department involved is the Department of Trade and Industry (DTI), which has general responsibility for company regulation and is the 'sponsoring department' for many individual industries, but other government departments are involved in regulation or oversight of industries that they sponsor (Grant 1982; Wilks 1996).

The main non-ministerial bodies concerned with regulation of competition policy are the Monopolies and Mergers Commission (MMC) and the Office of Fair Trading (OFT). The MMC was originally established by statute in 1949 as the Monopolies and Restrictive Practices Commission. It was renamed the Monopolies Commission in 1956 when responsibility for registrable practices was given to the Restrictive Practices Court. It was renamed again as the Monopolies and Mergers Commission in 1973 under the Fair Trading Act of 1973, which also set up the OFT. The MMC is classified by the government as an executive non-departmental public body. All its members are appointed by the secretary of state for trade and industry. At present, the MMC has a staff of ninety-six and a budgetary allocation of approximately £7.5 million wholly funded by government. It is 'independent' in the sense that its members have responsibility for the contents of its reports and these are published. However, it depends on other bodies to make references to it, and decisions on its findings are taken, not by the MCC itself, but by the government department or regulator that made the original reference.

The OFT is a non-ministerial government department set up in 1973. It is staffed by close to four hundred civil servants. Although it is a government department, advice to ministers from the head of the OFT, the director general of fair trading, is publishable, in contrast to the conventions concerning advice to ministers from civil servants. In addition, the director general makes public statements about desirable changes of policy. The OFT does have some powers of investigation and prosecution of its own, but among its roles are the receipt of references about uncompetitive practices from the new single-industry regulatory offices described in the next section and reference in turn to the MMC (Wilks 1996).

Privatization and the Formation of Regulatory Bodies

One of the ironies of the privatization program in Britain, which had as one of its objectives the withdrawal of government from involvement in the affairs of the industries, is that it has led to a substantial increase in one form of government intervention in industry, that of formal regulation. The removal of industries from state ownership necessitated an explicit regulatory regime, especially since privatization was not systematically used at the time of transition as an opportunity for breaking up monopolies and promoting competition, which could serve as at least a partial alternative to regulation. The subsequent history of the regulation of the earliest industries to be privatized is in part an attempt to inject competition, emphasizing the dynamics of the regulatory objectives, of the industry structure, and of developing technologies.

As each industry has been privatized, one or more separate regulatory bodies have been set up instead of the task being given to an existing body such as OFT or to a new utility regulatory agency supervizing all the industries. As Veljanovski has pointed out, the proliferation of regulatory bodies 'has, like the privatisation programme itself, evolved in a piecemeal fashion and has not been governed by a single set of clearly defined objectives' (Veljanovsky 1987, 174). Veljanovski also states that the government had originally asked the OFT to be the regulator of the privatized utilities, but that it refused to have its responsibilities widened in this manner.

Regulating Telecommunications

The Office of Telecommunications (OFTEL) was set up under the Telecommunications Act of 1984 to monitor and regulate telecommunications in the UK. Like the subsequent single-industry regulatory offices, OFTEL was modelled in part on the existing OFT (Veljanovski 1987, 175). OFTEL is a government department staffed by approximately 160 civil servants.

As the chapter by Cosmo Graham in this volume shows, the objectives set for OFTEL in regulating the telecommunications industry are multiple and conflicting, with some emphasizing the interests of the consumer and others the promotion of the industry. This provides some scope for the director general to choose which to emphasize, while focusing on the objective of promoting competition (National Audit Office 1996; Veljanovski 1987, 181–2). Telecommunications in Britain were until 1982 the monopoly of British Telecommunications, a nationalized industry that was part of the Post Office until 1981. British Telecom became a private limited company in August 1984. Mercury was given a licence to operate a telecommunications network in 1982, though British Telecom continued to be by far the larger in the new duopoly. Because of its lack of a nationwide door-to-door network, Mercury required connection to the British Telecom network, and the arrangements for this were one of the concerns of the new OFTEL. Other companies are involved in minor aspects of telecommunications services, such as cellular phones, and cable companies now also offer telecommunications services. OFTEL itself does not have powers to license new telephone companies; that power belongs to the DTI.

OFTEL took over the responsibilities previously held by the Post Office Users National Council in relation to telecommunications. However, the Telecommunications Act of 1984 provided for advisory committees on telecommunications for each of the four countries of the UK, appointed by the secretary of state for trade and industry. There are also two advisory committees on telecommunications for disabled and elderly people and for small businesses, which are appointed by the director general of telecommunications.

Until 1981, British Telecom had a statutory monopoly in the provision of attachments to the telephone network. However, even after the abolition of this monopoly, British Telecom itself was at first placed in charge of approving equipment that could be attached to its system, leading to complaints of long and expensive delays from other suppliers. Now, responsibility for approving equipment for connection to telecommunications systems lies not with OFTEL, but with the British Approvals Board for Telecommunications (BABT), which was set up on 7 May 1982 as a company limited by guarantee. It is not considered by government to be an official non-departmental body. Members of the BABT are drawn from DTI or OFTEL, the British Standards Institution, British Telecom, and major telecommunications trade associations. In its early years BABT relied heavily on the testing facilities of British Telecom, which itself was a supplier of telecommunications equipment, giving rise to continuing claims that delays in receiving approval were operating in the interest of British Telecom.

Regulation of the Gas Industry

The Office of Gas Supply (OFGAS), classified as a non-ministerial department, was established in 1986 under the Gas Act of 1986. This legislation also transferred the business of the nationalized British Gas Corporation to British Gas plc, which was privatized by share sale in December 1986. OFGAS is headed by a director general of gas supply. It was staffed at July 1989 by twenty-six civil servants, a small number considering the scale of the industry being regulated, but this has grown to over one hundred. The general function of OFGAS was initially to monitor the activities of British Gas as a public gas supplier. This includes the enforcement of the price formula to determine the maximum average price that British Gas is allowed to charge tariff customers. If OFGAS suspects unfair competitive practices, it must refer these to the MMC, which in 1988 found that British Gas was practising discrimination against industrial companies.

British Gas differed from British Telecom in that it was not merely a carrier but a provider of gas. It was therefore a monopoly carrier and a near-monopoly supplier. One of the other responsibilities of OFGAS is issuing authorizations to other suppliers of gas through pipes in Great Britain. As a result of a change in the regulatory regime in the mid 1990s, British Gas was obliged to separate its production and supply side from its pipeline carrying functions, and competition for domestic consumers was phased in. This followed an MMC investigation that illustrates the complex interaction of different bodies involved in regulation. There were two separate sets of references to the MMC, one from OFGAS and one from the government. In its submission to the MMC, OFGAS called for British Gas to be broken up into regional supply companies and a gas transmission business. The MMC recommended in 1993 that British Gas's domestic monopoly be ended and that it be forced to sell its trading activities.

The government decided to bring in a new gas bill to introduce competition in domestic gas supply and oblige British Gas to separate out, though not sell, its pipelines business.

The Gas Act of 1986 also set up a Gas Consumers Council that replaced the previous National Gas Consumers' Council and the Regional Gas Consumers' Councils. It has the power to investigate complaints from gas consumers, both domestic and industrial, but it has no powers to enforce remedies. The council can refer matters to the director general of gas supply.

Regulating Airlines and Airports

Prior to the privatization of British Airways, the airline industry was already regulated by the Civil Aviation Authority (CAA) established in 1971 under the Civil Aviation Act (Baldwin 1985). The CAA is classified by government as a nationalized industry. In addition to its regulatory functions, the CAA also provides a service in the form of air traffic control, which the outgoing Conservative government had in 1997 proposed to privatize, leaving the CAA as a more unambiguously regulatory body.

With the privatization of the British Airports Authority as a single company in 1987, the CAA took on the task of administering the regulations governing the now privatized airport company, though the government's special share embodied restrictions on ownership, control of the London airports, and the winding up of the company (Baldwin 1995, 66–74). The MMC has a larger role in relation to reviewing CAA proposals than is the case of other single-industry regulators. Important policy issues, such as designating which airports can carry transatlantic traffic, remain with the Department of Transport. Issues of domination by the privatized British Airways, including 'dirty tricks,' have been a recurring theme, and they have been handled through departmental decision and the courts in Britain (as is the case in the United States) rather than through the industry-specific regulatory structure.

Regulation of the Water Industry

Regulation of the post-privatization water industry in England and Wales from 1989 has been fragmented among a number of bodies. Price regulation and issues such as water pressure and compensation if water supplies are interrupted are the responsibility of the Office of Water Services (OFWAT). As the chapter by Booker in this volume shows, OFWAT is a non-ministerial government department and depends for its funding and control of staffing on the Department of the Environment. The first director general of water services was Ian

Byatt, a Treasury civil servant. Monitoring of the new pricing regime applies to previous private statutory water companies as well as the newly privatized water authorities. Regulation of mergers between water companies is not under the control of OFWAT; the MMC has the responsibility of making recommendations to the secretary of state for trade and industry. OFWAT does, however, have extensive fall-back powers to remove a water company that consistently fails to observe the terms of its official licence. Regulation of the quality of river water was allocated to the National Rivers Authority (NRA) and subsequently the Environment Agency, as discussed further below and in the chapter by Booker.

Regulation of the Electricity Industry

The extent to which the structure of newly privatized industries reflects the previous structure of each nationalized industry is emphasized by comparing the gas and electricity industries. The British Gas Corporation was a nationwide supplier and distributor of gas, and so is the successor privatized body. The electricity industry in England and Wales was split between a central generating board and regional distribution boards, while Scotland had two regional boards engaged in both supply and distribution. This is reflected in the post-privatization arrangements The existing English and Welsh regional distribution boards were privatized as individual companies, while the Central Electricity Generating Board was split into two generating companies and a national grid company. The grid company was initially owned by the regional electricity companies, but was subsequently floated. The two dual-purpose Scottish boards were privatized without separating out their supply and distribution functions. Partial liberalization of the market has subsequently led to new entrants into the electricity generation market.

The plans for privatization were complicated when it became clear in the summer of 1989 that nuclear power generation was not commercially attractive, and so the nuclear power stations were separated out into English and Scottish companies, which remained state-owned. The price formula imposed initially reflected the government's insistence that a proportion of power must come from the still nationalized nuclear power stations. The Scottish and English nuclear companies were subsequently merged prior to planned privatization in 1996. The older nuclear power stations, with the most imminent issues of decommissioning, will stay in public ownership.

The job of the Office of Electricity Regulation (OFFER) can therefore be seen as rather more complicated than that of OFGAS, since it involves adjudicating between supply and distribution companies, some of which are still be state-owned, and administering a price formula that contains the politically sensitive nuclear element. However, the advantage to OFFER is that information is likely to be easier to come by if there are multiple sources with competing interests. However, the subsequent mergers of regional electricity companies with other utility companies inject new scope for ambiguity.

Following the by now standard practice, OFFER is headed by a director general of electricity supply. The first director general was Professor Stephen Littlechild, who had been responsible for recommending to the government the RPI-X formula used for regulating British Telecom price increases (that is, the general rate of inflation minus a specified percentage for efficiency). This approach to regulation has been copied for other post-privatization regulatory regimes (though for water this was RPI+K because a water-quality cost had to added).

Coal Industry Regulation

The arrangements for the privatization of what by then was the rump of the British coal industry differed from what had become the standard pattern of a non-ministerial department single-industry regulator. The Coal Authority (a non-departmental public body) was established in September 1994 under the Coal Industry Act of 1994 to take over the licensing functions of British Coal, which had been both an operator of mines and the licenser of competitors. The bulk of the remaining pits, although offered in groups, were sold to a single buyer. The Domestic Coal Consumers Council was abolished and not replaced, presumably reflecting the modest extent to which the coal industry supplies domestic consumers directly rather than coal-fired power stations.

Rail Regulation

The regulatory regime for the privatization of British Rail reflects a substantially different approach to privatization by the government. The rail track was privatized separately, as was the freight operation (to a single purchaser). Passenger operations have been franchised for fixed periods in phases over 1996 and 1997. Following practices that are now standard, a non-ministerial department of the Office of the Rail Regulator was established. However, this office was not given the responsibility for overseeing the process of administering the franchising of the passenger operations. This was given to a separate Office of Rail Passenger Franchising, also a non-ministerial government department. Adding to the number of regulators involved, the Health and Safety Executive (a non-departmental public body, but one staffed by civil servants) retains responsibility for safety on railways through its Railways Inspectorate. Within its first three weeks of office, the incoming Labour government in 1997 indicated its intention of strengthening the regulatory regime for the railways.

The New Regulatory Regime for Privatized Industries

Although the process is only now reaching completion, some general comments about the regulatory arrangements for privatized industries can be made. First, most though not all of the new regulatory offices are listed as government departments and staffed by civil servants, and second, some depend on annual negotiations with their sponsoring department and the Treasury for their budgets. They cannot therefore be considered as being fully independent of government, even though the directors general have made full use of their right, not accorded to traditional civil servants, to make public statements about policy advice.

The regulatory agencies are 'dependent' on the firms and bodies being regulated for information; there is therefore a problem of what kind of relationship to develop with them. Full 'regulatory capture,' on U.S. lines, of the regulatory agencies by the industry being regulated is not likely because of lack of independent parliamentary budget and authorization committees on the U.S. Congress model. However, the traditional British regulatory style of private persuasion rather than vigorous application of formal powers might suggest scope for 'rounding the edges' of the application of regulation. Veljanovski (1987, 176–7) suggested a decade ago that a form of capture had already occurred, in that the soon to be privatized and regulated industries were intimately involved in discussions about the new regulatory bodies. The subsequent experience of OFTEL, OFGAS, and OFFER suggests that their directors general are quite happy to upset the industries being regulated – and possibly shareholders and MPs as well – but in the longer run there might seem to be the danger of a regulatory agency opting for a quiet life. Veljanovski also suggested that many regulatory agencies would display a life-cycle pattern of behaviour, beginning as aggressive regulators of the industry but over time becoming captured by those regulated as they begin to share some of the views of the industry (Veljanovski 1987, 177). However, since the initial launch of the regulatory offices, the regulatory regime has changed in the direction of breaking up monopolies like British Gas or injecting greater competition, with the result that the regulatory process over a period of a decade or so is not self-evidently or uniformly working to the advantage of the regulated industries in their original form.

Alternatively, the emphasis could be placed not on capture but on the 'interdependence' of the relationship among the wide variety of bodies and therefore on the complex networks of organizations that are involved in the regulation of the privatized industries. Even in relation to a single industry there may, as we have seen in the cases of telecommunications and water, be more than one 'single-industry' regulatory agency involved.

The single-industry regulatory offices have the power to enforce specific terms in the utility's licence, but not the power to enforce general competition law relevant to the industries they do regulate (National Audit Office 1996). Any detected abuses of monopoly have to be referred to the OFT or to the MMC (see Chapter 11 of this volume). If a regulatory office such as OFTEL wanted to modify the terms of the licence of a privatized utility and was unable to secure the agreement of the affected firm, it would have to refer this to the MMC. It may therefore be better to consider the new single-industry regulatory offices as a new layer of administration to complement the work of the now-strengthened competition agencies rather than as free-standing 'independent' regulatory agencies.

The complexity of the networks of regulatory bodies is increased when we take into account the new regulatory arrangements in the financial markets. As Chapter 6 in this volume, by Stephen Wilks, shows, financial regulation has a direct bearing on the privatized utilities. There are a number of reasons why this should be so. The first is the obvious one that initial and subsequent sales of shares have to conform to relevant regulations. Second, effective investor protection is a necessary condition for one of the aims of privatization, the expansion of individual share ownership. Third, the efficient operation of the price formulas in terms of their impact on the productive efficiency of utilities requires efficient capital markets. Fourth, rules about the handling of shares of privatized companies involved in takeover bids are highly relevant to changes in the structure of the utilities. Finally, if competition is indeed to be a possible long-term substitute for a legal framework of targeted regulation, then a regulatory structure in the financial markets that ensures a relationship between competitive effectiveness and financial market outcomes is essential.

One obvious point of comparison with the United States is the relative lack of involvement by the courts in matters concerning the regulation of utilities. The actions of all of the bodies involved are in principle subject to judicial review by the courts, but these have been relatively few in practice (National Audit Office 1996, 10). Thus the process of review, for example, by the MMC tends to adopt an administrative rather judicial mode.

An important characteristic of the regulatory arrangements for utilities is their evolution in the last decade. For example, when the arrangements were initially set up, the directors general had to administer the price formulas established by government. Each of the utility regulators has by now undertaken at least one price review, changing in the process the price controls that had been put in place at the time of privatization (National Audit Office 1996, 1). However, they have all chosen to retain the broad RPI-X approach. In some industries the whole nature of regulatory activity has changed; in the case of gas it has gone from regulating a single monopoly supplier and distributor to overseeing the introduction of competition in supplying domestic consumers.

There is a paradox in the institutional design for the regulation of the privatized industries: if the regulators are entirely successful in their aim of promoting competition, their existence would become unnecessary. This thought is probably enough to leave public-choice theorists aghast at the moral hazard involved. The paradox is in part resolved by the fact that the director generals are on short-term contracts.

Among the issues that have arisen in the years following the establishment of the privatized industry regulators is that of how far the 'independent' directors general are or should be accountable to ministers and Parliament, and there has also been a reopening of the issue of whether there should be a single regulator instead of one (or more) for each industry. Two major reports on the regulation of utilities were published in 1996. The first was a report from the National Audit Office on the work of the directors general of Telecommunications, Gas Supply, Water Services, and Electricity Supply. It was very much a review of how they had operated within their terms of reference, and it contains a wealth of information on this. Despite this limited remit, the report did draw a general conclusion about the regulatory form used: 'Single industry regulators for each industry, with powers to take decisions, and the use of the RPI-X formula, have resulted in speedier and less bureaucratic processes than might be attainable under more legalistic arrangements for the regulation of public utilities' (National Audit Office 1996, par. 6.1). In its final paragraph (6.2i), the report explored both the implications of the increases in competition in the regulated industries and the implications of mergers and acquisitions of regulated companies. It asked: 'If as a result of such structural changes, possible alternatives to the current system of industry specific regulation by single regulators were to be considered, what forms might these take?' Among the forms were regulation by a board of regulators for each of the industries, or by a board of the various regulators. The report asked whether these options would be a 'sensible insurance' against the overconcentration of power in one pair of hands or the 'dilution of effective decision making by one clearly responsible person?' (par. 6.2i). The comptroller and auditor general, who heads the National Audit Office, carefully refrained from suggesting answers to these questions.

The second report was commissioned by two research organizations, the

Hansard Society and the European Policy Forum (European Policy Forum 1996). The remit of the commission was concerned with the regulatory regime – the institutional, procedural, and constitutional aspects of regulation – rather than with substantive questions of pricing or the terms of privatization. The report concluded that on the whole the principle of independent economic regulation focused on economic objectives and free from day-to-day political intervention had worked well and should not be compromised in reforms. It noted that there were arguments for and against replacing individual regulators with panels of, say, three executive commissioners, or supplementing them with advisory boards of non-executive directors whose advice would be published. Its recommendation was the immediate establishment of advisory boards, with an eventual move to executive boards that might be triggered by the amalgamation of some regulatory bodies. The existence of separate regulatory bodies for each industry was seen as having had the advantage of making possible learning from varied experience. However, technological and market developments strengthened the case for some regulatory amalgamation, specifically that OFFER and OFGAS should be merged into an energy regulator after full liberalization of supply in 1998, and that OFTEL might be broadened into an 'Office of Communications' concerned with all the relevant infrastructure, though not with content.

The report recommended that the widely varying arrangements for consumer representation described earlier in this section under each industry should be standardized on the model of the Gas Consumers Council, with statutory independence, access to independent funding, and appointment by the secretary of state in consultation with the director general. The report also recommended parliamentary approval for frameworks for cross-subsidization of vulnerable groups, the strengthening of transparency and appeals procedures, and the recasting of competition law for the utilities so that, among other changes, there would be limitations on ministerial powers to veto references on utility mergers to the MMC.

Although it had opposed privatizations when in opposition, the Labour government elected in May 1997 did not seek to reverse the process. Apart from a windfall tax on the profits of utilities, its concerns were focused on strengthening what it saw as weaknesses in the current regulatory system. In its manifesto the Labour Party concentrated on general statements rather than specific pledges. It promised to reform competition law, with a tough 'prohibitive' approach to deter anti-competitive practices and abuse of market power. The promotion of competition in utilities was promised, but water was singled out as a case where tougher regulation was required. A need for open and predictable regulation was recognized, but no specific changes to regulatory structures were signalled until a Department of Trade and Industry report was published in March 1998.

New Regulatory Agencies in Financial Markets

Financial markets (commonly referred to as 'the City,' after the City of London in which much of the activity is concentrated) have undergone a major upheaval in regulation since 1979. This is sometimes confusingly referred to as 'deregulation.' However, the liberalization of markets that has undoubtedly occurred was sparked by government regulatory bodies and involved a new statutory basis to regulation of financial markets. The changes were precipitated by the OFT, which in 1978 referred the rule book of the Stock Exchange to the Restrictive Practices Court over its policy of minimum fixed commissions. Five years of legal battle between the Stock Exchange and the OFT followed. However, illustrating the OFT's lack of full independence, the result was a political compromise imposed by the then secretary of state for trade and industry, Cecil Parkinson (Moran 1988). Fixed commissions were to be eliminated, and membership rules for the Stock Exchange were to be relaxed in return for an exemption for the Stock Exchange from some restrictive practices legislation. In fact, wider changes were precipitated, including the abolition of the separation between brokers and jobbers, culminating in the so-called 'Big Bang' at the end of 1986. This led to major changes in the methods of operation of the Stock Exchange and other financial markets, and in turn to major restructurings in financial firms.

The other aspect of change was the new formal regulatory structure for financial services, the introduction of which was influenced by a series of major financial scandals and a report on investment protection commissioned by the government in 1981 and produced in 1984. The Financial Services Act of 1986 provided the first comprehensive statutory framework for the regulation of financial markets. Regulation had previously been largely dispersed, and it had relied heavily on self-regulation by individual markets. The conduct of an investment business without authorization was made a criminal offence. The power of authorization was given to the secretary of state for trade and industry, but the legislation allows that person to delegate most functions to a 'designated Agency.' This agency is the Securities and Investments Board (SIB). As Moran points out: 'The legal status of the SIB is, by design, ambiguous. It is incorporated as a private company, is funded by a levy on the industry, recruits its staff largely from the City ... But its chairman ... and its governing body are appointed jointly by the Bank of England and the Department of Trade and Industry; it exercises public powers (including powers of prosecution) delegated from the Secretary of State; and it will have to provide an annual report on the exercise of those powers' (Moran 1988, 21). Although officially designated by government as the principal body for regulating the financial markets, it is not considered by government to be a government body.

The SIB is not normally involved in the detailed regulation of individual firms. Instead, it has in turn licensed a number of self-regulatory organizations that have the responsibility for authorizing individual firms and monitoring their conduct. This part of the Financial Services Act came into operation in April 1988. The SIB has developed and reviews a set of model rules for the self-regulatory organizations and individual investment businesses. A chairman of the SIB explained the origins of this system as follows: 'The architects of the Financial Services Act were presented with a challenge. The need for regulation was scarcely accepted by many in the 1980s. Many people were doubtful, some downright hostile. Those who created the regulatory framework had to meet their objections. They had to breathe life into the system. They did so by offering significant independence to the front line regulatory bodies. These were, in essence, allowed to be self-governing' (Large 1997). The original self-regulatory bodies licensed by the SIB were the Securities Association (TSA) covering the Stock Exchange, the Investment Managers Regulatory Organisation (IMRO), the Association of Futures Brokers and Dealers (AFBD), the Financial Intermediaries, Managers and Brokers Association (FIMBRA), and the Life Assurance and Unit Trust Regulatory Organisation (LAUTRO). There are also a number of 'recognised professional bodies' that carry out similar functions in relation to the financial services activities of their members.

Many firms, because of the range of their activities, originally had to join more than one of the self-regulatory organizations. By the mid-1990s the list of self-regulatory organizations had shortened as a result of major restructuring to three: the Securities and Futures Authority (SFA), the Investment Management Regulatory Organisation (IMRO), and the Personal Investment Authority (PIA). The last was established in 1994 to deal with widespread dissatisfaction that arose because the existing structure did not provide a comprehensive regulatory body for firms or persons marketing products to individual consumers.

The coexistence of the recognized professional bodies with the self-regulatory organizations means that there is continuing fragmentation, though as pointed out elsewhere in this chapter such apparent fragmentation can also provide some information about differing regulatory regimes and enforcement mechanisms.

Although the self-regulatory organizations are formally private bodies, they have been given extensive immunity from civil writs for damages. As Moran notes (1988, 25), the drift of this and other amendments to the original bill 'has been to strengthen the public character of nominally private institutions.' The rule books of the new self-regulatory organizations were subject to scrutiny by the OFT, which severely criticized the proposed LAUTRO rule book. The OFT made reports to the secretary of state for trade and industry, who was responsible for deciding on whether to insist on changes.

Responsibility for administering the City's code covering share dealings and other aspects of takeovers remains with the Panel on Takeovers and Mergers (commonly referred to as the Takeover Panel), which was originally established in 1968. In 1978 the Takeover Panel was made responsible to the newly established Council for the Securities Industry, but when that body was wound up in 1985 as part of the new City regulatory regime it assumed sole responsibility for its functions. The Takeover Panel was originally created as a non-statutory body by the governor of the Bank of England in consultation with City bodies involved in the organization and functioning of the capital market. The Takeover Panel has no formal constitution and therefore no formal mechanisms for enforcement. It consists of a chair, two deputy chairs, a nominee of the governor of the Bank of England, a representative of the Confederation of British Industry, and representatives from a number of associations and organizations in the City. The Takeover Panel has a full-time staff headed by a director general. Although the Takeover Panel is a non-statutory self-regulatory body not considered to be a government body by the government itself, the Court of Appeal ruled in 1986 that it was subject to judicial review, the procedure by which the courts can review the actions of government bodies.

The other main aspect of financial market regulation not covered by the new SIB arrangements was the insurance market, including Lloyd's. Lloyd's itself underwent major changes in its regulatory framework in the Lloyd's Act 1982, which gave it new powers of self-regulation. Before 1982 all the members of the Council of Lloyd's were internal members. Between 1982 and 1987 the balance was 57 per cent internal, 43 per cent external (Baggott 1989, 441). Shortly after the 1982 act was passed, a series of scandals involving Lloyd's agencies emerged. The Bank of England persuaded Lloyd's to appoint an outsider, Ian Hay Davison, as chief executive at the beginning of 1983. Davison resigned in 1986 after a dispute with the chairman of Lloyd's about responsibility for the staff of Lloyd's (Davison 1987). However, his replacement was given powers similar to those sought by Davison. Political concern led to the government setting up an inquiry under Sir Patrick Neill into the regulatory arrangements at Lloyd's. The Neill Report was published in January 1987. It concluded that the balance of initiative rested too much with the working members of Lloyd's. As a result of the report, insiders became from July 1987 a minority of twelve among the twenty-eight Council members. The Neill Report also envisaged a more active role for the new nominated members in chairing and participating in the key regulatory committees. These changes were brought about by the agreement of the Lloyd's Council rather than through new legislation.

The new regulatory arrangements for the City established in the 1980s combined, in often ambiguous form, statutory regulation and self-regulation. The arrangements were complex, involving both a hierarchy of new organizations and continuing involvement by other regulatory bodies, including the DTI, the OFT, and the Bank of England.

Within three weeks of taking office in May 1997 the new Labour government announced a major upheaval in the regulatory arrangements. The SIB was to be placed on a new statutory footing and would absorb the three existing self-regulatory bodies that it supervized. It would also take over responsibility for banking supervision from the Bank of England (only two weeks earlier it had been given the power to set interest rates by the new Labour chancellor). It was still to be resolved whether the reformed SIB would also take over responsibility for regulating insurance (including Lloyd's) and building societies (currently regulated by the Building Societies Commission, a committee serviced by a non-ministerial department).

While the change announced by the Labour government is clearly a major one and marks a decisive move away from self-regulation in the financial markets, the proposed new arrangement did nevertheless build on existing ones. The new chairman of the SIB was to be Howard Davies, then deputy governor of the Bank of England, who was already a member of the SIB as a result of the existing cross-directorship arrangements between the SIB and the bank's Board of Banking Supervision (Large 1997). The new arrangements invite the drawing of a parallel with the U.S. Securities and Exchange Commission (SEC). A parallel between the situation in the two countries was certainly noted in the 1980s debate about city regulation, but was not explicitly referred to in the 1997 announcement, which in any case goes beyond the SEC model by incorporating bank supervision.

Environmental Protection

Environmental regulation in Britain has in the past been identified as having a distinctive non-legalistic style compared to regulatory regimes elsewhere (see Vogel 1986). However, since the late 1980s regulation has become more formalized and integrated, in part stimulated by the need for a new regulatory regime to cope with water privatization, and in part by the evolution of a professional ideology of 'integrated pollution control.' As in many other aspects of regulation discussed in this chapter, the regulatory regime and its organizational structure have evolved over the period instead of being the result of a single defining event, making it all the more difficult to trace the basis for the organizational forms adopted.

The process of privatization of water in England and Wales in 1989 was complicated by the fact that the regional water authorities had important regulatory functions over water pollution and quality as well as being water suppliers and sewage disposers. In fact, the water authorities were themselves major polluters of the rivers, illustrating the problems of combining the role of supplier and regulator in one set of organizations (Hogwood 1987, 166). The separation of these two roles was touted by the government as one of the major advantages of privatizing the industry, but logically there was no obstacle to separating the two functions even if the water supply and disposal functions had remained in public ownership. In addition to regional water authorities, there were twenty-eight private, though statutory, water-supply companies.

A further complication arose early in 1989 when the European Commission made it clear that it considered illegal a provision in the privatization bill to enable the secretary for state for the environment to continue to allow exemption of the privatized water authorities from European criteria on the cleanliness of drinking water. In September 1989 the European Commission decided to prosecute Britain for its failure to meet water-purity standards. The need for expenditure to improve the quality of drinking water and sewage treatment led the government to include as part of water privatization a so-called 'green dowry,' involving a write-off of £4.4 billion in loans and a cash injection of £1 billion. The price increase formula also provided for annual increases of the general rate of inflation plus 5 per cent, in contrast to the RPI-X formula used for previous privatizations. The price increase formula also allowed for the 'pass-through' of 'unavoidable' additional charges.

As the analysis by Booker in Chapter 12 shows, regulation of the quality of river water as well as direct responsibility for sea walls and river embankments became the concern of the NRA set up in September 1989 with extensive powers of prosecution. The NRA was initially headed by Lord Crickhowell, a former Conservative secretary of state for Wales. Of the authority's annual budget of £300 million about £70 million came from Treasury grants, with the rest provided from licences sold to private companies, including the new water companies.

A new Drinking Water Inspectorate was set up by the Department of the Environment at the beginning of 1990, and it remained there even after the establishment of the Environment Agency. When fully operational it was due to have a staff of twenty-three. However, it had to rely on the water companies themselves to do the sampling, with the inspectorate doing its monitoring by checking the records kept by the companies (Walker 1990). Inspectorates occupy a curious position in terms of independence in relation to government. They are employed and paid for by government departments, but have special roles that set them apart from normal civil servants. However, they may still be susceptible to political pressure. There have been allegations that the Inspectorate of Pollution (whose water division was taken over by the NRA) failed to prosecute water authorities for fear of jeopardizing their privatization (*Times*, 27 November 1989).

A major change in regulation of environmental and pollution matters took place in April 1996. Underlying it was the political-technocratic concept of integrated pollution control, a concept that also underlaid the earlier Environmental Protection Act of 1990 (Constitutional Reform Centre 1991, 512). Previously, separate regulation in England and Wales of rivers (NRA, a non-departmental public body), pollution inspection (inspectorate with the Department of the Environment), and waste regulation (local authorities) was given to the Environment Agency, which is a non-departmental public body. A similar development took place in Scotland, with responsibility for river purification (formerly given to non-departmental public bodies), the Scottish Industrial Pollution Inspectorate (within the Scottish Office, a government department), and waste regulation by local authorities being merged into a Scottish Environmental Protection Agency.

It is thus often tortuous to trace the influences on the organizational forms used for environmental regulation. In the case of the new environment agencies established in April 1996, one might expect to find reference to emulation of the Environmental Protection Agency in the United States, especially because that example had been cited in policy discussions in previous decades. The Scottish body is even called the Scottish Environmental Protection Agency. However, an examination of the consultation papers, the White Paper, legislation, and debate in Parliament about the formation of the Environment Agency shows no reference at all to policy emulation of the United States and very few specific references to the European Union dimension either. This is not the same as establishing that there was no emulation. The policy evaluation literature has established that even in the absence of a direct link between a report and an outcome, the context of a debate several years later may be affected by themes and findings that are not consciously drawn on.

Possible Explanations of Institutional Form

We now look at possible explanations for the variety of organizational forms that regulatory bodies in Britain take (Hood 1978). These include historical intertia, emulation, transaction costs, randomness, forms linked to the specific nature of regulation, fashion, and ad hoc additionality.

Historical Inertia

This explanation has a lot of initial plausibility: organizations simply continue with the form in which they are originally set up. Certain forms of organization were considered appropriate at different time periods. For example, non-ministerial departments in the form of boards or commissioners were more common before the early twentieth century, and so the form taken by the Charities Commission in regulating charities can be explained in this way. There are two major problems with this explanation. First, as we have seen above, many areas of regulation have undergone reviews of the activities of regulatory bodies, in some cases leading to new bodies, in others to replacement bodies of different organization type, sometimes with a continuation of existing organizational form but with changed legislative basis. Second, the explanation does not say why different organizational forms are adopted, even when bodies are set up in the same period. This is certainly true for the period since 1979.

Emulation

Emulation as an explanation argues that policy makers do not attempt to design a priori or even to find a model that best fits specified criteria, but that they look for examples of already established bodies that seem to offer an acceptable design (Hogwood and Gunn 1984). There are two major sources of emulation: copying previous examples from the same political system, and transferring organizational designs of bodies dealing with the same policy issues from other political systems.

There is no doubt that precedent is an important factor in determining organizational design in Britain. The British civil service will look for existing or past examples of an issue that appears to have similarities and will consider applying them to the case in hand. As we have seen, the OFT provided a model for the early single-industry regulatory bodies for privatized industries, and they in turn provided a model for later privatized industries. However, such models are not necessarily followed slavishly, as the case of the Coal Authority in particular indicates. Furthermore, the process by which a particular model is considered to be an appropriate precedent itself needs exploration.

Policy transfer is a topical subject (Rose 1993; Majone 1991). Two obvious sources for such emulation are the European Union and the United States as the largest developed country. However, establishing whether there has been explicit policy transfer, even in cases where there may be reason to expect it, can be difficult, as we saw in the case of the establishment of the Environment Agency in April 1996, where, despite the lack of immediate direct reference, a link from discussions over the previous decades can be established. The U.S. Securities and Exchange Commission (SEC) was cited as a model in the mid-1980s, but the form adopted at that time did not follow it, and the announcement of the 'Super SIB' in 1997 did not cite the U.S. example: indeed, the SIB went beyond the SEC by combining banking regulation with other forms of financial regulation.

There are examples of EU policy leading to a new regulatory body. The Meat Hygiene Service was established as a Next Steps agency in April 1995; this service is unusual in that it does not consisting of existing civil servants in a central government department but rather mainly of former local authority inspectors. The form of the body was not specified by the EU, but it was triggered by the need to implement its policy. It was noted above that EU regulations were relevant to the circumstances of water privatization and the establishment of the NRA, though it is not clear that they had any effect on the form of regulatory body adopted.

Transaction Costs

This approach derived from public-choice theory that the regulatory form adopted will depend on the costs and benefits perceived by legislators. In the form set out by Fiorina (1982), the choice is seen as being between delegating power to regulatory agencies or passing laws to be enforced by the courts. It therefore has little to contribute to an understanding of the particular organizational form chosen from the variety that is available. In addition to regulation through legislation enforced by the courts, Horn (1995) differentiates between independent commissions and executive agencies such as the Environmental Protection Agency. Legislators will have a number of considerations, including minimizing decision costs, avoiding political blame while being able to take political credit, desire for certainty of outcome (especially the possibility of different implementation in the future by political rivals), and assumptions about what the outcome will be. The regulatory agency form may allow for greater future involvement in the implementation process. According to Fiorina, the regulatory form chosen will be the result of the aggregation of the preferences of individual legislators. Though Fiorina's arguments are presented in a highly formalized manner, they rest on an assumption that legislation on regulation is determined by a highly atomized version of the U.S. Congressional model. In Britain, choices about legislative form are largely a matter for the executive.

Despite the U.S. orientation of the transaction-costs approach, it is possible to see some scope for insights derived from an approach that incorporates uncertainty and the risk preferences of policy formulators. For example, use of the ministerial department as regulatory body allows for direct political involvement in decisions – but it also enables opponents to do the same if they gain office in the future. Handing over implementation to an independent statutory body might preclude or limit intervention in individual cases, but would institutionalize the regulatory framework preferred by the current government. However, in the British system, new governments can, if they choose, simply introduce legislation to impose their own preferred form of regulation, though the need for legislative time is a factor. Approval of self-regulation minimizes opposition from those being regulated and makes possible the avoidance of blame, but it also reduces control over outcomes and can lead to future political problems if the system is seen as working in the interests of the industry rather than those of consumers or the general public.

Randomness

This explanation is in many ways the most attractive, if only as an exasperated reaction in trying to make sense of the diversity of organizational forms found in practice. Unfortunately, it is possible to find recurring patterns, such as the recent use of single-industry regulators, even if these patterns are far from complete or consistent.

Forms Related to the Specific Nature of Regulation

By the specific nature of regulation is meant here categories such as economic, professional, or sensitive (e.g., censorship, human fertility) arenas of regulation. This does seem to have partial explanatory power in explaining some of the variation between the different categories of regulatory concern, though not variations within the categories. For example, in sensitive issues such as censorship or judgments about artificial fertilization, the government prefers to distance itself so that the bodies regulating such activities are not government departments but non-departmental public bodies or even bodies that are not officially recognized as public bodies at all. For the regulation of professional conduct and standards in professions, the government largely prefers professional self-regulation, often endorsing this in statute. The problem area in terms of this type of explanation is economic regulation, where the full range of types of public bodies are involved.

Fashion

This is less a genuine explanation than an assumption that particular types of bodies are considered to be more appropriate than others at particular times. Particularly when combined with the historical inertia model, fashion might seem to explain variety. However, as we have seen, in recent years the full range of organizational forms has been used for regulatory bodies rather than a single fashionable type, such as Next Steps agencies in the early 1990s, though that fashion does explain why many but not all regulatory functions that already existed within departments have now been given agency form.

Ad Hoc Additionality rather than Synoptic Reappraisal

The main way of bringing these explanations together is to note that at no stage has the government attempted a synoptic overview of regulatory bodies or even of bodies operating in a policy area or type of regulation. Every time a problem or issue has arisen in which existing regulation is considered to be unsatisfactory or new regulation is required because of political developments (for example, privatization) or technological ones (such as scientific and medical advances), the regulatory form is considered on an ad hoc basis. This is not the same as saying it is considered in total isolation: particularly if a need is seen for a new regulatory body, there will be a (limited) search for something to emulate. Recent exemplars are likely to be noted more than older ones. Where an existing body is to be reformed, the tendency is to maintain the existing form. Even where there is a major structural change involving a number of different existing organizational types, the type of the predominant part may determine the type of the final body. This may be an explanation for the non-departmental public-body status of the Environment Agency, which took over functions from a large non-departmental public body (NRA), parts of a government department (Inspectorate of Pollution and other functions from the Department of the Environment) and local government (waste regulation).

Exceptions arise where there is a major institutional reform unrelated to regulatory body design, such as the establishment of Next Steps agencies within the civil service (Giddings 1995; Greer 1994). However, this reform did not involve a review of all existing regulatory functions to determine whether Next Steps agencies would be the most appropriate reform.

If we apply these general remarks to the development of regulatory bodies for the privatized utility industries, we can see that despite the lack of an initial master plan there is a clear pattern in the use of single-industry non-ministerial departments headed by individual director generals. This reflects the importance of emulation of precedents, initially of the OFT in the establishment of OFTEL, then of OFTEL as the model for later privatized utilities. Detailed variations in the internal structure of the regulatory bodies and associated consumer committees reflected the structure of the industry at the time of privatization. Underlying the choice of regulatory form was the key Conservative aim of making privatization appear to be successful and permanently established. Initially the stress was on the move to the private sector and the removal of state involvement: direct regulation by government ministers would have appeared to have been a contradiction. Although competition was often equated by the Conservatives with being in the private sector, the stress on the importance of *competition* was initially less coherent than the desire for *privatization*, though competition has subsequently emerged as the major emphasis of all the utility regulators.

Networks of Regulators

Particularly in examining the post-privatization regulatory arrangements and the regulation of financial services, we have seen that there are complex networks of organizations. These networks involve a wide variety of types of bodies, from ministerial departments to non-ministerial departments, non-departmental bodies, and bodies not counted by government as public even though they are performing a clear public function. Even in relation to a single industry there may, as we have seen in the cases of telecommunications and water, be more than one 'single-industry' regulatory agency involved. The complexity of the networks of regulation is increased when we take into account the new regulatory arrangements in the financial markets, because, as was outlined earlier in the chapter, financial regulation has a direct bearing on the privatized utilities.

The proliferation of bodies, often with overlapping remits, makes it tempting to regard the situation as administratively untidy and in need of rationalization. However, as Veljanovski argued early on, proliferation and overlap is not self-evidently less effective than a single central regulatory body and, in addition, there are potential advantages as well as disadvantages to competition between government agencies (Veljanovski 1987, 175–80).

Although the new regulatory bodies are often described as 'independent,' we have seen that in many cases their independence of governments is limited, that some depend on the industry being regulated for resources, and that all depend on the industry being regulated for information. A focus on whether or not any individual agency is 'independent' may not be the most helpful one. The full range of regulatory control often depends on the joint involvement of a number of regulatory bodies. An analysis of the effectiveness of the new regulatory regimes is therefore one of assessing the effectiveness of 'interdependence' rather than 'independence.'

Hancher and Moran (1989) stress the organizational complexity that we should expect in regulation, and this complexity is reflected in the discussion of networks and interdependency in regulation. Complexity, however, raises in even stronger form the debates in relation to individual regulators about accountability: how do you hold a network accountable?

Conclusions

This chapter has mapped out the range of regulatory institutions that exists in Britain in 1997 and has attempted to explore major developments since 1979. There has always been a diversity of organizational forms taken by regulatory bodies in Britain, but this diversity has developed further with the establishment of single-industry non-ministerial regulators and Next Steps agencies. In addition to the diversity of forms, we have seen the complexity of interaction of a number of bodies that are involved in the regulatory process, often involving bodies with different constitutional statuses. This complicates further the already difficult process of attempting to identify the explanations for organizational form and the relationships between organizational form and regulatory process in practice.

We have seen that there is no single simple explanation of institutional form. Rather, the best characterization is a pattern of dealing with each issue as it arises and either modifying the existing arrangements where they exist or looking to an apparent precedent in institutional form where a new body has to be established. There is no standard regulatory tool kit from which appropriate tools for different regulatory purposes can be taken. However, common patterns can emerge from common precedents.

Given that the Labour Party strongly criticized aspects of privatization and the regulatory regime for utilities when in opposition, we might expect that we would find party differences. However, the range of differences is less than fundamental, at least in terms of what organizational form to use. Existing single-industry regulators might be integrated, but in the same organizational form. The Health and Safety Commission survived eighteen years of Conservative government with trade-union representation. Differences have emerged under the new Labour government, particularly over the regulation of the City, but Labour (just as the Conservatives) has no coherent philosophy of the appropriate form for different types of regulation.

Is institutional form determined by a distinctive national style? The evidence presented in this chapter suggests that there has been a greater formalization of regulation in Britain in the economic and environmental fields than there has been in North America, though the self-regulatory approach lingers on in regulation of the professions and the media. There is a temptation to argue that the ad hoc nature of decision making about regulatory innovation or reform is distinctively British, but any student of comparative policy will be aware that Britain is far from unique. What does give a special British flavour is the lack of a systematic constitutional or law framework. As any observer of the United States will know, the presence of a constitutional framework neither ensures consistency nor constrains the imagination in proposing organizational forms, but the British system does have particular flexibility.

In looking for common international patterns arising from 'globalization,' we need to distinguish between shared problems and genuinely international influences in the form of problems or international institutions. An issue may be genuinely global – for example international financial markets – and therefore may impose some imperative for regulation, but this does not necessarily dictate the form that such regulation will take. We need to distinguish between cases of 'policy push,' such as European Union regulations on water quality, and 'policy pull,' where emulation is not necessarily entirely passive.

Greater insight into the issues raised in this chapter can be gained by comparing the institutional forms used in other countries for similar objectives, type of regulation, or policy area as is provided elsewhere in this book. Such a comparison can be hindered by the idiosyncrasies of constitutional form in each country. Nevertheless, such a comparison, however partial, helps to establish whether particular patterns or explanations for regulatory body forms have some generic power or is related merely to the history of particular countries. This chapter has shown pointers in differing directions: we should be suspicious of 'general' theories.

NOTE

1 Research for this chapter was assisted by funding from the Economic and Social Research Council for a project on 'The Audit of Accountability: Agencies and Their Multiple Constituencies,' funded under the Whitehall Programme. My thanks are owed to Murray McVicar for research assistance.

REFERENCES

Baggott, R. 1989. 'Regulatory Reform in Britain: The Changing Face of Self-Regulation.' *Public Administration* 67:435–54.

Baldwin, R. 1985. *Regulating the Airlines: Administrative Justice and Agency Discretion.* Oxford: Oxford University Press.
– ed. 1995. *Regulation in Question: The Growing Agenda.* London: London School of Economics.
Bishop, M., J. Kay and C. Mayer, eds. 1995. *The Regulatory Challenge.* Oxford: Oxford University Press.
Constitutional Reform Centre. 1991. 'Regulatory Agencies in the United Kingdom.' *Parliamentary Affairs* 44:505–20.
Davison, I.H. 1987. 'Lloyd's of London.' *Economist* 20 June 1987:77–80.
Department of Trade and Industry (DTI). 1998. *Fair Deal for Consumers.* Cmnd 3898. London: HMSO.
European Policy Forum. 1966. *The Report of the Commission on the Regulation of Privatized Utilities.* London: Hansard Society and European Policy Forum.
Fiorina, M.P. 1982. 'Legislative Choice of Regulatory Forms: Legal Process or Administrative Process?' *Public Choice* 39:33–66.
Giddings, Phillip, ed. 1995. *Parliamentary Accountability: A Study of Parliament and Executive Agencies.* London: MacMillan.
Grant, W. 1982. *The Political Economy of Industrial Policy.* London: Butterworths.
Greer, Patricia. 1994. *Transforming Central Government: The Next Steps Initiative.* Buckingham: Open University Press.
Hancher, L., and M. Moran, eds. 1989. *Capitalism, Culture and Economic Regulation.* Oxford: Clarendon.
Hogwood, B.W., 1987. *From Crisis to Complacency? Shaping Public Policy in Britain.* Oxford: Oxford University Press.
Hogwood, B.W., and L.A. Gunn. 1984. *Policy Analysis for the Real World.* Oxford: Oxford University Press.
Hood, C. 1978. 'Keeping the Centre Small: Explanations of Agency Type.' *Political Studies* 26:30–46.
Horn, M.J. 1995. *The Political Economy of Public Administration: Institutional Choice in the Public Sector.* Cambridge: Cambridge University Press.
Large, A. 1997. 'Regulation and Reform.' Speech delivered to the Society of Merchants, Trinity House, Tower Hill, London, 20 May 1997.
Majone, G. 1991. 'Cross-National Sources of Regulatory Policymaking in Europe and the United States.' *Journal of Public Policy* 11:79–106.
Moran, M. 1988. 'Thatcherism and Financial Regulation.' *Political Quarterly* 59:20–7.
National Audit Office. 1996. *The Work of the Directors General of Telecommunications, Gas Supply, Water Services and Electricity Supply.* Session 1995–6. House of Commons, 645. London: HMSO.
Peacock, A. 1984. *The Regulation Game.* Oxford: Basil Blackwell.
Rose, R. 1993. *Lesson-Drawing in Public Policy.* Chatham, N.J.: Chatham House.

Veljanovski, C. 1987. *Selling the State: Privatisation in Britain*. London: Weidenfeld and Nicolson.

Vogel, D. 1986. *National Styles of Regulation: Environmental Policy in Great Britain and in the United States*. Ithaca: Cornell University Press.

Walker, D. 1990. 'Inspector as Hero or Face-Saver.' *Times*. 29 January 1990.

Wilks, Stephen. 1996. 'The Prolonged Reform of United Kingdom Competition Policy.' In *Comparative Competition Policy: National Institutions in a Global Market*, edited by Bruce Doern and Stephen Wilks, 139–84.

5

No Longer 'Governments in Miniature': Canadian Sectoral Regulatory Institutions

RICHARD SCHULTZ AND G. BRUCE DOERN

This chapter examines the evolution of the core Canadian sectoral regulatory institutions in the transportation, energy, broadcasting, and telecommunications fields. It does so with a view to demonstrate both connections to and departures from developments in the United States. The essential analytical journey is one showing that, in the early twentieth century, Canadian and U.S. sectoral regulatory institutions were quite similar. Then, from the 1930s to about the end of the 1960s, a significant Canadian departure occurs. During this period the core Canadian sectoral regulators became virtual 'governments in miniature,' in that they were given broad ranges of functions, powers, and policy instruments that went well beyond narrowly defined regulation.

The three sectoral regulatory bodies, the Canadian Transportation Commission, later renamed the National Transportation Agency (NTA), the National Energy Board (NEB), and the Canadian Radio-television and Telecommunications Commission (CRTC), carried out a mix of functions. These included regulation making and licensing, adjudicative, and quasi-judicial tasks. However, they also included subsidy or spending roles and policy advisory and monitoring functions. Over this period as a whole, the three regulatory bodies were cast in various ways as planning and nation-building structures overseeing sectoral markets that typically included one major crown corporation (or state enterprise) and private-sector firms. The regulatory bodies were also multi-member commissions to ensure reasonable forms of regional and other representation in their deliberations and decisions. Though supervised by the courts and the Cabinet, the three main national regulators had considerable autonomy and evolved elaborate hearing processes that at times sought to be informal but that, because they were courts of record, tended to be lawyer-dominated and court-like in their own proceedings.

The title of the chapter evokes the nature of the transformation in the last two decades, namely a significant diminution of this status as 'governments in miniature' to the point where two of the regulators are mere shells of their former selves. The NTA and NEB, in particular, have been stripped to a narrower range of functions and to a greatly reduced number of commission members and staff. The CRTC has been less obviously affected for reasons to be presented below.

We argue that the causes of this transformation in the 1980s and 1990s cannot be attributed simply to a U.S.-style liberalized deregulation impulse. It was also the result of institutional factors, namely the actions of the political executive, which wanted to reclaim policy-making powers as a matter of both principle and power (Doern 1978; Schultz 1977; Johnson 1991; Thomas and Zajcew 1993). As we will see below, this transformation was not equally present in all three sectors, nor did it develop at the same time or pace, but it has been a pronounced development nonetheless.

The chapter is divided into five sections. The first briefly traces the early historical features of Canadian regulation and its relative similarity to the U.S. variety. The second section examines the change to the 'governments in miniature' era. The third and fourth sections deal with regulatory change as revealed by the diminution of the regulatory function, with brief looks at change regarding the NTA, NEB, and CRTC. In the third section these changes are linked to the initial actions of the Cabinet and ministers to reclaim policy powers. In the fourth section, the changes are linked to the somewhat later forces of deregulation and liberalizing markets. Conclusions then follow.

Canadian Sectoral Regulators in the Minimalist 'Policing' Era

The initial Canadian sectoral regulatory regime was similar in most respects to its American counterpart, which preceded it by more than a decade. In terms of its rationale or underlying purpose, as exemplified by both the railway and telephone regulatory systems, the regime in Canada had a relatively straightforward goal (Baldwin 1989; Armstrong and Nelles 1986; Babe 1990; Cruikshank 1991). Regulation was justified as necessary to control the potential for corruption and abuse of economic power that arose from monopoly or near-monopoly service provisions. In other studies, this has been described for Canada as a minimalist 'policing' regulatory function (Schultz and Alexandroff 1985), or, for the United States, as a 'market-corrective' regime (Eisner 1991).

Such regulation typically establishes not goals for the regulated but boundaries for economic behaviour, particularly concerning pricing and the differential availability of service. In the language of the statutes for regulations, regulated firms under a policing approach must only charge rates that are 'just and reasonable,' and they are not permitted to engage in 'undue discrimination' amongst customers.

This rationale for regulation, with its explicit preference for markets and its begrudging embrace of government intervention is inextricably linked to the design of the institutional mechanism for government intervention, which in Canada and the United States became the independent regulatory commission or agency. While the validity of the argument that regulation must be 'taken out of politics' can be exaggerated, in both countries the emphasis in institutional design was on impartiality and non-partisanship and hence the avoidance of politics, which was seen as leading to corruption, abuse, and favouritism (Willis 1941; Doern 1978; Hodgetts 1973).

Respect for private property, and more specifically respect for the right to private decision making over how to employ that property, was paramount in both countries. Constraints on decision making were to be at a minimum. To reinforce this objective, a relatively novel type of institution was created, the politically arm's-length, collective regulatory agencies. A dominant characteristic of these agencies was the fixed-term tenure bestowed on the individual regulators, which, though more restrictive than that given to members of the judiciary, was similar in intent. Regulators, like judges, were only to be removed 'for cause,' and did not serve simply 'at the pleasure' of their political masters as did other members of the state apparatus at the time.

The one major institutional difference between the original independent regulatory agencies in Canada and the United States was the power given to Canadian political authorities, in particular the Cabinet, to review regulatory decisions. Although this power was not in the original design proposals (McLean 1902), it was subsequently argued that, in a parliamentary system premised on ministerial responsibility, a totally arms-length relationship that allowed appointed officials to make final decisions was unacceptable (McLean 1902; Janisch 1978). Consequently, provision was made for appeals against regulatory decisions to the Cabinet as a whole and, subsequently, in some areas to the designated minister responsible for the agency.

It is worth noting that in the first instance, namely appeals to the railway regulatory agency, the appeal provision provided for rather extensive direct political control over individual decisions. Cabinet was given the power 'to vary or rescind' regulatory decisions, and not simply to set them aside or ask for a review. Subsequently, a rather variegated system of political appeals developed in terms of scope and constraints on the political authorities (Schultz 1977; Economic Council of Canada 1979, 1981), but the fundamental principle remained the same, reflecting a concern for responsible (in the parliamentary sense of the term) political control.

The original North American sectoral regulatory regime remained completely intact for more than thirty years. It was only in the 1930s, as governments grappled with the political consequences of the Depression, that it was challenged and ultimately supplanted. The next era, at least in Canada, evolved over thirty years, although most of its essential elements were in place by World War II. In terms of institutional design and particularly of the relationship between political and regulatory authorities, the new sectoral regime reflected the traditional principles for control, albeit with some modifications in techniques, given that individual Cabinet ministers were granted supplementary controls over some regulatory decisions in airline and broadcasting regulation.

The 'Governments in Miniature' Era

The primary changes in the regulatory regime in this thirty-year period involved the overall function of regulation. It is in this period that we see the most serious divergence between Canadian and U.S. sectoral regulatory systems. The Depression radically challenged prevailing conceptions of the role of the state in the economy, and thus it is not surprising that the traditional regulatory system was found wanting. The idea of the state as economic policeman, although not completely rejected, was perceived to be no longer sufficient. In particular, the reactive, case-specific, corrective focus was found wanting in the face of economic turbulence in sectors that were essential to the larger economic performance of the society and that entailed huge capital expenditures.

The result was the adoption of a much more positive role for regulation, one that stressed not reaction and correction for unacceptable individual corporate economic behaviour but anticipation and direction at the sectoral level. Eisner calls this an 'associational regime' (Eisner 1991) in the United States, whereas in the Canadian context it has been described as an approach in which first a 'promotional' and subsequently a 'planning' regulatory function was carried out (Schultz and Alexandroff 1985). Again, the new American and Canadian systems had much in common, but there were also some major differences.

Both started from the assumption that the role of the state is not simply to police individual corporations in regulated sectors but to promote a healthy and stable economy. Undergirding this assumption was a fear of what was presumed to be 'destructive competition.' The argument was that the economy and the country at large could not afford cut-throat competition in capital intensive, socially vital industries, such as the individual transportation sectors. Such competition was viewed as economically wasteful.

In the United States the response was 'an attempt to use regulation on a sector-by-sector basis to promote macroeconomic stability and growth. The goal was not to recreate markets but to compensate for their destabilizing effects' (Eisner 1991, 87–8). The result in sectors such as rail, trucking, and air transportation in the United States was a form of industrial policy, a promotional regulatory approach that in effect cartelized the sectors. Competition was to be managed, both inter- and intra-modally, as incumbent firms were protected through entry and exit licensing and pricing regulation. This produced 'government-sponsored protection from industrial overcapacity' (McGraw 1984, 211). Subsequently, when the fear of economic depression disappeared, it was this type of regulation that would come under intense scrutiny and criticism from economists and policy makers because of the costs it imposed on both consumers and the economy generally.

Canada also found the policing regulatory approach wanting in the 1930s in those sectors where natural monopoly was not to be found, although where it was found, most notably with telephones, policing regulation remained dominant. Canada's response, although superficially similar to that of the United States, was actually profoundly different, and the differences would only grow in the future. American regulatory responses were still rooted in a preference for free-market decision making. From this perspective, the 'associational regime' was but a further ameliorative step for markets, not a rejection of them in principle.

Canada, on the other hand, introduced its variant of promotional regulation not as a result of a preference for markets, but as a rejection of them, or at least of market competition, in some sectors. Promotional regulation in Canada reflected the view that regulation could also be a substitute for, or an adjunct to, public ownership for the pursuit of a broader, more comprehensive set of public policy goals than simply economic stabilization. In other words, the 1930s saw a fundamental divergence in the economic and public policy ideas and values undergirding regulation in Canada and the United States (Stanbury 1980; Tupper and Doern 1988; Strick 1990).

This divergence would grow significantly as Canadian policy makers embraced a much more positive role for state intervention through regulatory instruments in the economy. Although in the 1930s some of Roosevelt's advisers, such as Tugwell and Landis, viewed the introduction of a promotional or associational regulatory regime as a preliminary but necessary first step towards the use of regulation as a planning tool, Canada ultimately proved to be much more receptive to the idea.

Central to the divergence in views that emerged in the 1930s was the Canadian decision to create public enterprises in the transportation and broadcasting sectors. Public enterprises, in concert with the regulator, were created to pursue a broad mix of economic and non-economic objectives such as nation building, regional development, national unity, and cultural sovereignty, although this last term would not be popularized until the 1980s (Corbett 1965; Peers 1969; Stewart and Hull 1994).

The employment of public enterprises, but not full nationalization, as policy instruments nevertheless reflected a particular conception of the sectors in question. The enterprises were not perceived to be a collection of individual firms, or simply a mix of public and private organizations, each pursuing its own objectives within a set of stabilizing constraints, as was the case in the American model. Instead, they were deemed to be part of a single system, with both the private and the public economic actors either collaborating in the pursuit of public goals or alternatively with the former assigned a non-threatening status.

The differences between the original policing and the subsequent promotional and then planning regulatory eras in Canada and the United States are particularly striking in transportation, especially the rail and air modes, which were the two under federal jurisdiction, and in broadcasting. The changes in the goals or values in the 1930s were easily demonstrable in the broadcasting sector. The Canadian Broadcasting Corporation (CBC) was created, in part after the model of the British Broadcasting Corporation, to foster national consciousness, but it was established in concert with significant regulatory restraints being placed on the existing private broadcasters, most notably controls on their content and on the formation of private networks.

Similar objectives and constraints are to be found in the air sector and the introduction of airline regulation. In 1937 Canada created TransCanada Airlines (TCA) to be the 'chosen instrument' for Canada's airline policy objectives. In order to further TCA's capacity to act as such an instrument, the government gave it not only a national monopoly on the transcontnental trunk route but 'special status' before the regulator (Corbett 1965). This meant preferential treatment in its applications for any particular route in that, unlike other applicants, TCA was not required to argue 'public convenience and necessity' for its applications. Merely applying was deemed to be sufficient demonstration of valid public purpose.

Furthermore, disregarding the norms emphasizing impartiality that existed in the initial policing regulatory era, political authorities became intent on exploiting the full panoply of their powers, regulatory and otherwise, to protect and enhance the performance of their progeny.

Although Canada and the United States began to diverge in the 1930s over the role of regulation, both countries remained committed to the essential attribute of institutional design for the attainment of regulatory goals. If anything, the emphasis on independent, specialized impartial regulatory agencies was even more pronounced in the move to either promotional or planning regulation. As Thomas McGraw argues, 'the single overarching idea ... was the conviction shared by a majority of New Dealers that economic regulation by expert commissions would bring just results' (McGraw 1984, 212). Among the most articulate proponents of this idea was James Landis, whose work *The Administrative Process* was influential on both sides of the border.

Landis and his Canadian counterpart, John Willis (Willis 1941), defended the idea of an independent agency on grounds other than the traditional primary defence of impartiality and of taking issues 'out of politics.' Their common position was that regulatory agencies worked best when they were, in Willis's phrase, 'governments in miniature' that combined legislative, executive, and judicial functions and powers. Such a combination, linked, as it had to be according to these advocates, with specialization and expertise on the part of regulators and their professional staffs, was crucial if regulation was to perform effectively a function that went beyond policing. Unlike traditional regulation, the new regulation as propounded by Landis, Willis, and others, if it was backed by specialized experts, 'made it possible for an agency to offer direction and advice *in advance of regulatory action*' (McGraw 1984, 214, emphasis in original). It is precisely this forward-looking anticipatory approach that distinguishes promotional and planning regulatory systems from their remedial, corrective policing predecessors.

The Canadian preference for specialized independent agencies, created to serve a planning function, reached its zenith in the 1960s with the creation of 'super' agencies in the transportation and broadcasting sectors. In the former, the National Transportation Act of 1967 delegated the vast range of regulatory powers for all modes of transportation under federal jurisdiction to the Canadian Transport Commission (CTC), the predecessor of the NTA, with the regulator's explicit responsibility being that of 'coordinating and harmonizing the operations of all carriers.' The regulator was given little in the way of unambiguous effective policy guidance in its statute – the objective was an 'efficient, effective and adequate transportation system making the best use of all available modes of transportation at the lowest total cost.' If there were to be competition, it was to be competition 'among modes,' not between firms.

Furthermore, in a highly exceptional form of delegation, the CTC, a regulatory agency, was given the power to make regulations, that is, it was given a subordinate legislative power, without any political controls whatsoever. Finally, reflecting the emphasis on the cult of the expert, who was presumably depoliticized or at least once removed from immediate politics, the CTC was given the authority to be the primary policy adviser to the minister of transport on all transportation matters. The regulator, not the Department of Transportation, was designed and empowered to be the main policy maker (Langford 1976).

Similar developments were occurring almost simultaneously in the broadcasting sector. After relying for two decades on the CBC to regulate the private broadcasters and another subsequent conflict-riven decade with an independent agency with limited staff, the federal government created the Canadian Radio Television Commission (Stewart and Hull 1994; Raboy 1995a, 1995b). From our perspective, the creation of the CRTC in 1968 was important because it exemplified and codified the planning role of regulation and assigned it to an independent regulatory agency.

The CRTC was given an overriding and very broad regulatory goal 'to safeguard, enrich and strengthen the cultural, political social and economic fabric of Canada.' The regulator's anticipatory rather than remedial role was clear from the fact that it was empowered not simply to regulate the components of the broadcasting sector but to 'supervise all aspects of the Canadian broadcasting system.' Furthermore, its enabling statute explicitly used planning concepts when it declared the broadcasting system to be 'a single system ... comprising public and private elements.' Finally, like its transportation counterpart the CRTC was granted wide discretionary powers to make regulations to give force to the broad policy objectives, and it was subject to no political supervision or approval. Both agencies had a unique status in this respect within the universe of federal regulatory bodies.

The main sector that was a partial exception to the developments in transportation and broadcasting was that of energy. A specialized independent energy regulator was only established in 1959 (Lucas 1977; McDougall 1982; Doern and Toner 1985). Prior to that, the transportation regulator had a limited role in the regulation of interprovincial pipeline tolls. Ironically, in many important respects, energy regulation and the energy regulator, the NEB, became the model adopted for the other sectors in the following decade.

Almost from the outset, national energy regulation was more than simply policing in function, although there was a policing role given the presence of a monopoly in the carriage of oil and gas. By the time there was an acknowledged need for a national energy board, energy issues had become highly politicized as a result of a series of conflicts arising from federal-provincial and Canada–United States relationships. In particular, industry-wide issues, such as long- and short-term domestic supply and foreign exports, rather than firm specific actions, were the main concern.

The NEB's primary function from the outset was to be a sectoral planner that would use its powers to regulate not only interprovincial pipeline construction but especially the levels of exports of oil, natural gas, and electricity in order to protect Canada's long-term energy needs. The NEB, because of the limited policy guidance in its authorizing statute, was expected to become the primary draftsman of Canadian energy policy. Underscoring this responsibility and establishing the precedent that would shortly be followed in the transportation and broadcasting sectors, the NEB was made the federal government's primary policy adviser. It was mandated to monitor the current and future supply of and demand for Canada's major energy commodities and to recommend to its minister the measures it considered necessary or advisable in the public interest for the control, supervision, conservation, use, marketing, and development of energy and sources of energy.

In summary, by the late 1960s the essential characteristics of the Canadian regulatory regime were well entrenched in three of the four major regulated sectors. Regulation involved more than simply providing society's economic policeman. Government intervention by means of regulatory instruments was justified as a comprehensive tool to ensure economic stability and to protect and enhance the performance of public enterprises. Both these enterprises and, through regulation, private firms were employed to fulfil a wide range of exogenous objectives, such as national economic development and cultural sovereignty. Regulation was assigned a planning role to anticipate and create the conditions necessary for the attainment of those objectives.

Canadian Regulatory Change: Reclaiming the Control of Policy

By the mid-1990s the regulatory edifice, the complex of ideas and institutional relationships created only three decades earlier, had been largely torn down or significantly remodelled. The function of regulation had been drastically cut back, and in some cases removed completely. In addition, regulatory agencies, while still nominally independent, had their roles and powers redefined and restricted and their independence drastically curtailed.

Obviously many causal forces have been at work in the three sectors. Among these forces are federal–provincial disputes, Canadian–American conflicts, and private industry–public sector disagreements, not to mention such major international developments as the energy crisis in the 1970s, the subsequent inflation/stagflation economic cycles, and the regional trade agreements. In addition, some sectors, most notably telecommunications and broadcasting, were characterized by destabilizing technological changes that called into question the underlying market premises of the sector and the concomitant public-policy regimes.

The general transformation has been due to two overall forces: an effort by the political executive to reclaim policy and regulatory powers, and those of market liberalization and deregulation. In this section, we look at the former.

In brief, change occurred because of conflicts over the proper role of the independent regulatory agency, the limits of its independence, and the appropriateness of reliance on such agencies. Canadian regulatory agencies became entangled in intra-governmental disputes over control of the institutional levers of regulatory power, and the outcomes of these disputes influenced subsequent debates over the nature of the regulatory function and the degree to which agencies should be independent. Each sector saw the challenge unfold in somewhat different ways.

Energy Regulation

It is perhaps not surprising that the first disputes over the roles and powers of independent agencies should have arisen with respect to the youngest 'government in miniature,' the NEB. Compared to its counterparts in the transportation and communications sectors, this agency had no institutional history of either independence or centrality of function that could have protected it from the challenges it confronted very early in its operation.

Within a few years of its creation in 1959, the NEB emerged as a powerful independent regulatory body. In the words of its second chairman, the NEB was perceived to be 'the smallest shop with the biggest clout in town' (Dewar 1980, 30). In only its first decade of operation, the NEB appeared to have successfully carved out an exclusive policy and a regulatory space, an outcome that reflected both its power to make regulatory decisions and its role as the primary policy adviser to the federal government on energy issues. One measure of its power was the fact that it quickly developed as a closed regulatory shop that 'decided energy issues almost exclusively in response to the representations of the provincial governments and private companies which participated in its proceedings' (Doern and Toner 1985, 83). Other interested parties were not allowed in, and the federal government appeared to be content with both how the NEB operated and the quality of its policy advice.

Although the ramifications did not appear to be appreciated at the time, the decline of the NEB as the primary regulatory and policy actor within the federal government can be dated to 1966, for it was then that a bureaucratic rival and eventual successor emerged. The rival was the Department of Energy, Mines, and Resources, which brought together a number of technical units within Ottawa, but more importantly was assigned a role as a policy adviser to its minister on energy issues. In the first five years of its existence, the department did not appear to pose much of a challenge to the dominance of the NEB, in part because of its limited policy expertise. One sign of the potential for conflict emerged in early 1970, however, when the department began to lobby the government to restrict funds for the NEB for policy advisory personnel on the grounds that this was unnecessary duplication.

Within a decade, the NEB had been displaced as the primary bureaucratic agent in both the regulatory and policy sectors. One factor was the growing concern, played upon by officials within the department, that the NEB was too close to the industry and that consequently Ottawa was too dependent on industry information, which was channelled through the NEB (Doern and Toner 1985, 85). Another was that the quality and indeed accuracy of the NEB's advice and information were suspect. The energy crises, international and intergovernmental, that ensued after the 1973 oil embargo brought the dissatisfaction with the NEB to a head.

Within less than five years, not only had the Department of Energy, Mines, and Resources displaced the NEB as the primary policy adviser, but the government assumed some of the NEB's regulatory functions for itself and hived off other responsibilities for other agencies (Doern and Toner 1985, chap. 11). In addition, rather than delegating new responsibilities to the NEB as a consequence of the energy conflicts, the gederal government opted instead to create new regulatory instruments. In 1973, for example, using its power to approve NEB regulations, the Cabinet took over the power to issue export permits from the NEB. In 1975 Parliament passed the Petroleum Administration Act, which gave Cabinet, not the NEB, the power to regulate oil and gas prices. The same year saw the creation of a state-owned oil company, Petro-Canada, which was the result of governmental dissatisfaction with its existing 'windows' on the industry, including especially the NEB, which now appeared to be, if not captured, then far too sympathetic to the industry.

The displacement of the NEB as primary regulatory agency and policy adviser was completed in 1980 with the announcement of the National Energy Policy (NEP). Although the NEB had lost its monopoly status as policy adviser, throughout the 1970s it retained some status and role in the policy process. In 1980, however, it was completely isolated and excluded from the development of the NEP. Its chair, board members, and staff were not consulted by the political and bureaucratic officials in the drafting of the NEP, despite the fact that this was the most comprehensive set of regulatory initiatives in Canadian energy history.

Transportation Regulation

Similar developments occurred in the transportation sector. Within three years of the creation of the CTC as both a multi-modal planning regulator and a primary policy adviser to the minister of transport, the Department of Transport underwent a fundamental reorganization to become a ministry system (Langford 1976). Central to this reorganization was a desire by the department to claim its role as transport policy adviser within the federal government, a desire that would lead it into fundamental conflicts with the CTC. Some of these conflicts would involve the CTC's ability to thwart or frustrate departmental policy preferences, while others were caused by regulatory actions that led to intergovernmental battles.

Although there was not the fundamental reorganization in transportation regulatory instruments that occurred in the energy sector, there was nevertheless significant change. In the 1970s the primacy of the CTC's policy advisory role was scaled back considerably. No legislative mechanism was necessary as the Department of Transport simply reasserted itself and excluded the CTC when it wanted to do so. In addition, the government and the minister of transport used their political control over individual regulatory decisions, particularly in the air sector, to attempt to change regulatory policy (Janisch 1978).

Perhaps the clearest indication of the changed relationship occurred in 1984 when the minister of transport summarily ignored the CTC's recommendations on changes in air regulatory policy. On the day that the CTC issued its report after an extensive public hearing, the minister, without addressing the report, announced a major deregulatory initiative.

In addition to highlighting the inappropriateness of assigning a regulatory agency the role of primary policy adviser, the period saw the emergence of the first debate since 1903 over the effectiveness of traditional political-control mechanisms, especially in transportation policy issues. In the transportation sector, attention focused on the inadequacy of the one available mechanism for political control other than legislative amendments, namely the route provided by political appeals. Increasingly there emerged a consensus both within and outside government departments that the government should have a more immediate and effective power to control regulatory policy.

Broadcasting and Telecommunications

Simultaneously, similar controversies and conflicts emerged in the broadcasting and telecommunications sectors. Although the government, as has been indicated, was to speak ambitiously of designing a grand plan for all communications matters, in 1967 it was content to rely almost exclusively on regulatory instruments, particularly a well-endowed independent regulatory agency, to pursue its objectives. At the time of creating the CRTC, it is clear that the government saw the regulator as its primary instrument, superior even to its public broadcasting corporation, for the attainment of its broadcasting policy objectives.

However, as was the case in the other three sectors, shortly after an independent agency was endowed with a wide ambit of authority and responsibility as policy adviser, the political and bureaucratic environment changed dramatically. In 1969 the Department of Communications was created, and it saw itself as the prime actor in developing the comprehensive communications plan. As such, the department was now a rival seeking to supplant the CRTC as policy adviser. Soon a continuous series of conflicts ensued between the two. Some of these involved regulatory initiatives that caused public and consequently political opposition, while others were the result of broadcasting conflicts between Canada and the United States or of intergovernmental disputes, such as cable licensing. Perhaps the most explicit conflict was that involving the introduction of pay-television, which the minister in 1976 saw as inevitable but which the CRTC refused to license for as long as possible (Hall 1990).

As a result of these and other conflicts, pressure began to develop for a realignment in roles and responsibilities. Increasingly in this period, departments, government-commissioned studies such as those by the Economic Council of Canada (1979) and the Law Reform Commission (Janisch 1978), and Parliament itself all concluded that agencies had too much independence on policy matters. The result was a consensus that political authorities should have at their disposal the power to issue policy directives to individual regulatory agencies. Such a power, it was argued, would both confine independent regulatory policy making and place responsibility for such matters more directly and effectively in the hands of politically accountable authorities. Although there was no agreement on the scope of such powers or on the procedures to be employed, in the late 1970s the government introduced legislation in both the transportation and the communications sectors that would have empowered Cabinet to direct the agencies on policy matters (Schultz 1982). In both cases, however, the legislation was not enacted and the matter would remain unresolved for several more years.

Regulatory Change: Deregulation and U.S. Market Liberalism

The second major cause of change over the period as a whole was undoubtedly the combined forces of deregulation initiatives and U.S.-led market liberalism. In the mid-1980s the Conservative government of Brian Mulroney embarked on a number of deregulatory and regulatory reform initiatives in various sectors (Schultz 1988; Stanbury 1992). Although there were deregulatory initiatives under previous Liberal governments, there is no doubt that the most fundamental review and reformation of the regulatory regime in Canada followed the election of the Mulroney Conservatives in 1984. This reformation went well beyond the debate about the appropriateness of regulatory independence to include the ideas and values underpinning regulatory intervention and economic control. It is important to emphasize once again, however, that notwithstanding the rejection of the traditional principles for regulation, this rejection was not uniform across all regulated sectors. In some sectors, most notably broadcasting and telecommunications, the Conservatives remained firmly committed to the traditional principles justifying regulation or were only prepared to change the existing system at its margins. Second, deregulation, or qualified versions thereof, did not necessarily entail a complete rejection of regulation, or more generally a 'retreat of the state.' Instead, we find a recasting or reformulation of state objectives and principles, and a corresponding attempt to modify traditional regulatory instruments or substitute new, narrower, and more focused ones (Schultz 1988, 1994).

Energy Regulation

Energy was the first sector subjected to a new regulatory regime under the Conservatives, who believed that, wherever possible, markets and not governments should determine energy prices and output (Toner 1986; Butt 1986). These changes, however, were also strongly motivated by regional politics in Canada because Alberta and other western Canadian provinces had regarded the previous era of intervention from central Canada with great hostility. Consequently, the regulation of crude oil marketing and pricing, as well as the licensing of exports, was ended in 1985. Then gas prices were deregulated. Instead of relying on NEB regulations, the government chose to allow prices for both oil and gas to be set by buyer–seller relationships and negotiations. There was still a role for the regulator in the new regime, but, rather than that of a planner or even a policeman with considerable discretion, the NEB was confined to resolving disputes through arbitration between the contending parties. Its only remaining traditional regulatory function is that of licensing new or large expansions of pipelines.

The one area where there has been some growth in energy regulation is in the NEB's increased focus on environmental and occupational health and safety aspects of pipeline construction. The need for, and willingness of, the NEB to adopt this new emphasis can be attributed to four developments. First, federal policy now endorses sustainable development as a policy goal in all projects. Second, federal policy on environmental assessment, which had previously been based on guidelines, has now become statutorily required as a result of several court decisions (NEB 1995). The NEB has a vested interest in ensuring that such policies are implemented or regulated or both by it rather than by environmental departments. Third, the ageing Canadian pipeline system creates the potential for environmental problems that can subject both energy workers and the larger public to health and safety risks. In addition, the regulator, if it ignores its responsibilities in these areas, might also incur some liability for any consequences. Finally, it may be that there is an element of institutional survival in the embrace of the new social regulation. Regulators with less to do in their traditional realms may be seeking out interesting purposes in others.

A further change was that the NEB membership was reduced and its staff support greatly curtailed. Moreover, the agency itself was moved to Calgary, where it now functions in the midst of the oil industry. The agency is now almost totally funded by fees from industry rather than by the taxpayer.

Transportation Regulation

The transportation regulatory regime was further transformed in the 1980s. Particularly in the airline and railway sectors, U.S. deregulation initiatives were crucial because they caused a southern leakage of business from Canadian firms. Following the partial lead of the previous Liberal government, the Conservatives in 1987 abandoned not only the traditional air sector planning regime but rejected, except for a few areas, even a policing role for the regulator (Hill 1988). Only in northern Canada would the regulator henceforth have a role to play in licensing routes or in setting air fares. In the rest of the country, market forces would determine such matters. A similar approach was introduced for the interprovincial and international trucking sectors.

In the rail sector, the Conservative government almost completely deregulated railway rates by removing the banded pricing system of the previous twenty years and by allowing railways to establish confidential contracts with shippers, including the possibility of giving rebates, which had previously been illegal. Regulation of branch-line abandonment, which had continued under the previous regime, was reduced but not removed completely by the Tories. Henceforth, railways would be free to apply for permission to abandon an annual percentage of their total track system, and the regulator could only refuse requests under specified strict conditions. The new regime recognized that the railways would now be able to exercise considerable market power under certain circumstances, but rather than relying on traditional policing regulation the government introduced two major innovations that provided for a continuing albeit circumscribed regulatory role. Both innovations were directed at settling disputes between parties rather than at allowing the regulator to make public-interest determinations. One provided for mediation by regulators of disputes, while the other authorized the regulator to engage in final-offer binding arbitration if a railway and a shipper could not come to an agreement on a rate. Finally, again recognizing the potential for abuse by the railways but seeking to restrict the role of regulation, the new regulatory regime introduced a non-discretionary formula to set rates under very stringent and statutorily established conditions.

Recently, reflecting the new consensus on the role of regulation, the Liberal government further reduced regulation of airlines in northern Canada, such that we can now say that the airline sector is fully deregulated in terms of entry and price controls. Mergers and acquisitions involving transportation companies will no longer be reviewed by the transport regulator, but will be subject to both the Competition Act and the Investment Canada Act (Transport Canada 1995). In addition, the remaining constraints on railway branch-line abandonment have been relaxed. In particular, the annual percentage limit has been removed. As befits this reduced role, the agency was reduced to only three commissioners, and its staff and budget were similarly cut to the bone.

Although the new regulatory approach addressed the issue of regulatory independence indirectly by removing regulatory powers in several major areas and by confining and structuring its regulatory discretion in others, the government also addressed the issue of direct political control over the independent regulatory agency. Because there still might be the potential for regulatory policy making, under the new regime the government was empowered to issue directives on the remaining policy issues to the regulatory agency. Unlike proposals for a power like this one from previous governments, the Conservatives imposed a number of procedural requirements, including agency consultation and parliamentary scrutiny, on Cabinet use of this power (Scott 1990; Conklin 1991). One possible rationale for accepting such constraints might be that the government considered that these constraints might act as a hurdle, albeit one that could be jumped, for future governments that sought to change its deregulatory policy without parliamentary approval.

Broadcasting and Telecommunications Regulation

The Conservatives were much less ambitious when it came to the broadcasting and telecommunications sector (Globerman, Stanbury, and Wilson 1995; Schultz 1994, 1995a, 1995b). Unlike their pro-market efforts in other sectors, the Conservatives showed little inclination to adopt deregulation or even reduce regulation in telecommunications. The Conservatives were in office in 1985, for example, when the CRTC reversed its earlier pro-competition direction and rejected an application for telecommunications competition. There was no attempt by the Cabinet to overturn that decision, as it was empowered to do. Nor did the government encourage the CRTC to address the issue of rate rebalancing and cross-subsidization that was the single most important stumbling block to competition when the CRTC sought to avoid the issue. Indeed, it was a Conservative minister of telecommunications who declaimed about the 'déréglementation brutal' that he thought was characteristic of the United States, and vowed never to let it happen in Canada (Masse 1987). In all this period, the only exception to the general opposition from the government to competition came in the area of permitting liberalized resale of telecommunications services, and here one can confidently argue that it was internal division within the bureaucracy rather than a pro-competitive commitment on the part of the Cabinet that was the determining factor.

The telecommunications legislation proposed by the Conservative government in 1992 demonstrates the fundamental ambivalence towards competition in this area, as opposed to the determined advocacy of such a policy for the energy and transportation sectors. Although the legislation recognized the potential role that market forces could play in disciplining telecommunications providers and meeting consumer demands, the essential thrust was to impose a quasi-planning type of regulatory regime on telecommunications that was reminiscent of the one proposed fifteen years earlier by the Liberal government.

After declaring that 'telecommunications performs an essential role in the maintenance of Canada's identity and sovereignty,' the legislation stated that the primary policy objective was 'to facilitate the orderly development in Canada of a telecommunications system that serves to safeguard, enrich and strengthen the cultural, social, political and economic fabric of Canada' (Canada 1995). In short, while competition is mentioned, the emphases on non-economic objectives and on 'orderly development' are still cornerstones for a planning regulatory regime reminiscent of traditional airline and broadcasting regulation.

Although the regulator was given permission both to experiment with new regulatory tools such as price caps rather than rate-of-return regulation, and even to forbear from regulation where this was appropriate, there was no general commitment to the primacy of markets over regulation. At best, the legislation encouraged the regulator 'to foster increased reliance on market forces.' This approach should be compared to the same government's injunction in the National Telecommunications Act of 1987 that 'competition and market forces are, whenever possible, the prime agents in providing viable and effective transportation.'

In fact, the proposed telecommunications legislation was similar in intent to earlier arrangements in the airline industry in that it sought to plan, via regulation, the nature and extent of competition. The only difference, and one reflecting the conflicts in the 1970s on the subject of political control over regulatory policy making, was that the government proposed that it, and not the independent regulatory agency, would be the sector planner. This was to be accomplished by introducing a new licensing system for entry into the telecommunications sector. It would be unlike every other regulated sector for the previous thirty years in that the government proposed that the minister of communications and not the CRTC would have the licensing power. Although licensing would be guided by the statutory objectives, the minister proposed that he or she should be authorized, in a decision on whether to license or not, to consider 'any other factor' that he or she deemed to be important. In addition, the legislation gave the Cabinet the supplementary power to issue policy directives to the CRTC, although, unlike earlier proposals, these would be subject to some constraints and procedural safeguards. It was only widespread opposition and a determined Senate committee that led to the withdrawal of the ministerial licensing scheme (Janisch 1993).

Although new legislation was enacted near the end of the Mulroney era in the broadcasting sector, there was little resemblance between the new regulatory approach to broadcasting and the one the Conservatives had imposed in the energy and transportation sectors. In fact, in terms of the principles or ideas justifying regulation there was little that had changed since the creation of the original system in 1932 or its most recent version established in 1967. The core value was the continuing need to protect Canadian culture, now defined as cultural sovereignty, premised on the underlying fear that Canadian culture would be threatened if the planning role of regulation was altered. The new legislation almost repeated verbatim the Liberal policy statement of 1968. Furthermore, the regulator continues to be mandated to 'regulate and supervise' all aspects of the Canadian broadcasting system. The tools remain the same, including the right to impose Canadian-content quotas on broadcasting licensees and specific programming conditions and to restrict the carriage of non-Canadian services such as American specialty services. Practice in these realms has changed somewhat in that the CRTC has tried to regulate with fewer detailed rules.

Broadly speaking, however, the broadcasting regulatory regime is business as usual, which means that a planning regulatory approach continues. In fact compared to the other sectors, the one regulated sector that appears to have been largely immune from change has been broadcasting. The convergence of telecommunications and broadcasting, and particularly the emerging issue of the information highway, have resurrected concerns in some sectors about the vulnerability of Canadian culture and the need to take appropriate countermeasures. These concerns have, if anything, reinforced the planning approach, as the government has decreed by Order in Council that neither it nor the regulator will allow individual sectors to disappear whatever the technological developments. Furthermore, the central issue undergirding the broadcasting planning approach, the need to ensure a strong Canadian presence, has led both the CRTC (1995) and the government-appointed Information Highway Advisory Council (Canada 1995) to promote regulatory initiatives to ensure that the information highway is sufficiently Canadian in character. Similarly, regulation of new broadcasting distributions systems such as direct-to-home satellite systems has also emphasized Canadian-content concerns.

The only significant change in the broadcasting regulatory system introduced by the Conservatives addressed the long-standing issue of political control on policy matters. Mirroring provisions in the transportation and telecommunications legislation, the Broadcasting Act of 1991 sought to ensure that policy conflicts such as those that emerged in the 1970s could be resolved authoritatively. As of 1991, the Cabinet has been empowered to issue policy directions to the CRTC on any issue not involving an individual case. The recent CRTC–Cabinet conflict over the introduction of direct-to-home satellite services suggests that even this restriction is not particularly burdensome for a Cabinet determined to impose its will on the regulator, although the CRTC's decision also suggests that an equally determined regulator may not be without a will of its own.

Conclusions

Canadian sectoral regulatory institutions in the energy, transportation, and, to a lesser extent, broadcasting and telecommunications sectors have been transformed in the last two decades. They were once 'governments in miniature,' but that is no longer the case. Sectoral regulation and regulatory agencies as a whole are much diminished both as instruments and as institutions of governing. They no longer possess the range of instruments and functions that characterized the period from the mid-1930s to the late 1960s.

Comparisons of Canadian and U.S. regulatory development must be cognizant of all three periods covered above. The two regulatory systems were similar in the early decades of the century in that they were cast as minimalist 'regulatory policing' approaches that took markets as a given. The Canadian sectoral regulatory regime then parted company with its U.S. counterpart in that Canadian regulators became much more ambitious regulatory planners where markets or, at least competition, were eschewed in the name of broader developmental and nation-building goals. The last two decades have brought a third phase, in which somewhat greater institutional convergence is apparent, especially in the transportation and energy sectors.

The cause of this last phase of institutional transformation in Canada, however, was not a simple deregulatory impulse. The initial cause was state-led in that the political executive sought to reassert policy control and a realignment of institutional relations and accountabilty. For decades the appropriateness of delegating the primary decision-making and policy advisory roles to independent regulatory agencies, subject to only the most blunt and non-discriminatory forms of political control, was unchallenged, even unquestioned. In the 1980s and early 1990s governments have clawed back many of the levers of power.

The sectoral regulatory regime in Canada has also been influenced recently by deregulation and U.S.-led market liberalism. Market-oriented approaches are ascendant in all the utility sectors except broadcasting. It remains to be seen whether the traditional justifications for economic regulation, namely the abuse of market power and, for the specialized independent regulatory agency, the fear of political abuse, will ever regain the relevance they once had.

REFERENCES

Armstrong, Christopher, and H.V. Nelles. 1986. *Monopoly's Moment: The Organization and Regulation of Canadian Utilities 1830–1930*. Philadelphia: Temple University Press.

Babe, Robert E. 1990. *Telecommunications in Canada: Technology, Industry and Government*. Toronto: University of Toronto Press.

Baldwin, John R. 1989. *Regulatory Failure and Renewal: The Evolution of the Natural Monopoly Contract*. Ottawa: Economic Council of Canada.

Butt, Roger. 1986. 'Regulating Deregulation: The National Energy Board and Tory Energy Policy.' Unpublished research essay, School of Public Administration, Carleton University, Ottawa.

Canada. 1995. *Connection, Community, Content: The Challenge of the Information Highway*. Ottawa: Minister of Supply and Services.

Canadian Radio-television and Telecommunications Commission. 1995. *Competition and Culture on Canada's Information Highway: Managing the Realities of Transition*. Ottawa: Public Works and Government Services Canada.

Conklin, David B. 1991. 'The Broadcasting Act and the Changing Pathology of Cabinet Appeals.' *Media and Communications Law Review* 2:297–333.

Corbett, David. 1965. *Politics and the Airlines*. Toronto: University of Toronto Press.

Cruikshank, Ken. 1991. *Close Ties: Railways, Government and the Board of Railway Commissioners*. Montreal: McGill-Queen's University Press.

Dewar, Elaine. 1980. 'Groping in the Dark.' *Canadian Business*, May.

Doern, G. Bruce, ed. 1978. *The Regulatory Process in Canada*. Toronto: Macmillan of Canada.

Doern, G. Bruce, and Glen Toner. 1985. *The Politics of Energy*. Toronto: Methuen.

Economic Council of Canada. 1979. *Responsible Regulation*. Ottawa: Economic Council of Canada.

– 1981. *Reforming Regulation*. Ottawa: Economic Council of Canada.

Eisner, M.A. 1991. *Antitrust and the Triumph of Economics*. Chapel Hill: University of North Carolina Press.

– 1993. *Regulatory Politics in transition*. Baltimore: Johns Hopkins University Press.

Globerman, S., W.T. Stanbury, and T.A. Wilson, eds. 1995. *The Future of Telecommunications Policy in Canada*. Toronto: Institute for Policy Analysis, University of Toronto.

Hall, Richard. 1990. *The CRTC as Policy-maker*. PhD thesis, McGill University, Montreal.

Hill, Margaret. 1988. *Freedom to Move: Explaining the Decision to Deregulate Canadian Air and Rail Transportation*. Unpublished research paper, School of Public Administration, Carleton University, Ottawa.

Hodgetts, T.E. 1973. *The Canadian Public Service: A Physiology of Government, 1867–1970*. Toronto: University of Toronto Press.

Janisch, Hudson N. 1978. *The Regulatory Process of the Canadian Transport Commission*. Ottawa: Law Reform Commission of Canada.

– 1993. 'At Last! A New Canadian Telecommunications Act.' *Telecommunications Policy* 9: 691–8.

Johnson, David. 1991. 'Regulatory Agencies and Accountability: An Ontario Perspective.' *Canadian Public Administration* 34, no. 3:17–43.

Langford, John. 1976. *Transport in Transition*. Montreal: McGill-Queen's University Press.

Law Reform Commission of Canada. 1985. *Independent Administrative Agencies*. Ottawa: Law Reform Commission.

Lucas, A. 1977. *The National Energy Board*. Ottawa: Law Reform Commission.

Masse, Marcel. 1985. 'Looking at Telecommunications: The Need for Review.' Notes for an address to the Electrical and Electronic Manufacturer's Association, Montebello, Que., 20 June.

McDougall, John N. 1982. *Fuels and the National Policy*. Toronto: McClelland and Stewart.

McGraw, Thomas K. 1984. *Prophets of Regulation*. Cambridge: Harvard University Press.

McLean, S.J. 1902. 'Reports upon Railway Commissions, Railway Rate Grievances and Regulative Legislation.' In Canada. *Sessional Papers*, no. 20A.

National Energy Board. 1995. *National Energy Board Annual Report, 1994*. Ottawa: National Energy Board.

Partridge, John. 1983. 'Has the NEB Run Out of Steam?' *Canadian Business*, April.

Peers, Frank W. 1969. *The Politics of Canadian Broadcasting, 1920–1951*. Toronto: University of Toronto Press.

Raboy, Marc. 1995a. 'Influencing Public Policy on Canadian Broadcasting.' *Canadian Public Administration* 38, no. 3:411–32.

– 1995b. 'The Role of Public Consultation in Shaping the Canadian Broadcasting System.' *Canadian Journal of Political Science* 28, no. 3:455–78.

Schultz, Richard. 1977. 'Regulatory Agencies and the Canadian Political System.' In *Public Administration in Canada*, edited by Kenneth Kernaghan. 3rd ed. Toronto: Methuen.

– 1982. 'Regulatory Agencies and the Dilemmas of Delegation.' In *The Administrative State in Canada*, edited by O.P. Dwivedi, 89–106. Toronto: University of Toronto Press.

– 1988. 'Regulating Conservatively: The Mulroney Record 1984–88.' In *Canada Under Mulroney*, edited by Andrew B. Gollner and Daniel Salée, 186–205. Montreal: Véhicule Press.

– 1994. 'Regulation and Telecommunications Reform: Exploring the Alternatives.' In *Implementing Reforms in the Telecommunications Sector: Lessons from Experience*, edited by B. Wellenius and P. Stern, 133–50. Washington: The World Bank.

– 1995a. 'Old Whine in New Bottle: The Politics of Cross-Subsidies in Canadian Telecommunications.' In Steven Globerman et al. *The Future of Telecommunications Policy in Canada*, 271–88. Toronto: Institute for Policy Analysis, University of Toronto.

– 1995b. 'Paradigm Lost: Explaining the Canadian Politics of Deregulation.' In *Canada's Century: Governance in a Maturing Society*, edited by C.E.S. Franks. Montreal: McGill-Queen's University Press.

Schultz, Richard, and Alan Alexandroff. 1985. *Economic Regulation and the Federal System*. Toronto: University of Toronto Press.

Scott, Sheridan. 1990. 'The New Broadcasting Act: An Analysis.' *Media and Communications Law Review* 1:25–58.

Stanbury, W.T., ed. 1980. *Government Regulation: Scope, Growth, Process*. Montreal: Institute for Research on Public Policy.

– 1992. *Reforming the Federal Regulatory Process in Canada, 1971–1992*. Appendix to House of Commons, Standing Committee on Finance, Sub-committee on Regulations and Competitiveness. Issue no. 23 (December). Supply and Services Canada, chap. 5.

Stewart, Andrew, and William Hull. 1994. *Canadian Television Policy and the Board of Broadcast Governors, 1958–1968*. Edmonton: University of Alberta Press.

Strick, John. 1990. *The Economics of Government Regulation: Theory and Canadian Practice*. Toronto: Thompson.
Thomas, Paul, and Orest W. Zajcew. 1993. 'Structural Heretics: Crown Corporations and Regulatory Agencies.' In *Governing Canada: Institutions and Public Policy*, edited by Michael Atkinson. 115–48. Toronto: Harcourt Brace Jovanovich.
Toner, Glen. 1986. 'Stardust: The Tory Energy Program.' In *How Ottawa Spends, 1986–87*, edited by Michael Prince. 119–48. Toronto: Methuen.
Transport Canada. 1995. *Transport Canada's New Direction and the 1995 Budget*. Ottawa: Transport Canada.
Tupper, Allan, and Bruce Doern, eds. 1988. *Privatization, Public Policy and Public Corporations in Canada*. Montreal: McGill-Queen's University Press.
Willis, John. 1941. *Canadian Boards at Work*. Toronto: Macmillan.

PART TWO
INFLUENCES ON REFORM: INTERESTS AND IDEAS

6

Utility Regulation, Corporate Governance, and the Amoral Corporation

STEPHEN WILKS

The British system of utility regulation should be assessed as a whole. This seems an unexceptional position to take, but in fact many evaluations of regulation in the UK concentrate on the regulators, the regulatory agencies, and regulatory policies as if they were the whole story. They take the companies as given. This is a myopic approach. Domestically the system of utility regulation has been designed to deal with a particular sort of company operating within a particular market setting. British plcs have a high degree of autonomy and respond sensitively to the financial markets as well as to their product markets. Comparatively, it is short-sighted to juxtapose systems of regulation without also recognizing that the nature of the creature being regulated – the large company – also varies strikingly between countries. Moreover, the regulatory system is evolving rapidly, and that evolution can only be evaluated by reference to the relationship between the regulators and their client companies; just as the regulator's priorities, skills, and strategies change, so do those of the companies.[1]

This emphasis on looking at both sides of the regulatory relationship seems particularly appropriate in the British case, where we are studying the emergence of a new regime; it is a regime that was a direct response to the creation of a new class of private-sector companies, the utility companies that emerged from the process of privatization. Despite the fact that all the privatized utility companies were monopolistic or oligopolistic, and that they operated in heavily regulated markets and had public service obligations, they were nonetheless privatized as conventional British public limited companies (plcs) and floated on the stock market. In becoming plcs the utility companies were inserted into the British system of stock-market capitalism, which provides a set of priorities, a system of incentives, expectations about normal behaviour, and a model for how companies and corporate executives should define their function. Part of that model involves expectations about relations with government, which traditionally in Britain have rested on trust and negotiation between companies and regulators. It is not, however, clear that this traditional regulatory relationship can tolerate the strain put upon it by the magnitude of utility regulation or by the way in which British stock-market capitalism is evolving.

The private-sector company or corporation is more than simply a legal artefact, it is a legal person, but it does not of itself embody any principle of conscience, it is amoral. It is neither benign nor evil, and, in Bower's words, 'it is, perhaps the most important technological invention of our time, but it is only a tool and it has no intent. If we are not satisfied with the results of the legal personalization we call the corporation, we must change the guidelines provided for the managers who use the tool, or change the managers' (Bower 1974, 179). It can be argued that British companies generally have been given the wrong guidelines, and this chapter certainly argues that privatized utility companies have become too quickly and too thoroughly integrated into the system of incentives provided by the financial markets. It is a rather melodramatic argument, but it could be said that onto the blank sheet of corporate amorality has been inserted an overly emphatic rendering of stock-market morality in which profits, capitalization, and shareholder value receive priority. The utility companies have become 'more royal than the King,' and in so doing they create problems with which no regulatory system can adequately cope. From this perspective the 'crisis' of British regulation has to do less with the regulators and their powers, and more with the companies that are the targets of regulation. This chapter therefore presents a plea for reform of corporate governance to go hand in hand with reform of regulatory institutions.

The argument proceeds in five stages. It looks first at the design of the system of utility regulation that draws on a British tradition of negotiation and accommodation. Second, it suggests that the system is accountable, to an unhealthy extent, to the financial markets. Third, it speculates that companies are less and less likely to cooperate in negotiation. Fourth, it observes that the 'withering away' of regulation is unlikely and that the system requires improvement. Fifth, it suggests that improvement requires the design of successful strategies for negotiation and compliance, which in turn demands a change in the form of, or the guidelines for, the utility companies. In the discussion the experience of energy regulation is emphasized, reflecting previous research (Sturm and Wilks 1996, 1997).

Design of the UK Regulatory Regime

Principles

British economic regulation involves a striking combination of continuity in ideas (or traditions) and innovation in organizations. British traditions of public administration have consistently attached importance to the autonomy of the firm. This has rested on a deep-seated respect for property and the freedom to contract, combined with the legacy of a non-interventionist, minimal state. In practice this has translated into 'arms-length' regulation and has produced a regulatory style that is based on accommodation, mutual respect, and negotiation. Resort to litigation is exceptional, the judiciary has had a minimal role in regulating industry, and judicial review is unusual (Ogus 1994, 115–17). It is perhaps facetious to describe this as 'gentlemanly capitalism,' but Vogel's seminal work shows British regulation to be negotiated rather than adversarial (Vogel 1986) in a pattern that is also clear in the field of competition policy. British policy was highly tolerant of cartelization prior to the Second World War, and competition policy since 1948 has been 'persuasive' rather than interventionist. The Office of Fair Trading (OFT) has limited investigatory powers, virtually no sanctions, and an administrative approach to monopolies and mergers that depends ultimately on ministerial interpretation of the 'public interest.' The Monopolies and Mergers Commission (MMC) is particularly representative of this traditional style. It is a non-adversarial administrative body, and its investigations are undertaken by part-time specialists, who often share a business outlook and are sympathetic to orthodox business practice. These characteristics are important because the existing model of competition policy has had a substantial influence on the design of the utility regulatory structure; indeed, Helm (1994, 26) has argued that the MMC is the 'lynch-pin' of the regulatory system because of its role in encouraging compliance.

What may have begun as a style of regulation congenial to the propertied classes and a minimalist state has become fossilized in the realities of bargaining relations with the largest, wealthiest, and most influential organizations within the economy – big private-sector companies. As Hancher and Moran (1989, 275) have pointed out, 'The role of the large firm is unique. Whereas the regulation of the behaviour of individual "private" actors is concerned with the imposition of a public or general will on private citizens, large firms cannot be described as private "takers" of regulation ... They have acquired the status of "governing institutions."' They go on to conclude that 'Economic regulation of markets under advanced capitalism can thus be portrayed as an activity shaped by the *interdependence* of powerful organisations who share major public characteristics.' This highlights the onus on large corporations to behave responsibly and, indeed, the motif of self-regulation based on trust runs through the history of industrial and financial regulation (Ernst 1994, 68). The regulatory agencies have tended to be reactive – to take action when self-regulation has clearly broken down, a sort of regulatory version of 'management by exception.' These characteristics of autonomy, bargaining, and self-regulation place considerable moral and calculative responsibilities on the directors of large corporations. The emphasis is on uncoerced compliance – not necessarily with clearly specified and legislated obligations – but with acceptable standards of business conduct. This is a very distinctive British tradition. It is manifest in philosophies, in structures, in processes, and in norms – in short in every fibre of the regulatory regime. In this respect British regulation, like British capitalism, is 'exceptional' (Ingham 1994, 228–32).

Into this tradition of bargained regulation was abruptly inserted the privatized utilities and their regulatory counterparts from 1982 onwards. There is every indication that regulatory agencies were designed rapidly with a minimum of research and retrospection, almost as an afterthought and almost in an air of panic. The first agency, the Office of Telecommunications (OFTEL), earned less than a paragraph in the telecommunications white paper (DTI 1982), and Prosser (1989, 142) remarks that 'there has been remarkably little discussion of the rationale for regulation in relation to privatisation.' It appears that the discussion took place in an interdepartmental committee, with the main focus on the method of regulation and the main outside influence coming from the Austrian-School economist Stephen Littlechild. The institutional form selected was modelled on the OFT, which reflects the preoccupation with creating competition. Like the Director General of Fair Trading, the utility regulators are therefore single-person regulators with an 'Office' and responsibilities contained in industry-specific statutes. They operate administratively (rather than legalistically), and share the OFT's complex administrative relationship with ministerial departments, the MMC, and other regulatory agencies. Thus, while the utility regulatory agencies are radically new institutions, their mode of operation, norms of propriety, and constitutional status display great continuity with the civil service from which most of their staff come. Studies of the system in operation identify 'the British tradition of "bargained regulation"' (Maloney and Richardson 1995, 103), and, although regulators are loath to admit to bargaining with their clientele, it is a reality accepted by the designers of price regulation. Beesley and Littlechild (1992, 65) agree that 'there is greater scope for *bargaining* in RPI-X than in rate of return regulation' and that 'in short, X may be thought of as one of several variables in a political and commercial bargaining process.' This is not the economically rational one-off bargaining of a contract or sale (or a single prisoners dilemma game). It is a long-term bargaining relationship between powerful organizations that can take on features of 'good chap regulation' or, in more jargon-laden terms, 'relational contracting.'

What of the parties on the other side of the bargaining table? If little attention was given to the design of the regulatory agencies, even less was given to the legal structure and responsibilities of the plcs. The main criticism of the transformation of nationalized industries into private-sector companies has been of the size of the units selected. British Telecom (BT), British Gas, the power generators, and British Airways were privatized as monopolistic or oligopolistic undertakings. They were also privatized as conventional private-sector companies with legal obligations and governance structures like any other private-sector company – and for the same reasons. Just as fragmenting the industry would have reduced the acceptability of, and the returns from, privatization, so too would have peculiar governance obligations. The government's uncertainty as to how the companies would behave did cause them to introduce transitional safeguards in the form of unsold minority holdings and 'golden shares,' but it did not extend to examining a more appropriate legal structure for the companies. Such questions were simply off the agenda, this process was about expanding the private sector, not about reforming company law.

Influences and Inspirations

It is important to look at origins. Applying a biological metaphor, major organizations can be regarded as 'living organizations' that change and adapt, that develop habits and expectations, but that also develop according to an inherited genetic code. In this case, the 'genetic code' is made up of the ideas, the legislation, and the priorities that prevailed at the point of birth and were incorporated into the design of the organizations. Another way of expressing this is to talk about 'path dependency,' and British utility regulation shows increasing signs of strong path dependency as proposals for radical reform have steadily been modified in favour of incremental improvement. Most agencies implementing public policy have a design influenced by precedent, political goals, expediency, examples, and learning. Here we concentrate on the goals and the examples, particularly the example of the United States.

In a wry review, Stelzer (1991, 59–60) talks of the United States' 'virtual monopoly on regulatory nous' and on 'the wave of British economists, accountants, utility executives and sundry policy makers [who] descended on the USA seeking guidance from our experience.' He observes that the ideas have been reprocessed and have generated regulatory imports into the United States. How did British policy makers respond to North American ideas? In an earlier paper, Stelzer (1988, 70) suggested that the Conservative government was hostile to an American litigious style and displayed 'its deep seated aversion to "American-style" regulation.' It would surely be more accurate to conclude that the British government was hostile to some aspects of U.S. regulation, but also to maintain that the U.S. experience and the U.S. agenda were important formative influences. After all, Littlechild's PhD is from Chicago. This influence would not be surprising; the genetic code of American economic regulation reveals a family link with Britain.

The first U.S. independent regulatory commission, the Interstate Commerce Commission, established in 1867, was directly inspired by British debates over how to regulate the railways. In the disputes over direct parliamentary regulation of the industry, Gladstone's solution was his 1844 law that established principles of profit regulation, which fed directly into the American law of 1867. In a review of the history, Foster quotes Robson to the effect that the regulatory commission 'was Victorian capitalist democracy's notion of how to reconcile the public interest in a monopolist service of primary importance, with the profit making incentive of joint stock enterprise. The idea quickly spread to the United States' (Foster 1992, 44). In the early 1980s, with the Reagan-Thatcher honeymoon in its first flush, British policy makers looked for inspiration to the modern expression of Victorian values safeguarded in the United States.

British policy makers found reinforcement in the American experience, which helped to eliminate some options and to strengthen others. The reactions against the American practice are perhaps best known. The British government decided against a judicial process of regulatory accountability, it shied away from anything like the 1946 Administrative Procedures Act, and it decided against rate-of-return regulation. On the other hand it did adopt the model of the independent regulator and the goal of market efficiency. The independent regulatory commissions came into their own in the Progressive era. Eisner's interpretation of the period is one in which market solutions were emphasized, large corporations were criticized but were regarded as natural and beneficial, and corporations reacted positively to regulation (Eisner 1993, 28, 38, 40). Thus in the field of energy regulation, the Federal Power Commission dates from the 1920s. Such commissions had the key major attributes of independence, a combination of legislative, executive, and judicial functions, and expert staffs. The British agencies enjoy variations on each of these themes but pursued the economic efficiency goals of the Reagan era rather than the social concerns of the Progressives. In untangling the American influence on British practice we should be sensitive to the historical and sectoral variations in American practices. There is no one model but the British importers of American ideas found support for their emphasis on the market, on competition as the desirable end goal, and on the pre-eminence of economic efficiency, or rather, as Price remarks (1994, 95–6), of managerial effiency. The British importers also, of course, found reassurance in a system that regulated private-sector corporations that were autonomous, were dominated by shareholder interests, and pursued profits in a frank unabashed fashion. All the same, it was felt that British regulatory arrangements needed to be substantially different from those operating in the United States. But what about the companies? Were the British dealing with the same regulatory targets? Were British companies just like American companies? It seemed that it was assumed that they were, and indeed British utilities have become more and more Americanized. (In the case of seven regional electricity companies, of course, by 1997 they were American-owned.) Whether British companies do in fact respond like American utilities is a question touched on later in the paper.

To Whom Is the Regime Accountable?

During the period 1995–7 there was extensive criticism of the British regime of utility regulation, which prompted many proposals for reform and allowed the Labour Party to propose a windfall-profits tax. Lack of accountability has been a constant theme, but in considering this criticism there are two preliminary areas to be clarified. First, accountability takes many different forms. It can be legal, hierarchical, financial, legislative, or *ante* or *post hoc*. More important, it can also be normative. Most administrative theorists would put great weight on the normative aspects of accountability, which have always loomed large in Britain. The best guarantee of a job well done is a responsible and committed attitude by the employee or group of employees. This will be based on a set of tacit norms reflecting, for instance, recruitment, training, vocation, professional ethics, or a well-developed organizational culture in which incentive structures and peer esteem reward responsibility and commitment. It is all very well for public-choice and capture theorists to tell us that 'regulators are like other people, with the same utility maximisation function,' this is not how we expect them to be. In the regulatory game, 'people matter' (Stelzer 1991, 68). Government has taken great care to appoint 'upstanding' regulators, and when a whiff of suspect practices is in the air – as with the allegations that the lottery regulator Peter Davis had accepted free air flights – the media and the public are outraged (*Financial Times*, 20 December, 1995). Regulation should not throw the public-service baby out with the nationalized industry bathwater.

The second aspect is to ask what is accountable. Most attention is focused on the regulator, and in the British system of personalized regulation that is understandable. The regulators have stamped their personalities, beliefs, and styles on their sectors, and, perhaps to an unhealthy degree, a cult of personality has developed. Their pronouncements are couched in the first person, they express regulatory developments in terms of personal judgment, and they are the target for personalized attacks. But all this conceals the reality of shared regulation *within* government, shared with the OFT, the MMC, the minister, and the department. Thus the Hansard inquiry stressed that all statutory regulatory functions are shared with the Secretary of State, and expressed some surprise that 'little attention was paid by respondents to the decision-making procedures followed by the Secretary of State' (Hansard 1996, 38, 63). It could also be argued that regulatory responsibility is shared *outside* government with the industry itself. Under the old system, the nationalized industries were expected to meet standards of public service stretching from security of supply to universal service. Under the new post-privatization system, these standards are to be delivered by the regulator and by free competition within the market. The new regime therefore includes the regulator and the companies. The regulator simply cannot deliver the required standards alone; he or she depends on the companies responding sincerely to the regulatory framework, but further, the regulator might also expect reasonable levels of responsible corporate behaviour. Assessing the accountability of the regime involves examination of the structure, competence, and policies of the regulatory agencies, but it also involves examination of the structure, competence, and policies of the companies and looking at the regime as a whole.

To whom then, is the regime accountable, in theory and in practice? The theory is easy. The regulator is accountable to Parliament, sometimes directly, sometimes via the minister, on the basis of duties enshrined in statute. Via Parliament the regulator is accountable to the electorate. The companies operate under British law, and therefore under the 'ownership model' of corporate accountability, which holds simply that the board of the company is accountable to the general body of shareholders on the basis of a duty to maximize profits. This is the director's fiduciary duty to shareholders (Parkinson 1993, 74–5).

The practice is more complex and is at variance with the legal and constitutional theory. Accountability in practice is to those who wield power, and for the regulator this includes ministers and consumers. Ministers have more influence than at first appears. Their formal powers to amend licences, refer takeovers, and appoint regulators are important, but so too are their priorities and preferences. The Director General of Fair Trading has never fully developed his latent independence (Wilks 1996a), so too the utility regulators have shown substantial self-restraint. It would be interesting to know how much ministerial influence is direct and how much is based on anticipation by the regulators. Consumers, on the other hand, have less influence than at first appears, but expressions of consumer preference are important through the market and as magnified by the media and consumer organizations. All the regulators have mechanisms for consumer representation.

For utility companies the divorce of ownership and control means that accountability to shareholders is greatly attenuated. It is actually then rather difficult to say to whom corporate boards are accountable. From the left, Hutton (1996, xxii) talks of 'the unwritten constitution of British firms and their lack of accountability'; from the right, the economic idea of the firm as simply 'a nexus of contracting relationships' denies the very existence of the firm as an entity that owes any duty of accountability to anyone (Parkinson 1993, 178). A widespread concern about accountability in the wake of the Maxwell and BCCI scandals has, of course, fuelled the now intense British debate on corporate governance and the proposals contained in the Cadbury Report of 1992 and the Greenbury Report of 1995. Superficially, of course, wholly owned utilities are accountable to their parents (SWEB to Southern Group, Norweb to United Utilities, for example). That only pushes the question one stage back, although it can be an important stage if the parent companies are foreign multinationals as they now are with the majority of regional electricity companies. Business school theorists and contemporary reformers stress the idea of 'stakeholders,' so that directors should be concerned with suppliers, customers, employees, and so on. But, as discussed further below, the stakeholder principle is controversial and certainly does not form an explicit element in the strategies of utility companies. The post-privatization experience of accountability to employees, for instance, is salutory. Labour shedding, 'casualization,' decentralized bargaining, and union exclusion have all been seen (O'Connell Davidson 1994; Waddams-Price 1996, 172; Froud et al. 1996). In the public mind the accountability question reached scandalous levels with the pay increases given by British Gas to its chairman, Cedric Brown, who eventually was obliged to resign. Possibly of more concern is the National Grid case, where the windfall gains of directors through gratuitous share options raised disturbing questions about what lawyers coyly call 'improper managerial self-enrichment' (*Independent,* 25 November 1995).

So far, of course, the ghost at the feast has been the financial markets. Companies are accountable to the market, but utility companies have sufficient monopoly power or regulatory protection to be relatively unthreatened by the product market. The financial markets, however, are a different proposition. To a remarkable degree, British utility regulation has fallen victim to the dynamics of stock-market capitalism, and the regulatory regime has, through necessity and habit, become responsive to the financial markets.

The reality of accountability to the City is part of the regulatory genetic code. The privatizations were undertaken with the markets primarily in mind, City sentiment was a preoccupation, and the utility companies were structured to maximize their attractiveness to shareholders. In an interesting contribution, Veljanovski (1993, 59) has attributed semi-constitutional (or, in political theory terms, contractarian) status to the flotation prospectuses. He suggests that there was a 'regulatory bargain' between government and the shareholders that regulators should respect. After flotation, City analysts have been the most attentive students of utility regulation and of these implicit contracts. Reaction in the City to regulatory statements move the share prices of the utilities dramatically, and all the involved parties must be sensitive to the sheer scale of financial gain and loss involved in such price movements. Even in matters relating to the water companies, Maloney and Richardson (1995, 103) observe that 'the need to take note of the judgement of City investors has perhaps been even more important to the industry than the need to recognise its customers.' Similarly it was share price movements that prompted the electricity regulator to take the revolutionary step of revising the REC (regional electrical companies) distribution price controls in March 1995. This move by Professor Littlechild, which was greeted with shock and indignation in the industry, was prompted by revelations of the financial strength of the regional electricity companies flushed out by Trafalgar's bid for Northern. The story is now relatively familiar (see Newbery 1996; MacKerron and Boira-Segarra 1996, 105), but on the grounds for the revision Littlechild's press release notes that 'the companies argued that there is no new evidence which it is appropriate for me to take into account. However, share price increases since my original proposals in August constitute evidence' (undated but April 1995, 2). The floodlights of City attention have thus affected the processes as well as the content of regulation. Consultation that involves price-sensitive information must be handled with care, and impact on the share price is a constant consideration in all negotiation.

Market sentiment affects the content, the timing, and the legitimacy of regulatory decisions (the revision of the electricity distribution price review is simply the most dramatic example). This is seen in its effect on share prices but also in its effect on the market for corporate control. It is the possibility of takeovers that has the most profound effect on the directors and senior managers of utility companies. Once the golden shares in the RECs had lapsed, ministers adopted a permissive policy towards mergers, so that decisions on the structure of all the industries – but particularly electricity and water – were conceded to the financial markets. The electricity industry has seen an extraordinary takeover boom, in which eleven of the original twelve independent RECs had been taken over by autumn 1996. The restructuring was only slowed when the Industry Secretary, Ian Lang, very controversially prohibited REC takeovers by the two big generators against the advice of the MMC. We come back to the question of corporate control and industry structure below, but it is worth emphasizing the magnitude of City interests and financial incentives. The utility sector now accounts for about 17 per cent by value of London stock market capitalization and is therefore a major element in the investment portfolios of savings and pension funds. For directors and management, the use of share options within remuneration packages has created a preoccupation with share price and made millionaires of a number of fortunate directors who seemed qualified more by luck than by talent for such largesse. The impact of the City-centred financial systems has been a concern of theorists of Britain's relative decline for thirty years (Hutton 1996; Pollard 1984; Ingham 1984; Wilks 1997). Its impact on industrial investment, planning, and decision making has been widely discussed, and pathologies, such as 'short-termism' and insulation from industrial management, have been identified. Now this panoply of criticisms and diagnoses needs to be applied to the utilities sector. It can be suggested that in this context the most important, influential, and ubiquitous location of accountability is the financial markets. Helm (1994, 37) has observed that the British system 'has created significant regulatory arbitrage in capital and product markets, it has tended to benefit shareholders to an excessive degree and, in terms of outcome, has produced results consistent with capture.' This stress on the financial markets emphasizes the dominant relationship which is between the privatized companies and the market. To focus on the operation and reform of the regulatory agencies is to focus on only a part of the problem. In some ways the regulators have a quite impossible job. The 'targets' of regulation are therefore the utility companies themselves, but also the markets that provide the structure of pressures and incentives within which the companies operate. We go on to analyse these regulatory targets in more detail.

The Targets of Regulation – The Companies

In the British negotiated system of regulation it might be more appropriate to talk of regulatory partners rather than regulatory targets, but for the moment we will stay with the image of top-down regulation. At first sight it would seem that the obvious targets of regulation are the companies. This means senior management and the boards of directors, who may constitute a managerial cadre within each industry, moving between companies and sharing a common view of the industries' problems and responsibilities. Regulators may increasingly, however, find themselves dealing with a rapidly changing set of targets as companies merge or are taken over by other utilities, by conglomerates, or by foreign multinationals, so that new management with radically different expectations enters the industry.

If the British tradition of regulation is based on bargaining and accommodation, then we should see a distinctive regulatory exchange between regulatory agencies and their 'client' companies. The regulator will be prone to consult, to understand, to explain, and to compromise. Sanctions will be postponed pending remedial action, assurances will be accepted, and adversarial action will be exceptional. For their part companies will cooperate. They will explain their actions, provide information, give assurances on which they deliver, structure their organizations to be sensitive to regulation and to anticipate legitimate demands. This is a picture of uncoerced compliance. In most current regulatory thinking, compliance issues have been emphasized. Ayres and Braithwaite (1992, 20) contrast the two approaches of deterrence and compliance, and observe that 'today most, although by no means all, regulators are in the compliance camp ... whereas most regulation scholars are in the deterrence camp.' We can go on to explore whether the compliance model is still workable for British utility regulation by examining the company perspective.

Why should companies cooperate with the regulator? There are two groups of reasons, self-interest and social responsibility. The most powerful self-interest motivation is *reasonableness*. That the company regards the regulatory framework as sensible and equitable – one that facilitates forward planning and provides the legendary level playing field on which it can compete fairly with other companies. Regulation is seen as legitimate – a point we return to below. Related to this is the *reputational* argument. To breach reasonable regulatory provisions will affect the reputation of the company, which could have a knock-on effect with a commercial cost. The fact that in 1994–5 Norweb had the worst record on domestic disconnection of electricity and London the best should be a source of concern to Norweb directors (OFFER 1995, 31). Reputational damage can be hard to judge where the regulator's views may be critical in private but not articulated in public. Then there is the *defensive* self-interest motive for cooperation, namely that unless companies cooperate the regulatory regime will become more onerous. There is an excellent example of this in the field of power generation, which was unregulated until the regulator began to express concern about manipulation of the pool price by the dominant duopoly of PowerGen and National Power. Lack of any persuasive response led him in 1993 to insist on the disposal of 6000 MW of the sort of mid-merit generating plant that effectively sets electricity prices through the Pool (MacKerron and Boira-Segarra 1996, 108). Finally, we can turn to the most intriguing reason for cooperation, which is *aggressive* self-interest.

The aggressive self-interest argument is built on the premise that businessmen dislike competition and welcome regulation; they particularly welcome regulation that is influenced by business itself. This is, of course, the capture argument. It is an argument that has also captured the academic imagination and provided a fertile school of scholarship inspired by Stigler, whose dry observation that, 'as a rule, regulation is acquired by the industry and is designed and operated primarily for its benefit' (Stigler 1971, 3) seemed wonderfully to combine intuition and logic. There are no plausible cases of capture of the utility regulators, although regulatory capture is far from unknown in Britain (historically pharmaceuticals and agriculture provide good examples, as does the City Panel on Takeovers). It can, however, be argued that ministers were captured by forceful management during the privatization process and that the regulators began work with a regime that in terms of structure and price formulas was heavily biased towards industry and shareholder interests. It would be logical for the companies to pursue capture strategies by lobbying, careful selection of data, advocacy of favourable regulatory policies, and tactical cooperation.

The second group of reasons for companies to cooperate with the regulator arise from the social responsibility arguments. As mentioned earlier, the debate about whether corporations should leaven profit maximization with a concern for the social impact of their activities is tempestuous and complex. For efficiency theorists, the 'pursuit of profit within the law' *is* socially responsible, because it will maximize wealth, growth, and welfare. For theorists of the corporation as a social institution, the efficiency theorists offer unrealistic, and probably cynical justification for corporate greed. 'To argue,' said R.H. Tawney, 'in the manner of Machiavelli, that there is one rule for business and another for private life, is to open the door to an orgy of unscrupulousness before which the mind recoils' (Tawney 1938, 217). These are extreme renderings of opposed positions in an important and subtle debate that is well developed in the United States.

The social responsibility debate in Britain is far more recent and subdued (Lloyd-Smith 1995). Certain companies are regarded as responsible citizens (Pilkingtons, Marks and Spencer, the familiar list) and are encouraged by government initiatives such as 'Business in the Community,' but the British debate has centred on corporate governance rather than social responsibility. The popular concern about business corruption and executive remuneration has reinforced recourse to business self-regulation, as seen in the Cadbury Report, the Greenbury Report, and associated codes of conduct. The focus here has been on strengthening the legal model of corporate governance by trying to empower shareholders. Within the quite intense debate over corporate governance, the privatized utilities have acted as a catalyst. The issue of executive remuneration in the utilities prompted the Confederation of British Industries to set up a study group under Sir Richard Greenbury that was critical of remuneration practices in the utilities and elsewhere (Greenbury 1995). It produced a code of practice that is voluntary but that has been incorporated into the Stock Exchange Listing Rules (companies that do not comply risk prejudicing their listing). The report was widely regarded as useful but inadequate to cope with the problem, and it was very patchily implemented (*Utility Week*, 21 July 1995; Villiers 1995;

PIRC 1996). Nevertheless, despite these extensive inquiries, the question of the social responsibility of utilities has hardly been raised, which is odd.

Utilities have always been associated with a public-service responsibility, whether as private companies in the nineteenth century or as nationalized ones later in the twentieth – for very obvious reasons. They provide indispensable industrial infrastructure, they enjoy natural monopoly power, and they deliver the basic essentials of civilized life to individual families. This characteristic of the 'essentialness' of utility services is emphasized by Ernst (1994, 36), who remarks on the extraordinary change that 'commodification' has brought to perceptions of the utility industries. These features intrinsic to utilities mean that they have extensive opportunity to exercise social responsibility over a whole range of activities from disconnections to tariffs. Utilities fit Mintzberg's (1983, 13) categories of 'where social responsibility can work' – where cooperation and compliance with the *spirit* of regulation can make all the difference. Indeed, scrutiny of electricity company reports does reveal significant 'social' activities in relation to the environment, training of the workforce, involvement with the regional community, and substantial donations to charities such as Age Concern and Help the Aged, as well as liaising with them over access to energy for the elderly.

But such social responsibilities have received very limited reinforcement from the regulator, the market, or the government. There is perhaps an overreaction against the ethos of the nationalized industries, and an emphatic attention to market forces that downplays the traditional public-service ethos. Instead, as Ernst remarks, the utilities are portrayed as selling a simple commodity like any other. The cultural transformation of the utilities has been marked. They are adopting the practices and the priorities of the generality of quoted companies, and ideas of social responsibility appear to be regarded as secondary. Nonetheless, a sector recognized as being aware of its societal impact and operating according to norms of social responsibility could expect a lighter regulatory regime.

Self-interest and an ethos of social responsibility might incline companies to cooperate with the regulator, but there are also some powerful ideas at work that make cooperation reluctant or limited. The regulator will expect cooperation in four areas. First, the provision of information is fundamental and the question of information asymmetry is stressed by all economic theorists. The regulator will want routine information on accounts, investment, and technical performance, but also information on exceptional developments. The licences give regulators extensive powers to acquire information but they have to know what to ask for. Second, regulators will be receptive to new ideas and helpful initiatives from the companies. A constructive dialogue is essential. Third, they will need practical cooperation on day-to-day matters, such as providing information in an accessible format; and on compliance issues, implementing policies with commitment and on time. Fourth, the regulator will hope for support from the companies in their dealings with ministers, Parliament, the media, and consumers. The companies know where the bodies are buried and can make life very difficult.

The extent to which this cooperation is forthcoming is a function of the culture of the regulatory regime as well as a matter of rational calculation. As they select a level of cooperation, corporate executives will have a series of considerations in their (conscious or subconscious) minds. First, there is the fiduciary duty to shareholders. Loose or relaxed regulation is likely to facilitate profit growth, and there must be an interest in constructing a favourable regime. All cooperation will therefore be biased to the utilities' perceived self-interest. Second, in adopting this stance, executives are only doing what free-market economists expect (and indeed advise) them to do. It would be considered irrational for executives *not* to select and bias the information and ideas they provide. All Britain's current utility regulators come from an economic background and will discount tactical cooperation from the companies, which in this way are almost incited to play the textbook game of economic bargaining. A disciplinary grounding in economics appears to encourage those regulators who share it to seek to substitute impersonal competition for personal regulation. This deregulatory imperative has been noted by Eisner (1993, 177) in the United States. Third, the regulatory relationship is one of bargaining between big and powerful organizations. In the case of BT and British Gas, the companies, and their forceful chairs, were in a powerful bargaining relationship with ministers before the regulators were created. It almost appears as if these companies see themselves as the most powerful of the two adversaries, with talented staff and a commercial mission of national importance. In this setting one does not, in principle, gratuitously strengthen the hand of the adversary, and a constant pursuit of bargaining advantage is a feature of the relationship. Fourth, this tendency is reinforced by managerial reputation. Senior managers seek peer esteem for job satisfaction and for career advancement. A tough, calculating, and 'results orientated' approach to regulation is more likely to produce gratifying headlines such as the 'Baker the Roaster' story in *Utility Week*, which declared that 'National Power Chairman John Baker has roasted the regulatory regime with some fiery criticism. Recent events have made him turn up the heat' (23 June 1995, 17). Fifth, there is a lack of sanctions in the British system to punish non-cooperation. The option of revoking the licence is about as usable as a nuclear deterrent, and there are no equivalents of the U.S. administrative hearings that can call executives to account. The MMC is available to arbitrate on really intractable disputes, but this is a last resort, to be used only where normal relations have collapsed, and it is possibly even more time-consuming for the regulator than for the company. Finally, there is the option of appealing, of going behind the back of the regulator to the minister or to other influential political figures. Ministers have not always backed their regulatory watchdogs, most especially in the case of MMC merger references. Powerful industrialists know that they are likely to receive a sympathetic hearing and that some of the more extreme threats of the regulators lack credibility. James McKinnon, the first gas regulator, was willing to be confrontational, and experienced a stormy relationship with British Gas. Significantly his contract was not renewed, although his successor, Clare Spottiswoode, has also become fairly adversarial in her relationship with British Gas and its successor companies.

This section concludes, therefore, that the utility companies are problematic targets for regulation, a conclusion that accords with observation and anecdote. We do not have a thorough empirical study of cooperation and compliance that distinguishes between companies, between regulatory issues, between regulators, and over time. The popular impression, however, would be that companies have complied with the letter but not the spirit of utility regulation and that, even then, the compliance has been variable. The 1996 National Audit Office (NAO) Report does provide more detail but in a factual, non-evaluative fashion. It notes, for instance, that 'OFTEL has experienced considerable difficulty in obtaining information on which to monitor operations from both BT and other companies' and there is 'resistance by companies supplying information that may have strategic, tactical or commercial value.' The NAO echoes these points for each of the other regulators (NAO 1996, 109–10, 198, 248). The least cooperative relationship appears to have been in gas, and the general impression is that British Gas has been a difficult company with which to deal. The gas regulator has likened the relationship to a doctor with an obnoxious patient. They may not like dealing with that person but their Hippocratic oath and professional ethics require that they do everything possible to return that person to health. That British Gas can be obnoxious is clear. It has a reputation for being engineer-dominated, closed, autocratic, and dismissive. Extraordinarily, it also seems to have run a campaign of vilification against the actions and personality of the regulator (e.g., *Financial Times*, 8 October 1996). The acrimony between the regulator and the company was symbolized by British Gas's refusal to accept the proposals of the Office of Gas Supply (OFGAS) for the British Gas Transco price-control proposals in 1996. The proposals were then referred by the regulator to the MMC, and then caught up in the sensitivities of the 1997 general election. The issue illustrates perhaps some of the limits of the power of the utility regulators and the uncertainties that ensue when the relationship of trust and cooperation breaks down.

In contrast, the 'best' relationship is in water. Here the consensus that long-term regulation is unavoidable creates a need for accommodation, and here too there is a 'third force' in the form of the Pollution Agency (formerly the National Rivers Authority), with whom the relationship is more tense (see Chapter 12 by Alan Booker). Certainly the water regulator, Ian Byatt, has been seen as a reasonable, consistent, and informed official, with whom the companies can do business. In telecommunications the relationship has always seemed constructive, fuelled by a mutual recognition of the technological volatility of the sector and the constant need for flexibility, although during 1996 the relationship became more adversarial (see Chapter 14 by Cosmo Graham). Electricity is perhaps the most fascinating case, where regulating for competition has been taken furthest but where it was felt that the companies were running rings around the regulator, at least until the 1995 distribution price review (Sturm and Wilks 1997).

The Targets of Regulation – The Market

It is in their relationship with the market that the role of the British utility regulators appears both extraordinary and contradictory. The genetic code of the regulators gives them a teleological character: in electricity, gas, and telecommunications they have a legislative duty to promote competition. The end product should be the withering away of regulation; like income tax, utility regulation was intended to be temporary (Helm 1994, 22, 27; Beesley and Littlechild 1992, 76), also like income tax no realistic person now believes it.

It is surprising that the more extreme aspirations of the pro-competition advocates were taken so seriously. Ernst (1994, 183) nicely emphasizes this lack of realism by pointing to the 'competitive Utopianism' that underlay privatization (and he manages to quote Hayek in his support). From a theoretical point of view it is far from clear that competition in a neo-classical (or Austrian) style is the most effective form of industrial behaviour (see Doern 1996 for some comments on a huge literature), and in the case of natural monopolies it is simply beyond attainment. From the perspective of British business, the industries are located in an economy that is highly oligopolistic and whose competition authorities are under-resourced and often ineffective (Wilks 1996a). From a practical perspective, the process of restructuring the industry requires levels of intervention that would make a central planner hesitate, and, in any case, it can be achieved only with difficulty against the imperatives and priorities of the financial markets. Yet, despite these rather obvious drawbacks, the regulators, and particularly the electricity regulator, talked and behaved as if competitive markets would make them redundant, although by 1996 pronouncements referred less and less to this belief. This context militated against the creation of longer-term relationships with companies, it reduced the incentive for strategic planning of dealings with the industry (or design of the regulatory agencies), and it tended to create a hands-off posture on the part of the regulator who surrendered responsibility to the abstract market.

In relation to the attempt to substitute competition for regulation, electricity is important as the utility in which the most systematic attempt was made to restructure it to facilitate competition. The arrangements in England and Wales are among the most adventurous in the world (Sturm and Wilks 1997; Cross 1996), although they are following a model that had been widely canvassed within the industry. But the regulators have had repeatedly to intervene to try to secure or sustain a competitive structure. This can be seen in three major examples. First, Professor Littlechild insisted that the RECs sold their shareholdings in the National Grid Company in order to create an independent transmission company. Second, he also insisted on the sale of large amounts of generating capacity by PowerGen and National Power to increase competition in the generation market. Third, the Trade and Industry Secretary, Ian Lang, blocked the takeover by generators of two of the RECs (against the advice of the MMC), thus prohibiting an abrupt shift to vertical integration within the industry.

These interventions would not surprise 'institutionally-orientated' political economists. They are examples of regulators creating and constituting markets (rather than merely intervening in them). But do they speak of the strength or the weakness of the regulator? MacKerron and Boira-Segarra stress the strength, observing that 'a single individual was now sufficiently powerful as to shape the evolving structure of the generating industry, despite having no power in the Electricity Act,' and going on to say 'that while regulation might begin to fade away at some future moment, it was certainly becoming more powerful, and even arbitrary, in the short term' (MacKerron and Boira-Segarra 1996, 109). The weak version would suggest that regulatory interventions of this sort are a desperate attempt to head off a remorseless financial pressure for reintegration and larger units that will eventually produce major vertically integrated oligopolies. Whichever version is preferred, the reality is that with respect to industrial structure the regulator is in constant interaction with the financial markets and the pressures they exert.

In general, however, the financial markets have good cause to be grateful to the regulators, who have supervised a regime in which profits and share values have been buoyant and who also have provided complete security. The utility acts all require the regulators, in effect, to protect the profitability of the utility companies. The formulation in the Electricity Act of 1989, section 3(1), is that 'the Secretary of State and the Director shall each have a duty ... to secure that licence holders are able to finance the carrying on of the activities.' This is seen to require the ability to raise capital, which, in turn, requires a credit-worthy profits record. Thus the utilities become quite exceptionally safe and privileged investments. But the regulators' ambitions to restructure the industries along fully competitive lines are in constant danger of being frustrated by the markets that have undertaken finance-led restructuring through mergers and takeovers. With the acquiescence of ministers, it seems likely that many utility companies will be absorbed into larger or multi-utility groups and that others (especially in electricity) will be restructured into a few oligopolistic and vertically integrated super-utilities. When this happened in the United States in the 1930s it provoked the legislative breakup of the electricity industry. It would be curious if this cycle were repeated in Britain.

In utility regulation there is a reproduction of the great fault line in the British economy between the dynamics of the financial markets and those of the industrial markets. Even if one accepted that competition (and competition policy) could become an adequate substitute for regulation, then the influence of the financial markets would prohibit that outcome. This is seen most clearly in the area of industrial structure. There is close to universal agreement that the utilities have sub-optimal industrial structures to create competition, and the regulators have sought to create a more competitive structure. McGraw (1984, 305) wrote that 'more than any other single factor ... [the] underlying structure of the particular industry being regulated has defined the context in which regulatory agencies have operated'; that conclusion is echoed by Stelzer (1991), Vietar (1994, 310), and Bishop, Kay, and Mayer (1995, 1). But, in the British system, control over industrial structure is conventionally subject to shareholder preference and the market for corporate control, with the residual and reactive oversight of the competition authorities. If the regulators cannot control structure they are relegated to the second-order activity of remedying the more blatant abuses of monopoly power and managerial discretion. Perhaps, then, they should recognize the theoretical and practical inappropriateness of the competition utopia, and reconcile themselves to an indefinite but important continuing role of structural intervention and detailed regulation?

The Regulatory Deficit and the Crisis of Utility Regulation

The proposition is that Britain has designed and implemented a system of bargained regulation that demands trust between the regulator and the regulated and that requires cooperation from both sides. The importance of trust is now widely recognized. It has been stressed by Hutton (1996, 252), popularized by Fukuyama (1995), and theorized by Putnam (1993). The argument is that the regulators are continuing to operate within that normative framework but that the companies are not. The regulators are behaving as if a stable policy network were in place, while the companies are tending to behave as unconstrained adversaries, maximizing individual benefits. One should not necessarily 'blame' the companies and their boards for reacting in this way. They are amoral and responsive to the framework of incentives and pressures in which they are placed. The wrong framework has been chosen.

During 1996 the system was seen to be 'in crisis.' The symptoms of the crisis were widely noted and were summarized by John Kay in four – symbolic rather than substantive – events, namely the 1994 Electricity Distribution Price Review, which was spectacularly revised in March–July 1995; corporate activity in the financial markets, and especially the feverish merger activity after March 1995; executive pay and perquisites; and the 1995 drought and its impact on the public sense of indignation (Kay 1996).

The response to this crisis has, of course, been to press for reform, but the majority of the proposals for reform have concentrated on government and the regulatory agencies. Of equal if not greater importance is a need to reform the market framework within which the companies operate, and perhaps the companies themselves. This is particularly appropriate because the British system of bargained regulation is based on a method and a philosophy that appear to be being rediscovered in North America. The North American–inspired literature talks repeatedly of 'negotiated regulation' (Graham and Prosser 1991, 228), of the 'partnership concept' (Sparrow 1994, 228; Vietar 1994), and of 'responsive regulation (Ayres and Braithwaite 1992). This is also at the core of the British system. What would it take to revive it?

At this point, as we move into prescription, the discussion becomes more subjective and tentative. The suggestion is that reformers should look seriously at ways of increasing corporate compliance and corporate self-regulation. In turn this requires a leap of imagination, which many, especially neo-classical, economists will be loath to make: to recognize that corporations in general and utility companies in particular are social enterprises whose activities can be justified only insofar as they serve public or social interests. This is a position that gained increased salience over 1996–7 as a result of the Labour Party's debates on the merits of a 'stakeholder' economy and Will Hutton's hugely influential polemic on British economic and industrial policy. In his famous Singapore speech in January 1996, Tony Blair talked of his vision of the company as a community of partnership; Hutton's work explored this idea in the form of advocacy of 'stakeholder capitalism.' Hutton has been intensely critical of utility regulation, but just as the Labour Party began to back away before the 1997 election from the more radical reforms implied by stakeholder capitalism, so utility reformers began to stress the virtues of the established system.

At one end of the reform spectrum are the gradualists such as Peter Vass (see Chapter 10 in this collection) and Waddams Price (1996). At the more radical end of the spectrum are Hutton and John Kay who has emerged as an influential Labour Party adviser. Their views are usefully presented in Kelly, Kelly, and Gamble (1997). Thus Kay talks of the crisis in utility regulation, and conceives of a radical shift in the concept of the company. Waddams Price argues that the crisis is transitory and derives essentially from inadequacies in the early regulatory bargains. She feels that 'the regulators have done a remarkably good job' (1996, 178) and that it would be better to develop the existing system. Contributions to the debate have come from many sources, including a range of parliamentary inquiries. Thus, during 1996–7 the Committee of Public Accounts undertook a thorough investigation of utility regulation based on the NAO Report (PAC 1997; NAO 1996), while the Trade and Industry Committee undertook a range of more specific inquiries, including an important report on energy regulation (TIC 1997a, 1997b). Among the think tank studies, the report from the Hansard and European Policy Forum group is interesting (Hansard 1996). Published at the end of 1996, it comes from a distinguished, non-partisan group. It stressed the need for greater legitimacy but broadly supported the existing regime. Nonetheless, it made a series of sensible suggestions for improvement, some of them rather more than incremental, such as the proposal for ministers to issue a 'Social Policy Framework Document' to define the proper social responsibilities of regulators and their financial implications. The report is also interesting in its complete lack of any discussion of self-regulation, its exclusive focus on the regulatory apparatus within government, and the way in which corporate governance issues are totally ignored. In that respect it represents exactly the sort of reform agenda this chapter aims to confront.

In looking to improve corporate compliance and self-regulation, the task of the reformer is to exploit corporate amorality with a set of guidelines, incentives, and norms that lead the companies to pursue goals with a greater sense of social responsibility. There are many ingenious possibilities, some of which are explored in a North American setting by Pearce (1990) in an argument that parallels the one presented in this chapter. Here four areas are explored.

Reducing the Influence of the Financial Markets

It seems essential to reduce the concern of the companies with the capital market and to increase their concern with their customers. At the minimum, curbs on takeover activity could be considered. Mandatory referral to the MMC (as with water companies) is an option, and the Hansard Report endorses the idea of strengthening both the role of the Director General of Fair Trading and the MMC in the control of utility mergers. Hutton (1996, 303) similarly would make takeovers harder and would tighten up the rules operated by the City Takeover Panel. This proposal received support in the City as a result of CalEnergy's takeover of Northern Electric in December, 1996, where it was thought that the takeover rules enabled it to buy shares too cheaply. There was widely expressed support for moves to make hostile bids more difficult (*Financial Times*, 1 April, 1997). In the United States the question of takeovers will gain increased salience following the drastic deregulation of the electricity sector. A wave of mergers was being anticipated at the beginning of 1997 in the run-up to greater competition. A more ambitious approach would be somehow to involve stakeholders in commenting on, or even approving takeover and merger proposals. Precedents exist for this. Several American states have passed legislation to extend the constituency of interests to be considered when assessing a takeover and to make hostile takeovers virtually impossible.

Reform of Corporate Governance

It is likely that lasting reforms of corporate governance will come into effect over the next five years. These may be introduced voluntarily by the companies or the Stock Exchange, although experience with the Cadbury and Greenbury codes is not propitious. In any case the orthodox, City-inspired agenda for reform of corporate governance is very narrow, atavistic, and unlikely to meet the needs of a wider social responsibility. The orthodox approach is driven by the model of shareholder democracy (Parkinson 1993, 159), and seeks to overcome the pathologies created by the separation of ownership and control by increasing the influence of shareholders. Much wider definitions of corporate governance are possible. Woolcock (1996, 181) proposes a definition that considers how companies are embedded in the industrial and financial systems and that encompasses the relationship between managers and the various stakeholders in the company. In this spirit we can also consider whether the utility companies and the regulators could go further, falling short of full-scale revision of company law.

The regulators are unhappy about several aspects of corporate behaviour. They are also unhappy about the implications of takeovers and about how utility activities will be treated within larger corporate structures. In all the utility industries, internal organization and accounting practices are of great importance for regulatory scrutiny. The water and gas regulators have also taken measures to 'ring fence' licensed activities after takeovers, and the water regulator has called for separate stock-market listing of utility subsidiaries.

This level of interest and influence suggests that the regulators working together could insist upon internal changes in organization and process that would make the utilities more orientated towards regulatory compliance and social responsibilities. The range of possibilities is extensive, but three brief examples can be given. First, the regulators could insist on greater, and more systematic, disclosure of information to the public. The companies acts already require a limited amount of social disclosure (such as policy on employment of disabled persons). Many companies go beyond this to produce an environment report, and it would not be difficult to require utility companies to report on matters of social concern (Parkinson 1993, 374). Much of this material is already analysed and publicized through the specialized consumer organizations in each industry, but the consumer focus may not always overlap with wider social concerns (such as energy planning). This possibility perhaps requires greater emphasis in the light of the widely noted tendency, mentioned above, of utility companies to attempt to limit the amount of information they release.

A second possibility is to require mandatory consultation with certain groups over certain matters. The draft European Community Vredeling Directive envisaged more extensive consultation with employees, but the principle could be extended to other interested groups such as customers or suppliers. In stronger versions, a requirement for an external arbitrator (the regulator?) can be built in to compensate for the imbalance in negotiating power (Armstrong, Cowan, and Vickers 1994, 361). A third example is the idea of a specific compliance machinery within the company. All utility companies have extensive regulation divisions and senior managers who specialize in regulatory matters. In a very interesting discussion, Ayres and Braithwaite (1992, chap. 4) suggest the companies could take self-regulation to effective and credible levels if they also appointed corporate compliance groups reporting to a compliance director. Some companies are already moving in this direction with encouragement from the regulators.

Reform of Company Law

Tom Hadden (1977, viii) opens his company law text with the following formulation: ‘British company law is not unworkable. But it is tied to a conception of capitalism which has been discarded by all but the most ardent free-market economists. It has also ceased to reflect the realities of the commercial and industrial world.’ This was written before the ardent free-market economists staged an intellectual putsch, but the basic truth of Hadden’s statement has put company law reform back on the agenda. Pressures from Europe and the example of company law in other jurisdictions provide an important impetus. The more controversial aspects of the debate have revolved around greater worker involvement, the German model, supervisory boards, and the government's opposition to the Fifth Company Law Directive. Some British companies are sufficiently multinational to have to establish works councils, others are setting them up voluntarily, but all are embedded in a peculiarly British variant of capitalism that has nurtured the traditions of regulation outlined above (Wilks 1996). The British system of company law is intrinsic to this model and reforms will be slow and contentious (Parkinson 1993; Ireland 1996).

What does this imply for utility regulation? Kay and Silberston (1995) have advanced proposals for 'a new model of corporate governance' that would be based on the principle of 'trusteeship' and that would explicitly recognize the plc as a 'social institution with corporate personality.' This is not targeted specifically at utilities, although the utility question has clearly given impetus and form to the proposals. The plc concept would meet several of the concerns identified above, including insulation from the financial markets, greater awareness of a social role, wider consultation, and a framework that would be more congenial to regulatory compliance. Kay and Silberston's suggestions have been developed in an important contribution by Kay (1997) in which he refines proposals for implementing the trusteeship model. He proposes a new companies act that would 'establish a distinction between the PLC – the social institution with a corporate personality – and the owner-managed limited company' (137). Trusteeship managers would be required to sustain the company's assets rather than the value of its shares. They would be appointed by independent directors, not by shareholders. Under a reformed law the company would be strictly commercial, but would consider and respond to a wider set of stakeholder interests. Kay's concept would seem particularly relevant to utility companies, and his contribution will provide one of the foundations of the debate that can be expected in Britain over the possibility of moving to some form of stakeholder capitalism.

Negotiated Regulation

The more imaginative and creative reformers visualize regulation as a joint effort, a partnership that transcends the 'them' and 'us' distinction. This is a demanding concept that is challenging to more traditional lawyers and that demands a level of discretion many economists also find suspect. Nonetheless, this approach to regulation is very congenial to British traditions and presents interesting possibilities if market ideologies could be modified and public trust increased. It combines statutory and self-regulation elements.

The most interesting exposition comes from Ayres and Braithwaite (1992). They discuss the concept of 'coregulation' between companies, or industry associations, and the regulator, but their most interesting proposition deals with 'enforced self-regulation,' which is 'negotiation occurring between the state and individual firms to establish regulations that are particularised to each firm' (101). The mechanisms would draw on the corporate compliance groups and compliance director mentioned above. The compliance director could report to the industry regulator. This is a model that works in the field of financial regulation and also in areas like aviation safety where internal rules are approved by the regulator and can be the subject of legal action.

Of course, this is virtually what happens already in the case of telecommunications and gas, but it would be implemented under this model through changes in the internal organization of the regulated firms. This model would sit uncomfortably with the search for universal rules, stable regulatory regimes, and a faith in regulation through competition. It is based on an alternative philosophy of regulation, but given the defects in the present system and the change of government, perhaps it is an alternative that deserves sustained study. It is certainly an alternative that is widely canvassed (and practised) in North America.

Conclusions

This chapter has argued that the regulatory regime must be assessed as a whole to include both the government apparatus and the companies subject to regulation. It is a 'regime' rather than simply an administrative mechanism. The traditional British regime has allowed companies great autonomy and has pursued regulation through a relationship based on trust, bargaining, and compromise. This tradition has many virtues and is, in fact, highly compatible with current regulatory thinking on the importance of trust and compliance in the regulatory process. Yet the traditional British model is failing to deliver acceptable regulatory outcomes. It is suffering a series of policy failures, but, more important, it is suffering a crisis of legitimacy that has provoked well-nigh irresistible pressure for reform.

Reform of regulatory institutions is necessary. Some of the dimensions of reform are discussed in the chapters by Hogwood, Vass, Locke, Graham, and Booker in this volume. But in itself, reform of government will never be sufficient; it must also focus on the companies being regulated. This imperative takes the analysis of utility regulation into a wider theoretical context of the debate about variation between capitalist systems and the different role that companies play in divergent capitalist models (Wilks 1996b). It also places analysis in the context of a domestic political debate about the British political economy, the potential for stakeholder capitalism, the nature of corporate governance, and the reform of both competition law and company law. Indeed, the salience of utility regulation has imparted a considerable momentum to the debate on corporate governance. The utility companies have hardly been out of the headlines.

In considering the possibilities for reform of corporate governance to make companies more responsive regulatory partners, the 'amoral' nature of the corporation has been stressed. Since the 1850s in Britain, 'with the development of the modern doctrine of separate legal personality ... the company acquired a Renneresque neutrality, emerging as a colourless, empty vessel, in essence indifferent to any particular interest' (Ireland 1996, 28a). The interests that have filled this empty vessel have been overly dominated by the financial imperatives that are uppermost in the British system of stock market capitalism and that were powerfully reinforced from 1979 to 1997. The challenge for reformers is to make these companies more responsive and responsible. It is a challenge that has become a necessity in the 1990s as the delivery of public services has become entrusted increasingly to the private-sector (Wilks 1997) and as private sector companies become steadily more influential within the British polity. Utility regulation provides an important and appropriate arena within which responses to this challenge can be forged.

NOTE

1 The author gratefully acknowledges the support of the Economic and Social Research Council, which provided a Senior Research Fellowship.

REFERENCES

Armstrong, M., S. Cowan, and J. Vickers. 1994. *Regulatory Reforms: Economic Analysis and British Experience*. Cambridge, Mass.: MIT Press.

Ayres, I., and J. Braithwaite. 1992. *Responsive Regulation: Transcending the Deregulation Debate*. Oxford: Oxford University Press.

Beesley, M., and S. Littlechild. 1992. 'The Regulation of Privatized Monopolies in the United Kingdom.' In M. Beesley, *Privatization, Regulation and Deregulation*. London: Routledge, first published in 1989.

Bishop, M., J. Kay, and C. Mayer. 1995. *The Regulatory Challenge*. Oxford: Oxford University Press.

Bower, J. 1974. 'On the Amoral Organization.' In *The Corporate Society*, edited by R. Morris. London: Macmillan.

Cross, E. 1996. *Electric Utility Regulation in the European Union: A Country by Country Guide*. Chichester: Wiley.

Doern, B. 1996. 'Comparative Competition Policy: Boundaries and Levels of Political Analysis.' In *Comparative Competition Policy*, edited by B. Doern and S. Wilks. Oxford, Clarendon Press.

Department of Trade and Industry. 1982. *The Future of Telecommunications in Britain.* Cmnd 8610. London: HMSO.

Eisner, M. 1993. *Regulatory Politics in Transition.* Baltimore: Johns Hopkins University Press.

Ernst, J. 1994. *Whose Utility? The Social Impact of Public Utility Privatization and Regulation in Britain.* Buckingham: Open University Press.

Foster, C. 1992. *Privatization, Public Ownership and the Regulation of Natural Monopoly.* Oxford: Blackwell.

Froud, J., C. Haslam, S. Johal, and K. Williams. 1996. 'Stakeholder Economy? From Utility Privatisation to New Labour.' *Capital and Class* 60:119–34.

Fukuyama, F. 1995. *Trust.* London: Hamish Hamilton.

Graham, C., and T. Prosser. 1991. *Privatizing Public Enterprises: Constitutions, the State, and Regulation in Comparative Perspective.* Oxford: Clarendon Press.

Greenbury, R. 1995. *Directors' Remuneration – Report of a Study Group Chaired by Sir Richard Greenbury.* London: Gee and Co.

Hadden, T. 1977. *Company Law and Capitalism.* 2nd ed. London: Weidenfeld and Nicolson.

Hancher, Leigh, and M. Moran, eds. 1989. *Capitalism, Culture and Regulation.* Oxford: Clarendon Press.

Hansard. 1996. *The Report of the Commission on the Regulation of Privatised Utilities.* Chaired by J. Flemming, sponsored by the Hansard Society and the European Policy Forum. London: Hansard Society, December.

Helm, D. 1994. 'British Utility Regulation: Theory Practice and Reform.' *Oxford Review of Economic Policy* 10, no. 3:17–39.

Hutton, W. 1996. *The State We're In.* Revised ed. London: Vintage.

Ingham, G. 1984. *Capitalism Divided? The City and Industry in British Social Development.* London: Macmillan.

Ireland, P. 1996. 'Corporate Governance, Stakeholding, and the Company: Towards a Less Degenerate Capitalism?' *Journal of Law and Society* 23, no. 1:287–320.

Kay, J. 1996. 'Reviewing UK Utility Regulation.' Presentation to the Nottingham Business School Conference on Reviewing Utility Regulation, London, March.

– 1997. 'The Stakeholder Corporation.' In *Stakeholder Capitalism*, edited by G. Kelly et al. London: Macmillan.

Kay, J., and A. Silberston. 1995. 'Corporate Governance.' *National Institute Economic Review*, August.

Kelly, G., D. Kelly, and A. Gamble. eds. 1997. *Stakeholder Capitalism.* London: Macmillan.

Lloyd-Smith, S. 1995. 'Three Faces of "Corporate Social Responsibility."' In *Corporate Governance and Corporate Control*, edited by S. Sheikh and W. Rees. London: Cavendish.

MacKerron, G., and I. Boira-Segarra. 1996. 'Regulation.' In *The British Electricity Experiment: Privatization, the Record, the Issues, the Lessons*, edited by J. Surrey. London: Earthscan.

Maloney, W., and J. Richardson. 1995. *Managing Policy Change in Britain: The Politics of Water*. Edinburgh: Edinburgh University Press.

McGraw, T. 1984. *Prophets of Regulation*. Belknap: Harvard University Press.

Mintzberg, H. 1983. 'The Case for Corporate Social Responsibility.' *Journal of Business Strategy* 4, no. 2:1–18.

National Audit Office (NAO). 1996. *The Work of the Directors General of Telecommunications, Gas Supply, Water Services and Electricity Supply*. Session 1995–6. House of Commons, 645. London: HMSO.

Newbery, D. 1996. 'The Electricity Industry 1995–96.' In *Regulatory Review 1996*, edited by P. Vass. London: CRI.

O'Connell Davidson, J. 1994. 'Metamorphosis? Privatization and the Restructuring of Management and Labour.' In *Privatisation and Regulation*, edited by P. Jackson and C. Price. Harlow: Longman.

Office of Electricity Regulation (OFFER). 1995. *Report on Customer Services 1994–95*. Birmingham: Office of Electricity Regulation.

Ogus, A. 1994. *Regulation: Legal Form and Economic Theory*. Oxford: Clarendon Press.

Parkinson, J. 1993. *Corporate Power and Responsibility: Issues in the Theory of Company Law*. Oxford: Clarendon Press.

Pearce, F. 1990. '"Responsible Corporations" and Regulatory Agencies.' *Political Quarterly* 61, no. 4:415–30.

Pensions Investment Research Consultants (PIRC). 1996. *Greenbury One Year on: Rewarding the Board, Long Term Incentive Plans*. London: Pensions Investment Research Consultants.

Pollard, S. 1984. *The Wasting of the British Economy*. 2nd ed. London: Croom Helm.

Price, C. 1994. 'Economic Regulation of Privatised Monopolies.' In *Privatisation and Regulation*, edited by P. Jackson and C. Price. Harlow: Longman.

Prosser, T. 1989. 'Regulation of Privatized Enterprises: Institutions and Procedures.' In *Capitalism, Culture and Economic Regulation*, edited by L. Hancher and M. Moran. Oxford: Clarendon Press.

Public Accounts Committee (PAC). 1997. *The Work of the Directors General of Telecommunications, Gas Supply, Water Services and Electricity Supply*. London: HMSO.

Putnam, R. 1993. *Making Democracy Work*. Princeton: Princeton University Press.

Sparrow, M. 1994. *Imposing Duties: Government's Changing Approach to Compliance*. New York: Praeger.

Stelzer, I. 1988. 'Britain's Newest Import: America's Regulatory Experience.' *Oxford Review of Economic Policy* 4, no. 2:67–82.
– 1991. 'Regulatory Methods: A Case for "Hands Across the Atlantic."' In *Regulators and the Market*, edited by C. Veljanovski. London: IEA.
Stigler, G. 1971. 'The Theory of Economic Regulation.' *Bell Journal of Economics and Management Science* 2, no. 1:3–21.
Sturm, R., and S. Wilks, eds. 1996. *Wettberwerbspolitik und die Ordnung der Elektrizitätswirtschaft in Deutschland und Grossbritannien*. Baden-Baden: Nomus.
– 1997. *Competition Policy and the Regulation of the Electricity Supply Industry in Britain and Germany*. London: Anglo-German Foundation for the Study of Industrial Society.
Tawney, R.H. 1938. *Religion and the Rise of Capitalism*. London: Penguin.
Trade and Industry Committee (TIC). 1997a. *Energy Regulation 1996–97*. House of Commons 50–1. London: HMSO.
– 1997b. *Telecommunications Regulation 1996–97*. House of Commons 254. London: HMSO.
Veljanovski, C. 1993. *The Future of Industry Regulation in the UK*. London: European Policy Forum.
Vietar, R. 1994. *Contrived Competition: Regulation and Deregulation in America*. Belknap: Harvard University Press.
Villiers, C. 1995. 'Directors' Pay in the Utilities: An Ill Not Yet Cured.' *Utilities Law Review*, autumn:152–4.
Vogel, D. 1986. *National Styles of Regulation: Environmental Policy in Britain and the United States*. Ithaca: Cornell University Press.
Waddams Price, C. 1996. 'Corporate Governance and Management Under Regulation.' In *Regulatory Review 1996*, edited by P. Vass. London, CRI.
Wilks, S. 1996a. 'The Prolonged Reform of United Kingdom Competition Policy.' In *Comparative Competition Policy: National Institutions in a Global Market*, edited by B. Doern and S. Wilks. Oxford: Clarendon.
– 1996b. 'Regulatory Compliance and Capitalist Diversity in Europe.' *Journal of European Public Policy* 3, no. 4 (December):536–59.
– 1997. 'The Conservatives and the Economy 1979–97.' *Political Studies* 45, no. 4: 689–703.
Woolcock, S. 1996. 'Competition among Forms of Corporate Governance in the EC: The Case of Britain.' In *National Diversity and Global Capitalism*, edited by S. Berger and R. Dore. Ithaca: Cornell University Press.

7

Modelling the Consumer Interest

STEPHEN LOCKE

'We are all consumers – but not all the time, thank goodness'[1]

Because we are all consumers, it is often tempting to think that consumer interests are easy to identify. Most people have plenty of personal experience on which to draw, and there is no shortage of strong views on what should be done to help consumers get a better deal. Compared with the many other aspects of utility regulation, such as risk analysis, investment appraisal, and pricing policy, the consumer dimension seems relatively benign. It is all too easily added on as an afterthought in the belief that information campaigns and revamped complaints systems should do the trick.

Nothing could be further from the truth. Over time it has become clear that much of the work of regulators revolves around promoting and defending the interests of consumers. Provisions along these lines are indeed written into much of the relevant UK legislation. The problem, however, is that obligations of this kind have not necessarily been translated into practice in a systematic and rigorous manner. Yet there has been considerable policy development over the years in this area, at least in relation to general consumer policies if not the utilities as such. This chapter traces these developments and assesses how the experience of the UK utilities sector measures up.

The Broadening Consumer Agenda in Historical Context

It is easy to forget that, even in its simplest form, consumerism is a relatively recent phenomenon. Until the mid-twentieth century, the interests of consumers were normally found bracketed together with the interests of taxpayers, electors, citizens, and clients, all of whom would be seen as making up the public interest. Politicians would normally see themselves as natural mediators of consumer wants, based on democratic elections and regular contacts with constituents, and senior public officials could rely on a broad political consensus on where the public interests lay. In such circumstances, fine distinctions between the consumer and citizen, let alone between different categories of consumers, probably did not matter too much. Few if any situations arose in which an explicit consumer interest was called upon to be defined.

Even the advent of independent consumer organizations did little to change this situation at first. The UK's main consumer organization, the Consumers' Association, publishers of *Which?*, was inspired by the success of a parallel initiative in the United States. The American initiative was devoted to the ideal of impartial scientific testing as the basis for informed consumer decision making: 'If a million citizens could be persuaded to invest one dollar each year for verified facts about their purchases, wonderful things could be done. In relation to services rendered, scientific work is normally the cheapest thing in the world' (Chase and Schlink 1927, 252). This thinking inspired the establishment of the world's first major consumer organization, Consumers Research (later Consumers Union) in the United States, which started publishing independent and impartial product research in its magazine *Consumer Reports* in 1936. It was not until after the Second World War that other Western countries followed suit, but they then did so in quick succession in the late 1950s and early 1960s, starting with Sweden, and then continuing with the UK, France, Australia, Germany, and the Netherlands. The overwhelming emphasis in all of this work was on public information and objective research. In the UK, there was a very direct line of continuity from the highly successful public information campaigns conducted in wartime (for example, 'Export or Die,' 'Work or Want,' and 'Eat up Your Greens') and the export drives that followed soon after the war ended. The 'supply' of consumer information was generated by a number of key journalists on major Fleet Street publications such as the *Observer*, long-established technical bodies such as the British Standards Institution, the Treasury (anxious to improve the quality of British goods on sale abroad), and independent bodies such as women's organizations. The 'demand' came from the ignorance and weakness of shoppers used to wartime austerity but faced with more and more goods coming into the shop and increasing volumes of advertising (Roberts 1982).

Against this background, it is not surprising that much contemporary policy development took a very restrictive view of the consumer interest. For example, the government-appointed Committee on Consumer Protection, set up in March 1959 (the 'Molony Committee'), confined its remit to shoddy goods and sharp sales practices and to promotion of consumer education and information in order to bring about a better informed and more discriminating public (Committee on Consumer Protection 1962). Its work led directly to the establishment in 1963 of a government-appointed and funded Consumer Council to look after the interests of the consumer.

During the 1960s the consumer interest – at least inasmuch as it was defined by the actions of policy makers – substantially widened as the need for wide-ranging legislation to protect consumers became clear. The joint efforts of the Consumer Council and the Consumers' Association bore fruit in the form of landmark legislation, such as the Trade Descriptions Act of 1968, which was devoted explicitly to making misdescriptions of goods and services a criminal offence.

But even here, the consumer interest was largely seen as confined to the 'high street,' and it was not until the 1970s that the wider aspects of the consumer interest came into play. A key development was the establishment of a new director general of fair trading under the Fair Trading Act of 1973. The responsibilities of the director general were deliberately cast in general terms: (1) an 'active' duty to deal with the economic interests of consumers – specifically by reviewing and collecting information about consumer goods and services, with a view to establishing any practices which adversely affect the consumer's economic interest; (2) a 'passive' duty to receive and collate evidence prepared by other people about any activities which adversely affect the consumer interest – whether on the economic side or in relation to health and safety matters (Fair Trading Act 1973, sect. 2.1). While these activities may of themselves seem to be rather limited – lead responsibility for policy legislation is of course left with the secretary of state – the breadth of the consumer interests that the director general considers is interesting and important. A broad conception of economic interests has allowed the Office of Fair Trading to take up a number of wide-ranging policy issues far beyond the traditional 'high street' agenda, involving sectors as diverse as financial services, estate agents, funeral directors, and holiday timeshares.

The establishment of the OFT heralded a rapid development of interest in the broader aspects of consumerism, spurred by the establishment in 1975 of the government-funded (but non-statutory and operationally independent) National Consumer Council (NCC), with a clear remit to consider the full range of consumer economic as well as legal interests, and to cover the public as well as private sectors. The NCC is also explicitly committed to take on board the interests of all consumers, and particularly those of the inarticulate and disadvantaged, who needed a body to speak for them and ensure that they were protected (National Consumer Agency White Paper 1974).

Developments of this kind paved the way for a rapid broadening of the consumer agenda in each of the UK's main consumer organizations in the 1980s and 1990s. For example, both the Consumers' Association and the NCC took on board and published reports on the consumer interest in international trade and the Uruguay Round of the General Agreement on Tariffs and Trade and on competition policy. Both organizations have also carried out assessments of various aspects of the Common Agricultural Policy and the single European Market. And they have been active participants in the debate on utility privatization and regulation. In areas of this kind – seemingly far removed from the experiences of shoppers in the 1950s – it has become essential to adopt a tight and rigorous definition of the general consumer interest and how it is best served. This has become a central focus in the work of the Consumers' Association and NCC, although the process is inevitably an evolutionary one.

In this work, both organizations have been able to draw on general models of the consumer interest developed in the UK and internationally.

Milestones in Defining the Consumer Interest

A number of policy-making bodies have attempted to set out guiding principles to help identify the consumer interest. In practice, these do not amount to much more than a series of headings, but they have nevertheless informed, whether explicitly or implicitly, most attempts to analyse the consumer interest in a given situation.

The 'Kennedy Principles'

Most general assessments of the consumer interest can be traced back to the so-called 'Kennedy Principles,' named after a speech given by President Kennedy in 1962. These enunciate very clearly what consumers can expect – whether through regulatory action or the voluntary action of companies – from the goods and services that they buy and use in a free society.

1/*Choice*: Consumers vary in their needs and preferences, and they are often the best judges of what suits them. In general, the wider the choice, the greater the consumer benefit. In an open market, choice also encourages competition between suppliers, improved efficiency, and better value for money.

2/*Information*: Without accurate, relevant, and understandable information – whether through product labelling, advertising, impartial research studies, newspapers, or consumer publications – choices cannot be exercised effectively. As well as damaging the consumer interest, information failures also encourage misallocation of resources and economic inefficiency.

3/*Safety*: Even rational, informed choices can end up damaging the interest of the consumer if the product or service in question is unsafe, which usually requires the establishment of minimum standards through regulation of some kind.

4/*The right to be heard*: Consumer voices and concerns need to be adequately reflected in the decisions taken by public and private institutions (Kennedy 1962).

These basic principles have stood the test of time remarkably well; they have proved amenable to adaptation and amendment in the light of new problems and priorities. For example, 'information' may be widely taken to include publicly provided information and consumer education as well as narrow information about particular products or services. 'Safety' can extend to immunity from damage to economic as well as physical interests, such as when consumers' advance payments or investments are at risk.

Furthermore, these concepts can extend, with only minor modification, to the provision of services by the public sector and by bodies such as monopoly utilities, even though this was clearly not the emphasis in 1962.

The European Community's 1975 Council Resolution on Consumer Policy

This unpromising sounding title covers a very far-reaching set of consumer principles – and an associated program of consumer-protection – based on the Kennedy principles as applied to the European Union's first consumer protection program, which was agreed in principle at the Heads of Government Summit in Paris in October 1972 (European Council 1975). It provided a very clear framework for subsequent consumer policy making by the institutions of the EU. The document opens with a recognition that 'the consumer is no longer seen merely as a purchaser and user of goods and services for personal, family, or group purposes, but also as a person concerned with the various facets of society which may affect him whether directly or indirectly as a consumer.' It then goes on to explain that the need for a clearly articulated consumer policy arises from a domination of: (1) the complexity of goods and services offered to the consumer by an ever widening market, and (2) the imbalance between suppliers and customers – arising, for example, from technological change, market expansion, improving communications, new forms of retailing, mergers, cartels, and other competitive restraints – which has made it more difficult for the demand side to play an active part in the mass market (European Council 1975, 1).

The document then sets out five principles, which may be broadly summarized as follows:

1/*The protection of health and safety*: Goods and services offered to consumers must present no risk to their health and safety. Where any risks arise from a foreseeable use for which goods and services are put, consumers should be appropriately informed. Where unforeseeable risks arise, there should be simple procedures for withdrawing goods and services from the market.

2/*Protection of economic interests*: Purchases of goods or services should be protected against the abuse of power by the seller, in particular against one-sided standard contracts, unfair exclusions, high-pressure selling methods, misleading advertising, and attempts to limit choice. There should be access to after-sales service and spare parts needed to carry out repairs.

3/*Advice, help and redress*: Consumers should receive advice and help in respect of injury or damage resulting from the use of defective goods or unsatisfactory service. They should also be entitled to proper redress for injury or damage by means of swift, effective, and inexpensive procedures.

4/*Consumer information*: Consumers should have sufficient information available in order to assess the basic features of goods and services on offer, make rational choices between competing offers, use products and services safely, and claim redress for any damage or injury resulting from the product or service. In addition, facilities should be made available to educate children, young people, and adults to act as discriminating consumers, capable of making informed choices and to be conscious of rights and responsibilities.

5/*Consultation and representation*: When decisions that involve consumers are being taken, the latter should be allowed to express their views, in particular with organizations concerned with consumer protection and information (European Council 1975, 1–16).

It can be seen that these principles represent a significant broadening of the consumer agenda as compared with that of 1962. One additional principle has been included, that of redress, that is, recognition that even with the best laid plans, transactions can go wrong and damage the consumer. In addition, two of the other principles are significantly augmented: economic interests to include protection against abuses of market power and misleading statements, as well as consumer choice; and information to cover consumer education, as well as information about products and services.

This document was then followed by a second consumer program adopted in 1981 and by a series of three-year action plans running from 1990 onwards. All have been within the broad context set by the first consumer program, but it is interesting to note that this consumer activity was not explicitly provided for in the Treaty of Rome, which contains almost no mention of consumers in its original form. Nor was much made of the consumer interest in the *Internal Market: White Paper* of the Commission of the European Communities published in 1985. The Council of Consumer Ministers passed a resolution in May 1986 inviting the Commission to prepare a paper on proposals to integrate consumer interests more closely into policy making in the whole range of European Community areas, including agriculture and competition, but progress in this area has been extremely slow.

One significant milestone on the European front has, however, been the incorporation of a new article in the Treaty of Rome as a result of the Maastricht Summit in February 1992. This article (129a) commits the EC to the attainment of a high level of consumer protection, and effectively – if somewhat tangentially – binds the key thinking behind the first consumer program into the Treaty of Rome itself, although it could be argued that a more explicit recognition of the basic consumer principles is still needed.

The UN Guidelines for Consumer Protection

Like the consumer protection work of the Commission of the European Communities, the UN guidelines had their origins in the 1970s when the UN's Economic and Social Council recognized the importance of consumer protection in economic and social development. The preparation of the guidelines followed intensive lobbying from the International Organisation of Consumer Unions, leading to a formal request from the Economic and Social Council to the secretary-general. After detailed consultation with the governments concerned, the full guidelines (running to forty-six paragraphs) were adopted by the General Assembly in April 1985 and published in 1986 (UN 1986).

The guidelines follow very closely those adopted by the European Council of Consumer Ministers, but with some additions. The additions include a principle based on safety and quality standards (that might in other circumstances be bracketed with physical safety), a principle related to distribution of essential goods and services, and a health principle. Of these additions, the most interesting from the point of view of the public utilities is the distribution-facilities principle, which might loosely be translated into an 'access' criterion and which has clear implications for debates on universal service in the utilities.

The UN guidelines have been much debated over the years, and it is quite widely recognized that any revised version would need to contain rather more about the control of monopolistic abuses and also about environmental protection and sustainable consumption. But as an official document, negotiated with a number of governments and endorsed by the UN General Assembly, the guidelines are so far without equal as an international statement of the consumer interest and how it should be reflected in policy. They have had a wide-ranging impact on the development of consumer-protection legislation in many developing and emerging economies.

Some Other Key Sets of Consumer Principles

In addition to the general initiatives set out above, aimed at setting a broad framework for the development of consumer policies, there have been three key areas where sets of principles have been devised as a means of establishing the consumer interest: competition policy, international trade, and public services.

Competition Policy

At both the European and UK levels of government, established competition policies have made a number of references to the consumer interest. At the European level, Article 85(3) of the Treaty of Rome sets out a general prohibition on restrictive practices, subject to a specific exemption of agreements or practices that 'contribute to improving the production or distribution of goods or to promoting technical or economic progress while allowing consumers a fair share of the resulting benefit.' In practice, the calculation of consumer benefits, which is carried out by Directorate General IV, is rather cloudy and is sometimes discharged out with the help of firms that have applied for the exemption. In addition, the term 'consumer' does not necessarily apply to the private citizen or to end-use, but may be confined to the immediate purchaser. A further problem is that consumer organizations are not necessarily consulted about proposed exemptions (National Consumer Council 1995). But the legal requirement is there nonetheless.

On the UK side, the main legal reference in the competition provisions of the Fair Trading Act is to the public interest rather than the consumer interest, and the criteria have been widely criticized as too vague and therefore open to a very wide range of interpretations (Locke 1994; Wilks 1996). But it is worth recording this example of the enshrinement in UK legislation of the public interest as being based on the desirability of:

1/maintaining and promoting effective competition
2/promoting the interest of consumers, purchasers, and other users in respect of prices, quality, and the variety of goods and variety of goods supplied
3/promoting the reduction of costs and the development of new techniques and products through competition, and of allowing new competitors into the market
4/of maintaining and promoting the 'balanced distribution of industry and employment'; and
5/of maintaining and promoting 'competitive activity in markets' outside the UK on the part of UK producers (Fair Trading Act, 1973, sect. 84).

Of these, the last two have nothing directly to do with the consumer interest, but the first three clearly do. The second, in particular, recognizes the importance of the economic interests of consumers, and defines this in terms of price, quality, and range of choice. There is, however, little official guidance on how these principles should be applied or which of them should take precedence in particular cases (with the exception of the guidance – the 'Tebbitt doctrine' – on mergers issued in July 1984 by the then secretary of state for trade and industry, which stressed the overriding importance of competition). In practice this interpretation is left mainly to Monopolies and Mergers Commission (MCC) when referrals are made to it.

International Trade

Here most of the running on the impact of trade restrictions on the consumer interest has been made by the Organization for Economic Cooperation and Development (OECD). In April 1985 the OECD's Ministerial Council approved an 'indicative checklist' for the assessment of trade policy measures (OECD 1985). One clear implication behind this development was that a more rational approach to trade policy at the national level would raise awareness of the domestic costs of protection and therefore tend to narrow the range of issues needing to be resolved at the international level, and so help to halt protectionism and to resist continuing protectionist pressures (Long 1989).

A specific objective of the checklist is to ensure that the costs to consumers of trade policy measures such as quotas and tariffs are fully itemized in terms of, for example, their effect on prices in general, their impact on specific groups of consumers, their effects on the availability and quality of products, and their impact on the structure and competitive process in the domestic market in question. Several of the items in the list deal with interests other than those of the consumer, such as those affecting local producers, employees, and government revenues. But explicit items in the checklist include:

- What is the expected effect of the measure on the domestic prices of the goods or services concerned and on the general price level?
- What are the direct costs of the measure to consumers as a result of the higher prices that they must pay for the product in question and the reduction in the level of consumption of the product? Are there specific groups of consumers that are particularly affected by the measure?
- What is the likely impact of the measure on the availability, choice, quality, and safety of goods and services?
- What is the likely impact of the measure on the structure of the relevant markets and the competitive process within those markets?

This author is not aware of this checklist being used in relation to any developments other than trade policy, but in principle it would be perfectly possible to do so, for example in relation to mergers and other developments affecting domestic markets. The endorsement of the checklist by OECD implies that all the member governments support its application and accept the logic behind it (even if their collective memories are sometimes hazy on this point).

The Consumer Interest in Public Services

This policy has developed significantly with the implementation of the UK's Citizen's Charter, which enshrines a set of 'principles of public service' applicable, at least in theory, to all areas of public service, including privatized utilities (*Citizen's Charter White Paper* 1991). The principles were included in the government's white paper launching the Charter Initiative, and have subsequently been modified in the light of comment and experience (Doern 1993). The principles are:

1 / *Standards*: Explicit standards for the services that individual users can reasonably expect are set and their publication is monitored. The actual performance results against these standards are published.

2 / *Information and openness*: Full and accurate information is readily available in plain language about how product services are run, what they cost, how well they perform, and who is in charge.

3 / *Choice and consultation*: The public sector should provide choice wherever

practical. There should be regular and systematic consultation with those who use services. User views about services, and their priorities about improving them, need to be taken into account on final decisions on standards.

4/*Courtesy and helpfulness*: Users should receive courteous and helpful service from public servants, who will normally wear name badges. Services should be available equally to all who are entitled to them and run to suit their convenience.

5/*Putting things right*: If things go wrong there should be an apology and a full explanation, a swift and effective remedy, and well publicized and easy-to-use complaint procedures with independent review wherever possible

6/*Value for money*: There should be efficient and economical delivery of public services within the resources that the nation can afford, and independent evaluation of performance against standards (*Citizen's Charter Second Report* 1994, 2).

The context of these principles is of course slightly different from the general frameworks of the 'Kennedy Principles' and those of the EC and the UN, but the similarity of many of the dimensions will be very clear.

Towards a Single Set of Consumer Principles

Pulling together all the various principles and ideas arising from the initiatives described in the previous section is not particularly difficult, and can provide us with a single set of principles against which the consumer interest can be assessed. This model takes as its starting point the 'classical' notion of consumers as 'ordinary members of the public in their role as purchasers and users of goods and services.' In other words:

- It explicitly excludes business consumers, concentrating instead on ordinary members of the public.
- It excludes what might be termed citizen interests, confining attention to members of the public 'in their role' as purchasers and users.
- It covers users as well as purchasers (that is, it goes well beyond the 1950s notion of the consumer as shopper, to cover, for example, users of goods and services provided free at point of sale and members of households who are not in fact purchasers).
- It makes no distinction between the public and private sectors.
- It explicitly includes services as well as goods.

The interests of consumers defined in this way can then be classified under five main headings, plus a sixth one needed to ensure that the other five are effective. Taken together, these headings can be seen to encompass all of the developments in consumer-policy thinking described above, thereby taking us at least as far as the early 1990s.

1/*Access*: The key principle here is of access to essential goods and services of appropriate quality and supplied in an appropriate manner (which can be taken to include the principles of courtesy, helpfulness, etc., of the Citizen's Charter). This principle applies most obviously to essential public services, but it may be held increasingly to apply also to certain private services that are becoming more important as the boundaries of the state retreat.

2/*Protection of economic interests*: The essential notion here is that consumers should get a fair deal from what they pay for. In most situations, consumers themselves ought to be the best judge of this, and can get the fairest deal through the exercise of clear choices in open, unrestrained markets characterized by vigorous competition. But where competition is not possible, other mechanisms are necessary to ensure that consumers get appropriate levels of quality and receive value for money. This will normally also require some form of validation against agreed standards for the performance of public providers, regulators, and others not subject to market discipline.

3/*Information and education*: These are the elements necessary to ensure that choices are made effectively, and also that, in areas where choice is not possible, those responsible (including government departments and other public bodies) are fully accountable and transparent in their actions. 'Education' in this context can be interpreted in terms of consumer education rather than education for employment or citizenship. By the same token, education relates not just to children and young people but also to all those likely to make complex consumer decisions.

4/*Safety*: As suggested above, this needs to be interpreted in the widest possible sense. It extends most obviously to issues of physical safety and the management of foreseeable and unforeseeable risks; similarly it applies to the development of standards to establish minimum levels of risk agreed to by all concerned. But, less obviously, it extends to other forms of safety, such as the safety of a customer's assets, whether held in the form of a deposit against goods or services or in the form of investments. A distinction is clearly needed here between foreseeable risks (such as losing money on the National Lottery, against which consumers cannot expect to be protected) and unforeseeable risks (such as failures resulting from regulatory lapses or unfair trading practices, against which consumers can clearly expect to be protected).

5/*Redress*: This extends from redress in its very simplest form, such as the effective handling of complaints, right through to the provision of affordable, accessible, effective, and efficient systems of access to justice using the courts and other bodies that are independent of the supplier. As the Citizen's Charter principles make clear, this concept plainly applies to the public as well as the private sector where there is a commitment to 'swift and effective remedies' when things go wrong.

6/*The right to be heard*: This is more of a 'supporting principle' than a key underlying criterion – it is necessary, rather, as a means of making all the other principles effective. It extends to direct consultation with consumers themselves, on a regular and systematic basis, using surveys, focus groups, and similar techniques as a means of establishing people's experiences and priorities for improving what is on offer. But it extends also to consultation with organizations that have a legitimate interest in promoting the use of the views of consumers and users, ranging from generalist national consumer organizations through to local amenity societies and special interest groups. The key requirements in such circumstances is that groups seeking to represent the consumer should not do so on the basis of their own prejudices or personal experiences; instead, they should seek to establish the facts through the rigorous analysis of the consumer interest on the basis of the five other principles and of supporting evidence.

The actions of bodies such as Consumers' Association and the NCC have been closely guided by this kind of framework over the last twenty years or so. The NCC has, for its part, added a seventh principle, that of equity and the prevention of arbitrary and unfair discrimination against consumers, either as individuals or in groups, which reflects closely its concern with the less advantaged (Whitworth 1994). The list has proved particularly useful in helping to isolate issues entirely outside the consumer arena (including most questions relating to religion and morality, for example); it has also proved very useful in helping to filter out the consumer dimensions from such complex issues such as broadcasting regulation and the provision of the state education that otherwise lead consumer researchers into very deep water.

A further refinement is that it is possible to use this kind of framework as a basis for asking a whole series of key questions such as:

- How many consumers are affected by the dimension concerned?
- Which categories of consumers are affected?
- To what extent are they affected and how large are any of the detriments any of them suffer?
- What kind of assistance would any proposed policy measures give along each of the dimensions concerned?

This is still far short of a detailed statistical model (which would be unrealistic), but it does provide a basis for clarity and intellectual rigour.

Some Self-evident Shortcomings

These principles provide at least a starting point for analysing consumer interests in relation to any given area of public policy, and they are considerably more robust than anything else currently available. But there are risks in pursuing this kind of analysis on a mechanistic basis, and a degree of perspective and general common sense is essential. There are also some concerns that these principles do not cope sufficiently well with some of the blurring of the boundary between consumer interest and citizenship that has become evident in areas such as environmental regulation. This section sets out some of the key problems and outstanding issues.

The Status of the Consumer Principles

At various points (e.g., both in President Kennedy's speech and in the European Council resolution in 1975) the references are to 'rights' rather than principles. This cannot literally be true, under common law at least. In the UK legal system they can only become rights where they have been clearly established by case law or enacted in legislation. For the most part the picture is heavily fragmented, the main exceptions being where major horizontal legislation, such as the Unfair Contract Terms Act of 1977 and the Consumer Protection Act of 1987, have materially altered consumer rights to information or redress across a whole range of sectors. Unfortunately, however, this kind of misunderstanding can cause confusion in debates with policy makers who have a background in Roman law; it may also cause some confusion among consumers themselves, who may be under the illusion that they have more extensive rights than is in fact the case.

Differential Effects on Different Groups of Consumers

This is a very thorny issue. The general framework provided by the consumer principles says nothing about the respective rights of different groups of consumers (except, possibly, under the 'access' criterion, where implicitly the most vulnerable consumers are supposed to be provided access to essential goods and services). This is a really difficult area for consumer organizations and, implicitly, for regulators too. Neither is in a good position to make value judgments about the merits of claims from different parts of society. Ultimately, it is for the political system rather than consumer policy makers to resolve this kind of issue. Yet it often arises in a very uncomfortable form. As well, in addition to the obvious example of the respective claims of different income groups (even if the need for a degree for social justice in consumer policy is accepted, what kind of weight is given to the interests of the very poor as opposed to the others on below-average incomes?), parallel issues arise from the respective interests of different age groups, rural versus urban dwellers, different regions of the country, and, most intractable of all, future as against current consumers. Again, these are really matters for the political system to resolve, but they often arise in the context of consumer protection and regulatory policy.

The Weighting of the Different Criteria

There may well be circumstances where a particular policy proposal will promote the interests of consumers along one of the dimensions but reduce them along another. In areas such as the public utilities, this may most frequently arise through the conflict between the 'access' and 'economic interests' principles: it is generally held that the development of fully competitive regimes will reduce cross-subsidies and therefore make it impossible to provide access to the least profitable customers. This issue has arisen with particular force in debates at the EU level over universal service in telecommunications and postal services. The first objective in such circumstances has to be to secure hard information about the extent of any likely gains and of possible losses. But of the theoretical possibility of such a trade-off, there can be no doubt.

Similarly, there is a long-standing trade-off between the consumer's economic interests and the principle of safety and risk avoidance. In theory it is possible to spend almost limitless amounts of money (e.g., to prevent transport accidents), but in practice a compromise has to be found based clearly on public expectations and the best possible available information.

What about Consumers' Own Views?

The sixth 'supporting' principle makes it clear that consumers should be listened to. But it is no less essential to maintain a clear distinction between consumer views and the consumer interest. There are strict limits on what can fairly be expected from ordinary members of the public, especially in dealing with complex technical issues. It is particularly hard for individual consumers to assess hypothetical propositions that do not relate directly to their own experiences. It is hard for them to make trade-offs between different priorities, especially where some do not affect them directly. It is difficult to get them to take on board levels of risk, especially those relating to very remote probabilities of cataclysmic events. Some of these issues can be tackled, at least indirectly, through 'focus groups' designed to assess qualitative reactions of small panels of people to particular propositions; some progress has also been made in developing 'citizen's juries,' where complex issues are put to a cross-section of the public and debated for a day or two before final views are recorded. But techniques of this kind are extremely expensive and self-evidently need to be confined to the largest and most intractable problems. For most day-to-day issues there is no substitute for engagement at a technical level with those who are clearly empowered to represent the consumer interest, on the assumption that they too will play by the rules and stick to rigorous use of the principles and objective data to support their case.

That said, there are a number of areas where carefully judged consumer research can do much to fill out the picture, such as determining measures of acceptability (e.g., of competing undesirable outcomes), levels of concern about existing shortcomings, views on how to help the vulnerable, actual experiences of using goods and services, and levels of knowledge about what is provided and what kinds of choices are available.

Consumers versus Citizens

In theory the distinction between consumers and citizens ought to be clear. Members of the public only become consumers when they purchase or use goods and services; citizens can be defined as 'members of the public exercising the rights and fulfilling the obligations which have been given to them by the state and society at large.'

This definition leaves many citizen issues, such as abortion rights, gun control, the ordination of women priests, the defence of the realm, and the rights of prisoners, far outside the consumer domain. Similarly, it highlights the fact that many consumer acts, such as small-scale purchases of goods and services, have only a very minor citizenship element. But there are overlaps, and these are becoming more important, especially in the light of increasing concerns about environmental problems and other externalities such as traffic congestion and burdens on public finances. These make it more difficult to take a 'pure' consumerist view in relation to major purchases such as cars and houses and in relation to activities that use up significant public resources. In such circumstances, it is impossible to ignore the fact that the act of consumption also raises citizenship obligations and cannot be viewed in isolation. Thus there is little in the consumer principles that would suggest any restraint on the ability of consumers to use their cars whenever they want to and without restraint, but this proposition clearly needs to be tested against the wider issue of citizenship responsibilities and the ability of other consumers to meet their needs, whether in the short or long run. Again, many of the issues are ultimately political, but there is much that consumer organizations and regulators can do to ensure that the issues are transparent and that the various interests clearly analyzed.

The Consumer Interest and UK Public Utility Regulation

The Regulators' Statutory Obligations

All the utility regulators in the UK have some kind of obligation to ensure that the interests of consumers are somehow protected. But these obligations vary considerably in their nature, and also in the level of prominence given to the consumer interest as opposed to other interests (Consumers' Association 1996). Some examples are the following.

1 / *Civil Aviation Authority (CAA) (Airports Act, 1986)*:

To further the reasonable interests of users of airports within the UK

This is a general obligation apparently equal in importance to the promotion of the efficient economic and profitable operation of airports and the encouragement of investment.

2 / *The Office of Water Services (OFWAT) (Water Act, 1989)*:

To ensure that the interests of customers or potential customers of licensed water and/or sewerage undertakers are protected as regards the prices of services provided, particularly those in the rural areas, and ensure that there is no undue preference or discrimination in fixing charges.

To ensure that the interests of customers or potential customers are also protected as regards other terms of supply including quality of service provided.

To ensure that the customers of licensed undertakers are further protected as regards the benefits that could be secured for them by the application in a particular manner, or any of the proceeds of a disposal of any protected land or of any interest.

Although these three items are relatively detailed, they are 'secondary' objectives below the two primary ones of ensuring the provision of water and sewerage services and that the companies concerned are able to finance their activities.

3/*Office of Electricity Regulation (OFFER) (Electricity Act, 1989)*:

To ensure that the prices charged to tariff customers by public electricity suppliers for electricity in Scotland are not differentiated by area.

To protect the interests of consumers of electricity supplied by licensees in respect of

- prices charged and other terms of supply, taking particular account of customers in rural areas
- continuity of supply
- the quality of the electricity supply services provided, taking particular account of the elderly and disabled.

Like the obligations of OFWAT, these for OFFER are secondary, coming behind those of ensuring that all reasonable demands for electricity are met and that licence holders are able to finance their activities, and of promoting competition in the generation and supply of electricity.

4/*Office of Telecommunications (OFTEL) (Telecommunications Act, 1984)*:

To promote the interests of consumers and purchasers of telecommunications services in the UK (particularly the elderly and disabled) in respect of prices, quality and variety of services and apparatus.

Again, this is a secondary objective, coming behind the primary objectives for OFTEL of ensuring that telecommunications services are provided throughout the UK and that those providing such services are able to finance their provision.

5/*The Office of Gas Supply (OFGAS) (Gas Act, 1986)*:

To protect the interests of consumers of gas supplied through pipes, in respect of prices and other terms of supply, continuity of supply, and the quality of the supply services provided.

To protect the public from dangers arising from the transmission or distribution of gas through pipes or from the use of the gas supplied.

These again are secondary objectives coming behind those of ensuring that reasonable demands for gas are met in all those areas where it is economical to provide it, and to ensure that the companies concerned are able to finance the services in question.

Issues Arising from Comparisons of the Statutes

Setting out the consumer protection obligations in the above manner illustrates graphically the piecemeal nature of the UK approach to regulation. Several questions and issues arise from such a basic review.

Should the Promotion of Consumer Interests Be a Primary or Secondary Objective?

It is striking that nowhere in the primary objectives of OFWAT, OFFER, OFTEL, or OFGAS is there any reference whatever to consumers, users, or customers. This appears to fly in the face of long-standing national and international commitments to place consumer interests high on the list in making of public policy and to define them in clear, unambiguous terms. Even the Fair Trading Act's much-criticized public-interest principles go further than this. Closer inspection confirms that consumer interests are partially (if only implicitly) reflected in the primary objectives through the reference to provision of services. But this is done in a very incomplete way; for example OFFER, OFTEL, and OFGAS have duties to ensure that 'all reasonable demands' are met within the sectors for which they are responsible, yet there is no guarantee that 'reasonable demands' will coincide with consumer needs. In the case of water, the service provision element is incorporated through a requirement to ensure that services are provided 'in every area' of England and Wales, but not necessarily to every household or even to all those households that 'reasonably demand' it. The clear implication is that consumer interests have been treated as an add-on rather than as a fundamental dimension to the thinking of the regulators. This is made worse, in turn, by a confusion between ends and means. Some of the primary duties, such as the promotion of competition in the generation and supply of OFFER's objectives, are in fact not objectives at all but means to an end. The same could arguably be said of the obligation to ensure that companies providing services are able to finance their provision: if there is already an obligation to meet the interests of consumers by ensuring that services of appropriate quality are provided, it should logically follow that in any privatized system those providing the services should be able to finance them.

Customers: Users or Consumers?

The objectives of OFFER, OFTEL, and OFGAS all relate to consumers, but those of OFWAT relate expressly to 'customers.' This suggests that OFWAT may not have any obligations to those users of water supplies who are not in fact customers, which is odd as this would appear to exclude, for example, those living in rented accommodation whose landlords pay the water bills, and also those members of households who are not themselves responsible for paying the bills. The obligations of the CAA in relation to airports are the broadest and refer to 'users,' which quite properly in this context would appear to cover both business and residential consumers, as well as those who have no contractual relationship with the airport or any associated services (such as meeters and greeters).

Which Consumers?

This again is something of a 'dog's breakfast.' OFWAT's objectives are the only ones to refer explicitly to current and future consumers ('the interests of customers or potential customers'); for the other regulators, any obligations to safeguard the interests of future consumers must be assumed to be implicit. There is a similarly confused treatment over the interests of consumers living in particular parts of the country. OFWAT and OFFER are explicitly required to take special account of the needs of consumers in rural areas, while OFTEL has a remit that extends only to services in rural areas, not to those who live in them, which is not quite the same thing. OFGAS has no explicit rural responsibilities, although this may be a reflection of the slightly different nature of the gas market and the relatively low number of rural connections to the gas mains.

There is a similarly schizoid treatment of the interests of disadvantaged consumers. OFFER is obliged to take particular account of the elderly and disabled in relation to the quality of services supplied; OFTEL has to pay particular heed to the interests of elderly and disabled people in relation not only to the quality of service but also to the variety of services and to prices and apparatus. Meanwhile, OFGAS and OFWAT have no such obligations, and their respective statutes are silent about the interests of disadvantaged consumers other than the elderly and disabled.

Which Consumer Interests?

It is helpful in analysing the interests served by the regulators' statutory responsibilities to use the general consumer principles set out earlier, as these pinpoint the gaps very clearly.

1/*Access*: This is mostly provided rather indirectly through the 'all reasonable demands' criterion in the remit of OFFER, OFTEL, and OFGAS, and through the geographical criteria of OFWAT and OFTEL. But these basic principles fall a long way short of a general access principle, which would need to relate to 'access to services of appropriate character and quality to meet the essential needs of consumers.' Even if the latter was made subject to some kind of reasonableness test, a criterion on these lines would represent a big step forward from what we have at present.

2/*Protection of economic interests*: This, understandably, is much more comprehensively covered. OFWAT, OFFER, OFTEL, and OFGAS all have obligations to ensure that consumer interests are protected in relation to prices for services provided and in relation to other aspects of supply, including the quality of service. In addition, OFFER and OFGAS have obligations to ensure continuity of supply, while OFTEL has a further objective of ensuring that there is a variety of services on offer in the interest of consumers and purchasers. OFWAT also has an obligation to ensure that consumers benefit from disposals of assets such as land. There is, however, no explicit principle regarding principle choice built into the original statutes; this is not surprising, because in each case it was expected that domestic consumers would continue to be faced with monopoly suppliers for some time to come. Incorporation of consumer choice has come about only through subsequent policy statements and (in the case of gas) additional legislation.

3/*Information and education*: This is surprisingly absent from any of the statutory obligations of the regulators, although it is an issue that has arisen with increasing frequency as consumer choices – whether of differing tariff packages from existing suppliers or of choosing between alternative suppliers – have increased.

4/*Safety*: This is an explicit obligation in the case of OFGAS, but not in relation to the other regulators. To some extent the omission is because safety is assured by other agencies and through other legislation (e.g., in the case of water through the Environment Agency, which controls river pollution and the quality of drinking water). But it is surprising that it is not included at least as a secondary principle, given that many decisions on pricing and investment can have significant implications for safety in one sense or other.

5/*Redress*: This is also noticeable by its absence from the list of key obligations of the regulators. Again, this absence is partly a result of provision elsewhere (e.g., through the small-claims procedures in the county courts), but it is surprising that there is no explicit obligation in this area, at least to ensure that effective and independent redress mechanisms are available in each of the sectors concerned.

6/*The right of consumers to be heard*: This is not covered in the key obligations of the regulations – indeed it would be slightly surprising if it was – but it does feature elsewhere in the relevant legislation, for example, in the requirement to establish customer-service committees in the water industry. There is however no general requirement to ensure that available mechanisms achieve a fully effective representation of the consumer interest.

How Much Does All This Matter?

In practice, the UK's utility regulators have proved rather more effective in promoting the consumer interest than might have been expected at the time when the original privatization legislation was passed. This has been particularly true of OFTEL, which has effectively advanced the promotion of consumer interests to a primary objective: 'In carrying out [these] functions ... our focus is on the customer. OFTEL's aim is for customers to get the best possible deal in terms of quality, choice and value for money. Our main means of achieving this is by promoting effective and sustainable competition. More competition will lead to real choice – three or more operators or service providers knocking at the door offering a full range of services at a price to suit the customer' (OFTEL 1996). The author has not come across similarly explicit statements of consumer interest from the other regulators – at least not statements that go beyond obligations included in the relevant legislation – but there has been no shortage of evidence of the regulators' willingness to take a tough line with industry interests in successive price reviews, as the evidence of the scope for efficiency savings has continued to mount.

The problem is that this tough approach has generally been a reflection of political pressures – coupled with serious concerns about accountability – at the same time that the role of the regulators has come under ceaseless scrutiny from parliamentary select committees, the National Audit Office, independent inquiries, and the media. It does not emerge from any rigorous definition of the consumer interest as enshrined in legislation, and it would be much easier for the regulators to take a less pro-consumer line at a time when public attention is diverted elsewhere or where the general circumstances are complex and confusing. The fact is that, under the present arrangements, consumers have no guarantee that their interests will be fully protected in all of the regulators' day-to-day decisions; they are heavily dependent on the preferences of individual directors general and on particular combinations of circumstances.

Two further problems arise from the failure to apply consumer principles rigorously to the utilities sector. One is that some consumer interests become too easily overlooked. A classic example is the provision of information about competing tariffs or service providers. Consumer associations can and do provide some of this information, but they do not have the resources to do the task comprehensively, nor can they be required to provide this kind of information even where it is demonstrably in the public interest. In the first instance, responsibility for information ought to rest with regulators, but they rarely have resources to do the job. If the regulators had a clearer statutory remit to ensure the provision of balanced, objective, and independent information for consumers, it would be very much easier for them to get the resources to ensure that this task is carried out. But in present circumstances there is little that can be done beyond hand-wringing and exhortation.

A second problem is rather more fundamental. One of the uses of the consumer principles is that they can help to establish the limits of a purely consumer-based approach: there are many problems that cannot be solved purely on the basis of consumer criteria but that require the incorporation of wider citizen concerns (the discussion on self-evident shortcomings above gives some examples). In particular, it is very difficult to use the consumer principles as a basis for establishing the respective claims of different groups of consumers, such as current versus future consumers, urban versus rural, young versus old, etc. Similarly, there is often no 'consumer' solution to the weighting of the different criteria (e.g., price versus quality or safety). These are by and large political issues to be resolved through the political system. But a persistent problem in the UK regulatory experience has been the loading of what are in effect political decisions onto the independent regulators. This has applied particularly in the water sector, where OFWAT has been confronted with some extremely thorny issues on the level of investment necessary to provide for water supplies of sufficient quality, and on who should pay for that investment. Given the massively conflicting interests involved, especially between current and future consumers, there are strong grounds for believing that this kind of issue should be dealt with by elected politicians rather than by independent regulators. In principle, many tariff issues raise similar conflicts of interests; that they have not done so on a major scale is probably a testimony to the enormous efficiency gains that have been achieved in the UK utilities sector since privatization, which are in turn a testimony to the gross inefficiency of the nationalized industries they have replaced. But the scope for such gains is likely to diminish over time, and future conflicts of interest between different groups of consumers are extremely likely to increase.

Conclusions

Utility privatization in the UK was born out of a wide range of motives, including the raising of revenue for the Exchequer, the spread of share ownership among the public, and the need to get future public investment off the public-sector balance sheet. The promotion of the interests of consumers originally came a long way down the list.

As the regulatory system has developed, it has proved necessary to develop a clearer focus on how the consumer interest should be defined as a basis for making major decisions on, for example, pricing and universal service. But the development of models of the consumer interest has been piecemeal and heavily dependent on the interests and concerns of individual regulators, often under the strong influence of day-to-day political pressures.

The statutory obligations in this respect are a confusing mishmash and provide little help as a basis for day-to-day guidance. Even more problematic has been the apparent willingness to leave what are in essence political decisions involving trade-offs between the interests of different groups of consumers in the hands of independent and supposedly objective regulators.

The way forward has to be based on a much more rigorous definition of the consumer interest, one based on principles long developed in the general consumer policy arena and widely applied by governments worldwide, as well as by a range of international bodies. The six key principles outlined earlier – access, economic interests, information, safety, redress, and the right to be heard – are not difficult conceptually, and they can do a lot to help clarify the general consumer interests in any given situation. They also expose a number of gaps in the current UK regulatory approach, which can claim many successes in promoting the consumer interests, but only at the cost of too many problems being swept under the carpet.

NOTE

1 Dame Rachel Waterhouse, 'New Frontiers for Consumerism,' *Royal Society of Arts Journal* 136, no. 5383:465.

REFERENCES

Chase, Stuart, and F.J. Schlink. 1927. *Your Money's Worth: A Study in the Waste of the Consumer's Dollar*. New York: Macmillan.

Citizen's Charter White Paper. 1991. Cmnd 1599. London: Cabinet Office, July.

Citizen's Charter Second Report. 1994. Cmnd 2540. HMSO: London, March.

Commission of the European Communities. 1985. *Completing the Internal Market: White Paper from the Commision to the Council*. Brussels: Commission of the European Communities.

Committee on Consumer Protection. 1962. *Final Report*. [Chaired by J.P. Moloney.] Cmnd 1781. London: HMSO.

Consumers' Association. 1996. *Submission from Consumers' Association*, to the Commission on the Regulation of Privatised Utilities. March.

Doern, G. Bruce. 1993. 'The UK Citizen's Charter: Origins and Implementation in Three Agencies.' *Policy and Politics* 21, no. 1:17–29.

European Council. 1975. *European Council Resolution of 14 April 1975 on a Preliminary Program of the European Economic Community for a Consumer Protection and Information Policy*. 18 (c92/1):1–16.

Kennedy, John F. 1962. *Speech to the US Congress*, 15 March.

Locke, Stephen. 1994. 'A New Approach to Competition Policy.' *Consumer Policy Review* 4, no. 3:159–68.

Long, Olivier. 1989. *Public Scrutiny of Protection: Domestic Policy Transparency and Trade Liberalisation*. London: Trade Policy Research Centre.

National Consumer Agency White Paper. 1974. Cmnd 5726. London: HMSO, September.

National Consumer Council. 1995. *Competition and Consumers*. London: National Consumer Council.

Office of Telecommunications (OFTEL). 1996. *A Guide to the Office of Telecommunications*. London: OFTEL.

Organization for Economic Co-operation and Development. 1985. *Indicative Checklist for the Assessment of Trade Policy Measures*. Press Release, 29 May 1985. Paris.

Roberts, Eirlys. 1982. *Which? 25, Consumers' Association 1957–82*. London: Consumers' Association.

United Nations. 1986. *Guidelines for Consumer Protection*. Publication no. E86.IV.2. New York.

Waterhouse, Dame Rachel. 1988. 'New Frontiers for Consumerism,' *Royal Society of Arts Journal*. 136, no. 5383:465–74.

Whitworth, Diana. 1994. 'Promoting and Representing the Consumer Interest.' In *The Consumer Revolution*, edited by Robin John. London: Hodder & Stoughton, 15–26.

Wilks, Stephen. 1996. 'The Prolonged Reform of United Kingdom Competition Policy.' In *Comparative Competition Policy: National Institutions in a Global Market*, edited by Bruce Doern and Stephen Wilks. London: Clarendon Press, 139–84.

8

The Theory and Practice of Regulation in Canada and the United States: Opportunities for Regulatory Learning in the United Kingdom

MARGARET M. HILL

The conventional wisdom is that the last decade has been marked by the introduction of a radically new and elaborate system of regulation in the UK. The growth of regulation is normally portrayed as part and parcel of the privatization of a number of previously nationalized sectors. This perspective is understandable, but it ignores the legacy of government regulation in Britain prior to the 1980s. In the eyes of a North American observer of regulation, what is happening in Britain in the mid-1990s is neither new, nor surprising. Accordingly, what we are witnessing is the more definitive *recognition* of a UK regulatory state.

The move to a regulatory state raises fundamental questions. Some are primarily theoretical and conceptual, while others have a more practical bent, concerned mainly with improving the efficiency and effectiveness of regulation. Regardless of the kind of question, the rich and well-documented experience with regulation in Canada and the United States is a unique learning resource for anyone interested in understanding better the political economy of regulation in Britain. A readily identifiable regulatory literature offers important insights into the kinds of questions that ought to be asked in the UK context and suggests conceptual and methodological tools to assist in finding answers. Regulatory developments in Canada and the United States also establish concrete terms of reference for considering the likely political, policy, management, and institutional implications of the emergence of a more recognizably regulatory state in the UK. Some of this North American regulatory experience has been fully examined by students of regulation in the UK, but some has not.

This chapter seeks to address this latest version of regulatory bypass. Drawing on the concept of policy learning, the chapter examines the relevance of the theory and practice of regulation in North America for the UK. The first section discusses policy learning and its application to the regulatory area. The remainder of the chapter explores two related questions: What to learn? and Why learn? In addressing these questions, the chapter draws attention to some of the lessons that might be extracted by scholars and practitioners from the recent history of regulation in Canada and the United States.

Policy Learning and Regulation

The Concept of Policy Learning

Public-policy making is often characterized as an exercise in technical problem solving or, alternatively, as a process of raw political conflict where interests compete with one another to influence policy outcomes. In recent years, students of public policy have increasingly embraced a third perspective. This perspective emphasizes the ideas, beliefs, paradigms, and values undergirding public policy and sees policy making as intellectual 'puzzling' (Heidenheimer, Heclo, and Adams 1990).

The concept of 'policy learning' falls squarely within this school of thought. Heclo (1974), Sabatier (1987), Rose (1991), Hall (1993), Etheredge (1981), and others contend, in fact, that policy making is a process of policy learning. The common theme in this literature is that policy actors from all corners of a policy community regularly look to experiences in other fields and jurisdictions for inspiration during the course of their day-to-day activities and in the larger processes of policy reform as well.

The motivations for policy learning are manifold. Policy makers often expand their tool kits by incorporating the latest innovations in policy, program, or process design. They may seek to understand why certain means or techniques work while others do not, or to draw conclusions about the use of a particular policy instrument. There is also what might be called 'high order learning,' where policy actors look to experiences elsewhere for guidance in settling on the hierarchy of goals and objectives for their policy domain.

The learning literature has recognized weaknesses. As Howlett and Ramesh (1995, 175–8) tell us, there is confusion about who learns, about what is learned, and about the effects of learning. The confusion is both conceptual and empirical.

Accordingly, it is useful to differentiate among the various potential learners in a policy community. Howlett and Ramesh emphasize that policy actors are not created equal when it comes to learning. The insistence in the policy community's literature on differentiating kinds of policy actors is equally relevant in the learning context. Furthermore, how well regulatory actors and entire policy communities learn – their *learning capacity* – depends on a variety of factors, including attitudes towards learning, the ability to absorb and process information, and the level of integration in the policy community (Howlett and Ramesh 1995, 177–8).

Our understanding of policy learning is improved as well if we distinguish the *substance* of learning from the *process* (e.g., via study, experience, or teaching). These two dimensions of learning are likely to have their own peculiar dynamics in different policy fields (e.g., health-care and telecommunications regulation), when different policy instruments are employed (e.g., spending and regulation), and when different policy actors are mobilized. In addition, our models of policy learning must allow for the possibility on the process side that policy outcomes may converge with or without policy learning (Hoberg 1990).

There is a clear need, too, to test the learning framework empirically. The general model may make intuitive good sense; nevertheless, detailed evidence of policy learning has yet to be identified and compiled systematically. It is therefore important to ask what concrete evidence there is, if any, that policy actors actually learn.

Learning and Regulation

The above discussion suggests a series of questions to apply in any given regulatory context: Who learns, What do they learn, How do they learn, and Why do they learn. The case for examining regulation through the lens of learning becomes even stronger when we consider that preliminary evidence suggests that learning is in fact characteristic of the regulatory area. Majone's recent assessment (1991) of the sources of regulatory policy making in Europe is a case and point. He argues that American regulatory philosophy and practice has had a substantial influence on European regulation, particularly in the development of European competition policy and the growth of European Community regulation during the Community's formative years, in the burst of social regulation in the 1970s, and again in the 1980s era of deregulation.

Majone detects the American influence in several places. He notes that so-called 'American regulatory techniques,' such as entry and price regulation, licensing, and standard setting, are found in a number of European regulatory systems. He also observes that overall subtantive policy is influenced as well, as for example in the telecommunications area, where the regulatory approach in Europe 'has been influenced, up to now, more by the American model than by EC regulation' (Majone 1991, 94).

Further evidence of regulatory learning comes from Raab's work on data protection in Britain. Raab (1993) conceives of the implementation of data-protection policy as a continuous learning process intended to acquire new capacity for behaviour. In this model, as Raab stresses, 'it is not only the regulators, but the regulated and the lay public as well, whose learning is a crucial determinant of success' (Raab 1993, 46).

Majone and Raab deal explicitly, albeit in different ways, with the question of regulatory learning. It is also true, however, that evidence indicating regulators, regulated parties, the public, and even regulatory systems can and do learn is captured in existing studies of the politics of regulation and merely needs to be brought to the fore. Recent research on Canada's 1988–92 pesticide registration review, for instance, hints at the potential for regulation-related learning in a major exercise in regulatory reform (Hill 1994). In fact, the pesticide case may illustrate that such learning among governmental and non-governmental actors is a prerequisite for successful regulatory reform.

Finally, the case for examining regulation from a learning perspective is especially strong at the present time. There is growing recognition that regulatory officials and other actors in the policy community not only behave like policy learners but also consciously engage in learning. This both reflects and is consistent with the internationalized nature of regulatory policy and policy making in the late 1990s. Moreover, with continued pressure on regulators in all countries to cut back and 'do more with less,' learning may be an eminently sensible way to achieve the long-sought objective of what in Canada is called 'smarter regulation.' Majone's observation that 'the ability of policy makers to innovate often depends more on their skill in utilizing existing models than on inventing novel solutions' (Majone 1991, 79) is perhaps more true today than ever.

Learning from the North American Experience

The fundamental premise of this chapter is that regulation in Canada and the United States offers a basis for regulatory learning in the UK. The focus is on the learning that can be achieved by academic scholars and regulatory officials. However, as suggested earlier, it should always be kept in mind that learning is a phenomenon that applies across the entire policy community, including among business and consumer groups.

A discussion of the relevance of the North American experience for regulation and for regulators in the UK must also be prefaced with a caution. Generalizing from single cases is a perennial quagmire for students of policy and regulation (Timney Bailey 1992). In addition, as Ogus advises, 'American [and Canadian] regulatory institutions, processes and styles are often very different from their British counterparts,' and this necessitates being exceedingly careful when drawing conclusions about the UK using North American modes of analysis (Ogus 1994, preface).

The danger Ogus identifies is not merely a matter of terminology. Models of government programs and policies cannot simply be lifted out of their original context and transplanted into another. Policy makers must be sensitive to and respect the ordinary need to emulate, not copy, which implies that programs and policies must be tailor-made in light of the political, social, economic, and institutional environment of the 'importing' jurisdiction. The relevance of North American experiences for regulation in the UK is conditioned by this same environment.

Finally, we are misguided if we think solely in terms of learning from 'the North American experience' with regulation. There is often no monolithic experience as such, as the remaining sections of the chapter confirm. Regulation has often followed different macro-level patterns in Canada and the United States. It has also frequently developed in different ways in the same fields in the two countries. Moreover, a focus on a North American experience risks masking not only the distinctiveness of learning in many areas of regulatory activity in Canada and the United States, but also the considerable cross-jursidictional emulation that has historically transpired between the regulatory systems on either side of the Canada–U.S. border (Hoberg 1991).

What to Learn? The Study of Regulation in North America

This section begins the chapter's consideration of the *what* question. The aim is to illustrate the overall body of principles, concepts, and theories that drives the analysis of regulation in North America. The section examines two central concepts, regulation and the regulatory state, and then three different theoretical perspectives on regulation, namely the agency case-study literature, private interest theories of regulation, and regulation as a policy instrument. The section also highlights some of the major developments in regulatory theory since the 1980s.

Regulation has been a pillar of governance in Canada and the United States since the origins of both countries. Primative regulatory systems were set up in the nineteenth century to standardize weights and measures and to protect citizens against such things as poisons and adulterated food. Similarly, policy makers have often relied on regulation in their nation-building strategies, as well as those for provinces and states.

Systematic academic scholarship on regulation is a much more recent phenomenon. Lowi, writing in the late 1960s and very early 1970s, drew attention to the unique politics associated with the regulatory functions of government (Lowi 1969, 1972). Investigating his well-known proposition that 'policy determines politics' – and its converse – quickly became the *modus operandus* for a relatively small group of scholars from politics, economics, public policy and administration, law, sociology, and other equally diverse disciplines.[1] What they shared was an interest in better understanding what James Q. Wilson (1980) labelled 'the politics of regulation.'

Today the study of regulation in North America deals more generally with the political economy of regulation. There is an extensive literature. The topics covered range widely, from why and when governments use regulation, the effects of regulation, and the regulatory process to regulatory policy and decision making in specific areas, patterns of interest group behaviour in regulatory regimes, and national styles of regulation. Moreover, analysis is informed by a valuable set of concepts, principles, and theoretical approaches.

It is equally important to note that the field of regulatory studies retains its multi-disciplinary character.[2] Trespassing between disciplines is widely considered essential if genuine insight is to be gained into the special dynamics of regulatory policy and policy making. It is also judged to be essential for good theory construction.

Before delving into the principles, concepts, and theories underlying the study of regulation, an additional cautionary note is in order. The so-called 'North American' literature is not limited to studies of regulation in Canada and the United States or to research by North American scholars. Especially after the mid-1980s, the study of regulation had a distinctly – and very welcome – comparative bent. The analysis of the theory side of regulation in the following sections makes use of the 'North American' label as a matter of convenience and also to underline that regulation is recognized as a legitimate, free-standing field of inquiry in North America.

Regulation and the Regulatory State

What is the study of regulation all about? In short, What is regulation? Surprisingly, perhaps, there remains a degree of ambiguity about the meaning of the central concept (Schultz and Alexandroff 1985, 2–5). Fortunately, this ambiguity is not serious. The North American literature typically conceives of and treats regulation as a distinct tool of government, one that involves the imposition of rules by government, backed up by the use of penalties, that are intended specifically to modify the behaviour of individuals and firms in the private sector and in realms of private action.

The concept of regulation has been refined still further. One of the oldest distinctions in the literature is between *economic* regulation and *social* regulation. Eads and Fix (1984), McGarity (1986), and others claim that social and economic regulation are inherently distinct types of regulation, differing in their focus (i.e., rules on prices, rates of return, entry, and exit versus rules on the conditions under which goods and services are produced and sold and the characteristics of the goods and services themselves). They differ also in the scope of coverage (i.e., sectoral versus horizontal), in the perceived legitimacy of their use by government, and in the policy considerations and interest groups they invoke. While the economic/social distinction may be useful from a conceptual and analytic standpoint, it is extremely difficult to sustain fully in practice, given that all economic regulation has social consequences and all social regulation has economic impacts. Much of contemporary regulation amounts to what Nemetz, Stanbury, and Thompson (1986) term 'hybrid' regulation.

Another common thread in the North American literature is the attention paid to the multifunctional nature of regulation (Economic Council of Canada 1979). The classic rationale for regulation is technical efficiency. Governments constrain choices in the economy and society in order to remedy market failures, such as natural monopoly, imperfect (i.e., asymmetric or costly) information, and externalities, and therefore to improve overall allocative efficiency. Regulation driven by the pursuit of these aims has come to be known as 'public interest' regulation.

Subsequent analysis has shown, however, that the objectives for regulation are often not public-interest related, but instead are at their core political- and private-interest oriented. This largely economic literature shows us that regulation is a highly effective way to redistribute income and wealth in society, mainly because it is largely hidden and *appears* to be inexpensive as a result of the low direct government expenditures and the largest portion of the costs being borne by the private sector (Stanbury and Lermer 1983). Redistribution and other political functions of regulation are the basis for many private-interest perspectives on regulation. Stigler's famous contention that, 'as a rule, regulation is acquired by the industry and is designed and operated primarily for its benefit' (1971) is among the best-known propositions about regulation.

The other crucial concept in the study of regulation in Canada and the United States is the 'regulatory state.' The post-war period in North America has been marked by a massive change in the way governments conduct the business of governing. In particular, governments have embraced the practice of subdelegating significant regulatory power and authority to their bureaucracies in more and more areas of economic and social activity. The executive arm of government continues to set broad goals in statutes that constrain private decision making, but specific ministers (and, in practice, their officials) are empowered under the legislation to make and amend the detailed regulatory framework that defines precisely how the specified goals will be achieved. Scholars in North America have come to call this phenomenon 'government by regulation,' or the emergence of the regulatory state.

The literature stresses that the regulatory state raises serious questions about accountability and control. Ministers are authorized to issue and revise regulations without parliamentary (or congressional or presidential) approval. Where the chosen means for regulation is a specialist agency operating at arm's-length from ministers and the legislature, the scope to interpret the general mandate conferred by Parliament or Congress during the course of regulatory decision making is especially problematic.

The main line of defence of government by regulation is usually exceptionally pragmatic. Government by regulation is considered by many to be highly efficient and effective given the complex agendas facing modern policy makers. Proponents of the private-interest view of regulation emphasize instead that the regulatory state offers politicians an easy way to distance themselves from contentious policy issues, and regulatory officials a means to aggrandize their power.

Agency Case-Study Literature

Much of the early academic work on regulation was classically institutional. The central goal was analysis of particular regulatory realms and, to a much lesser degree, an explanation of regulation as such. The object of study tended to be government regulatory bodies and the processes and procedures of regulatory policy and decision making. Typical of this genre were case studies of the Progressive era innovation in American government organization, the independent regulatory commission, and of its Canadian version, the independent regulatory agency.

Most of the agency case-study literature examines either the administrative rationales for governments choosing the agency mode, or the interests that will be served by this choice. It is frequently argued, for example, that politicians and bureaucrats are convinced the independent regulatory agency is institutionally more competent for certain purposes. This is the claim in the analysis by Ackerman and Hassler (1981) of the institutional framework for clean-air regulation in the United States, where the origins of independent regulatory agencies such as the Environmental Protection Agency are traced to the acceptance by policy makers of a series of New Deal ideas about how regulatory administration could be made more efficient and more effective if responsibility for regulation was given, not to the executive branch of government or the courts, but rather to an appointed collective body operating at arm's length from political control.

Studies of independent agencies in Canada have generally taken a similar approach, despite the fact that the tradition of cabinet and parliamentary government means that Canadian regulatory agencies have never been as independent as their American namesakes (Doern 1978). If there is a dominant explanation of the origins of Canadian sectoral regulatory agencies, it is that they have historically been chosen as a way to depoliticize highly contentious and divisive regulatory issues by relieving politicians of responsibility for resolving them. Other reasons are also said to have been behind creating agencies. Many relate to the presumed ability of the mode to improve regulation through a clear division of labour between elected officials and expert regulators, enlarged opportunities for public participation, and greater flexibility in decision-making and operating practices (Doern 1978; 1979).

The original literature on agencies remains important today because it raised for the first time some of the classic issues of regulation. It shows us in very concrete terms, for instance, the multifunctional nature of the activities performed by regulatory agencies. Agencies regulate private-sector behaviour, but they also typically engage in other activities related to governance, such as quasi-judicial decision making, subsidy allocation, and mediation.

Case studies of regulatory agenices also remind us that, having decided to regulate, governments must still settle on the organizational arrangement or mode for regulation. Governments can be considered to have a choice between regulation by an executive department of government, by an independent agency, or by self-regulation. The modes are distinguished by where they vest regulatory responsibility – in, respectively, a minister, a collective board, or the industry itself. The agency literature pays particular attention to the ways in which collective boards with wide discretionary powers and operating at arm's length from the executive violate traditional principles of political accountability, responsibility, and control.

Last, but not least, research on agencies is the original pre-Stigler source for ideas about regulatory capture. In his famous study of the U.S. Interstate Commerce Commission, Bernstein (1955) proposed a 'life-cycle' theory of agency behaviour. Agencies were said to pass naturally and inevitably from youth through to old age. In the latter stage, public support for the agency is greatly diminished and the agency becomes vulnerable to domination by the regulated interests, or what Bernstein called 'regulatory capture.' The notion of capture was later extended to include capture by other members of the policy community, including bureaucrats. Capture theory in its various guises informed much of the later literature on regulatory failure (Wilson 1980; Makkai and Braithwaite 1992).

Private-Interest Theories of Regulation

A revolution in thinking about government regulation was launched with the publication of a series of books and articles by Posner, Stigler, Wilson, and Stiglitz in the mid- to late 1970s. This work, taken together, was the origin of the private-interest school of regulation. It also set in motion the groundwork for a much more theoretically oriented study of regulation.

Posner's seminal 1974 article, 'Theories of Economic Regulation,' built on earlier work by Stigler (1971), and thereby firmly extended the economic analysis of law into the regulatory area. The essential point was that, to understand regulation we must identify who benefits from it. Posner claimed that the answer to the question of who benefits explains which interest groups are likely to mobilize and seek to influence regulatory policy and decision making. More specifically, he stressed that the existence and form of regulation can be predicted as a response by politicians to the demands of interest groups who will derive benefits from the measure.

Posner, Stigler, and other economists offered what was basically a supply and demand interpretation of government regulation. The approach was used to illustrate the extent to which regulation confers direct benefits on producers, and is technically inefficient. It also revealed that many regulatory measures that ostensibly protect more generalized interests, such as consumers or the environment, actually serve to generate economic rents for the industries or firms subject to regulation.

Wilson (1980) added another dimension to the private-interest perspective, arguing that both benefits and costs – and winners and losers – had to be incorporated into theories of regulation. Wilson's main contention was that the distribution of costs and benefits of regulation determined which groups in society competed to have influence in the regulatory process. In any given instance, the benefits and the costs of regulation could each be highly concentrated or highly diffused. Wilson reasoned that the situation of highly concentrated effects (benefits or costs) created a strong incentive for affected groups to protect or advocate their interests in regulatory policy and decision making. This suggested a natural linkage between the study of regulation, and research and writing on interest-group politics.

Regulation as Policy Instrument

A third body of literature on regulation emerged as a result of, and alongside, the development of a general theory of instrument choice (Doern 1978). As Linder and Peters explain, governments 'have a number of tools at their disposal for exercising their influence over the economy and society. These tools range from simple exhortations to complex tax and benefit schemes' (Linder and Peters 1989, 35). Regulation is a key instrument within this spectrum of choice. The basic contention of instrument-choice theory is that the various instruments are substitutable and that the policy process involves governments choosing among them. Choice may be in part based on efficiency. The primary factor, however, is political rationality *writ large.*

The theory of instrument choice posits that choices about the preferred policy instrument are resolutions of courses of action rationally pursued by political actors – politicians, bureaucrats, and interest groups – seeking to maximize their self-interest. The key to unlocking the choice, it is claimed, lies in understanding the political rationality of the three games dominated by these actors. Explanation of the choice of instrument is therefore sought in the leading actors in each game through the quantity and quality of information available to them, the formal and informal rules under which they operate, and the goals they pursue as holders of offices and as self-maximizing individuals.

A leading example of the instrument-choice perspective as it applies to regulation is the 1982 study by Trebilcock, et al. for the Economic Council of Canada. This study attributes the heavy use of regulation in Canada and elsewhere to the instrument's perceived low cost in comparison with other instruments. Trebilcock and his colleagues examine in great detail the political rationality of politicians choosing between the agency mode for regulation and the much more traditional regulation by executive department. The goal assumed to dominate in the process of choice is re-election. Among the speculations is that politicians consider the departmental mode to be more responsive to political will, and therefore turn to it when they anticipate having to make constant marginal adjustments in regulatory policy, or even when the main policy objectives for regulation have been settled but the costs to be incurred in ensuring that regulatory officials maximize the appropriate objectives are calculated to be low relative to the agency mode.

Despite allowing scholars to think about regulation in a new, dynamic, and expressly comparative way, the instrument-choice perspective has several important weaknesses. Empirical analysis has been limited for the most part to the question of why *politicians* choose regulation. The interests that regulation can serve for other policy actors, such as regulatory officials and other bureaucrats, and for private-sector organizations and individuals, have been ignored. The latter approach suggests treating the choice of regulation as a policy community-wide exercise, not one restricted to a closed shop of elected representatives.

Another advantage of extending the instrument-choice theory of regulation beyond politicians is that it encourages us to question the decidedly secondary importance Trebilcock and his colleagues assign to technical efficiency. For some actors, considerations other than political rationality may be relevant, such as their familiarity with regulatory administration or their prestige in the regulatory process. Moreover, the downplaying of technical efficiency in instrument-choice theory may be especially problematic in an era of restraint in government. At such times, it seems reasonable to think that the calculus of instrument choice is likely to put a premium on achieving efficiency and effectiveness rather than other sorts of rationality.

Regulatory Theory in the 1980s and 1990s

A concerted effort has been underway since the early 1980s to strengthen even further the theoretical side of the study of regulation in North America. This reflects, in part, a simple desire by regulatory scholars to keep pace with developments in policy theory. Another key factor has been the proliferation of deregulation initiatives (especially in the United States) and regulatory reform initiatives (especially in Canada).

Scholars turned their attention in the opening years of the 1980s to the determinants of regulatory outcomes. The outcomes to be explained ranged widely. Moreover, there was considerable debate in the literature about what the main determinants were in each case and how they exercised their influence. One of the strengths of this literature as it emerged was its explicit comparative base.

An early contribution to the latest generation of literature stressed the importance of political institutions and political and administrative values in determining regulatory outcomes.[3] Brickman, Jasanoff, and Ilgen (1985) concluded in their highly regarded study of toxic chemical regulation in the United States and Europe that the distribution of regulatory power within government and between state and societal interests (e.g., whether it is fragmented or highly concentrated) and between legal and bureaucratic practices are leading factors in regulatory outcomes. The authors claimed that the structural characteristics of the regulatory system 'are conditioned in turn by the larger context of state–society relationships,' especially different conceptions of the appropriate role of government in society (Brickman et al. 1985, 307). The significance of these factors for regulatory outcomes lies, according to these authors, in their intermediary effects on the nature of interest-group politics and the types of policy analysis entering the regulatory process.

Similar arguments were made by Kelman (1981) and Badaracco (1985). Kelman explained differences in the American and Swedish processes for occupational safety and health regulation in terms of different traditions of business–government relations. To account for similarities in other outcomes, he referred to a common professional ideology among regulatory officials. Badaracco's study of vinyl chloride regulation found that particular patterns of institutional arrangements 'load[ed] the dice' in favour of either cooperative or adversarial regulatory processes.

While these early studies greatly advanced our understanding of regulation in modern capitalist societies, they were still not without significant shortcomings. Of particular note was the crudeness of the models of the politics of regulation. Highly selective sets of explanatory factors and imprecise causal relations between variables generated interpretations that were not only out of step with the complex realities of regulation, but also hindered assessing the comparative importance of different determinants of regulatory outcomes and integrating knowledge.

To help remedy these shortcomings, Derthick and Quirk (1985) used a more sophisticated argument about how convergence between three main variables – leadership from regulatory agencies that were independent of the political executive and unconstrained by rigid mandates and from the courts, economic analysis that was successfully transplanted into political debate, and ineffective industry lobbies – explained deregulation in the airline, trucking, and telecommunications sectors in the United States. The account by Harris and Milkis (1989) of major shifts in trade and commerce and environmental regulation in the Reagan years was based on a conceptual distinction between quantitative shifts in regulation, which result from incremental adjustments in regulatory policy, and qualitative shifts, which emerge from a clash between new and old ideas about the regulatory regime and consequent institutional change. Vogel (1986) also made a very significant contribution to the push for rigorous statements about the determinants of regulatory outcomes in his comparative analysis of how the characteristics of political regimes influence national styles of regulation.

The search for more scientific explanations of regulatory outcomes has lately taken yet another step forward under the guidance of scholars inspired by innovations in policy theory. Much of this work is related to the challenge of explaining the new pattern of politics of pesticide regulation in North America. The overhaul of the American pesticide regulatory system in the mid-1980s intrigued students of public policy and regulation because it defied several long-standing tenets of interest-group theory and the private-interest perspective on regulation. It proved particularly difficult to use existing analytic approaches to explain why long-time adversaries were suddenly willing to compromise over the terms of a new regulatory system and join forces to present Congress with a predigested proposal for statutory reform arrived at through private negotiations. The pesticide case also raised important theoretical questions about the effectiveness of the Reagan administration's attack on regulation.

For Bosso (1987, 1988) and Nownes (1991), the overriding question was why Congress did not legislate a new regulatory framework despite the formation of a powerful pro-reform coalition of non-governmental interests. Both scholars took their cue from recent developments in policy theory and looked to the post-war pesticide policy subsystem for an explanation. According to Bosso, the answer lies largely in the dynamics of a temporary coalition representing environmentalists and the chemical pesticide industry, the factors driving its formation, and the politics of compromise precipitating its premature demise. A highly fragmented policy process, he says, also stands in the way of Congress moving expeditiously on policy proposals prepackaged by private interests. Nownes presents an even more subtle account of regulatory reform in the pesticide policy community by incorporating a distinction between the agenda-setting and alternative specification phases of the policy process.

The integration of policy community-based analysis with studies of regulation continues – and strengthens – the North American tradition of seeing regulatory scholarship in inherently multi-disciplinary terms. As Bosso and Nownes suggest, the policy-community approach casts vital light on the determinants of regulatory change. For them, the concern is with the constraining power of policy communities in what outwardly appears to be a period of rampant deregulation. A recent examination of pesticide regulatory reform in Canada indicates that trespassing into the policy community domain is equally instructive for understanding how the choice is made about the mode for regulation (Hill 1994). Hoberg's recent work (1993) also owes much to policy community analysis. Its emphasis on the institutional and ideational bases of regulatory politics has greatly facilitated systematic comparisons of regulatory systems and outcomes.

Finally, it is crucial to appreciate the role the practical empirical world has played in strengthening the theoretical side of the study of regulation in the 1980s and 1990s. Regulatory developments in Canada and the United States exposed the inadequacies of many of the existing theories of regulation. Derthick and Quirk (1985) were among the first to recognize the problem. As they noted, the leading schools of thought were unable to explain, let alone predict, the rise of what was loosely called the deregulation movement.[4] They seemed wholly unable to account for the formation of powerful user-group coalitions that were in favour of less regulation since, in the old theories, users were assumed to have vested interests in maintaining the status quo from which they derived considerable benefits (Hood 1994). Pressure for reform from the regulators themselves was similarly ignored.

Not surprisingly, then, the 1980s wave of regulatory change in North America led to a significant rethinking of the concept of 'deregulation.' Not all sectors deregulated to the same degree. Students of regulation adjusted accordingly, and began to refer to a regulatory continuum grounded at one end with full-blown, highly interventionist government regulation, and at the other with the absence of regulation or, put another way, complete reliance on market forces. Deregulation represented a move along the continuum towards the market end. The milder notion of 'regulatory reform' was coined for changes that landed the regulatory system somewhere between the two end points of the continuum. The main advantage of the revised terminology was that it moved beyond the dangerous tendency to see regulation in simple 'more' or 'less' terms.

The new, more subtle conceptualization of (de)regulation was extended to macro-level studies of the regulatory state. In Canada, especially, the notion of different mixes of regulation offered a much more accurate picture of what had happened during the 1980s and, indeed, what continues to happen in the 1990s. There might be less economic regulation in some sectors; there were also instances, however, where social regulation was being increased, sometimes to compensate for reduced economic regulation (e.g., airline and rail safety). As Schultz (1990) pointed out, the Canadian regulatory state was not disappearing, but was rather being 'recast.'

Two key American regulatory scholars have 'looked backed' at the North American experience in the 1980s with a view to systematically assessing the state of theories of regulation. Peltzman (1989) identifies serious gaps in the theorizing regarding alternative models for regulatory organization and the impact of organizational structure on regulatory performance. For Kahn (1990), the need – a growing one – is to be able to explain and understand what he calls 'asymmetric' (de)regulation. By this he means not only the phenomenon of differential experiences across the regulatory terrain, but also the increased interpenetration of markets by regulated *and* unregulated firms (e.g., in the case of telecommunications carriers and cable operators).

What to Learn? The Practice of Regulation

Regulatory learning is hardly just the preserve of regulatory scholars. We also need to examine some of the major developments and innovations in the world of regulatory practice in North America over the past two decades. Practice has sometimes changed in response to fresh conceptual and theoretical insights. On other occasions, regulatory practitioners have carved out their own direction as a result of the very pragmatic need to make regulatory programs and policies work. This section focuses on four issues related to regulatory practice: the management of regulation, the effects of restraint in government, proposals for regulatory flexibility, and regulation and competitiveness.

Regulation had become a discredited instrument in the eyes of many policy actors as early as the late 1970s. The theme of regulatory failure, by now predominant in the academic literature, spilled over into government. Analysts and policy makers on both sides of the Canada-U.S. border viewed regulation as a leading cause of double-digit inflation and of the continent's poor and still-declining economic performance. The maze of bureaucratic red tape associated with many regulatory systems was blamed for bringing the economy to a standstill, especially by the small-business lobby.

Other manifestations of regulation's failure became widespread as well. These included:

- The increased ability of regulated interests and others to bypass regulatory systems, often owing to technological developments (e.g., microwave technology versus plain old telephone service)
- The perceived inability of regulation to achieve even the simplest policy objectives
- Massive unaccountable and unresponsive regulatory bureaucracies that engaged not just in implementation but also in policy making
- The size of the regulatory burden, as measured by the 'true costs' of regulation, and government's apparent preference for taxation by regulation

Regulation had also failed from an ideological standpoint. Neo-conservatism gained currency in the United States and, to a lesser degree, in Canada throughout the 1980s. For its proponents, continued resort to regulation was incompatible with the substantially reduced role for government in society and the economy that they considered both necessary and desirable.

In the mid-1990s, regulation has been remarkably transformed in North America. It is now increasingly conceded that new forms of regulation, not its absence, *may be* the best means to achieve public policy goals in some of the areas where government is perceived to have continuing responsibilities. The about-face is partly attributable to the kinds of significant advances in knowledge of the political economy of regulation that were described in the previous section. A more important factor, however, has been the acceptance by policy makers that regulation is a tool of government, that it, like other tools, can be used more or less effectively, and that it must, in fact, be managed in light of fiscal and other realities.

Managing Regulation

Regulatory management is distinct from deregulation and regulatory reform.

Deregulation focuses principally on the quantity of regulation, and regulatory reform on the quality of regulation. Regulatory management, on the other hand, embraces a longer-term view of regulation and the regulatory state. It is concerned with government- and state-wide issues such as the aggregate costs of regulation, consistency and coordination among regulatory systems and priorities, alternatives to traditional command and control regulation, accountability, and transparency. The management perspective on regulation rests on a relatively sophisticated appreciation of the political economy of regulation.

It is fair to say that in both Canada and the United States regulatory management has matured into an integral element of the central management functions of government. This can be seen very clearly in the development of government-wide regulatory processes. While the Canadian and American models have often been driven by significantly different political contexts, they have evolved in broadly similar directions over the past decade in terms of their essential institutional arrangements and the complementary management tools that have been adopted.

Consider the Canadian case. In the early 1980s the federal government was responsible for 146 different regulatory programs, employing 34,500 officials (Canada 1986b). The cost of administering these programs was estimated to be $2.7 billion. The true cost of regulation was closer to $30 billion when compliance costs for the private sector were taken into account. Against this backdrop, the Canadian government launched a concerted, explicit policy for improving regulatory programs and policies.

The federal regulatory policy was announced in February 1986 (Canada 1986a) and updated in 1992 (Canada 1992). The policy embraces the theme of 'smarter regulation,' and it obliges departments and agencies to undertake regulatory impact analyses (a close cousin of the economist's cost-benefit methodology) to show ministers and the public that the benefits of regulation 'clearly outweigh' the costs. The policy also introduced a number of reforms designed to enhance public participation in the regulatory process, such as prepublication of all upcoming regulatory initiatives in the *Canada Gazette*, a Citizen's Charter of Regulatory Fairness, obligatory periods for public comment, and an annual Regulatory Plan.

Responsibility for implementing the federal regulatory policy resides with a central review body that is charged with managing regulation across the government. This body, the Regulatory Affairs Division of the Treasury Board Secretariat, acts as a gatekeeper to Cabinet for all regulatory initiatives, and performs other functions related to horizontal regulatory review, such as providing policy leadership and advice to departments and agencies, undertaking evaluation of regulatory programs and policies, liaising with the private sector, facilitating inter governmental consultation, and developing expertise in regulatory affairs across the government through training activities and programs.

The federal regulatory policy hinges on the idea that regulation is much like other governing instruments in at least one key respect. With its use subject to much closer scrutiny, supporters argue that the overall effectiveness, efficiency, and fairness of government regulation can be achieved. Scrutiny is supposed to come from ministers and Cabinet (through the Special Committee of Council, which is responsible for approving new and revised regulations), from departmental and agency regulators, from regulatory analysts at the Regulatory Affairs Division, from regulatees, and from the general public. The regulatory policy also places its faith in using scrutiny by quantitative assessment to improve regulatory outcomes and outputs and, thereby, to achieve efficiency gains in the economy.

There is long-standing debate in Ottawa and elsewhere about the extent to which the federal regulatory policy has been successful. The Auditor General evaluated the 1986 reforms after they had been in place for two years (Canada 1989, 343–57). While praising the objectives and the extent to which the reforms had clarified the lines of accountability for processing regulations, the Auditor General's report was highly critical of how the reforms had been implemented, especially in four major regulatory departments. It recommended, among other things, that the central review agency strengthen its role by selectively conducting in-depth reviews of the regulatory impact analyses done by departments and the information they submitted for the annual regulatory plan. A 1991–2 assessment of the federal regulatory process undertaken for the House of Commons Standing Committee on Finance adopted a more general line of criticism, contending that the greatest need was for improved regulatory analysis throughout the regulatory system (Stanbury 1992).

In the United States, concerns about improving political accountability for regulation and centralizing and coordinating regulatory priorities led to the establishment of a government-wide regulatory review process centred in the Office of Management and Budget (OMB) and therefore subject to presidential oversight. The foundation of this process was set in February 1981 with the promulgation of President Reagan's Executive Order during the administration's first week in office (Eads and Fix 1984). It created a set of substantive principles for all regulatory agencies (i.e., federal departments and executive branch regulatory agencies) to follow 'to the extent permitted by law.' This included the following requirements: that 'regulatory action shall not be undertaken unless the potential benefits to society for the regulation outweigh the potential costs to society'; that 'among alternative approaches to any given regulatory objective, the alternative involving the least net cost to society shall be chosen'; and that 'major' regulations shall be accompanied by a regulatory impact analysis. The order also established a formal but relatively undefined mechanism for OMB oversight of the agencies' regulatory activities.

The regulatory review process assumed a more defined shape over the next decade (McGarity 1991; Pildes and Sunstein 1995). With promulgation of Executive Order 12498 in 1985, the regulatory agencies were required to submit annual regulatory plans to OMB for review and *de facto* approval. This made possible the publication of the Regulatory Program of the United States, which every year contains a detailed discussion of all proposed regulatory actions that might be costly or controversial and which constitutes another tool for planning and coordinating regulatory priorities across the executive branch agencies (OMB 1994).

The latest major changes to the regulatory review process are a by-product of President Clinton's commitment to reinvent the U.S. government. Executive Order 12866, issued in September 1993, declares that 'only such regulations as are required by law, are necessary to interpret the law, or are made necessary by compelling public need, such as material failures of private markets to protect or improve the health and safety of the public, the environment, or the well-being of the American people' should be put into effect (reprinted in 5 U.S. Congress Supplement 1993). The order directs the regulatory agencies to assess available alternatives to regulation and to pay greater attention to issues of risk when making regulatory decisions.

Perhaps the most significant aspect of the Clinton administration reforms, however, is the effort to clarify the allocation of authority among the executive branch agencies, the White House, and the OMB's Office of Information and Regulatory Affairs (OIRA). OIRA's status in the regulatory process has long been uncertain and, not surprisingly, contentious from the standpoint of the agencies and private-sector actors. In recognition of this, Executive Order 12866 outlines specific procedures regarding OIRA review. For instance, the order sets a ninety-day time limit on the review process, requires OIRA to provide a written explanation if it decides to return a regulatory proposal to an agency for additional review, and obliges OIRA to keep a publicly available log of all written communications and all substantive oral communications with people outside the executive branch.

But regulatory management involves more than government-wide review processes. It also encompasses intra-organizational reforms, or changes in the way regulation is dealt with inside government departments and agencies themselves. In Canada the leading federal regulatory departments – Agriculture and Agri-Food, Industry, and Transport – have undertaken comprehensive regulatory audits since 1992 to assess the effectiveness of their programs and policies.

Where necessary, the departments have publicly rejustified their regulatory activities. This is considered a basic step in 'tackling the regulatory burden' (Canada 1992).

The Clinton reforms in the United States include other types of intra-organizational approaches to improving regulatory management. Executive Order 12866 establishes the agencies as the principal regulatory decision makers. It also requires each regulatory agency to appoint a regulatory policy officer who will be involved 'at each stage of the regulatory process' and will be responsible for furthering the regulatory philosophy and principles enunciated by the president. As Pildes and Sunstein (1995) suggest, this may signal a shift towards the view that a regulatory process where power resides disproportionately in a central OIRA-like body is neither the only blueprint for the reinvented American regulatory state nor the preferred one.

The latest innovation in managing regulation in Canada is inspired by the increasingly popular public management concept of 'service quality in government.' The 1992–3 report of the House of Commons Standing Committee on Finance recommended using management standards or the general principles of quality service to improve the implementation of federal regulation (Canada 1993, chap. 7). The committee recognized that ongoing regulatory reform depended on sustaining crucial momentum across government, and contended that the management standards approach would greatly assist the process of institutionalization.

The idea of using ISO 9000–like management standards in the federal regulatory process was endorsed formally by the Treasury Board Secretariat in 1994 (Canada 1995, App. B). Standards have been written and implemented for four aspects of the regulatory process after extensive discussion with departments and stakeholders in the private sector: policy development and analysis, consultation, notification, and training in regulatory affairs. The hope is that standards will offer an avenue for enhancing the management of regulatory programs (e.g., by forcing regulators to assess a fuller range of reasonable alternatives, both regulatory and non-regulatory, when contemplating regulation), but also for establishing a stronger framework for accountability and audit.

Restraint in Government

In one crucial sense, budgets have traditionally had very limited influence on the regulatory activities of governments in North America. The size of direct expenditure programs is constrained by appropriations and ultimately by government tax revenues. Regulation, on the other hand, is an off-budget item. The total costs associated with regulatory programs and policies are not reflected in the government budget. Instead, these kinds of programs and policies are 'paid for' by the firms and individuals who must comply with them.[5]

Regulation's deceptive low cost has meant, in the past, that regulatory decisions could be – and were – made without regard to budgetary cost factors. The situation is fundamentally different in the 1990s age of restraint in government. With restraint, regulators, like other public administrators, are required to 'do more with less.' In the case of regulatory officials, the challenge translates into regulating better – and sometimes less – and at a reduced cost to the taxpayer and the private sector.

One of the most common strategies in Canada for cutting back in the regulatory area is cost recovery. With cost recovery, those who are regulated are required to contribute to the direct costs of providing regulatory 'services.' This approach has helped regulators such as Canada's Health Protection Branch sustain million-dollar cuts to their operating budgets without abandoning their regulatory obligations. Nonetheless, it raises significant concerns about the potential for capture, about fair and equal access to the regulatory process, and about which costs are shared. These concerns have been heightened by recent research suggesting that, in the pesticide and drug areas in Canada at least, some parties are willing (and able) to pay for more efficient and effective regulatory service from government (Hill 1994). The literature on regulatory negotiation also presumes, and indeed shows, that stakeholders are prepared to shoulder part of the financial burden of designing regulatory programs and systems (Fiorino 1988).

Another strategy for reducing government spending in the regulatory area is reforming the organizational arrangements through which regulatory programs and policies are delivered. Senior policy makers in Canada have long been intrigued by the possibility of consolidating regulatory programs concerned with food inspection into a single agency. The magnitude of savings to be derived from this kind of reorganization is unfortunately highly uncertain. What *is* clear, however, is that governments are being forced to design regulatory systems that are organized and operate along non-traditional lines (involving, for example, delegations of power to the private sector or alternative methods for ensuring compliance) and that the implications of the service-delivery perspective on regulation – where regulation is considered a service provided by government to various clients – have not yet been carefully evaluated (Sparrow 1994).

The realization that pressures to reduce government spending will not abate in the foreseeable future has raised fears in many quarters of 'reduced' regulation. Reduced regulation is often equated with less government intervention in areas where citizens continue to want protection from the rigours of free market forces. However, reduced regulation also points to the real possibility of less effective regulation, especially at the compliance and enforcement end. Compliance and enforcement activities tend to be the most expensive items for government in administering a regulatory program or policy. At the same time, reducing resources in this area of the regulatory process has potentially far-reaching effects, since compliance and enforcement are critical to the overall legitimacy of government's use of regulation.[6] The challenge for regulators, as many in North America have already discovered, is to maintain overall compliance and enforcement levels with fewer resources. This may call for novel approaches based on such things as random sampling and monitoring compliance records, both techniques now used by Agriculture and Agri-Food Canada's Food Production and Inspection Branch.

Trebilcock identifies an interesting dilemma. He observes that there are at least three possible scenarios in this period of government restraint. Governments may be tempted to substitute forms of largely off-budget regulation of private-sector activity, 'even if expenditure instruments are technically the most efficient means of realizing given policy objectives' (Trebilcock 1994, 70). Another option is that governments may rely on ill-advised forms of self-regulation for professionals and business, 'the costs of which are entirely off-budget but which may be either ineffective or may foster antisocial forms of collusion.' Last but not least, he suggests that politicians may resort to taxes rather than regulation, mainly because taxes have revenue-raising potential.

Trebilcock's logic rests on the Stiglerian insight that regulation shifts the costs of public policy onto individuals and firms, and therefore seems to allow government to find ways to pursue social and economic goals without boosting government spending. The general message, Trebilcock tells us, is that the choice facing regulators and policy makers generally has changed and that the technical, distributional, and political implications of using regulation must undergo a major reassessment as we reinvent the regulatory state.

Related to Trebilcock's underlying fear of increased resort to regulation is the concept of 'regulatory budgeting.' Proposals for a regulatory budget are not new in Canada or the United States. There was, however, a resurgence of interest in Washington in 1995–6. The basic idea is to create a mechanism analogous to an expenditure budget for regulation. The regulatory budget would set a limit for the total 'regulatory outlays' for each agency (i.e., the total compliance costs agencies could impose on the private sector). The agencies would then be required to decide, within this framework, which rules they could afford and which they could not. Supporters of regulatory budgeting contend that this framework offers an effective way to estimate and control the aggregate costs of regulation. They also believe that it increases accountability to the public by facilitating the measurement of performance. Recent discussions in the U.S. Congress suggest, however, that the primary advantages of a regulatory budget are political, just as Trebilcock's re-evaluation of the use of regulation would lead us to believe.

Regulatory Flexibility

Regulators in North America are currently considering a variety of means to improve further the effectiveness of government regulation through what is called 'regulatory flexibility.' The idea is very simple: that in designing and operating regulatory systems what matters most is achieving results (i.e., performance), not how the results are achieved.

The surge of interest in regulatory flexibility is attributable to several developments. In part, it reflects the dissatisfaction of policy makers with traditional styles of command and control regulation and especially the high costs of using them. The regulatory flexibility concept is also, however, rooted in shifts in the realm of regulatory ideas. The notion of flexibility shows again the influence that managerialism is having on regulation and regulators in North America. From a legal perspective, the concept of regulatory flexibility manifests a wider trend from autonomous to responsive law.

Regulatory flexibility was the basis for Canada's proposed Regulatory Efficiency Act[7] (Martin 1995). This legislation would have given ministers with regulatory responsibilities discretion to approve alternative means of achieving stipulated regulatory goals, provided health, safety, and environmental objectives were met equally well or better. Such discretion would normally have been activated in response to changes in technology, products, or processes that were unanticipated by the original drafters of the regulatory system. The act would have entitled those regulated to submit 'compliance plans' to the relevant minister outlining how they would meet their regulatory requirements in the new circumstances. If approved, these plans would have become part of the regulatory framework.

The bill's architects and proponents contended that it offered a regulatory version of 'having your cake and eating it too,' that it would have lowered the costs of compliance and improved overall compliance. Opponents, on the other hand, saw it as continuing the regulatory state's dangerous trend towards unaccountable, private-interest government. One of the principal concerns was that regulated parties would not have equal access to the resources necessary to propose alternative schemes for compliance.

Regulation and Competitiveness

In the 1990s regulation's link with competitiveness has spawned yet another new phase in 'reinventing regulation.'[8] The link between regulation and a strong, internationally competitive economy is now arguably the most compelling rationale for regulatory reform among policy makers in North America.[9] Multinational firms consider the favourableness of the regulatory environment when they make location and marketing decisions, with consequent implications for domestic levels of investment and employment. Furthermore, regulations can constitute significant non-tariff barriers to trade. Where they do interfere with the free flow of goods and services, national regulators are generally obliged under world and regional trade agreements such as the General Agreement on Tariffs and Trade (GATT) to take steps to remove them.[10]

The competitiveness rationale for effective management of regulation has champions at the senior most policy levels. In Canada it was a major theme in the 1992 report of the federal Steering Group on Prosperity and in Industry Canada's 1995 policy paper on 'Building a More Innovative Economy.' U.S. president Bush directed his Council of Competitiveness to take the lead in implementing regulatory reforms to ensure that new regulations hurting growth in the economy were stopped and that those contributing to growth were speeded up. Vice-President Gore's National Performance Review and his subsequent Common Sense Task Force also embraced competitiveness as a driving factor in the search for reinvented regulation.

Finally, the connection between regulation and competitiveness has had a direct effect on the tools used by national regulators. In the past, regulation and its reform have been considered in principally domestic terms – for example, how to improve public participation in the regulatory process, or how to do better regulatory analysis. The competitiveness push, combined with the ongoing need to reduce government spending, leads regulators to resort more and more often to what might be called an international division of labour in the regulatory area. Regulatory officials in both Canada and the United States increasingly rely on the techniques of mutual recognition and harmonization with regulatory standards set in other countries. This is necessary to meet trade obligations, and may also coincidentally lead to savings in administrative costs in the long run. Again, however, policy makers have reservations. The international division of labour associated with regulation may constrain national sovereignty in inappropriate ways, for instance by limiting the ability of national regulators to promote and achieve domestically determined policy and program goals.

Conclusions: Possible Lessons for Regulation in the UK

Learning can plainly be about specific regulatory techniques and processes and the circumstances in which they are more or less likely to be employed successfully in the UK. This version of regulatory learning has happened in the past, most famously in the early Thatcher years, when the American rate-of-return concept was investigated and adapted in the price-cap model used for public utility regulation. Similar cases of learning can be found in other areas of regulation in the UK, such as food safety.

Despite these developments, regulation remains, on the whole, a relatively undeveloped area of theory and practice in the UK. The most significant academic contributions have come from economists and legal scholars (Majone 1991; Ogus 1994). The economists have tended to be mainly concerned with market structures, the principles of price regulation, and public utilities. Legal scholars, for their part, have generally been interested in the procedural aspects of regulation. Evaluations of regulatory programs and policies, work on institutional questions, and conceptual and theoretical development are less present than in Canada and the United States.

The state of the field in the UK is perhaps readily explained. On the one hand, the British preference for nationalization in the post-war, pre-Thatcher years was simply inconsistent with a concern about regulation. It was assumed that publicly owned corporations, combined with ministerial discretion, would always 'behave in the public interest. And, if they strayed, the elected minister to whom they putatively reported would quickly bring them into line' (Stelzer 1990, 59). No formal regulation or regulatory framework was accordingly deemed necessary.

Institutional factors are also part of the explanation. Regulation and regulatory policy making have always had very low visibility in Britain because of the cabinet focus for policy and decision making and the attendant traditions of secrecy and confidentiality in a parliamentary system of government (Majone 1991). Scholars who might otherwise have 'seen' and investigated regulation have also been hampered by the regular mixing of regulatory and non-regulatory policy objectives that goes on, by the prevalence of informal procedures in regulatory decision making in the UK and of British conventions regarding the machinery of government (such as a preference for granting regulatory functions to ministers and their departments rather than specialized regulatory bodies) and by an approach to statutory drafting that leaves little room for delegated legislation and statutory instruments (Ogus 1994).

If a fuller investigation of the emerging UK regulatory state is the objective, it is useful to recall the two questions that have driven the chapter's analysis – What to learn? and Why learn? – and what the North American experience suggests in response. Consider initially the What to learn? question. The chapter has revealed the existence of a well-developed regulatory literature and two comparatively mature regulatory states across the Atlantic. At the heart of both developments is the emergence of concepts, principles, and models that have been used to improve our understanding of the political economy of regulation, including, for instance, the theory of instrument choice and the principles of regulatory management. This set of analytical devices and organizing principles is the terrain most fertile for regulatory learning in the UK. The potential for learning is especially strong in the absence of a fully developed made-in-Britain alternative.

Equally important on the learning front, the North American regulatory experience provides a basis for drawing out the full extent of the UK regulatory state. In the eyes of a North American student of regulation, much of the UK regulatory state is hidden artificially. The British custom is to see little difference between law and regulation or between different kinds of policy and decision making, and this, in turn, translates into a definition of regulation in the UK that appears to be limited, arbitrarily, to regulation by the new regulatory offices. In fact, as other chapters in this book show, there is a long history of government regulatory activity in Britain, and the newly created utility regulatory offices are only the latest organizational form. It seems only appropriate that the scope of the study of UK regulation should be adjusted to enable the total nature of the regulatory state in Britain, in all its complexities, to be laid bare and investigated.

Broad theoretical concerns aside, it is certainly important not to overlook the lessons that might be drawn from specific areas of the North American regulatory experience. Many of these have been discussed in earlier sections of the chapter, such as alternative organizational arrangements for regulation with different loci of responsibility, accountability, and control, the role of stakeholders and pressure groups in the regulatory process, and the techniques and processes for managing regulation, from parliamentary oversight to training programs in regulatory affairs.

Another slice of the North American experience may be especially apposite for Britain. An extensive literature and practice has developed in Canada and the United States relating to regulation and intergovernmental relations (e.g., Schultz and Alexandroff 1985; Hoberg 1991). This may be a useful starting point for thinking about the regulatory implications of Britain's membership in the European Union.

We are now left with the why question. The case for regulatory learning is an efficiency argument, at least in part. Distilling lessons from the experiences of other jurisdictions, other fields, and even other periods of time is a way for policy makers to avoid mistakes and take advantage of successes. But learning has other rationales as well. The cross-fertilization of regulatory models and approaches is likely to produce innovative analyses in the academic community and innovative solutions in the world of regulatory practice. Moreover, increased familiarity in the UK with the concepts, principles, models, and theoretical perspectives informing the study of regulation in North America lays the groundwork for accumulating knowledge about the political economy of regulation in the UK in a way that is maximally conducive to genuinely comparative (i.e., cross-country) and global analyses.

Stelzer reminds us that learning is a two-way process, from North America to the UK and from the UK to North America. This chapter has focused on the former. The latter should not be disregarded. 'Serious students of regulation on both sides of the Atlantic,' Stelzer writes (1991, 60), 'are hoping that a process of continued intellectual cross-fertilisation is now underway.' At its best, the learning process is more akin to a merger than a bypass. Furthermore, the process must extend beyond narrow regulatory techniques to the general study of regulation and the regulatory state. The North American regulatory experience examined in this chapter ought to be seen, in short, as a valuable source for guiding the intelligent (re)thinking of regulation that must be undertaken in the late 1990s in the UK, Canada, the United States, and elsewhere.

NOTES

1 For a fascinating, Pulitzer Prize–winning analysis of the development of the study of regulation in the United States as seen through the eyes of three eminent regulators (Louis D. Brandis, James M. Landis, and Alfred E. Kahn), see Thomas K. McCraw, *Prophets of Regulation* (Cambridge, Mass.: Belknap Press 1984).

2 The benefits of the multi-disciplinary approach to understanding regulation are pointedly illustrated in Roger G. Noll, ed., *Regulatory Policy and the Social Sciences* (Berkeley: University of California Press 1985). See especially Noll's own piece, 'Government Regulatory Behavior: A Multidisciplinary Survey and Synthesis,' 9–63.

3 It also reminded us of the limits of the term 'North American literature on regulation.'

4 On the general problem of explaining policy reversals in the regulatory area and elsewhere, see Christopher Hood, *Explaining Policy Reversals* (Buckingham: Open University Press 1994), especially chapters 1 and 2.

5 These costs are substantial. It has recently been estimated that the costs of regulation in the United States total $668 billion per year, or about $7,000 per household.

6 The issue of compliance has very slowly been taken up by a very small number of regulatory scholars. A key contribution is Sparrow (1994). See also Ayres and Braithwaite (1992). It is interesting to note that compliance is an area where some of the leading analyses have come from scholars in the UK.

7 An Act to Provide for the Achievement of Regulatory Goals through Alternatives to Designated Regulations and through Administrative Agreements, first introduced in Parliament in late 1994. The proposed legislation has encountered numerous obstacles and, as of September 1996, it was unlikely that the bill would be reintroduced in its present form.

8 The term derives from David Osborne and Ted Gaebler's best-selling *Reinventing Government* (New York: Plume 1993). Policy makers in North America rely on the rubric of 'reinventing regulation' to symbolize the ongoing need for regulatory reform.

9 Nonetheless, the impact of competitiveness forces on regulatory decision making has occasioned very little serious analysis from scholars. An exception, a suggestive but preliminary one, is Donald Haider, 'The United States–Japan Gateway Awards Case of 1990: International Competition and Regulatory Theory,' *PAR* 56, no. 1 (Jan.–Feb. 1996): 9–20. Haider contends that theories of regulation do not currently take adequate account of global industry forces and interests in domestic regulatory decisions.

10 Note, in particular, the World Trade Organization Agreement on Technical Barriers to Trade, the North American Free Trade Agreement's Articles on Technical Barriers to Trade (chap. 9), and Article 405 of the Canadian Agreement on Internal Trade.

REFERENCES

Ackerman, Bruce A., and William T. Hassler. 1981. *Clean Coal/Dirty Air*. New Haven: Yale University Press.

Ayres, I., and J. Braithwaite. 1992. *Responsive Regulation: Transcending the Deregulation Debate*. Oxford: Oxford University Press.

Badaracco, Joseph L., Jr. 1985. *Loading the Dice: A Five-Country Study of Vinyl Chloride Regulation*. Cambridge, Mass.: Harvard Business School Press.

Bernstein, Marver. 1955. *Regulating Business by Independent Commission*. Princeton: Princeton University Press.

Bosso, Christopher J. 1987. *Pesticides and Politics: The Life Cycle of a Public Issue*. Pittsburgh: University of Pittsburgh Press.

– 1988. 'Transforming Adversaries into Collaborators,' *Policy Sciences*, 21, no. 1:3–22.

Brickman, Ronald, Sheila Jasanoff, and Thomas Ilgen. 1985. *Controlling Chemicals: The Politics of Regulation in Europe and the United States*. Ithaca: Cornell University Press.

Canada. 1986a. Office of Privatization and Regulatory Affairs. *Regulatory Reform Strategy*. Ottawa: Supply and Services Canada.

– 1986b. Task Force on Program Review. *Regulatory Programs*. Ottawa: Supply and Services Canada.

– 1989. *Report of the Auditor General of Canada to the House of Commons*. Ottawa: Supply and Services Canada.
– 1992. *Budget of the Government of Canada*. Ottawa: Department of Finance.
– 1993. House of Commons. Standing Committee on Finance. *Regulations and Competitiveness*. 1st Report of the Sub-Committee on Regulations and Competitiveness. Ottawa: Supply and Services Canada, January.
– 1995. *Regulatory Policy 1995*. Ottawa: Treasury Board.
Derthick, Martha, and Peter J. Quirk. 1985. *The Politics of Deregulation*. Washington: Brookings Institution.
Doern, G. Bruce, ed. 1978. *The Regulatory Process in Canada*. Toronto: Macmillan.
– 1979, 'Regulatory Processes and Regulatory Agencies.' In *Public Policy in Canada*, In edited by G. Bruce Doern and Peter Aucoin. Toronto: Macmillan, 158–89.
Eads, George C., and Michael Fix. 1984. *Relief or Reform: Reagan's Regulatory Dilemma*. Washington: Urban Institute Press.
Economic Council of Canada. 1979. *Responsible Regulation*. Ottawa: Economic Council of Canada.
Etheredge, Lloyd S. 1981. 'Government Learning: An Overview.' In *The Handbook of Political Behavior*, edited by S.L. Long. New York: Plenum.
Fiorino, Daniel J. 1988. 'Regulatory Negotiation as a Policy Process.' *Public Administration Review* 48, no. 4 (July–August): 764–72.
Francis, John. 1993. *The Politics of Regulation: A Comparative Perspective*. Cambridge, Mass.: Blackwell.
Hall, Peter A., 1993. 'Policy Paradigms, Social Learning and the State: The Case of Economic Policy-Making in Britain.' *Comparative Politics* 25, no. 3, 275–96.
Harris, Richard A. and Sidney M. Milkis. 1989. *The Politics of Regulatory Change: A Tale of Two Agencies*. Oxford: Oxford University Press.
Heclo, Hugh. 1974. *Modern Social Politics in Britain and Sweden: From Relief to Income Maintenance*. New Haven: Yale University Press.
Heidenheimer, Arnold J., Hugh Heclo, and Carolyn Teich Adams. 1990. *Comparative Public Policy: The Politics of Social Choice in America, Europe and Japan*. New York: St. Martin's.
Hill, Margaret M. 1994. 'The Choice of Mode for Regulation: A Case Study of the Federal Pesticide Registration Review 1988–1992.' PhD thesis, Carleton University, Ottawa.
Hoberg, George. 1990. 'Risk, Science and Politics: Alachlor Registration in Canada and the United States.' *Canadian Journal of Political Science* 23, no. 2 (June): 257–77.
– 1991. 'Sleeping With an Elephant: The American Influence on Canadian Environmental Regulation.' *Journal of Public Policy* 2, no. 1 (January–March): 102–32.
– 1993. *Pluralism by Design: Environmental Policy and the American Regulatory State*. New York: Praeger.

Hood, Christopher. 1994. *Explaining Policy Reversals*. Buckingham: Open University Press.

Howlett, Michael, and M. Ramesh. 1995. *Studying Public Policy: Policy Cycles and Policy Subsystems*. Toronto: Oxford University Press.

Kahn, Alfred E. 1990. 'Deregulation: Looking Backward and Looking Forward.' *Yale Journal on Regulation* 7, no. 2:325–54.

Kelman, Steven. 1981. *Regulating America, Regulating Sweden: A Comparative Study of Occupational Safety and Health*. Cambridge, Mass.: MIT Press.

Linder, Stephen H., and B. Guy Peters. 1989. 'Instruments of Government: Perceptions and Contexts.' *Journal of Public Policy* 9, no. 1 (Jan.–March): 35–58.

Lowi, Theodore. 1969. *The End of Liberalism*. New York: Norton.

– 1972. 'Four Systems of Policy, Politics and Choice.' *Public Administration Review* 32: 298–310.

Majone, Giandomenico. 1991. 'Cross-National Sources of Regulatory Policymaking in Europe and the United States.' *Journal of Public Policy* 11, no. 1:79–106.

– 1996. *Regulating Europe*. London: Routledge.

Makkai, Toni, and John Braithwaite. 1992. 'In and Out of the Revolving Door: Making Sense of Regulatory Capture.' *Journal of Public Policy* 12, no. 1 (Jan.–March): 61–78.

Martin, James K. 1995. 'Performance-Oriented Regulatory Programs: A Way to Modernize Regulatory Systems.' Presentation to the New South Wales Regulatory Review Conference, Sidney, Australia, 21 June.

McGarity, Thomas O. 1986. 'Regulatory Reform in the Reagan Era.' *Maryland Law Review* 45, no.2:253–73.

– 1991. *Reinventing Rationality: The Role of Regulatory Analysis in the Federal Bureaucracy*. Cambridge: Harvard University Press.

Nemetz, Peter N., W.T. Stanbury, and Fred Thompson. 1986. 'Social Regulation in Canada: An Overview and Comparison With the American Model.' *Policy Studies Journal* 14:580–603.

Nownes, Anthony J. 1991. 'Interest Groups and the Regulation of Pesticides: Congress, Coalitions, and Closure.' *Policy Sciences* 24, no. 1:1–18.

Office of Management and the Budget (OMB). 1995. *Regulatory Program of the United States Government*. Washington: US Government Printing Office.

Ogus, Anthony I. 1994. *Regulation: Legal Form and Economic Theory*. Oxford: Clarendon Press.

Peltzman, Sam. 1989. 'The Economic Theory of Regulation after a Decade of Deregulation.' *Brookings Papers*: 1–59.

Pildes, Richard H., and Cass R. Sunstein. 1995. 'Reinventing the Regulatory State.' *University of Chicago Law Review* 62, no. 1 (winter):1–129.

Posner, Richard. 1974. 'Theories of Economic Regulation.' *Bell Journal of Economics and Management Science* 5 (autumn):335–58.

Raab, Charles D. 1993. 'Data Protection in Britain: Governance and Learning.' *Governance* 6, no. 1:43–66.

Rose, Richard. 1991. 'What Is Lesson-Drawing?' *Journal of Public Policy* 11, no. 1:3–30.

Sabatier, Paul. 1987. 'Knowledge, Policy-Oriented, and Policy Change.' *Knowledge* 8:649–92.

Schultz, Richard. 1990. 'Privatization, Deregulation and the Changing Role of the State.' *Business in the Contemporary World* 3, no. 1 (autumn):25–32.

Schultz, Richard, and Alan Alexandroff. 1985. *Economic Regulation and the Federal System*. Toronto: University of Toronto Press.

Sparrow, Malcolm. 1994. *Imposing Duties: Government's Changing Approach to Compliance*. Westport, Conn.: Praeger.

Stanbury, W.T. 1992. *Reforming the Federal Regulatory Process in Canada 1971–1992*. Appendix SREC-2 to Canada. House of Commons. Standing Committee on Finance. *Minutes of Proceedings and Evidence*. Issue no. 23, December.

Stanbury, W.T., and George Lermer. 1983. 'Regulation and the Redistribution of Income and Wealth.' *Canadian Public Administration* 26, no. 3:378–401.

Stelzer, Irwin M. 1990. 'Two Styles of Regulatory Reform.' *American Enterprise* (March–April):68–77.

Stigler, George J. 1971. 'The Theory of Economic Regulation.' *Bell Journal of Economics and Management Science* 2 (spring):3–21.

Timney Bailey, Mary. 1992. 'Do Physicists Use Case Studies? Thoughts on Public Administration Research.' *Public Administration Review* 52, no. 1 (Jan.–Feb.):47–54.

Trebilcock, Michael J. 1994. *The Prospects for Reinventing Government*. Toronto: C.D. Howe Institute.

Trebilcock, Michael J., Douglas G. Hartle, J. Robert S. Prichard, and Donald N. Dewees. 1982. *The Choice of Governing Instrument*. Ottawa: Economic Council of Canada.

Wilson, James Q. 1980. *The Politics of Regulation*. New York: Basic Books.

9

Resurgent Regulation in the United States

JOHN FRANCIS

This chapter explores an apparent paradox in recent American politics: this is an era of deregulation, yet at the same time new regulatory regimes continue to form (Ayres and Braithwaite 1992; Harris and Milkis 1989). The paradox is in fact apparent on both sides of the Atlantic. In the 1980s, as the British state withdrew from the direct ownership of important sectors of the economy through privatization, the state began to create (and continues to create) a series of regulatory regimes (Baldwin 1995; Vass 1994; Veljanovski 1991). Calls for deregulation in the United States have been juxtaposed with extensive new regulatory regimes such as the Americans with Disabilities Act and anti-smoking initiatives. Indeed, a number of policy areas, both social and economic, have witnessed the expansion of regulatory regimes. If this is an age of retreat from regulation, why is there such regulatory vigour? The explanatory argument offered in this chapter is that the sources of regulation in the United States are in large measure independent of the forces that have driven deregulation. There is a disjunction between the creation of regulatory regimes and the dismantling or significant reduction of other existing regulatory regimes. This observed disjunction requires some exploration if we are to develop an analytical grasp of the interplay between regulation and deregulation in contemporary American politics.

Deregulation shares many of the same assumptions that underlie privatization, or, the retreat of states around the world from direct involvement in economic production. Deregulation is based, in part, on fundamental shifts from the predominant judgment in the middle decades of this century that the state had the capacity to serve as an effective mechanism for redressing the problems of the market place. Regulatory regimes are brought into existence by a far greater range of conditions than the forces promoting deregulation. A somewhat flight-of-fancy example might make this point. In the last few years a number of western American states have greatly expanded the regulations governing the operation of hot-air balloons. Licensing is required for operators, and permissible flight patterns over nearby communities are prescribed. This regulatory growth is, undoubtedly, a response to the increasing popularity of ballooning and to its potentially intrusive presence in the lives of others. This rise in regulation has occurred in western states, where scepticism about governmental intrusiveness runs fairly high.

Nonetheless, the architecture of these new regulatory regimes is structured in significant ways by the deregulatory critique. Market-driven models of regulation have, for example, gained in popularity at the expense of traditional rule-based compliance models, as became evident in the Clean Air Act of 1990. Market themes are clearly present in a number of recent regulatory regimes.

This chapter begins with a brief review of the arguments that have been successfully deployed to promote deregulation in America. It then examines the recurring conditions that not only sustain existing regulatory regimes but also initiate new ones. The subsequent sections examine four regulatory areas where significant debate and development has taken place in the United States to illustrate the interplay of factors shaping contemporary regulation. These areas are: (1) the regulatory protections provided disabled Americans in the past decade; (2) the technological changes in telecommunications that have opened up new modes of delivery and new possibilities for communication, but have also brought new demands for regulation; (3) the erosion of traditional boundaries in the provision of financial services, as well as the rapidly growing internationalization of capital movement; and (4) the debate over the expectations for property use and the constraints set by environmental regulation on land use. The analysis of these four areas suggests that demands for regulation remain strong. How such regulation is to be implemented, however, is very much open to debate.

The Era of Deregulation

The deregulatory movement has its impetus in contemporary scepticism over the capacity of the state to play the commanding role it played so effectively in the immediate post-war decades. Specifically, the call for deregulation draws from two traditions of critique. First is the view that regulation is ineffective, frequently to the point of perversity. The claim of these critics is often that regulation may achieve just the opposite of what was legislatively intended. The second is the concern that regulation obstructs economic growth.

On the first point, critics argue that regulation has failed because the agencies in charge of regulation are often captured by the forces that they are charged to regulate. Moreover, if they are not captured, they are certainly overwhelmed.

The steady elaboration of regulations and the expanding number of goals that have been set for regulatory agencies have proved burdensome, in the eyes of these critics. The consequence is that an overburdened regulatory administration actually results in 'underregulation.' In short, the simple objectives of regulation cannot be achieved by attempting to meet a panoply of goals, the result then being the paradox of underregulation (Breyer 1993).

The second point, that regulation is hazardous to economic growth, has come to be politically the most persuasive argument in support of deregulation. The claim is that economic growth is obstructed by regulation. These critics identify the market, in its pursuit of growth, as the engine that drives economic advancement. From this critical perspective, regulation is a burden on the economy, at least on specific sectors of the economy. In the United States the debate over whether economic drag is imposed by regulation is often focused on the small-business sector. This sector is judged less able to manage the cost of regulation, and at the same it has come to be seen as the engine of job creation and, therefore, as a stimulus to economic growth.

This critique of regulation, which is found on both sides of the Atlantic, plays out differently in federal systems than in unitary systems. It frequently appears that the critique of the state's regulatory role may be separated by the level of government involved. In the present era, scepticism is at its most intense about the long-standing and commanding role of the national state in providing budgetary and programmatic leadership to resolve contemporary issues. Some critics of the regulatory role performed by central governments are, nonetheless, prepared to grant a significant regulatory role to subnational units of government (Francis 1993).

The current presumption is that when the state needs to play a regulatory role, that role is best performed at the subnational level. This presumption is manifest in the demand for a regulatory shift away from the centre. This shift to the subnational arena raises two concerns: first, the budgetary implications for states undertaking an increased regulatory role are significant; second, many current regulatory issues are not easily captured in a limited political or geographical space. The lament of many American state governors in recent decades is that the federal government's commitment to regulatory regimes has not been matched by budgetary commitments. Regulatory regimes requiring budgetary allocations that are not forthcoming are, in the view of state leaders, unfunded mandates.

Sustaining Regulation

The historic arguments advanced for state regulatory intervention are, as has been noted, diverse, and appear to have a wider range of sources than is found in the deregulatory movement. This chapter concentrates on four frequently employed contemporary arguments for regulatory intervention: fairness, technological change, risk reduction, and what is broadly understood as the appeal to the public interest. What these arguments have in common in the advocacy of regulation is that they draw attention to an apparent weakness in the market and the belief that the market will be unable to address the concerns raised. Moreover, these four concerns are often interactive as ideas in the formation of regulatory regimes.

Fairness

The interaction of the arguments for regulation is quite apparent in the question of fairness as a factor in promoting regulation. Over the past decade, for example, there have been sharp rises in cable television rates. Such rate increases remove cable service from the realistic reach of needy citizens. The question of fairness arose when it became apparent that a significant minority of the population could not afford cable television. Thus, demands for rate regulation have immediately followed sharp increases in cable rates. Another example is the introduction of new health-care procedures. Suppose, for example, an effective but expensive genetic screening test for breast cancer were developed. A number of regulatory questions would then follow. Who should have access to the new technologies? How should the level of risk inherent in such procedures be determined? Should such procedures be licensed to provide quality standards? Should medical administrators be required to supply the service to those who can least afford it at a regulated rate?

Technology

Technological innovation is often followed by demands for new regulations. The remarkable changes that have taken place in telecommunications open up dramatic new possibilities to consumers. Often such innovations call into question existing regulatory regimes, which have been tied to then-current telecommunications technologies or specific geographical areas. Technological change may lead to the breakdown of existing product barriers, or may provide new products and services that transform existing markets. Technological change may also have broad political geographical consequences, as new products transform our understanding of time and space. The development of the railway, for example, provided an attractive, steady, and sure system of transport for heavy products, but raised the spectre of a single supplier with little interest in constraining costs or expanding services. For some observers, perhaps the modern cable supplier is the contemporary equivalent of the nineteenth-century railway.

Current examples of technological changes that challenge existing regulatory regimes are particularly evident in telecommunications and financial services. The role of technological change is increasingly apparent in telecommunications, where traditional walls between wireless services and services by wire have collapsed. In financial services, traditionally distinct areas such as brokerage houses and banks have converged in the range of services they offer. The political consequences are significant: as dynamic markets blur lines, subnational and even national jurisdictions lose their respective administrative credibility. In financial services, the internationalization of capital flows has seriously challenged existing national regulatory structures.

Risk Reduction

The goal of reducing risk is the other side of the task of restoring consumer confidence (Breyer 1993). Sustaining consumer confidence is the aim of the establishment of regulatory standards for specific products or services such as food, drugs, or financial transactions. Risk-reducing regulation is often driven as much by producer interest as it is by consumer interest. In many cases regulatory proposals arise from the providers of the products and services themselves. New issues in risk regulation are ever occurring. During the past several years, E. coli outbreaks from undercooked food or unpasteurized fruit juice have induced new regulations governing food-product preparation. Often the providers of the products are the first to seek an official vetting of what they sell in order to reassure the public that the product acquired by the consumer meets a specified set of standards that minimize risk.

Public Interest

In political analysis, public values are often thought to carry much less weight in discussions of policy than was the case in past generations. But a review of Congressional debates suggests the continuing force of appeals to public values. The character of a specific community in extending recognition and regulatory protection to the values it judges important is powerfully persuasive in Congress and in many state legislatures. Examples of policy makers privileging a specific set of values as community values or, more forcefully, as the nation's public interest range from the creation of parks and monuments to the limitation of the content of speech. One frequently controversial example is in land-use planning, and through it deciding when community values should outweigh individual choice in determining property use (Fischel 1995).

In a number of social regulatory areas, there remain broad levels of popular support and deep commitment on the part of specific constituencies to particular regulatory regimes. Some of most comprehensive and extensive environmental regulatory regimes, such as those for clean water and air quality, possess fairly solid levels of support (Hoberg 1993). Even one of the most deeply divisive areas of regulation in the United States, the protection of endangered species, continues to enjoy support. Although the Endangered Species Act is commonly portrayed by its critics as obstructing economic development and discouraging productive human activity, nonetheless it continues to enjoy a measure of broad support in American public opinion and deep support of specific, strong environmental constituencies.

The interplay of these four factors in promoting regulation is pervasively apparent. They do not always produce new regulation, but recent examples suggest the presence of a powerful interplay of fear, innovation, fairness, and community values. To take just one area, proposals for the regulation of the content of telecommunications are increasing in debates over whether to restrict what comes over the Internet, what is broadcast in children's television, and what is communicated on a college campus (Klingler 1996).

In summary, regulation is sustained by events and constituencies that are largely independent of the forces advocating deregulation. For the past two decades, as Paul Pierson has pointed out (1996), countries on both sides of the Atlantic have undertaken budgetary retrenchment. Yet it is apparent, when outlays in recent years are examined, that the rising political demand to scale back the welfare state in Europe has been largely ineffectual. Pierson's explanation is that the successful resistance to budgetary cutbacks is in large measure to be attributed to the fact that the groups favouring cutbacks are distinct from the web of communities that are now woven into the fabric of the welfare state and are committed to its sustenance. There is a reasonable parallel to the conflict over the regulatory state, where advocates of regulation form constituencies distinct from those arguably more broadly grounded favouring of regulatory regimes.

Illustrations of Contemporary Regulatory Regimes

The past decade has been characterized by debates over regulatory regimes and over growing demands for deregulation that have often been intense. The examples taken up in this section have all been recent and heated. They are by no means exhaustive of the regulatory debates in the United States, but they are clearly important, and they illustrate the impetus for regulation that in a number of areas may be the product of inertial conditions, while at other times is the result of dramatic social and economic change. Yet the argument in this chapter is that the factors that sustain or promote regulation are distinct from the forces that have driven deregulation. The concerns about fairness, technological change, risk reduction, and public values discussed above are recurrent themes in the examples. At the same time, there is an insistent interplay between the concerns driving regulation and demands for growth and the commitment to the private sector. This interplay has structured the challenges and often the architecture of the regulatory regimes discussed in this section, which are those in the areas of telecommunications, financial services, and environmental regulation, and those that ensued from the Americans with Disabilities Act. These four areas also illustrate the general proposition that regulation is driven by constituencies and communities. In the case of the Americans with Disabilities Act, the sustained and energetic efforts of its supporters were greatly aided by the absence of strong opposition in the general population. In the environmental regime, the situation is substantially different, for existing regimes are under challenge by groups vigorously opposed to them, and confronted by groups and public opinion broadly supportive of the existing regimes.

The Creation of a New Regulatory Regime: The Americans with Disabilities Act

Over the past several decades, interest among public-policy makers in the difficulties facing people with disabilities has grown. Dealing with these disabilities may require transportation systems, redesigned entrances into public buildings, workplace education, and extensive changes in many areas of social and economic relations. The argument that is frequently advanced for regulatory intervention is that the disabled, through no fault of their own, face barriers that restrict their opportunities to participate in society.

George Bush, when asked to comment on which domestic initiative of his presidency gave him the most pride, responded with the American with Disabilities Act. The act was a piece of legislation that was also strongly supported by Senator Dole (Seelye 1996) who said that among his proudest achievements in his thirty-five years in Congress was helping to enact it. Dole defended bipartisanship in disabilities issues and endorsed accessibility as a good thing for business. The act is a remarkable piece of regulatory legislation, easily as extensive as affirmative action in its impact on employment opportunities and businesses. It is an act with significant budgetary implications for both the private and public sectors. Indeed, it is framed more broadly than Title VII, the employment discrimination title of the Civil Rights Act. According to the Americans with Disabilities Act, the term 'disability' means a physical or mental impairment that substantially limits one or more major life activities or is perceived as so doing. Examples of people with these impairments range from the hearing or visually impaired, to the recovering drug addict or alcoholic, and to a person regarded, however incorrectly, as having a contagious disease. The act does not extend regulatory protection, however, to individuals using illegal drugs (Huefner 1991). It forbids discrimination in access to and participation in public programs and services, transportation, employment, and public accommodations. Nondiscrimination is understood to mean the removal of barriers to full participation. The act requires, to the maximum extent possible without undue hardship, the removal of architectural, communication, or transportation barriers that obstruct participation of the disabled in the economy. The regulatory objectives go beyond what might be understood as striking down traditional discrimination against a vulnerable group, to a regulatory regime that facilitates participation by the disabled throughout society and the economy (Watson 1994). The act also provides for auxiliary services and aids to assist the disabled in securing important governmental services such as education. The goal is that by regulation the diverse group identified as the disabled will not only have discrimination removed, but will be assisted in participating in mainstream American life. It is estimated that approximately 10 per cent of the American population have disabilities that fall within the parameters of the act (Burkhauser and Daly 1994). As a regime, the Americans with Disabilities Act is undoubtedly a very significant regulatory initiative of the past decade. It has had, and continues to have, massive implications for regulation on every level of government. It is thus all the more remarkable that support for it remains bipartisan.

Technological Change and Telecommunications

There is little question that the introduction of new technologies has raised formidable challenges to the set of regulatory regimes that took shape with the development of television in the aftermath of the Second World War. From television to the Internet, rapid technological changes have swept the telecommunications industry in recent decades. The regulatory regimes of the 1950s, 1960s, and 1970s were characterized by clear segmentation of services. Newly released films were shown in theatres. Film production and distribution companies were not allowed to own chains of movie studios. An important distinction was drawn between made-for-television films and film distribution through theatres. Actors rarely shifted between the two forms of entertainment. Television itself could best be described as a regulated market with a high threshold for entry. Three great broadcasting companies dominated the television market, but they were restricted from major ownership of local stations. Independent stations operated at the margins of the industry, and the not-for-profit public television stations held only a small share of the audience. With such segmentation and high entry thresholds, regulatory concerns in television focused on issues of public access and fairness.

Radio was a far more competitive market with a good deal of segmentation. Music and news largely dominated the medium. As with television, the regulatory issues in radio were often issues of public access and fairness. During the same period, telephone service was a regulated national monopoly. The principal regulatory issue in the latter area was the nature of cross-subsidization between long-distance and local telephone services. The telephone services monopoly was vertical as well as horizontal, for it extended to the manufacture and development of telephone equipment (Cohen 1992).

The regulation of telecommunications was for many decades guided by the Telecommunications Act of 1934. Relying on existing models of regulation in the public utilities industry, the act focused on the common carrier as a transmitter of communication. The common carrier was regulated to provide the consumer with just and reasonable charges and protection from unreasonable discrimination (Crandall and Waverman 1995; Klingler 1996). By the 1970s, it had become apparent to critics of the telecommunications industry that competition was an increasingly viable option for the provision of telephone service. Through the confluence of technological change with the changing regulatory climate, the regulatory regime substantively shifted to economic models of regulation by means of the introduction of competition. By the end of the 1970s, judicial action had broken the monopoly of American Telephone & Telegraph over local service, and facilitated interstate competition (Teske 1990; Brock 1994). In the early 1980s the rise of cable television not only provided a challenge to the three major television networks, but was itself challenged by the interest of telephone companies in providing video entertainment through the telephone lines. By the Cable Act of 1984 Congress provided protection to the new cable firms from the telephone services.

In the 1990s computing reached a level of consumer access that once again introduced a significant change in telecommunications. The Internet provided a great array of communications around the globe with words and video images. By the middle of the 1990s the distinctions that were so important in the 1950s no longer held. Films moved easily and quickly from movie houses to television. Films on video cassette could be rented for home consumption, and often made more money for the producer than film-house distribution. The written word could be faxed over phones, and videos could be transmitted as well. The proliferation of telecommunication technologies has paradoxically led to convergence, in that any one medium is capable of transmitting a greater range of communications than in the past. This mixture of technological change and shifting regulatory models provides the backdrop for the contemporary debates over the regulation of telecommunications. During the 1980s home computing became increasingly accessible to the middle class. Home computing, along with the academic and business use of computers, introduced a new dimension to telecommunications. The creation of the Internet has led to rapid communication by computer throughout the 'plugged-in' world. For growing numbers of people, the 'net' became a vast public forum for an ever expanding number of topics and, thereafter, a market place for an increasingly diverse array of products and services.

The intersection of technological change and competition through the rise of the VCR, cable, and satellite provided consumers with unprecedented choices. Moreover, if hundreds of channels offered insufficient choices, then consumer could turn to video cassette libraries. This rise in segmentation is, of course, consonant with the increased number of choices achieved by technology. Yet there is something of a paradox in this segmentation, for technological innovation has allowed the convergence in delivery of the same product from traditionally distinct telecommunications industries. Telephone lines can deliver film, written communication, and cable-like television. The emergence of the Internet created in one location a technology that combines the market place, personal communication, and entertainment. The changing environment brought by technology and new perceptions of competition has produced a new environment for regulatory change, but has by no means meant the end of regulation (Pavlik 1996). In 1996 Congress passed and the president signed the Telecommunications Reform Act, undoubtedly the most sweeping act in sixty years of modern telecommunications regulation. By any measure, powerful regulatory impulses were at work in the 1996 act (Klingler 1996). The general structure of the mechanisms for licensing broadcasters remains unchanged. What has changed is that cross-ownership is now permitted. Television networks can own cable companies and vice versa. Klingler points out that the renewal of a licence is simply based on whether the station serves the public's interest, not on whether the licensee possesses a major market in one or more areas or is deeply involved in more than one form of telecommunications. In this sense, the act may be fairly judged to be a deregulatory initiative; the changed regulatory regime for telecommunications no longer evidences the fear of a dominant carrier that was there in the past. What best characterizes the act, however, is that it embraces a common regulatory direction for telecommunications as a whole rather than a segmented regulatory strategy for a series of discrete industries.

In the current regulatory regime, considerations of fairness are the apparent in the control over programming. Discrimination is prohibited in the distribution of the programming that is controlled by cable operators. Regulatory concern over content is also an important theme in the act; channels that broadcast shows with images judged obscene or indecent must be scrambled Perhaps the greatest regulatory issue in telecommunications is where considerations of fairness meet the free market. Can the federal government require cable operators to carry public television and other programming that the operators would not if left to their own preferences? The question pits considerations of market control against the exercise of freedom of speech. By compelling a major telecommunications firm to carry a wide range of broadcasters, a possible consequence is that the firm's freedom of speech is constrained, while the federal government is enabled to regulate the adverse effects of discrimination found in concentrating telecommunications power. The core regulatory principle that has resulted from legislation and court decisions is that access to cable may be imposed on the cable operator as long as it is neutral in content. Regulation for access is thus permitted so long as it does not have undue impact on free speech. This Supreme Court–induced reconciliation between regulatory fairness and free speech allows for the traditional component of regulation to continue unabated in telecommunications by protecting such values as access, non-discrimination, and interconnection, and so we would need to conclude that the traditional impetus for regulation, fairness, is an animating force in the 1996 act (Klingler 1996).

Undoubtedly the Internet is one area of telecommunications that is growing so rapidly and in so many different directions that it seems to defy existing regulatory strategies. For example, efforts such as in the Communications Decency Act of 1996 by Congress to censor content on the Internet have met challenges in the courts. The rise of the Internet is a force for energy and innovation, but it also seems chaotic. It is apparent that the Internet is raising a series of regulatory issues at a rapid rate. Should gambling be permitted over the Internet? Should abusive speech be allowed? Should the sale of goods and services go unsupervised? The Internet suggests impressive possibilities for deception and abuse. The risk of chaos is somewhat reminiscent of the early days of radio, when broadcasting was open to all who possessed sending and receiving units, and the risk of insult and injury became apparent to some observers of telecommunications. (Mackie-Mason, Shenker, and Varian 1996).

As in the early days of radio, there is growing demand in Congress and elsewhere to regulate the Internet in an ever expanding number of areas. Taken as a whole, discrete constituencies can be accumulated into an effective coalition for building a regulatory regime that clearly could turn out to be a powerful supplement to the Congressional action of 1996.

Technological Change and the Internationalization of Financial Services

Perhaps a useful way to think about financial services in the United States is to understand two distinct movements: the steady rise of New York in dominating stock-market transactions and merchant banking within the nation, and the rise of New York as a world financial centre. Both trends are obviously related. The sign of a major financial centre is its capacity to raise significant pools of money for capital investment. The hallmark of financial centres is speculative investment.

The consonant regulatory concern of speculative investors is confidence. Do investors have confidence in the claims that are made on behalf of the investment opportunities that they are being offered? In the 1930s the Securities and Exchange Commission was in part created as a means to return confidence to small investors in the stock market. In the 1980s the junk-bond market and insider trading (investors possessing information not available to others) threatened confidence in the market. The rise of mutual funds, which combine multitude of small investors in large pools for fund managers, probably cushioned the risk to investor confidence during the 1980s. What is proving a greater challenge is again the combination of technological change and the privileging of competition by the deregulatory critique.

Financial centres such as New York and London are still world centres, but impressive changes have taken place. People who search for capital do not need to travel to these cities, for capital will find them as it moves with technological ease around the globe in the search of suitable interest rates and favourable rules of transaction. Great financial centres, both old and new, compete for business and seek to outbid other cities in providing the technologies and regulatory accommodation to attract financial transactions. The other side of the coin is that a number of cities such as Tokyo and even London have concluded that changing the rules to allow openness to new technologies may also shake investor confidence. It is in the internationalization of financial services that regulatory regime creation is still very much a desired outcome, as American commentators have observed. Such internationalization is, nevertheless, elusive in its realization, at least when regimes are constructed within the borders of the United States that in fact need to be constructed as transnational entities. Some view the current debates in financial regulation as evidence of a retreat by the state or at least critical political communities from the regulation of financial services. Just as persuasive a case, however, can be made for the view that changes in technology exacerbate difficulties in establishing workable regulatory regimes. Such difficulties may be observed in a growing number of problems in financial regulation. Money has no doubt always moved across borders with more ease than most states would prefer. The international movement of money is far easier today than it has ever been in the past. Electronically, money moves rapidly and globally in search of profits. The transactions frequently elude regulatory costs imposed by various states. During the 1980s it became apparent that money travelled with relatively few restrictions around the globe. That decade was also a time when the role of the central banks took on new importance for states seeking to maintain some authority in financial affairs. The United States confronted a distinctive dimension of financial regulation: the historical role developed by the states in the regulation of banking. The fear was that powerful national banks would pursue interests independent if not antagonistic to the interests of local communities. The rediscovery of national banking, in both the national and international economies, has been a major development of the last decade. It now seems clear that the role of subnational regulation has been reduced by the construction of immense financial entities that can compete worldwide and assemble the financial base needed to realize this competitive goals.

Perhaps the fear of national banking has been reduced, just as competition has been strengthened, by the breakdown of barriers among various sorts of financial services, such as merchant banks, savings institutions, and brokerage houses. There is an increasing convergence in the range of financial services provided by a wide range of financial organizations. Arguments for competition have broken down barriers that restricted who could sell shares in specific stock markets, for example. The volume of U.S. trade in equities has grown 40 per cent in each year since 1984. Daily non-equity trading is estimated at $1.3 trillion. The growing diversification in financial products has led to the blurring of lines between public and private markets and the growing irrelevance of geographic borders; as a result, existing regulatory structures that are geographically based appear to be increasingly out of date.

There is clear convergence in many of the issues that have reshaped telecommunications and financial services. The uses of the Internet in financial transactions are clearly growing. With this growth comes new challenges to the scrutiny of financial transactions: 'As concern grows about electronic money laundering, cybercounterfeiting and banks runs on the internet [,] regulators in the United States and around the world are scurrying to catch up with the rapid development of electronic money' (Hansell 1996). The secretary of the Treasury, Robert Rubin, has likewise expressed concern about the use of the Internet for cross-border money laundering and tax evasion.

Like the free speech issue, the potential for fraud on the Internet has raised significant Congressional concern. But here the issue is complicated not only by the transborder problem of regulators being unable to track funds moving from one country to another but also by the introduction to electronic deposits and transfers. The federal government is asked on the one hand to transmit payments electronically to individuals, which raises what is already the major concern of protecting the consumer and assuring the security of the recipients of the funds, but on the other hand there is the concern that the security given to the recipients may also provide anonymity to potential criminals seeking to secure cheques for which they have no legitimate claim.

The issue of competition in the worldwide financial service market, in conjunction with the domination of computer-assisted financial services has not reduced the interest in the necessity of regulation but rather has increased it.

A Regime Resisting Deregulatory Challenge: Property and Environmental Regulation

Beginning in the late 1960s and continuing at a significant pace in the 1970s, a remarkable series of federal environmental statutes came into effect in the United States (Hoberg 1993). These include laws governing air and water quality, as well as controls over land use, wetlands, and coastal lands, and protection for endangered species. Taken as a whole, an environmental regime was structured that is woven into decision making on land use at every level of government.

These regulatory regimes have significant implications for the sale, development, and use of property. There can be little doubt that over the years, land use and property values have been affected by these regimes. A local community may define itself through a land-use plan as residential or as rural or in a manner designed to attract economic investment. Local, state, and federal environmental agencies are charged with wetlands preservation, air quality, and water standards (Kincaid 1995).

The last two decades have witnessed the rise of the property rights movement in a number of states (Fischel 1995). The movement seems to be principally motivated by the judgment that in a number of areas environmental regulation is a serious constraint on the use of property and the freedom of the property market (Gotlieb 1989). The environmental regulatory statutes that have generated the greatest resistance are those for wetlands protection, endangered species preservation, and historical preservation. The property rights movement as manifested in Congressional and state-wide initiatives seeks exemption from selected environmental restrictions. The exemptions are sought in part on grounds of disproportionality: that the costs and burdens of protecting an endangered fish or tortoise, to take an example, are so high that a property owner is left with little latitude to use affected properties even as vacation homes or to sell for profit. Property, in the view of such critics, is transformed into a social responsibility rather than an opportunity for its owner. The problem for the larger community is that the issues of economic growth and redirection seem to be removed or at least reduced by regulatory restraints that are not necessarily of the community's making. The traditionally strong relationship between markets and property use is attenuated (Altshuler and Gomez-Ibanez 1993). The relationship between property and environmental regulation plays out in two distinctive and not necessarily complementary ways. On the one hand, it is argued that property owners, in addition to suffering a loss of autonomy, are assuming the social costs of environmental regulation. If, for example, the goal is wetlands preservation and the land the state wishes to preserve might, through draining, be developed for residences, should the state compensate the landowner for the constraints it has imposed? What, if any, is the relationship between what is described as a 'taking' – that is, the state taking ownership rights – and the imposition of a regulatory regime on the owner that severely directs or curtails use? The strategy of the property rights movement is to establish that regulation, at least in some areas and at certain levels of constraint, represents a 'taking' of property by the state (Yandle 1995).

The other dimension of this argument that often proves to be a troubling issue in regulatory discussions is land-use planning as expressed in zoning rules. The argument is often advanced that communities should be able to define the quality of their lives by restricting lot sizes an establishing a balance between residential and commercial uses. But such restrictions generate many of the same issues faced by environmental regulation – that is, they reduce the market possibilities, prospects, and, of course, the autonomy of the property owner. If zoning to achieve community use is a recognized value, how should it be distinguished from the constraints on land imposed by environmental regulation? (Rudel 1989). Recent decisions of the U.S. Supreme Court on the takings issue reflect these tensions (Fischel 1995). In a coastal wetlands case, the court concluded that regulatory restrictions on an owner's plans for building constituted a taking and required compensation. In an Oregon case, a community was prepared to grant a commercial variance to a business owner if the owner would dedicate land for selected amenities, including a bicycle path adjacent to the property; the court found that exchange a form of extramural taxation by regulation.

These rulings should and perhaps did give encouragement to critics of the environmental regulatory regimes. In a number of states and in Congress, efforts were undertaken, by initiative and referendum as well as by statute, to strengthen property owners' discretion at the expense of land-use regulatory regimes by requiring compensation for economic losses caused by regulation protecting endangered species, wetlands, and air quality. To date, none of these efforts has been enacted into law, although their supporters continue to urge the passage of legislation. Challenges to the existing federal environmental regimes were played out in a bill introduced in the 1995–6 Congressional session. The bill would have required a review of all the direct or indirect costs to industry of environmental legislation. If a review were not completed within 180 days, the regulation would cease to take effect. A small agency such as the Mine Safety and Health Administration reviews eighty dangerous chemicals and carcinogens per year. In addition, the bill would compel all regulation to be assessed through cost-benefit analysis. Many people, however, strongly questioned if certain values could easily be calculated. Any single scale of values in dollars as a measurement was unlikely to improve analysis. In June 1996 the bill was abandoned.

It is apparent that the kind of serious challenge to the environmental regulatory regimes created in the 1970s that the bill represented has been largely frustrated. This particular challenge did not succeed, in large measure because it failed to mobilize broad opinion in its favour for exempting property owners from the regimes. Instead, the result has been the converse – a rekindling of support in electoral circles for the existing regimes.

Conclusions

It is a reasonable inference that what is sometimes regarded as a unidirectional trend towards deregulation covers genuine confusion over how to develop a regulatory regime in areas of technological change that make traditional borders elusive. Borders that once separated industries from one another, as well as borders between nations, have eroded to the point that new regulatory regimes need to be constructed. At the same time, the traditional concerns about risk as well as about community interests combine to resist challenges to environmental and telecommunications regulations.

Undoubtedly, the most interesting recent example in the United States is the Americans with Disabilities Act, where a new regulatory regime has been consolidated. The act is an example of a recent regulatory regime that has been brought about by the traditional forces for regulation. Regulations enacted as a result of moral pressure from an organized minority, in conjunction with moral acquiescence, has created the most important civil rights regulatory regime since affirmative action. Regulation thus remains an important force in American politics, albeit in forms responsive to the deregulatory critique.

REFERENCES

Altshuler, Alan A. and Jose A. Gomez-Ibanez. 1993. *Regulation for Revenue: The Political Economy of Land Use Exactions*. Washington: The Brookings Institution.

Ayres, Ian, and John Braithwaite. 1992. *Responsive Regulation: Transcending the Deregulation Debate*. Oxford: Oxford University Press.

Baldwin, Robert B., ed. 1995. *Regulation in Question: The Growing Agenda*. Cambridge: London: Law Department, London School of Economics and Political Science.

Breyer, Stephen G. 1993. *Breaking the Vicious Cycle: Toward Effective Risk Regulation*. Cambridge: Harvard University Press.

Brock, Gerald W. 1994. *Telecommunication Policy for the Information Age*. Cambridge: Harvard University Press

Burkhauser, Richard V., and Mary C. Daly. 1994. 'The Economic Consequences of Disability: A Comparison of German and American People with Disabilities.' *Journal of Disability Policy Studies* 5:25–53.

Cohen, Jeffrey E. 1992. *The Courts and the Divestiture of A.T.& T.* Armonk, N.Y.: M.E. Sharpe.

Crandall, R.W., and L. Waverman. 1995. *Talk is Cheap: The Promise of Regulatory Reform in North American Telecommunications*. Washington: The Brookings Institution.

Fischel, William A. 1995. *Regulatory Takings*. Cambridge: Harvard University Press.

Francis, John G. 1993. *The Politics of Regulation*. Oxford: Basil Blackwell.

Francis, John G., and Leslie P. Francis. 1997. 'Land Use in European and North American Communities: The Limits to Autonomy.' In *Archiv für Rechts- und Sozialphilosophie*, edited by Rex Martin and Gerhard Sprenger. Stuttgart: Franz Steiner.

Gotlieb, Alan. 1989. *The Wise Use Agenda: A Task Force Report Sponsored by the Wise Use Movement*. Bellevue, Wash.: The Free Enterprise Press.

Hansell, Saul. 1996. 'Regulators are Turning a Spotlight on Cybermoney's Snags.' *New York Times*, 19 September 1996:C18.

Harris, R.A., and S.M. Milkis. 1989. *The Politics of Regulatory Change*. New York: Oxford University Press.

Hoberg, George. 1993. *Pluralism by Design: Environmental Policy and the American Regulatory State*. New York: Praeger.

Huefner, Dixie. 1991. 'Brief Summary of Selected Portions of the Americans with Disabilities Act of 1990, P.L. 101–336.' Presentation at the Annual Convention of the National Association of Counties.

Kincaid, John. 1995. 'Intergovernmental Costs and Coordination in U.S. Environmental Protection.' In *Federalism and the Environment: Environmental Policy Making in Australia, Canada and the United States*, edited by K. Holland, F.L. Morton, and B. Galligan. Westport, Conn.: Greenwood Press.

Klingler, Richard. 1996. *The New Information Industry: Regulatory Challenges and the First Amendment.* Washington: The Brookings Institution.

Mackie-Mason, R., J.S. Shenker, and H.R. Varian. 1996. 'Service Architecture and Content Provision: The Network Provider as Editor.' *Telecommunication Policy* 20:203–19.

Marzulla, Nancie G. 1994. 'Property Rights as a Centralizing Organizing Principle.' In *Environmental Gore: A Constructive Response to Earth in the Balance*, edited by John Baden. San Francisco: Pacific Research Institute of Public Policy.

Mathews, Jessica T. 1996. 'Weakening States and More Powerful Non-State Actors.' Presentation to the Council on Foreign Relations, Pacific Council on International Policy, Second Annual Retreat, San Francisco.

Pavlik, John V. 1996. 'Competition: Key to the Communications Future.' *Television Quarterly* 28:35–45.

Pierson, Paul. 1996. 'The New Politics of the Welfare State.' *World Politics* 48:143–79.

Rudel, Thomas K. 1989. *Situations and Strategies in American Land Use Planning*. Cambridge: Cambridge University Press.

Seelye, Katherine Q. 1996. 'Dole Turns to a Pet Cause: People with Disabilities.' *New York Times*, 14 August 1996:A11.

Skrzykl, Clare. 1996. 'Deregulation by Default.' *Washington Post National Weekly Edition*, 4–11 March 1996:6.

Teske, Paul Eric. 1990. *After Divestiture: The Political Economy of State Telecommunications Regulation*. Albany: State University of New York Press.

Vass, Peter, ed. 1994. *Regulating the Utilities: Accountability and Processes*. London: Centre for the Study of Regulated Industries.

Veljanovski, Cento. 1991. *Regulators and the Market: An Assessment of the Growth of Regulation in the UK*. London: Institute of Economic Affairs.

Watson, Sara D. 1994. 'Analysis of the Implementation of the ADA.' *Journal of Disability Policy Studies* 5:1–24.

Yandle, Bruce, ed. 1995. *Land Rights: The 1990s Property Rights Rebellion*. Boston: Rowman & Littlefield.

10

Regulatory Reform and Relations among Multiple Authorities in the United Kingdom

PETER VASS

The regulation of privatized network industries and utilities in the UK is a complex and controversial process.[1] The regulated sectors have different characteristics, different interests are affected by the regulatory processes adopted, and the position of the regulators themselves is different from the traditional structure of accountabilities that operated with respect to nationalized industries and public corporations. In addition, a sophisticated system of incentive regulation has been created that operates on a dynamic, transitional path, and relies on regulatory discretion, flexibility, and balanced judgments. This system is susceptible to political manipulation by interest groups, which are able to exploit public expectations, inexperience, and preconceived ideas. Terms such as profit, monopoly, and public service will in themselves conjure up strong images and associations from the past. The calls for regulatory reform and the analysis of relations among multiple regulatory authorities have therefore to be set within a clear framework of objectives that can be used to test and examine the developments in regulation and evaluate the prospective outcomes.

The chapter therefore starts with an outline of the UK regulatory model and the objectives to be achieved. It is then followed by sections on the multiplicity of actors in a tripartite model of responsibility and on regulatory harmonization of methodological procedure and practice. It ends with conclusions on reform and accountability. In places, reference is made to the technical detail of economic and financial regulation, detail that it is important to understand if a clear judgment is to be made on the success or failure of the regulatory process.

The System of Incentive Regulation in the UK

The new system began with the privatization of British Telecom (BT) in 1984, followed by the remaining 'network' industries over the period to 1997. The

TABLE 10.1 Privatization and regulatory offices

Year	Industry	Regulatory office and regulator
1984	British Telecom (BT)	Office of Telecommunications (OFTEL) Director General: Sir Bryan Carsberg, successor to Don Cruickshank
1986	British Gas	Office of Gas Supply (OFGAS) Director General: Clare Spottiswoode, sucessor to Sir James McKinnon
1987	British Airports Authority (BAA)	Civil Aviation Authority (CAA) Director General: Malcolm Field, successor to Sir Christopher Chataway
1989	Water and Sewerage (England and Wales)	Office of Water Services (OFWAT) Director General, Ian Byatt
1990–6	Electricity (Great Britain)	Office of Electricity Regulation (OFFER) Director General: Professor Stephen Littlechild
1993	Electricity (Northern Ireland)	Office of Electricity and Gas Regulation (OFREG) Director General: Douglas McIldoon
1996	Railway Infrastructure	Office of the Rail Regulator (ORR) Rail Regulator: John Swift
1996–7	Rail Passenger Franchises	Office of the Passenger Franchising Director (OPRAF) Franchising Director: John O'Brien, successor to Roger Salmon

only significant business to remain in 'public' ownership is the Post Office. The sequence is shown in Table 10.1, with the names of the accompanying regulatory office and the regulator. Typically each privatization established a non-ministerial public body to act as the office of the appointed regulator, usually known as the director general. The important development was that the powers and duties of regulation are vested in the individual regulator. The regulator is appointed by the secretary of state for the sponsoring department, but is independent within the statutory duties set out in the respective privatization act.

The statutory duties essentially define the objectives of regulation, but they are set, both for the individual regulator and comparatively between them, in a way that has caused much misunderstanding and public comment. Primary and secondary duties are referred to, and these have on occasion been adduced as proof that regulators might either be susceptible to capture because they are obliged to have regard to the interests of regulated companies, or that their judgments necessarily balance the interests of shareholders and customers. Most attention has been paid to the duties that require the regulators to ensure that the companies can finance themselves. Notwithstanding the use of primary and secondary duties, it is clear that the duties themselves are general in nature and leave the regulator with considerable discretion. Regulators must have regard to the duties, but the only test with respect to whether or not a particular judgment is consistent with them is likely to be the test under judicial review of whether it was so unreasonable that no reasonable person could have made it. In the complex practice of regulation, this would be a particularly stiff test for someone appealing against a regulatory decision, and in practice the courts have not become involved.

The regulatory framework was designed, therefore, to move the regulatory functions further away from the political process and the involvement of politicians, and to give sufficient room for the practice of regulation to evolve, particularly as the regulatory mechanisms to be implemented were new. It is at this point, therefore, that we should ask, what are the objectives of regulation against which regulatory practice and procedure can be evaluated? The following suggests that the primary objective is consumer protection.

Customer Protection

The utilities and network services provided to secure water supply and disposal, energy (gas and electricity), transport, and telecommunications are, for the most part, essential services with a strong public interest element. This is not only for reasons such as public health and the environment, but also to achieve for citizens the possibility of full participation in a modern society. Universal access at an affordable price has become part of the modern political agenda and scheme for the achievement of human rights. It is not surprising, therefore, that regulators' statutory duties include duties to ensure that all reasonable demands for supply are met, that regard must be paid to the needs of the elderly and of those who live in rural areas, and that services must be provided at a common price to all users irrespective of where they live. This is the context for regulation in the UK – effectively a system of public services privately provided.

The next question concerns the discipline on the providers of these privately provided essential services, first, not to abuse their monopoly power and, second, to encourage efficiency. One answer is that where consumers have choice, that is, where there is competition, then the discipline of the market will protect consumers. However, two factors must be taken into account; first, the services might be natural monopolies, such that it would be wasteful to encourage competition; second, at privatization the industry privatized normally has an effective monopoly, even if there is an intention to introduce competition in the longer run.

It is important to distinguish, therefore, between those services (or businesses) for which encouraging direct competition would be inappropriate (e.g., the high voltage transmission and distribution systems) and those that might be competitive after a transitional period (e.g., supply and generation of electricity). There is unfortunately no hard and fast rule! Technological developments in telecommunications have eroded the idea of a natural monopoly in the copper wiring for local access, but even without direct competition in the product market, competition in the capital markets to take over inefficient operations may provide an equivalent discipline on management. Such competition in the market for corporate control has developed strongly, particularly in the electricity sector, once the Government lifted its restrictions (through owning a special or 'golden' share) on the percentage of shares that could be acquired by one shareholder.

Regulatory duties include statutory requirements to promote, facilitate, and secure competition, but this needs to be seen as a means rather than an end in itself. The fundamental objective of regulation – whether by competition or other means – is to protect the customer from the abuse of monopoly power. There are two parts to this regulatory question, however, that are often insufficiently distinguished when comparing the traditional system of rate-of-return regulation with the modern system of incentive regulation by periodic price capping (typically known as the RPI-X system, where RPI is the retail price index and X is a composite factor that ensures the price cap takes account of the regulators' forecasts of improved efficiency and any changing quality of service requirements). First, the objective is to ensure that companies cannot abuse their monopoly power by charging more than the current long-run cost of supply for a reasonably efficient company, based on current knowledge and technology. This can be achieved either by annual rate-of-return regulation that controls profits or by periodic price capping. The second objective is to provide incentives to companies to improve efficiency further than the current forecasts of the long-run cost of supply. If this can be achieved, then overall national welfare is assumed to be increased.

However, to achieve efficiency improvements there will have to be incentives for suppliers to do other than provide a service at the prevailing level of costs (unless one relies on a general argument that a public-service ethos will always encourage managers to seek the most cost-effective service on behalf of customers and the public). The incentive is economic profit, measured from better performance than the regulator's forecasts, where economic profit is defined to be profit over and above that necessary to earn a normal rate of return and therefore to be able to meet the firm's cost of capital. This second element – which comprises the incentive regulation component of the UK system – is the key feature compared with the more traditional systems of rate-of-return regulation found in the United States, which have as their primary rationale the control of monopoly power. Both systems can control the abuse of monopoly power, but the UK system of price regulation rather than profit regulation aims to achieve improved efficiency too. The question then arises, who gains from the improved efficiency, customers or shareholders?

Surrogate Competition and Profit-Sharing

The model of incentive regulation is one that seeks to mimic, or be a surrogate for, a competitive outcome. Perfectly competitive markets put a ceiling on the price for a given quality, and so the regulator sets a price control for a period that gives the maximum price increase allowed, one year's tariffs compared with another (i.e., the RPI-X system). Given the maximum prices, the company has an incentive to cut costs and therefore earn additional profits. Excess profits would not last indefinitely in a competitive system but be competed away, thereby redistributing the rewards of innovation and efficiency. The regulator therefore sets the price cap for a limited period, and takes advantage of the fact that if the company responds to the incentive of profit to improve efficiency further, then that reveals new information on costs, which the regulator can use at the next periodic review to reset maximum prices. If the new information is improved costs, then the next set of maximum prices will be lower than they would otherwise have been. The benefit is therefore passed from being economic profits retained by the company to lower prices for the consumer. The fundamental logic of a periodic price control system is therefore to share economic profits between shareholders and customers, something that has not been widely understood.

In practice, therefore, a periodic system of price capping is a profit-sharing system, and it is the length of the period between reviews that determines the equitable balance between gains to shareholders and customers. Most important in the context of the politics of incentive regulation is to recognize that the system is not a 'zero sum' game (i.e., either shareholders or customers win), but one where, if incentives and regulation work properly, both sides can win. It is in this context that the purpose of profit needs to be better understood (Byatt 1996).

In part this problem is the result of the timing of the distribution of rewards, with accounted profits coming first, followed by lower prices at the 'periodic' review. But it also arises from the public's confusion over the element of regulatory purpose, which is concerned with the control of monopoly power compared with the element that provides the incentive to achieve further improvements in efficiency. The former stigmatizes monopoly profits as a bad thing, and if the regulated industries are monopolies, then any excess profit must also be bad. The fact that the baseline of profit is controlled by regulation and that the purpose of being able to earn excess profits *ex post* is to achieve the provision of new information on costs, not the abuse of monopoly power, is little understood. And the fact that it is little understood leads to a crisis of consent over the system, which we shall return to later when considering the debate on reform.

Reconciling Accounting and Cash Flow

Finally, in terms of regulatory mechanics, it is also important to note that the forecasting procedure for setting the price cap is a means by which cash flows can be reconciled with rates of return. The regulator makes a forecast of capital and operating expenditures necessary for an efficient company to ensure that the quality of service is maintained. The forecast is for the period up to the next review. The series of expenditures is then converted to a single present value by discounting at the agreed cost of capital for the company. This, when added to the opening value of assets for the period, and deducting the value of capital employed at the end of the period, gives the total costs that need to be covered by allowed revenue within the review period. The profile of allowed revenue is optional (e.g., a cut in prices now followed by a lower decline) as long as the present value of the revenue stream, discounted by the cost of capital, is equal to the present value of costs (OFFER 1996).

It is the process of discounting at the agreed cost of capital that ensures the business will be able to pay the necessary interest and dividends to remunerate investors for having financed the company's capital. Accounting concepts and practices merge with the economic cash-flow analysis because the opening and closing asset values will be built up from previous capital expenditure and the amount invested at privatization, less an allowance for capital consumption (i.e., depreciation). The profile of depreciation chosen will affect the distribution of consumer charges over time, but not conflict with the underlying objective of ensuring that the business can finance itself at the cost of capital. We shall see in the section on convergence and methodology, however, that this core methodology has become a critical area of debate because of differences in approach by regulators and through the introduction of market valuations for assets.

The Multiplicity of Regulatory Authorities

Many have analysed the failures of nationalization, and Sir Christopher Foster has incorporated their insights into a broader sweep that starts with rail regulation in the nineteenth century and finishes with the developing policy of natural monopoly regulation for privatized 'network' industries since the flotation of BT in 1984 (Foster 1992). His book contributes to the debate on whether there was a clear and well-defined policy on utility privatization and regulation from the beginning, or whether it, like Topsy, just grew? A book about practical governance, it demonstrates that, although the detail was necessarily painted in as experience evolved, what has happened is consistent with the broad agenda of Conservative political philosophy promoted by Mrs Thatcher. To the critics of pragmatism and regulatory evolution, he answers, 'What is the point of hard and fast rules without experience?'

Nevertheless, pragmatism can still be guided by a broad framework of principles, and the principles of privatized natural monopoly regulation could be clearly identified from the beginning, or could be logically deduced. The objectives of economic regulation having been dealt with, the following section examines the institutional division of responsibility that was designed to create 'independent' regulation with clear responsibilities. It is referred to here as the tripartite model.

The Tripartite Model

The explicit attempt to distance the day-to-day supply of 'network' services from political involvement of the kind that dogged the nationalized industries required a 'technocratic' institutional structure, given that public regulation would still be required to protect the consumer. This structure would require due accountability within a policy framework set politically and enshrined in a broad codification by the law.

The important point, therefore, is to note that while the process of regulation is carried out independently of the government on a day-to-day basis, this should not be taken to mean that the government should be divorced from policy or that the accountability of regulators is necessarily compromized. Debate about regulatory responsibility should therefore be conducted in the wider context of Parliament and government at one end of the spectrum, responsible for policy and the public interest, with the consumer and the general public at the other end. The independent regulators and regulated companies are therefore to be seen as intermediaries, responsible for policy implementation within the broader framework that sets the objectives and criteria by which their activities can be judged.

This is illustrated in Figure 10.1, the arrows showing some of the main directions of responsibility. In particular, it draws attention to the division of the implementation of regulation into three main areas (the tripartite model),

FIGURE 10.1 The UK tripartite model of regulation

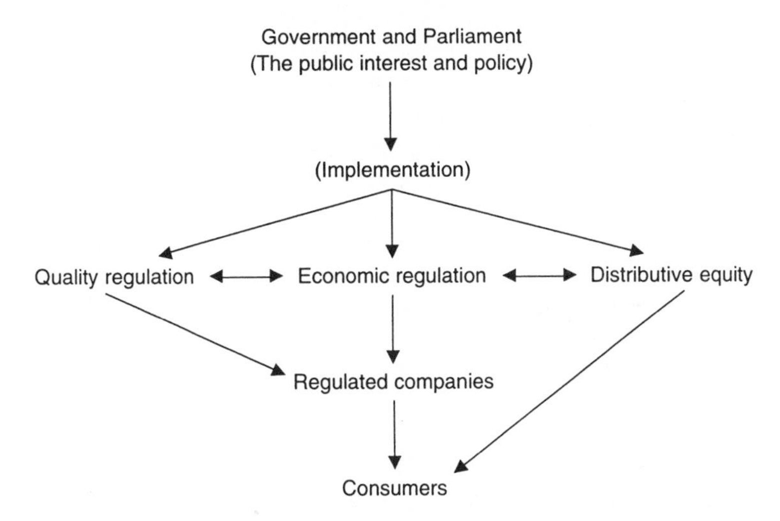

although the division of responsibility between them is not always completely clear, which is discussed further below.

The separation of regulatory responsibilities was required to provide a clearer operational focus to regulation, and in principle it should improve accountability and minimize conflicts of interests within a regulatory agency. The debate on the tripartite division of responsibility was probably most discussed as part of water privatization in 1989, when the dual responsibilities of the regional water authorities for operational services and environmental control was split, giving environmental control to the newly formed National Rivers Authority (NRA, part of the Environment Agency after 1 April 1996). As the chapter by Alan Booker in this book shows, this division helped ensure that the newly privatized water companies did not have the conflicts of interests that would arise from acting, as it was often said, as both 'poacher and gamekeeper.'

While there was no clear government blueprint, the tripartite model allows for a clear distinction between three key dimensions of policy for which different regulatory authorities must take responsibility, although each is about a common issue, that of correcting for market failure: (1) economic efficiency, (2) quality of service specification, and (3) distributive and social justice. With respect to distributive and social justice, the term market failure simply means that the purchasing-power outcome from an unregulated market is one that is not acceptable politically, and hence regulatory agencies step in to correct it in some way (e.g., the Department of Social Security with income support).

Economic regulation is designed to protect consumers from monopoly power. Incentive-based price-cap regulation both protects against monopoly power and promotes long-run efficiency and innovation. Where the business is a natural monopoly, then 'surrogate' competition by regulation remains in perpetuity; where the business is potentially competitive, then regulation that promotes or facilitates the introduction of self-sustaining competition may, in due course, itself be able to wither away. Tariffs should reflect costs, which means statutory non-discrimination clauses. These factors are primarily the responsibility of what have become known as economic regulators, as set out in Figure 10.1 above.

Price, of course, has no meaning without specifying the quality of service to which it refers. Quality of service has various dimensions, including quality of product, continuity of service, environmental impact, and interface with the customer.

The first three have significant cost implications with a distinctive economic aspect, notably the problem of making optimal decisions with public goods, such that, at the margin, the economic benefit of a quality standard equals its economic cost. Standards that are too high raise problems of affordability for essential services; standards that are too low compared with what people are willing to pay reduce the quality of life. Economic regulators have responsibility for setting certain standards, particularly those related to the customer interface and continuity of service, while decisions related to health and safety and environmental impacts have separate institutional regulation (the 'horizontal' regulation of Regime II in the terminolgy of Chapter 2). Once these latter standards are set, it is incumbent on the economic regulator to allow private suppliers to recover costs from customers. Typically, the quality regulators are a direct government responsibility, whether centrally as standard setters (e.g., EU environmental standards) or via enforcement institutions such as the Drinking Water Inspectorate and the Environment Agency, which incorporates the National Rivers Authority, the Inspectorate of Pollution, and waste authorities (Booker elaborates on these tradeoffs in Chapter 12).

Economic regulation (assuming established public-good standards) that promotes incentives to efficiency based on cost-reflective tariffs, erodes cross-subsidies. The tripartite model therefore did not expect economic regulators to be agents of social justice; issues of income distribution, affordability, and income support would remain with government and the social security system. In effect, the government retains the role of distributive regulator. This division in responsibility was clearly expressed, for instance, in early OFTEL annual reports (Burns 1995). However, it is clear that over time economic regulators have been drawn into questions of affordability and universal access, in part to deal with public-service obligations that must be maintained in spite of the introduction of competition, and in part because the government itself has had operational rules that conflict with regulatory equity, such as only paying average levels of income support when water bills vary widely on a regional basis. Public and political pressure then focused on the regulators, forcing them to act.

Five Key Themes

Five aspects that have emerged from the operation of the tripartite model with multiple regulatory authorities and devolved economic regulation are relevant to subsequent questions of whether, and how, to reform the regulatory system. This is because the public perception of these issues in particular has suffered from misunderstanding and has been an area on which public commentators have often pre-judged the issue.

Enhanced Transparency

The fact that different regulatory responsibilities fall to separate institutions, even though they are linked financially in their consequences for customers or particular classes of customer, means that the opportunity for public debate – and hence the possibility of improved public understanding – has been increased. Improved transparency has provided a firmer foundation for achieving public consent for the new system. Alan Booker's account in chapter 12 of the public debate from 1991 to 1994 between NRA and the economic regulator OFWAT over the 'cost of quality' is a clear example, one that led to an improvement in ministerial accountability, given that the government had to declare its responsibility to try and make rational – or at least explicit – environmental decisions. The most important outcome of this debate was that the Environment Act, which set up the Environment Agency with effect from 1996, has an explicit requirement for standards to be set on a cost-benefit test. It is fair to say now that the distinction between economic and quality regulators in terms of the financial context and policy perspective is less than it was.

Comparative Regulatory Competition

Independent sectoral regulation of the network industries has demonstrated many features of competitive evolution towards best practice. Regulatory procedures and the content of consultation papers have benefited from cross analysis and quotation and from the interchange of regulatory staff (e.g., moves by senior economists, such as Dr Eileen Marshall's from OFFER to OFGAS, and Chris Bolt's from OFWAT to ORR). The experience has been codified, where appropriate, as in the Competition and Service (Utilities) Act of 1992, where the powers of the regulators to set quality of service standards was harmonized and competition requirements reinforced. Such convergence is itself a test of the framework of principles for incentive regulation. An instance is the need for a clear separation of natural monopoly from potentially competitive businesses and the post-privatization restructurings that have been a consequence; another is the regulatory pressure to improve on the structures inherited from privatization, most notably British Gas, which has finally de-merged into its trading arm (Centrica) and its natural monopoly business (TransCo) as part of the international company (BG plc), each with separate listings on the stock exchange. BT has had internal accounting separation in spite of remaining a single entity. Regulators have regular meetings and there have been proposals for a college of regulators from the water regulator, Ian Byatt. The benefits of this process argue against consolidation of regulators into a composite regulatory agency.

The Accountability Debate and Special Interests

The tripartite model, with devolved responsibility to 'independent' economic regulators, has been cited as a loss of democratic accountability. This does not seem to have been the case, either in theory or in practice. The experience of regulators appears to be one of heightened accountability for their actions (Vass 1994), and if accountability is the process by which those responsible for decisions can be subjected to public scrutiny and debate about the decisions they have made, then the assertion seems to have little substance. In fact, it seems more plausible to argue that, often, those who play the loss of accountability card are simply making the point that they do not agree with a particular regulatory decision or with privatization in general. These are legitimate views, but they are a separate issue from accountability. In a fundamental sense the 'independent' regulators have a 'lagged' line of accountability to the democratically elected government and ministers who appointed them. If there is a failure of regulation, reappointment need not follow. In the meantime, due process, proper systems of consultation and publication of information, and the general requirement on regulators to give reasons for their decisions (which in practice is observed), can serve well the interests of public accountability.

One under-researched area is the accountability of the regulated companies for the way in which they lobby in the regulatory system. The companies have criticized the powers of regulators regularly, but it is important to analyse their criticisms objectively and recognize the companies' own self-interest in protecting their monopoly power. This analysis has to be balanced against constructive and sensible criticisms of potential regulatory flights of fancy, however theoretically respectable.

One major misunderstanding concerns the issue of information asymmetry between the company and the regulator. The 'incentive' regulatory system is, essentially, an adversarial system, and some degree of allowed asymmetry has to exist, otherwise companies would have no incentive to outperform the regulators' forecasts. A regulatory system that allows economic profits to be earned provides the context in which company managers will explore the opportunities to outperform, without knowing in advance whether those profits can be achieved.

It is not a question, therefore, of asking a company how efficient it can be and expecting it to tell the regulator truthfully. It probably doesn't know the answer itself. The issue is to provide the incentive context by which the opportunities can be explored. The danger is that if the perception of information asymmetry is pushed too far, it questions the legitimacy of incentives and economic profit, and may lead to a situation whereby the regulatory framework emphasizes rate-of-return and encourages company managers simply to comply with the regulators' forecasts.

EU and UK Regulatory Philosophy

Public-service obligations have also been a strong European argument for preserving publicly owned national monopolies, in spite of the development of funding arrangements for ensuring that all players in the market place contribute to meeting the cost of social obligations. Recent initiatives by the EU, and its intention to achieve the single market in goods and services, have demonstrated that utilities are not a special case and that they cannot rely on public-service arguments to protect their monopoly power. Article 90 is not an avenue for exclusive rights, and any protection afforded has to be shown to be proportionate to the need and not achievable by other means that are consistent with the single-market provisions (Hancher 1996). The lesson of the UK versus the EU experience to date is not, perhaps, so much one of an underlying difference of opinion about the appropriate framework for regulating utilities, but one about the means to progress from a wide continental consensus on the place of national monopolies in providing public services to one in which the public service obligations are retained, but within a framework of private provision and management. The speed of development of the directives to liberalize utility markets will reflect the power of entrenched special interests (i.e., the national monopoly suppliers) who, quite naturally, have been the major defenders of the existing regime. For the EU itself, and the Commission, there is also the need to minimize the bureaucratic distance from the impact of their decisions on member states.

The process of formulating directives needs to have a more explicit element of public communication – and hence accountability – if the special interests of particular member states are not to delay the likely long-term outcome, given the framework and objectives set by the treaties. An example would be the recent UK Environment Act, whereby explicit statutory reference is made to the need to consider costs and benefits in arriving at environmental standards.

Consumer Protection Is Paramount

We noted earlier that the statutory duties of the economic regulators set out primary and secondary duties. One primary duty is to ensure that the privatized businesses can finance themselves (i.e., 'earn a reasonable rate-of-return'). Consumer protection is often termed a secondary duty. These semantic distinctions have caused enormous confusion and public doubt, most notably by reinforcing the belief that regulators are there to serve the needs of companies, or at best to balance the interests of the companies with those of the consumer (Vass 1995).

Regulatory practice, however, has constantly emphasized the primary aim of consumer protection, and it would seem more appropriate to characterize regulation as having a primary objective, subject to certain constraints. The constraints themselves, however, are aimed at long-run consumer protection (a constraint to ensure finance is, in practice, to stop a position of prices that are too low in the short run, which would endanger long-run continuity of supply). Hence the legislation might have more clearly said that its primary objective was consumer protection, *subject to*: (1) the ability of an efficient provider to secure the minimum necessary rate-of-return, and (2) to meet all reasonable demands for supply.

The proof of the primary objective of consumer protection is found most distinctly in the consultative texts issued by the regulatory bodies for periodic reviews of price caps and in the annual reports prepared by regulators, most notably their overviews and introductory statements. It is important, nevertheless, to distinguish the question of what the regulator's primary objective might be from the question of whether the regulator has done his or her job well. Much public criticism of the regulators about their roles in apparently balancing the interests of the companies more favourably than those of the customer comes from the *ex post* observation of excessive profits. The performance of regulators in achieving their primary objective is a different issue, one to be addressed from the question of their *ex ante* intentions.

The primary objective of consumer protection, and the use of terms such as 'reasonable' or 'no undue' discrimination indicate that the separation of economic from social and distributive justice is likely to be imprecise. Also, the legislation may incorporate specific constraints, such as 'having regard to the needs of the young, the old, the disabled or those living in rural areas.' While it is clear that regulators have developed a social and community dimension to their activities, particularly with respect to affordability, an underlying theme is still that the vast majority of customers are 'economic' customers for the companies, and they either require proper management of the customer-company interface or can be rationalized through having wider economic benefits, for example, network externalities in telecommunications. Where uneconomic universal service obligations have to be met, the question is a practical one of designing schemes that create 'fair' competition.

Relationships between Economic Regulators

Ministers appoint sectoral regulators for a fixed term. It is not surprising that the regulators are drawn from a relatively small pool, and that there are certain common characteristics among them. Ian Byatt (OFWAT) and Clare Spottiswoode (OFGAS) had Treasury connections; Sir Brian Carsberg and Sir James McKinnon (respectively the first telecommunications and gas regulators) had regulatory experience of setting accounting standards; Don Cruickshank (OFTEL) had management experience in a public service body, the National Health Service; and Professor Stephen Littlechild (OFFER), as well as Carsberg and Byatt, have academic links and specialisms that focus on economic and financial regulation. John Swift, QC (ORR), may be an exception, both by having been appointed prior to privatization and by being a lawyer.

The regulatory system has evolved within a strongly articulated defence by the regulators of 'incentive' regulation with periodic review of price caps, typically every five years. The tensions of the untypical first period following privatization, particularly in water and electricity, have led, however, to some fragmentation of the regulators' consensus. OFGAS, in its price review for 1997 of the natural monopoly business, TransCo, has introduced annual formula profit-sharing proposals and pay-as-you-go proposals that are a significant departure from accepted regulatory practices (Burns, Turvey, and Weyman-Jones 1995). British Gas and Transco have indicated their willingness to accept formula profit-sharing, but they are strongly opposed to the pay-as-you-go.

There are a number of arguments against formula profit-sharing:

1 / erosion of incentives;

2/change in the equitable balance of the existing periodic price-cap system (see in particular Viehoff 1995);
3/loss of statutory rights for companies if they participate in symmetrical loss sharing;
4/loss of stability and continuity, increasing the probability of renegotiation of the terms of the regulatory contract; and
5/weakening of discipline on regulators themselves to achieve a balanced judgment on the price cap

There are also strong arguments against pay-as-you-go, which undermines the proper relationship of revenue to accounted costs. The existing approach blends a cash-flow model (which forecasts an internal rate-of-return equal to the cost of capital) and appropriate current consumer charges based on the following: (1) operating costs; (2) current cost of consumption of assets (measured by depreciation); and (3) financing charges based on what the investors actually paid for the assets (O'Neill and Vass 1996).

It is curious indeed that the gas regulator should have been reported in the press as saying that one reason for a pay-as-you-go approach is that a regulated company cannot be trusted with the money when it is a cash generator (i.e., when depreciation plus retained profit exceeds capital investment). Ian Byatt, the water regulator, has participated in the public consultation by OFGAS and written to the *Financial Times*. The debate raises the fundamental question: what limits are there on independent regulation, particularly when the decisions in one sector could have ramifications for regulatory practice in the others? Earlier we have noted the benefit of evolution, but the wider test is always that evolution takes place within the framework of regulation set down by the government and under which the regulators were appointed.

Who guards the generic framework of regulation within which the 'club' of regulators work is therefore becoming an important question. There are a number of institutional responses to that question.

First, the Monopolies and Mergers Commission (MMC), in the absence of a specific code of regulatory practice and particularly on the methodology for resetting X at periodic review, has played an important role. Companies that do not accept a regulator's proposals to amend the licence can appeal to the MMC, and in the case of the BAA, it is the MMC that carries out the price review following a reference from the CAA. Its reports on BAA (first and second periodic review), Scottish Hydro's appeal from OFFER, the appeal of South West Water and Portsmouth Water from OFWAT, and the British Gas inquiry in 1993 have amply demonstrated its role. The MMC itself, however, is but one element in the regulatory chain, and the government can decide not to accept an MMC recommendation, as it did in the case of restructuring British Gas. It preferred, for reasons of industrial policy, to retain an integrated British Gas, while introducing competition more quickly than had been recommended in the 1993 report. Each decision provides a potential precedent and clarifies the underlying principles of regulation. Similar reasoning can be applied to the decisions not to refer takeovers to the MMC (which provides a discipline on management through the capital market), except where vertical reintegration might pose a threat to competition in the market. Overall, however, the effectiveness of the MMC as an appeal mechanism for the companies and as a bastion against arbitrary regulatory power must be maintained, and it would be inappropriate if regulators were able to disregard the substance of MMC decisions. That has to be reserved for the government.

Each case, of course, has to be judged on its merits. Professor Littlechild's reopening of the electricity distribution review in 1995 may be seen as having broken the regulatory contract. More to the point, it demonstrated that regulation exists within a framework of public consent. Properly carried out, the logic of the regulatory system can secure consent, and be defended politically. When an error of judgment is made, particularly if it comes at a time of strong public disaffection, the regulatory reality is that regulation has to match political reality. The Trade and Industry Committee supported the reopening of the review in its subsequent inquiry into aspects of electricity supply, but it asked why the process had led to an outcome that could not prevail. It concluded that the same outcome should never be allowed to happen again. The effect on regulators, I am sure, has been salutary, and it is unlikely that the same pattern of incidents could happen again because information gathering and the audit of companies' financial and engineering circumstances will be suitably rigorous. As we know, it is the exception that proves the rule.

Similar arguments can be applied to self-regulation and corporate governance. The fiasco of the 1995 British Gas annual general meeting in London Docklands, when public concern over executive salaries was at its height and the chief executive became dubbed Cedric the Pig, will have strengthened the understanding in all regulated companies that their core business is one of public services, privately provided. Companies that are mindful of the long-run security of the business and value to shareholders would do well to be proactive with the City in this regard rather than be reacting to unrealistic pressure to raise dividends on a speculative path that is beyond what is consistent with the underlying political context for the regulatory framework.

Government and Parliamentary Oversight

With hindsight, the most notable omission from the regulatory system has been a post-privatization role for government, particularly as government remains at the centre of the tripartite model of regulatory responsibilities. The incentive regulatory system of price caps is politically sophisticated – based as it is in part on the idea that excess profits in the present are the quid pro quo for lower prices in the future. To achieve public consent requires continual public reinforcement of both the message and the facts of improved performance. Belatedly, the government now recognizes this (Jack 1996), and it is noteworthy that Ian Byatt is now suggesting that the government should, on occasion, review the basis of regulation and initiate a public debate (Byatt 1996). In a system where essential public services are privately provided, government, regulators, and companies have a collective responsibility to promote public understanding as a basis for long-run public consent. The question of governments issuing general guidance to regulators is now more open.

Second, Parliament's select committee system has been an important procedural tool for ensuring accountability. The Public Accounts Committee (PAC), through the National Audit Office (NAO), carries out 'value for money' exercises on regulatory bodies, the sectoral committees shadowing the sponsoring departments (i.e., Trade and Industry, Environment, and Transport) call regulators before them, and particular themes, such as remuneration, have been explored by the Employment Committee. What is absent, however, is an effective cross-sectoral review of regulation overall, although the PAC has commissioned a comparative study of regulatory procedure from the NAO. This study is unlikely to question directly the policy of regulation, although the NAO report on the work of the regulators raised some fundamental questions relevant to the issue of reform (NAO 1996).

The Treasury and Civil Service Committee could have been a candidate for providing the cross-sectoral review, but, given the changes made during the 'Machinery of Government' exercise in 1995 when Michael Heseltine was made deputy prime minister, it would seem appropriate to consider the Cabinet Office, with its general responsibilities for deregulation, contracting out, citizens' charters, and public service. The new Public Services Committee of the House of Commons might be the appropriate committee to undertake occasional reviews of utility regulation, principles, and practice, set as this would be in the wider context of government as facilitator and regulator rather than owner and provider.

Convergence and Methodology

The most substantive issue with respect to relations between the economic regulators and the MMC is the methodology for resetting X at periodic reviews in order to determine the price caps. This issue will be examined in the following section.

The government was responsible for setting the price controls at privatization for the period until the first review by the respective regulators. The methodology on which the price caps were set is uncertain, and even if a cash-flow requirements model was used, it probably became just one element in the overall decision on the share price and the profile of price caps. City opinion had to be met for a successful sale, and the management of the privatized companies had to be a party to the agreement, because their views were a significant input into city confidence.

What is not in question is that state assets were sold at less than their current replacement value, that is, at a discount. This is not of itself a problem (the original discount might have been entirely appropriate, given the prevailing level of nationalized industry tariffs), but in practice it has been the source of much disagreement in subsequent regulatory debates, and it has highlighted the fact that inadequate guidance was given by government on the methodologies and procedures for regulators who were asked to reset X at periodic reviews.

Since no guidance was given to regulators about how the methodologies used at privatization were to be carried through to the process of resetting X, each regulator has adopted a different scheme, and it has been left to the MMC to establish the practice through its various reports on references that have arisen because companies did not accept the regulators' proposals for licence changes. Unfortunately, the MMC procedure does not create a legal precedent, and so the implications for methodology that arise in one report might subsequently be overturned (as we have seen in the MMC report on British Gas in 1997, compared with 1993).

The Disputed Areas

Various elements have contributed to the overall confusion, the most important of which are:

- The treatment of the discount at privatization and its implication for rates of return and the profile of charges
- The carry-over of investors' expectations at privatization into subsequent periods
- The carry-over of outperformance in order to maintain incentives to efficiency and the impact of various types of annual profit-sharing scheme
- Disaggregation of economic profit into controllable and uncontrollable sources, and the question of clawback of illegitimately earned economic profit
- Market values versus accounting roll-forward as the basis for determining opening and closing asset values

The cash-flow model implies that allowable revenue is cost driven, that is, that regulators allow natural monopoly service providers sufficient revenue to cover their costs and earn the minimum necessary rate-of-return required to remunerate investors (lenders and equity). It is a natural conclusion from this to expect asset values in subsequent periods to be based on what investors paid for the assets at privatization and to be rolled forward for subsequent capital spent, less an allowance for depreciation, which represents the capital value used up through providing services. The water regulator fundamentally took this approach. Others, notably in the energy sector, took the view that market values were relevant, even though there is an inherent circularity because the market values are determined to a considerable extent by the level at which the regulator sets the price caps. Market values also capitalize investor expectations about outperformance by the companies, and will rise if, post-privatization, the cost of capital falls significantly. This happened, if only because the regulators' duties to ensure that the businesses can finance themselves put an effective ceiling on risk once privatization had occurred.

The use of market values was a convenient means by which to allow the carry-over of investors' expectations at privatization, instead of putting into operation an immediate convergence model that immediately passed on the benefits of a fall in the cost of capital to consumers. The issue of using-market values is at the heart of the debate about whether the government under priced the shares at privatization, and, if it did so, whether there is any obligation on regulators to carry over the higher rates of return for investors that this implies into subsequent regulatory periods. In general, regulators have allowed some carry-over, but the 'regulatory contract' has clearly been imprecise (MMC 1995a). However, when allied with the public dissatisfaction over high utility profits in the transitional period following privatization, the approach adopted by Professor Littlechild became unsustainable at the time of the first distribution review for the regional electricity companies in England and Wales (OFFER 1995). The uprating of 50 per cent in the market value of assets had to be reduced to 15 per cent in the light of the MMC's Scottish Hydro-electric inquiry. With a lower valuation placed on the capital value of the businesses, then clearly a lower level of revenue was indicated to service that capital value, and this proved to be the major technical source of the additional price cuts in 1996 that flowed from the reopening of the distribution review (MMC 1995a).

It is unfortunate, however, that the use of market values continues as a surrogate for dealing with the problem of the discount at privatization. It would have been clearer if the distinction between the accounted net book value, based on the current replacement cost for a modern-equivalent asset, and the regulatory book value, for the purposes of determining allowed revenue, had been enshrined in the regulatory terminology from the beginning. Companies could then have argued correctly for current cost depreciation as the basis for profiling consumer charges between regulatory periods, while equity would have been maintained by regulators, ensuring that the rate-of-return on assets related only to the regulatory book value, that is, what investors have paid for the assets. The logic is that each customer should pay, in the year of receiving the utility service, for three things: the current operating cost; the measured current replacement cost of the assets used up in providing the service to them (i.e., depreciation), given these are long-term industries; and the necessary financing costs of the assets (dividends and interest), based on what investors actually paid for the assets.

This issue is at the heart of the debate between OFGAS and British Gas with respect to the reference to the MMC on the 1997 TransCo price review (OFGAS 1996). OFGAS argued that depreciation should be based on the discounted acquisition value. It is appropriate that OFGAS should not allow a full rate-of-return on current replacement cost, but the equitable halfway house – which in effect underpinned the results of the 1993 MMC inquiry into British Gas – appears to have been lost in an acrimonious debate about whether shareholders are being penalized. This is in part because the MMC's approach in 1993 was not based on a clear methodology, which arguably resulted in a windfall gain for shareholders because the rate-of-return abatement applied only to the return on pre-privatization assets and not to assets acquired after privatization (MMC 1993). To avoid a windfall gain, either the abated return has to be carried through to each review period or the depreciation on pre-privatization assets has to be based on acquisition costs.

In fact, the real issue is about intergenerational equity between consumers. The OFGAS proposals mean lower prices today and higher prices tomorrow. The hybrid model – with current cost depreciation and an abated rate-of-return effected through an annuity deduction from each period's allowable revenue in perpetuity (for an ongoing gas business) – would give a steady price over time and be consistent with the idea of consumers paying for those assets they consume on an ongoing basis. Given that OFGAS is responsible for securing supply competition, its approach to determining TransCo's charges is open to the accuzation that TransCo will be cross-subsidizing all gas suppliers, and hence artificially holding down prices and making new entrants look more profitable.

Variance Analysis

In general terms the incentive system of price caps requires that regulators only look forward and do not seek to claw back past profits from outperformance, otherwise the incentive to outperform is destroyed. Nevertheless, little attention has been paid to the fact that some clawback could be warranted where a company deliberately manipulated its spending on which allowable revenue had been granted. This means that regulators should have developed a more transparent system of 'variance' analysis in order to disaggregate the out-turn economic profit and divide it into those sources that were in the control of the companies' management and those that were not.

Uncontrollable variations – which can lead to excessive windfall gains or losses – are best dealt with by explicit adjustments in the price-capping formula in order to eliminate them or make them more cost-reflective. In practice this is an area where regulatory discretion has been allowed such adjustments to be implemented with the longer-run benefit of helping to secure public consent for the system, since people react strongly to evidence of excess profit. The main area of controlled variation that was underestimated was slippage in the capital program. Far more attention is now being given to the detailed forecast capital program that underpins the allowed revenue. Where this has not been carried out or where it is not a result of identifiable capital efficiencies, then the clawback of allowable revenue in the next period is legitimate where the economic profit earned has been significant. The Northern Ireland electricity regulator was one of the first to tackle this issue explicitly in the Northern Ireland Electricity price review for 1997, which was also referred to the MMC. The rail regulator has also made it clear to RailTrack that significant underspending of the agreed capital program will be unacceptable.

Finally, evidence that the incentives to efficiency are not as strong under a periodic price capping system as previously thought has meant that consideration has to be given to carrying over some economic profit from outperformance in the previous period. If so, allowable revenue in the forthcoming period would be based on forecast costs plus a proportion of economic profit from the previous period. The debate on profit-sharing, however, has been conducted for the most part in terms of introducing an annual formula profit-sharing (say on a fifty-fifty basis) in order to overcome public resistance to economic profits being earned by regulated companies.

The problem is that incentives to outperform are eroded at the same time as the public's desire to see more (or less) economic profit earned is assuaged. One alternative would be to extend the price-capping period in order to restore the incentives, but this would be risky because there are general advantages in having a regulatory review after five years. A better alternative, which has been pursued by the water regulator, is to encourage the companies to voluntarily accelerate the return of benefits to customers when the company is outperforming. This would improve the relationship between the company and the customer, and the mechanism might be as follows: the company would underutilize the maximum price cap allowed by the regulator, but the economic value of that underutilization would be compounded forward and added to the allowable revenue for the next period. In this way, the profile of profits and return of benefits would be made to run in parallel rather than in series, with profits coming first. Consent for the system would be more likely to be forthcoming, but the overall economic benefit of incentives to efficiency would be maintained. Although this proposal remains controversial, the regulators have in general declared that they are against introducing annual formula profit-sharing schemes (Vass 1996).

Conclusions

Utility regulation is a complex division of responsibilities between regulatory agencies operating within a system of checks and balances, and collective responsibilities for improving public knowledge as a basis for public consent. The regulatory system has to be flexible enough to evolve and retain public consent, while being contained within a broad framework of principles that can ensure stability and the maintenance of incentives to efficiency. The key feature of the UK model is incentive regulation through periodic price control rather than profit control. The incentive to improve efficiency is set within an equitable framework of profit-sharing. As competition is introduced, regulation of retail businesses can be withdrawn, and the regulator can concentrate on being a sectoral competition authority unless the general competition authorities take over responsibility. To date the sectoral and general regulators have worked in a complementary fashion. This is notwithstanding the confusion that has ensued from the secretary of state overturning the recommendations of the MMC on allowing some vertical reintegration in the electricity industry on the grounds that there was insufficient supply competition, and this has probably made the MMC more cautious in allowing takeovers and mergers, even though competition in the capital markets is an essential part of incentive regulation.

Technocratic independence in non-elected public bodies would appear to be essential for regulators to achieve effective incentive regulation, and due accountability does not appear to have been sacrificed. The most important thing is to learn the lessons from the comparative experience of sectoral regulation and its development. This is important for many countries that are deciding how to proceed. Independent regulation with powers vested in an individual regulator has been shown to have advantages in speed and effectiveness of public communication.

The relevance of this conclusion is perhaps demonstrated by the progress of

New Labour's policy. The party started with calls for re-nationalization, progressed to a policy of tougher regulation, and ended in office with an emphasis on the need for continuity in regulation and the development of policies that encourage the discipline of competition wherever possible. The only distinctive policy that is still there is the windfall tax aimed at clawing back past profits, although other ideas such as introducing panels of regulators also remain (Department of Trade and Industry 1998).

There are two main areas where improvements could be made in the regulatory process. The first is in the improvement of public knowledge and codification by: (1) occasional government inquiries into comparative regulation; (2) cross-sectoral parliamentary committee (the candidate would be the Public Service Committee); (3) presentational improvement of RPI-X to RPI-Po-X+Q, which separates the passing on of outperformance from the previous period from the forecast productivity improvements (X) and the change in quality standards (Q); and (4) recasting statutory objectives of regulators, such as the Duties of Regulators (Consumer Protection) Bill).

The second area is through improved corporate governance and regulatory consistency. This would be achieved by: (1) the adoption of accelerated benefit schemes whereby underutilization of price caps is rolled forward for addition to the allowed revenue in the subsequent periodic review, thereby preserving incentives and empowering companies to improve the relationship with customers; (2) written statements of methodological practice to be adopted by regulators, which would provide a firmer framework for appeal to MMC or judicial review; and (3) clearer divisions between the core and non-core business in holding company structures.

The call by the National Consumer Council (NCC) to establish independent consumer committees on the lines of the Gas Consumers' Council is not a reform that would be consistent with the above, given the emphasis on the regulators' substantive primary duty of consumer protection. The NCC can continue to play, along with the Consumers Association, a general research and advocacy role for utility consumers. It is interesting to note that the Trade and Industry Committee of the House of Commons, just prior to the 1997 election at which the Labour Party gained a landslide victory, broadly endorsed the framework of incentive regulation with cross-party support (Trade and Industry Committee 1997). Other commentators also seem to be concentrating their reforming zeal on procedural and administrative areas (European Policy Forum 1997). Given widespread concern over the remuneration of utility executives (the 'fat cats'), there is also a focus on ethical management (Employment Committee 1995). More radical proposals have focused on changing the form of the corporate organization to one based on stakeholder or cooperative models (Kay and Silberston 1995). For the time being, however, in the spring of 1998, both the regulators and the regulatory system remain largely unchanged.

NOTE

1 Part of this chapter reflects my work as a specialist adviser to the House of Commons Trade and Industry Committee for its 1997 report on energy regulation (Trade and Industry Committee 1997). I am writing this chapter in my personal capacity.

REFERENCES

Burns, P. 1995. In *Proceedings of the 1995 Academic Forum*, edited by P. Vass. London: Centre for the Study of Regulated Industries.

Burns, P., R. Turvey, and T.G. Weyman-Jones. 1995. *Sliding Scale Regulation of Monopoly Enterprises*. Discussion Paper no. 11. London: Centre for the Study of Regulated Industries.

Byatt, I. 1996. 'The Evolving Regulatory Agenda – Where Is It?: Discussion on Public Acceptability and the Regulation of the Water Industry.' Paper presented to the Anglian Water Seminar, OFWAT, 26 March.

Department of Trade and Industry (DTI). 1998. *Fair Deal for Consumers*. Cmnd 3898. London: HMSO.

Employment Committee. 1995. *The Remuneration of Directors and Chief Executives of Privatized Utilities*. Session 1994–5. House of Commons, 159, Third Report. London: HMSO.

European Policy Forum. 1997. *The Report of the Commission on the Regulation of Privatized Utilities*. Chairman, John Fleming, Rapporteur, Dr Mark Thatcher. London: Hansard Society for Parliamentary Government.

Foster, C. 1992. *Privatization and the Regulation of Natural Monopoly*. London: Blackwell.

Hancher, L. 1996. 'Utilities Policy and the European Union.' *CRI Regulatory Review*. London: Centre for the Study of Regulated Industries, Chap. 8.

Jack, M. 1996. *Utility Regulation: A Political Perspective*. CRI Occasional Lecture no. 1. London: Chartered Institute of Public Finance and Accountancy.

Kay J., and A. Siblerston. 1995. *Corporate Governance*. London: National Institute Economic Review, August.

Monopolies and Mergers Commission (MMC). 1993. *British Gas plc: Reports under the Gas Act 1986 on the Conveyance or Storage of Gas and the Fixing of Tariffs for the Supply of Gas by British Gas plc*. Vols. 1–3. Cmnd 2314–16. London: HMSO.

– 1995a. *Scottish Hydro-Electric plc: A Report under Section 12 of the Electricity Act 1989*. London: HMSO.

– 1995b. *South West Water Services Ltd: A Report on Adjustment Factors and Infrastructure Charges for South West Water Services Ltd.* London: HMSO.

National Audit Office (NAO). 1996. *The Work of the Directors General of Telecommunications, Gas Supply, Water Services and Electricity Supply*. Session 1995–6. House of Commons, 645. London: HMSO.

Office of Electric of Electricity Regulations. (OFFER). 1995. *The Distribution Price Control: Revised Proposals*. Birmingham: Office of Electricity Regulation.

– 1996. *The Transmission Prices Control Review: of the National Grid Company, Fourth Consultation Paper and Final Proposals*. Birmingham: Office of Electricity Regulation.

Office of Gas Supply (OFGAS). 1996. *1997 Price Control Review: British Gas's Transportation and Storage: The Director General's Final Proposals*. London: Office of Gas Supply.

O'Neill, D., and Peter Vass. 1996. *Incentive Regulation: A Theoretical & Historical Review*. Research Report no. 5. London: Centre for the Study of Regulated Industries.

Trade and Industry Committee. 1997. *Energy Regulation*. Session 1996–7. First Report. House of Commons, London: HMSO.

Vass, Peter. 1994. 'Accountability of Regulators.' In *CRI Regulatory Review*. London: Centre for the Study of Regulated Industries.

– 1995. 'Consumer Representation: Integration or Independence?' In *CRI Regulatory Review*. London: Centre for the Study of Regulated Industries.

– 1996. 'Profit Sharing and Incentive Regulation.' In *CRI Regulatory Review*. London: Centre for the Study of Regulated Industries.

Viehoff, I. 1995. *Evaluating RPI-X*. NERA Topics 17. London.

PART THREE
SECTORAL VERSUS FRAMEWORK REGULATORS: CONVERGING AND COLLIDING REGIMES

11

Approaches to Managing Interdependence among Regulatory Regimes in Canada, the United Kingdom, and the United States

G. BRUCE DOERN

This chapter examines key institutional approaches to managing interdependence among regulatory regimes, in particular between competition regulators and sectoral utility regulators in the telecommunications sector. Accordingly, it takes up one of the thematic conclusions reached in both Chapter 2 and the analysis of UK regulatory institutions by Hogwood in Chapter 5. The examination in this chapter looks at the core institutional approaches of the United Kingdom, Canada, and the United States, but with some reference to the the European Union as well (Wilks 1996; Wilks and McGowan 1996; Scott 1996).

As previous chapters have shown, the institutional relationships between competition regulators and sectoral regulators such as the energy, transportation, and telecommunications regulatory bodies have changed considerably in the last decade. In the United States and Canada these areas of regulation have historically involved natural monopoly or utility regulation and were often legally exempt from many aspects of general competition law; hence they were also often exempt from the activities of competition authorities, or were left alone by such authorities. Competition laws, however, are framework or horizontal in nature, and cut across, in principle at least, all sectors of the economy (Doern and Wilks 1996).

In the UK, the regulated utility sector was established largely in the wake of the massive Thatcherite privatization program, with the regulators themselves receiving partial competition mandates as well as becoming subject in part to the general competition regulator (Beesley 1995; Veljanovski 1991). In the European Union, competition regulation was one of the first areas of real regulatory strength but was never assessed by a set of arm's-length sectoral regulators in the manner of the United States and Canada (Wilks and McGowan 1996; Doyle 1996; Scott 1996). In the late 1990s the two regulatory realms – sectoral and competition frameworks – are converging and colliding because of an expansion and strengthening of competition regulation and because of the extensive or partial break-up of natural monopolies resulting from the combined impacts of technological change, privatization policies, and deregulation initiatives (Crandall and Waverman 1995; Helm 1995; Ernst 1994). Many of the economic aspects of these changes have been examined but there is much less concerted analysis of the institutional issues and relationships.

As a prelude to other case studies in Part Three, this chapter examines four approaches that have been utilized to help manage or influence the relationships between competition regulators and sectoral regulators. The four approaches are: (1) advocacy and representation rights of the competition regulator in the proceedings of the sectoral regulator; (2) 'regulated conduct' defence doctrines and concepts of regulatory forbearance; (3) mechanisms of appeal by firms from the sectoral regulator's decisions to competition regulators; and (4) private legal action. These approaches are, of course, not the only institutional mechanisms for managing interdependence. Broader and often quite subtle processes exist within the cabinets, executive branches, and legislative arenas of the jurisdictions in question.

A crucial reality of these approaches is that they apply to a range of regulatory realms, and hence, even though this chapter uses the telecommunications sector as an illustration, their institutional behaviour and outcomes can never be fully understood in relation to just one sector. The chapter's illustrative focus on the telecommuncations sector is largely because it is the one that is undoubtedly experiencing the most rapid forms of change, involving both complementarity and collisions between the two regulatory regimes (Mansell 1993; Crandall and Furchtgott-Roth 1996; Vietor 1994). Institutional change is also occurring rapidly, though not as fast as the technological and competitive forces.

At the centre of the telecommunications competition policy conundrum is a dual notion of 'convergence' (OFTEL 1995; CRTC 1995; U.S. Information Infrastructure Task Force 1995). Broadcasting and telecommunications (telephone) are converging into each other's worlds. But convergence is also occurring between competition and telecommunications regulators, especially because the vital politics of transition are centred on the question of whether the competition allowed should be full, fierce, and free, or fair, workable, and, in effect, 'managed' (Brock 1994).

It is clearly the digital-based technological revolution that is most forcefully propelling this sector towards a pro-competitive position and away from traditional sectoral utility regulation (Crandall and Waverman 1995). The core technological change is the increased capacity and flexibility made possible by the switch from analogue to digital signals. This is what, ultimately, is allowing both the broadcasting and cable industries and the telephone industry to get into each other's business, and what is producing the vast new array of telecommunications and information products and services (U.S. Information Infrastructure Task Force 1995).

The analysis proceeds in three steps. The first section examines key concerns about efficiency and accountability and how these norms may be harmed if relationships between sectoral and competition regulatory institutions are not considered carefully and are not, in some fashion, coordinated or clarified. A central political issue is also raised, namely whether it is the state as an interested party that gets to determine how such inter-regime institutions are realigned or whether private interests, are becoming more assertive about institutional design. Private interests, in his instance, refer mainly to business interests, but larger consumer and citizen interests, as traced by Locke in Chapter 8, are also important.

The second section of the chapter examines in turn the four institutional approaches listed above, and in each case links them briefly to situations in the telecommunications sector in the three jurisdictions. The final section offers overall conclusions.

Managing Interdependence: Efficiency and Accountability Concerns

A logical starting point for the analysis is to probe further the general question about why anyone should be concerned about the institutional relations between competition and sectoral regulators. After all, many Western countries have had to live with the jurisdictional complexity of a multi-regulator world for decades (Doern 1978; Meier 1985; Ogus 1994). Firms, interest groups, and consumers have had to navigate their way through a mélange of regulators without apparent major problems. Moreover, when looked at in terms of democracy and accountability, the various regulatory institutions were all approved by elected governmental bodies, and thus in implementing their regulatory actions they should know full well that legislators were broadly aware not only of potential conflicts between laws, but also that each regulatory law was, in its own terms, desirable. In short, according to this argument, a pluralist political system produces pluralist multiple regulators who must work out accommodations with each other, but whose total actions cannot and perhaps even should not be coordinated in some overall sense.

Economic Efficiency and Competitiveness

The broadest argument against this line of thinking is that in a world of globalized markets and with an increasingly internationalized set of policy processes, no country can afford to have such a rambling ad hoc regulatory system as a whole (Purchase and Hirshhorn 1994). There is simply, in the language of economists, too much dead-weight loss to the economy. It is only the rent-seeking interests living off lax regulatory complexity that profit from such a status quo approach. The rent-seekers are, in this negative portrait, the firms, lawyers, accountants, lobbyists, bureaucrats, and other kinds of regulatory professionals who feast on the system. Regulators ultimately live in a world of myriad 'cases,' and the more complex regulation is, the more cases there will be and the more income for the rent-seekers. But such a system does not enhance the total growth and adaptability of the economy in the face of international competition (Bishop, Kay, and Mayer 1995).

This economic need is the focus of what Levy and Spiller refer to as building an appropriate level of 'commitment' to deal with the 'rules versus discretion' choices inherent in a fast changing telecommunications field (Levy and Spiller 1996). Commitment refers to a form of firm political-institutional support that allows investment to be attracted so that firms can deliver the services needed or essential to virtually every citizen, but that also allows the benefits of technological change to occur. A lack of attention to institutional design contributes to uncertainty; moreover, it creates barriers to investment in an overall sense, not only by a nation's own firms but also, and perhaps even more importantly, by foreign firms contemplating investment in the United Kingdom, the United States, Canada, or elsewhere.

Democratic Accountability

There is also a democratic parallel to the dead-weight loss argument. It is that this dense regulatory complexity also produces a lack of accountability, cynicism in political life, and a lack of respect for democratic political institutions (Ayres and Braithwaite 1992). If there is no overall discipline in thinking about policy and implementation about the overall regulatory system, then not only is there simply bad or ineffective policy but there is also a significant loss of basic democratic accountability. However, the difficulty is that accountability must be understood at several levels.

For example, consider accountability in the Cabinet and parliamentary government in the UK and Canada. Accountability in its broadest form under Westminster-based systems of Cabinet and parliamentary government involves a set of processes whereby elected ministers are held accountable to Parliament, and officials to ministers (Stone 1995; Sutherland 1991). The Cabinet and its ministers are responsible for all policy, and, in addition, ministers are accountable for all decisions made within the ambit of such policies. Accountability for individual decisions is supposed to apply even though officials have been the de facto decision makers in many individual situations. Thus, in theory ministers would resign over major errors of omission or commission.

Accountability in the above system tends to centre on the notion of 'answerability,' or having to account for what is being done. The occasions for giving an account are numerous and can include Parliamentary question period in the House of Commons, scrutiny before parliamentary committees, supplying information to national auditing bodies, internal reporting to the central fiscal and political agencies of the government, and specialized reporting on matters such as human rights and privacy. Ultimately, however, these systems of accountability are underpinned by the larger dual imperative of the potential for a government to be defeated if it does not command the confidence of the House of Commons.

But, in itself, this central parliamentary aspect of accountability does not answer all the questions that many ask about the concept of accountability, particularly in regulatory realms (Stone 1995; Vass 1994; Burton and Duncan 1996). Obviously, differences in political systems arise. In the United States a separation of powers imposes a different configuration of concepts than is found in parliamentary systems. EU institutions not only have more nascent accountability regimes but they are also executive-dominated.

Still further questions about accountability arise. These include: accountability to whom? accountability for what? and accountability over what time frame? The issue of whom accountability is owed to can be posed because many players think that accountability should also be to the citizens or interests most affected by a regulatory policy. The question of what accountability is for raises difficult concerns about whether the 'what' refers to precise and measurable performance criteria, to criteria related to democratic processes (e.g., the right to have hearings and be consulted), or to some combination of both performance and process. The issue of the relevant time frame is important because the occasions for accountability can be annual or even monthly, and thus short-term accountability reporting regimes may distort real accountability simply because many policies and regulations are, by their nature, long-term in their consequences (e.g., price review periods) and in the time they need to mature. For example, the issues relating to convergence in the telecommunications sector are crucially driven by issues of 'how fast' it should occur.

One does not have to ask too many basic questions before it is realized that in practice there are many kinds of accountability within and among a set of sectoral and framework regulatory bodies. Any further loss of clarity arising from a failure to consider inter-regulatory relations can only make things worse in terms of democratic accountability. But making accountability clearer is not an easy or self-evidently defined task, and accountability may not gibe with simplistic efficiency criteria either.

While all of the above economic and political arguments are compelling in a globalized economy, they do not produce easy answers or straightforward road maps to the 'simplification' of competition versus sectoral regulatory institutional relations. Nor do they do indicate how much of the coordination of the state's regulators can or should be done by the state itself or by private interests and citizens through private actions of various kinds. The first option can involve further choices as to which part of the state one is talking about (the executive, the legislative bodies or the courts), and it raises the issue of whether the state can, in fact, 'regulate its regulators' (Martin 1995). The second option, on the other hand, can produce many kinds and degrees of private action (legal and political) with vastly varying degrees of transparency and power in the actions taken.

To ask questions about who might 'coordinate' the interacting regulators, let alone interacting regimes of regulators, is to ask simultaneously questions about political power. And the most elementary aspect about power is that it is continuously contested. The importance of multiple regulatory venues is bound to produce a complicated political game. Competition and sectoral regulators may use each other in threats to a given industry or firm that, if it does not act appropriately, it may receive an even more unfavourable decision from another authority. Similarly, affected private interests may play off one regulator against another to postpone action or to obtain a favourable conclusion. Obviously, there are real limits to such gamesmanship in that there are some mechanisms of real or attempted coordination among competition and sectoral regulators.

Institutional Approaches for Managing Relations between Competition and Sectoral Regulators

Each of the four institutional approaches listed above are examined in this section, first in a general way, since they affect many sectoral regulators, and then with brief references to the telecommunications sector. Some of the approaches are identified with particular countries more than others, and hence must be seen to emerge from nationally specific histories and institutions. But the approaches as a whole are also suggestive of broad mechanisms that might be adapted to conditions elsewhere or that simply show different kinds of politics at play and institutions at work and under stress.

Advocacy and Representation in Sectoral Regulatory Proceedings

The first institutional approach is one that provides opportunities for the competition regulator to appear before sectoral regulators and to advocate or raise concerns about competition in the given sector, either in general or, possibly, on a given case being considered. Canada is the main jurisdiction to emphasize this approach.

Under the provisions of Canada's Competition Act (sections 125 and 126) the director of investigation and research (who heads the Bureau of Competition Policy) is authorized to make representations to, and give evidence before, federal and provincial boards (the latter, by invitation), commissions, or other tribunals. The minister of industry may also direct the director to make such representations (Doern 1995; Monteiro 1993).

Over the years, this advocacy role has been carried out many dozens of times in the transportation, energy, and telecommunications sectors. Recently the range of sectors being examined has extended to agriculture, sports, the professions, and banking. The competition regulator's advocacy was often the only and very lonely voice in some sectors in the early 1980s (e.g., in transportation), but then the activity gained momentum as other pressures for competition took hold in the wider economy in the late 1980s and in the 1990s (Doern 1995; Monteiro 1993).

The Canadian model of using the competition regulator as an advocate in sectoral regulatory hearings has certainly been resorted to often in the telecommunications sector. A 1993 study shows that of the total of 175 interventions in the period between 1976 and 1992, 60 were in the communications sector (Monteiro 1993, Table 1). In assessing the effectiveness of interventions, the study used several indicators of success, one of which was to examine the decisions of the telecommunications regulator and to see whether they were favourable or not towards the arguments advanced by the director of investigation and research. For the communications sector, the study concluded that thirty of the sixty decisions were favourable, eleven were partially favourable, and twelve were unfavourable. The remaining seven were either pending or withdrawn (Monteiro 1993, 168).

The study recognized that there were controversies over which indicators of success to use, and, moreover, that the sectoral regulator's reasons for favourable responses related to many sources of argument and political and economic pressure. Nonetheless, it is not at all unreasonable for the Canadian competition regulator to claim some credit in keeping up the pressure for 'the competition case,' and it is certainly true that there is far more competition in the Canadian telecommunications sector now than a decade ago. Indeed, competition is a stated goal in the Telecommunications Act of 1992, a point that the competition regulator has increasingly referred to, indeed highlighted, in annual reports (Industry Canada 1995, 1996).

The Canadian advocacy approach involves an institutionalized form of representation. Other countries and jurisdictions also have vehicles for inquiries, albeit of a more ad hoc nature. For example, the EU's Regulation 17 makes provision for the Commission of the European Union to conduct general inquiries into an economic sector. But, while inquiries have been carried out in sectors such as petroleum and telecommunications, general inquiry powers are rarely used as overt tactical devices to advance competition or other goals, largely because in the EU the interests of many nations are involved rather than just private or interdepartmental interests.

Regulated Conduct Defences and Regulatory Forbearance Concepts

A 'regulated conduct' defence is a doctine used in courts by sectorally regulated firms as a defence against allegations by a competition regulator about a particular anti-competitive action. Regulatory forbearance refers to a doctrine whereby a regulator chooses not to regulate, or is prohibited by law from doing so, or forbears from regulating in situations where the facts in a particular kind of market situation indictate that effective competition exists. This dual doctrine-based approach can be seen as a pair of operating concepts centred in law and practice that can either facilitate or limit competition in a selected case by case manner.

The regulated defence doctrine and the concept of regulatory forbearance should also be seen as linked in that they have an overall wrap-around effect to help define the boundaries of behaviour in inter-regulatory arenas. One such effect is largely in the realm of criminal offences, but with tendencies to link behaviour to very specified activities. The other is more oriented to civil or economic situations but also is confined to particular kinds of product or service markets where, if competition exists, the regulator shall not or should not regulate.

When seen as a discretionary act by a sectoral regulator, regulatory forbearance becomes a practice that reduces or possibly eliminates rules or practices imposed on an industry or a regulated firm (Janisch and Romaniuk 1985). Such acts of discretion must not be contrary to the purposes of the main terms of the parent regulatory law. However, forbearance can also be made mandatory in that, as in current Canadian and U.S. telecommunications laws, it is specified that if a finding of fact shows there is effective competition, then the telecommunications regulator 'shall' forbear. This provision was put into the Canadian and U.S. statutes because the ability to forbear was sometimes seen to be illegal, in that the presumption was that the regulator had a duty in law to regulate.

All of the jurisdictions surveyed have some version of these practices, whether or not they are sanctioned as working doctrines or not. In other words, some form of legal defence can be be mounted if firms are accused of anti-competitive behaviour (especially criminal behaviour) when in fact they believe they are functioning under the rules of a sectoral regulator. There is simply no way to determine the number of instances in court or regulatory proceedings that regulated conduct defences have been used in the telecommunications sector. Implicitly, in every instance where a firm is challenging the alleged anti-competitive behaviour of a dominant utility, the latter is making some kind of loosely defined regulated conduct defence. But it must be reiterated from our earlier discussion that this doctrine is used primarily in criminal offence matters involving anti-competitive behaviour.

On the other hand, the concept of regulatory forbearance has been frequently practised in the telecommunications sector. The Janisch and Romaniuk analysis (1985) observed its emergence in Canadian telecommunications in the early 1980s, initially in a discretionary way. Recently, the Canadian Radio-television and Telecommunications Commission (CRTC) has defended its record by arguing that it had 'forborn from regulation with respect to terminal devices, cellular and other wireless services and a variety of competitive private line services' (Colville 1996, 9). The CRTC has also 'established criteria for forbearance for the telephone companies long distance services' (Colville 1996, 9). These requirements flow from changes introduced in the Telecommunications Act of 1992 specifying that the CRTC must forbear in situations or markets where, as a finding of fact, it determines that effective competition exists. Prior to this change, there was some legal uncertainty as to whether the CRTC could forbear unless it was specified by statute.

In the United States, the Communications Act of 1934 specified that the Federal Communications Commission (FCC) had to regulate all interstate services. However, for many years the FCC regulated only the rates of dominant carriers, such as AT&T. New, smaller entrants such as MCI and Sprint did not have their rates scrutinized (Crandall and Waverman 1995, 54). Regulatory forbearance, was extended in 1985 to the point where the FCC would not even accept tariff filings from new entrants. Court action launched by AT&T ended this forbearance, when the courts ruled that the 1934 law imposed a duty to regulate (Crandall and Waverman 1995). The new 1996 telecommunications legislation specifies that such forbearance shall occur where the facts warrant (Bureau of National Affairs 1996).

In this regard, the practice of regulatory forbearance has taken on a particular importance in the telecommunications sector as an institutional device to facilitate increased competition. While the concept of forbearance is understandable in the context of rapid change, it is a curious concept that in other respects, if not defined clearly in law, could simply be viewed as the regulator exercising normal discretion. In effect, if it practised a general form of forbearance the regulator would simply be saying that it could have regulated but it did not regulate at all or not to the degree that its statute allows. For example, the act, of establishing 'criteria for forbearance' is itself a regulatory act, in that the regulator is establishing guidelines for its own behaviour. Compare this action, for example, with the competition regulators of Canada and the United States, which have published 'merger guidelines.' These guidelines are simultaneously actions of regulation and discretionary forbearance.

Forbearance must also been seen in relation to the kinds of results that have emerged in the UK cases that are discussed in the next section. Under the UK process the sectoral regulator, and at times the Monopolies and Mergers Commission (MMC), jointly determine where to act and where to, in effect, 'forbear.'

Appeals or Actions from Sectoral to Competition Regulators

The third approach is one that enables appeals to be made from sectoral regulators' decisions to competition regulators. The best example here is found in the role of the UK's MMC in relation to public utility regulators (MMC 1994; Liesner 1995; Odgers 1995).

The main responsibility for regulating the utilities lies with the regulators such as the Office of Telecommunications (OFTEL), the Office of Water Services (OFWAT), and the Office of Gas Supply (OFGAS) (Vass 1994; Beesley 1995). But the various legislative acts for each sector also provide for a role for the MMC, basically when there is a disagreement between the regulator and the regulated utility firm. References to the MMC may also occur under the Fair Trading Act of 1973 and the Competition Act of 1980. The 'utility reference' provisions vary across the utility sectors, but basically consist of three types: modifications of licence conditions, determination of water charges and airport references, and mergers between water companies. There are also provisions whereby the secretary of state (the minister of trade and industry) may direct the MMC not to proceed with licence modification references made under the telecommunications, electricity, and railway acts.

The MMC process on licence modifications is triggered when the regulator and the utility cannot agree. It is then the regulator who takes the issue to the MMC. After a hearing process that might take about six months before a report is made, the MMC must report to the regulator 'whether any of the matters referred operate, or may be expected to operate, against the public interest' (Liesner 1995, 3). The public interest test is not quite the broad test set out in general UK competition policy laws, but it must relate to the duties, as established by the sectoral law, of the regulator and the secretary of state. If there are adverse public-interest effects, the MMC must also advise whether the adverse effects could be remedied by changes to the licence, and if so, how. The MMC must give reasons for its decisions.

On the other hand, if the MMC concludes that the matters referred to it are not contrary to the public interest, then its decision is final and the regulator cannot amend the utility's licence. Where modifications are proposed, some modifications must be made, but the particular modifications proposed by the MMC are not binding on the regulator.

It is important to stress that under these procedures the MMC cannot initiate its own inquiries, and that the MMC is independent of the government and of the Office of Fair Trading. To date the MMC has carried out ten licence modification and charge determination inquiries in the telecommunications, gas, electricity, and water sectors. Utility references, however, are a growing part of the MMC's overall mandate.

While the utility reference process is relatively new (a product of the last decade), it has garnered criticism of various kinds, both about the process and, not unexpectedly, about decisions in particular cases. Even the chair of the MMC has expressed criticism in at least two areas. First, the legislation is often, as he put it, 'unnecessarily inconsistent' across the various utility sectors (Odgers 1995). Thus pricing references are final in the water sector but not in the electricity sector. Second, the criteria and approaches used in common elements of decision making vary across the utility fields. Such variation exists in crucial aspects, such as asset valuation, risk assessment, appropriate rates of return, rates of convergence, and assessments of efficiency. Key utilities are also critical of the process in that it can be quite time-consuming and can generate uncertainty. At the same time, however, some victories have been won by firms seeking to gain commercial freedom from the strictures of monopoly power.

The telecommunications competition regulatory process has certainly made use of the UK's MMC appeal process. In 1988 a reference made under the Telecommunications Act required the MMC to investigate and report on the provision by British Telecom (BT) of chatline and message services. The MMC found that the provision of premium rate services over the BT network significantly impaired the value and quality of the telephone service and operated against the public interest (Liesner 1995, 5). The MMC recommended modifications to the BT licence. Following a consultative process initiated by the regulator, OFTEL, the regulator introduced new licence conditions broadly similar to those suggested by the MMC.

A similar pattern of events happened in a 1995 reference on telephone number portability (Liesner 1995, 7). The MMC concluded that the absence of portability resulting from BT's cost recovery practices was against the public interest. The MMC recommended modifications to the BT licence. As a result, the regulator announced a statutory consultation based broadly on the MMC recommendations.

More significantly, the MMC has become a possible player in a range of convergence, interconnection, and competition-defining issues. These involve multifaceted processes and discussions, but, early in 1996, also included the possibility that OFTEL would refer some items to the MMC. BT and OFTEL were at loggerheads over just how far and how fast competition should occur and how regulatory systems should be changed (*Independent*, 3 February 1996, 16).

The essence of OFTEL's demands for a modified BT licence included new omnibus fair-trading or competition powers that would have enabled the regulator to act swiftly against any alleged abuse of monopoly power by BT. This would have included no right of appeal except through the courts. BT would also have had to give competitors adequate notice of new services and products enabling them to respond. In addition, OFTEL proposed a reduced rate of return on capital as the basis for calculating the next phase of price caps.

BT's opposition to the OFTEL positions was multifaceted and strong (*Financial Times*, 3–4 February 1996, 20). It wanted competition powers administered through normal competition authorities, with the MMC's role intact or even strengthened. It argued that lower rates of return would not only adversely affect profits, but would also make it more difficult to attract capital for investment. And BT was strongly opposed to any requirement that it give notice to its competitors about new services.

Following an eighteen-month negotiation process, agreement was reached between BT and OFTEL, thus obviating a reference to the MMC. Among the provisions in the deal were changes that would reduce the proportion of BT's regulated revenues from about 65 per cent to 25 per cent (*Sunday Times*, 4 August 1996, sect. 2, 1). Significantly, however, BT has decided to seek a court ruling to block the new general competition regulatory power that OFTEL insisted should be a part of the licence renewal agreement.

Private Action and the U.S. Model

In the approaches sketched above, it is largely the state or its regulatory players that are the exercisers of decision making and discretion. Put more broadly, it is the state managing its own stable of competition and sectoral regulators. Pressure points for private political action certainly exist, but not wide realms of real or institutionalized private action. It is the United States that supplies the widest realm of genuine private action as a way to deal with sectoral versus competition sectoral relations (White 1988; Eisner 1991; Peters 1996).

For every single action pursued by U.S. competition authorities, there are ten pursued by private firms and citizens. Under section 4 of the Clayton Act, 'any person who shall be injured in his business or property by reason of anything forbidden in the antitrust laws may sue therefor.' The law also provides for treble damages plus costs, including legal fees. The opportunity to obtain treble damages is intended to be an incentive to plaintiffs to identify uncompetitive acts and to take the time and risk involved in bringing a case to court. Class-action suits can also be brought by otherwise dispersed and risk-averse consumers.

The main U.S. antitrust authorities, the Antitrust Division of the Department of Justice and the Federal Trade Commission (as well as the fifty state governments), cannot prevent, and in many respects have little to do with, private antitrust cases (Peters 1996). Firms found guilty in government-led cases can subsequently be sued privately. Private cases are brought through the general U.S. court system. A government antitrust regulator can, however, act as an amicus curiae and offer views in some cases.

Because private cases are motivated by self-interest, the public interest in promoting competition could lie with either the plaintiff or the defendant depending on the case. Many commentators point out that the purpose of such private-action enforcement mechanisms is to support competition, not the competitor. But many of the decisions do not enhance competition.

The provisions for private action in other jurisdictions pale by comparision. Since 1986 the Canadian Competition Act contains a provision in section 36 that allows for private action arising from anti-competitive conduct. More specifically, the section states that 'any person who has suffered loss or damage as a result of: a) conduct that is contrary to any provision of Part VI of the statute; or b) the failure of any person to comply with an order of the Tribunal or another court under the Act may sue.' Actual losses or damages (but not treble damages) can be recovered, plus court-allowed costs of any investigation and of the proceedings. Under provision (b) no cause of action arises until the Competition Tribunal has made an order in respect of the transaction and the order has been violated. There is also provision in the Canadian legislation for six citizens to ask that the director of investigation and research inquire into an alleged offence. Such requests must be carried out by the director though, to date, they have been few in number. Moreover, the director has the monopoly in reviewable matters as to what can be taken or challenged before the Competition Tribunal.

The EU, the UK, and some other individual European countries have similar quite restricted avenues for private action, certainly no positive incentive equivalent to the treble damages provision.

Without doubt, when it comes to private action the U.S. penchant goes well beyond its statutory provisions. The political-economic and legal culture of the United States simply encourages the general right to take legal action. And it is clearly both a blessing and a curse. Private-action mechanisms greatly expand the opportunity to enforce competition laws, and in the U.S. case these are laws that are already very much oriented towards competition. But at the same time, the system can produce a severe clogging of the courts and many decisions that reward competitors rather than competition.

In any given utility sector, however, the U.S. system of private action cannot be judged only on the basis of the volume of decisions. One or two cases alone may profoundly change the mix and extent of regulation. This is clearly the case in the telecommunications field, where private actions eventually produced the court-ordered break-up of AT&T, the emergence of the Baby Bells, and the radical transformation of the U.S. telecommunications industry (Crandall and Waverman 1995; Vietor 1994; Brock 1994).

A product of American pluralism and populist capitalism and democracy, the U.S. style of private action is often easy to dismiss because of its extreme form. Many countries are understandably wary of U.S. excesses in litigation, especially when oiled with the incentive of treble damages and contingency fees. Thus reform in other countries may turn on whether more than single damages are allowed. As always, the fear is that a private-action realm, even a muted version, will help competitors but not necessarily competition. On the other hand, this system is likely to continue in the United States, and thus Canadian and Mexican businesses in a North American Free-Trade Agreement context may have to be armed with roughly the same competition policy weapons. More cases launched from private sources may also help to establish precedents, and thus clarify key parts of the law faster than under the current approach. When considering private action in a more literal political rather than legal sense, it is crucial to see that it is a broad phenomenon and that it is simply increasing because of more complaints being lodged by firms with their national competition regulators.

The above four approaches are by no means the only ways in which interregulatory regime relations are managed. For example, overlaying relations in most governments are an array of somewhat less formal processes that include coordination between sectoral and competition regulators (concordats and memoranda of understanding), Cabinet-level accommodation on key cases and policies, and ongoing government-wide regulatory review processes. However, the four approaches that are examined attempt to deal with an inter-regulatory regime phenomenon that is of increasing importance.

Conclusions

This chapter has examined four institutional approaches for managing inter-regime regulatory relations, with a special focus on competition versus sectoral regulation, and illustrative attention has been given to the telecommunications sector.

It is not difficult to see why there is a growing view present that basic inter-regime regulatory relations and institutions should be reformed so as to promote as clear a form of accountability and as transparent a set of processes as possible. Underlying pressures and concerns about efficiency and competitiveness in a global economy are evident. In this compelling context, firms, interest groups, citizens, consumers, regulators, and legislatures should have a more transparent view of what the relations among regulators are and what their interconnected roles involve. Some of the more perverse kinds of rent-seeking can undoubtedly be minimized by a concerted look at the inter-regime problems. The current inter-regulatory relations have evolved incrementally, and have been given insufficient thought as to how they can be reformed in a more concerted fashion.

At the same time, however, the chapter has shown that accountability concepts and systems are far from single-dimensional in nature. The questions of accountability – To whom, For what, and Over what time frame? – produce many possible institutional answers. Moreover, the chapter has shown that the nature of existing sectoral versus competition regulatory institutional relations is such that one regime will not, in some final sense, institutionally prevail and triumph over the other. Compared to even a decade ago, there is certainly a noticeable and largely desirable movement in favour of the competition regulator vis-à-vis its sectoral cousins. But this is a trend, not a total victory, and it varies in the countries examined, whose ideas of competition and capitalism differ to a considerable extent.

With respect to the Canadian use of advocacy and direct representation approaches by the competition regulator, there is likely to be a continued value in such mechanisms, whether they are systemic, as in Canada, or somewhat more ad hoc, as they are elsewhere. The value of the approach is that it is transparent and relatively consistent, and thus it forms a regular and persistent source of fairly objective criticism and commentary that may help steel the nerves of sectoral regulators (and their parent ministries), which are otherwise potentially subject to much pressure from interests that seek at least their own survival under regulatory protection if not 'the quiet life.' However, as an institutional mechanism it may not be sufficient on grounds of efficiency, simply because it is too leisurely and is centred on persuasion rather than on direct regulatory powers as such.

The analysis shows that there is an overall and linked logic to the use of both the regulated defence doctrine and the concept of regulatory forbearance. Both are legal and operational practices that seek to define the boundaries of competitive and allowable anti-competitive behaviour of particular kinds. Regulated defence doctrines focus on criminal offences that are, however, confined to particular activities. Forbearance concepts refer more to civil-economic areas that are, however, also specified in terms of particular markets for goods or services. Together the two concepts help to shape boundaries and behaviour at a time when the sectoral and competition regimes converge and collide.

Of the two concepts, regulatory forbearance is the more active pro-competitive device, and it is a positive force in promoting competition. Where the duty to forbear is enshrined in statute form, its value in terms of accountability is maximized. On the other hand, discretionary regulatory forbearance practices are more dubious. They are undoubtedly a source of some adaptive flexibility, but discretionary forbearance is too prone to legal uncertainty and to the regulator's own biases to preserve its own roles even when it is not needed.

The UK-based approach of appeals from sectoral regulators to competition regulators is obviously a unique product of that country's highly discretionary 'public-interest' – oriented competition policies and sectoral regulatory institutions. However, it has considerable merit on grounds of accountability in that its reports are in the public domain. It suffers from weaknesses, however, in that it can take considerable time for the full process to unfold. The concordats among UK regulators are not made public, but should be. Moreover, greater care should be taken to ensure that the nature of concurrent competition powers are made more consistent across sectoral regulatory domains.

With respect to private action, the chapter has show that this is an approach preferred only in the United States, though it is by no means the only one employed in the panopoly of regulatory institutions. However, given globalization and given the pace of technological change, especially but not exclusively in the telecommunications field, there is likely to be an increasing pressure to provide more direct avenues of private action in all three countries. Indeed, various kinds of private complaints that can trigger investigations by competition authorities and sectoral regulators are seen to be growing in all jurisdictions. More explicit U.S.-styled private-action approaches need not take on the extreme form of the U.S. model of treble damages (single damages may suffice), but the public interest may well lie in ensuring that competition and sectoral regulatory enforcement is itself competitive.

In a larger overall sense the chapter has suggested reasons for inter-regime accommodation and mutual recognition that go beyond our competition and telecommunications examples. First, competition authorities are not the only framework regulators of industrial sectors, including the telecommunications sector. Intellectual property, privacy, and other social and business framework areas of regulation are also involved. Accordingly, there is both an analytical and practical danger in thinking of the issues of inter-regime relations only in terms of the interplay between sectoral and competition regulators.

Last but not least the chapter has emphasized the contested political nature of any effort to redesign inter-regime regulatory relations. The state (national, state, or provincial), and international entities have a pivotal interest and role, but private interests are also increasingly assertive about what kinds of changes will be tolerated and what balances of efficiency and accountability will be supported. In short, no institutional reform package will be simply 'designed' from on high. Rather it will be significantly a series of continuing sectoral- and framework-level negotiated outcomes with very mixed efficiency and accountability outcomes.

REFERENCES

Ayres, Ian, and John Braithwaite. 1992. *Responsive Regulation: Transcending the Deregulation Debate.* Oxford: Oxford University Press.

Beesley, M.E., ed. 1995. *Utility Regulation: Challenge and Response.* London: Institute of Economic Affairs.

Bishop, Mathew, John Kay, and Colin Mayer, eds. 1995. *The Regulatory Challenge.* Oxford: Oxford University Press.

Brock, Gerald W. 1994. *Telecommunications Policy for the Information Age.* Cambridge: Harvard University Press.

Bureau of National Affairs. 1996. *Antitrust and Trade Regulation Report.* Vol. 70, no. 1748, 8 February. (Telecommunications Reform Bill, 102 and 122–79.)

Burton, Paul and Sue Duncan. 1996. 'Democracy and Accountability in Public Bodies: New Agendas in British Government.' *Policy and Politics.* Vol. 24, no. 1 (January): 5–16.

Canadian Radio-television and Telecommunications Commission (CRTC). 1995. *Competition and Culture on Canada's Information Highway: Managing the Realities of Transition.* Ottawa: Public Works and Government Services Canada.

Colville, David. 1996. 'The Changing Role of the CRTC.' Paper presented to the Globe and Mail Insight Conference, Toronto, 30 January.

Crandall, R.W., and Harold Furchtgott-Roth. 1996. *Cable TV: Regulation or Competition?* Washington: Brookings Institution.

Crandall, R.W., and L. Waverman. 1995. *Talk is Cheap: The Promise of Regulatory Reform in North American Telecommunications.* Washington: Brookings Institution.

Doern, G. Bruce, ed. 1978. *The Regulatory Process in Canada.* Toronto: Macmillan of Canada.

– 1995. *Fairer Play: Canadian Competition Policy Institutions in a Global Market.* Toronto: C.D. Howe Institute.

Doern, G. Bruce, and Stephen Wilks, eds. 1996. *Comparative Competition Policy: National Institutions in a Global Market.* Oxford: Clarendon.

Doyle, Chris. 1996. 'Effective Sectoral Regulation: Telecommunications in the European Union.' *Journal of European Public Policy* 3, no. 4: 612–28.

Eisner, M.A. 1991. *Antitrust and the Triumph of Economics.* Chapel Hill: University of North Carolina Press.

Ernst, John. 1994. *Whose Utility? The Social Impact of Public Utility Privatization and Regulation in Britain.* Buckingham: Open University Press.

Helm, Dieter. 1995. *British Utility Regulation: Principles, Experiences and Reform.* Oxford: Oxera Press.

Industry Canada. 1995. *Director of Investigation and Research, Annual Report for Year Ending March 31, 1994.* Ottawa: Supply and Services Canada.

– 1996. *Director of Investigation and Research, Annual Report for Year Ending March 31, 1995.* Ottawa: Supply and Services Canada.

Janisch, Hudson N., and B.S. Romaniuk. 1985. 'The Quest for Regulatory Forbearance in Telecommunications.' *Ottawa Law Review* 17: 455–89.

Levy, Brian, and Pablo T. Spiller, eds. 1996. *Regulations, Institutions, and Commitment: Comparative Studies of Telecommunications.* Cambridge: Cambridge University Press.

Liesner, Hans. 1995. 'The Role of the MMC in Utility Regulation.' In *British Utility Regulation: Principles, Experiences and Reform*, edited by Dieter Helm. Oxford: Oxera Press.

Mansell, Robin. 1993. *The New Telecommunications.* London: Sage Publications.

McCahery, Joe, W.W. Bratton, S. Picciotto, and Colin Scott, eds. 1996. *International Regulatory Competition and Coordination.* Oxford: Oxford University Press.

Meier, K.J., 1985. *Regulation: Politics, Bureaucracy, Economics.* New York: St. Martins.

Monopolies and Mergers Commission (MCC). 1994. *1994 Review.* London: HMSO.

Monteiro, Joseph. 1993. *Interventions By The Bureau of Competition Policy.* Ottawa: Bureau of Competition Policy, Industry Canada, September.

Odgers, Graeme. 1995. 'What is the Role of the MMC in the Utilities Sector?' Paper presented to the Adam Smith Institute Conference on the Future of Utilities, London, 12 December.

Office of Telecommunications (OFTEL). 1995. *Effective Competition: Framework for*

Action: A Statement on the Future of Interconnection, Competition and Related Issues. London: Office of Telecommunications.

Ogus, Anthony I. 1994. *Regulation: Legal Form and Economic Theory*. Oxford: Clarendon.

Peters, Guy. 1996. 'United States Competition Policy Institutions: Structural Constraints and Opportunities.' In *Comparative Competition Policy: National Institutions in a Global Market*, edited by Bruce Doern and Stephen Wilks, 40–67. Oxford: Clarendon.

Purchase, Bryne, and Ron Hirshhorn. 1994. *Searching for Good Governance*. Kingston: School of Policy Studies, Queen's University, chapt. 9, 10.

Scott, Colin. 1996. 'Institutional Competition and Coordination in the Process of Telecommunications Liberalization.' In *International Regulatory Competition and Coordination*, edited by Joe McCahery, W.W. Bratton, S. Piccioto, and Colin Scott, 381–413. Oxford: Oxford University Press.

Stone, Bruce. 1995. 'Administrative Accountability in the Westminster Democracies: Towards a New Conceptual Framework.' *Governance* 8, no. 4 (October): 505–26.

Sutherland, Sharon L. 1991. 'Responsible Government and Ministerial Responsibility: Every Reform Has Its Own Problem.' *Canadian Journal of Political Science* 24: 91–120.

U.S. Information Infrastructure Task Force. 1995. *Intellectual Property and the National Information Infrastructure*. Washington: Department of Commerce.

Vass, Peter. 1994. 'The Accountability of Regulators.' In *Regulatory Review 1994*, 199–211. London: Centre for the Study of Regulated Industries.

Veljanovski, Cento. 1991. *Regulators and the Market: An Assessment of the Growth of Regulation in the UK*. London: Institute of Economic Affairs.

Vietor, Richard H.K. 1994. *Contrived Competition: Regulation and Deregulation in America*. Cambridge: Harvard University Press.

White, L.J. 1988. *Private Antitrust Litigation: New Evidence New Learning*. New York: Free Press.

Wilks, Stephen. 1996. 'The Prolonged Reform of UK Competition Policy.' In *Comparative Competition Policy: National Institutions in a Global Market*, edited by Bruce Doern and Stephen Wilks, 139–84. Oxford: Clarendon.

Wilks, Stephen, with Lee McGowan. 1996. 'Competition Policy in the European Union: Creating a Federal Agency?' In *Comparative Competition Policy: National Institutions in a Global Market*, edited by Bruce Doern and Stephen Wilks, 225–67. Oxford: Clarendon.

12

The Office of Water Services and the Interaction between Economic and Environmental Regulation

ALAN BOOKER

In the UK, prior to 1989, when the water and sewerage services were privatized, the interaction between economic and environmental regulation was hidden from view. The former regional water authorities were both regulators and operators (Maloney and Richardson 1996). They enjoyed substantial autonomy in defining and financing their statutory functions. Government influence over water charges was maintained through the application of financial constraints on the authorities, such as external finance limits and a target current cost return on assets. This chapter examines the regulatory arrangements that were established at the time of privatization and how they have developed since then. In particular, it analyses how the openness and transparency that resulted from the separation of operational from regulatory functions has worked in practice.

Drawing on the framework by Doern in Chapter 2, this chapter examines broadly the interplay between four generic regimes that are at work wherever we see regulatory activity. The complex interaction between economic and environmental regulation within the UK illustrates and develops the understanding of how these four regimes come together in practice and interact with each other, often in a largely informal way.

These interactions have required the development of administrative as opposed to statutory arrangements to facilitate the achievement of practical outcomes that are consistent with the concept of incentive regulation (O'Neill and Vass 1996). In that context it is important to note that the UK government is responsible for setting up the regulatory framework and for reviewing the way regulators undertake their duties. Regulators are responsible for their actions in carrying out their own duties. Interactive mechanisms work through cooperation between regulators who need to work together to fulfil their separate duties.

As earlier chapters have shown, the regulatory framework for water is one of a number of sectoral regulators that were established by government to supervise the former state monopolies following their privatization (Maloney and Richardson 1996). The Office of Water Services (OFWAT) supports the director general of water services (or, the director) who is the independent economic regulator for the water sector.

Within the confines of this chapter it is not possible to explain fully the nature of some aspects of the regulatory framework. Customer representation and protection is one such aspect. Another is the need for, and scope of, environmental and economic regulatory data and information (OFWAT 1995). Such information is supplied by the water companies to regulators, who publish it in a form that is useful to customers to show the performance of their water supplier compared with others. The use of comparative information as a basis for comparative competition is a significant feature of economic and environmental regulation in the UK.

In monitoring the performance of the companies, the economic regulator has focused his attention on quality, quantity, and service outputs for customers rather than on activity or financial inputs. However, the regulator does need to collect capital cost information as a basis for decisions when setting forward-looking price caps. This could be in terms of yardstick or benchmark costs derived from estimates or actual costs. Adequate, reliable, and consistent information is the lifeblood of regulation of monopolies, whether regulation is conducted along incentive lines or on some other basis.

The chapter concentrates on water regulation in England and Wales, and is divided into three sections. The first sets out the nature of the four regimes as they apply to environmental and economic regulation in the UK. The second section examines the regulatory relationships that result from the framework. Finally, conclusions are drawn as to options for improving the UK model and for developing aspects of the international regime that are inadequately formulated if at all.

The Regulatory Framework: The Four Regimes

We look first at the four regimes. In brief, Regime I is the economic regulatory function of the director general of water services. Regime II is the quality regulatory function fulfilled by the quality regulators, the Environment Agency and the Drinking Water Inspectorate. Regime III is the government executive regime for managing regulation. In the context of this case, this means in particular the arrangements to manage the interface between economic and environmental regulation. Regime IV is represented by the regulation of environmental standards within the European Community.

Regime 1

Economic regulation in the UK is built on the concept of incentive regulation (RPI-X), that is primarily about setting price limits at a level that provides incentives for companies to improve performance and reduce costs. The approach adopted for setting price limits is not a matter that is discussed in this chapter, but it provides the context within which relations between OFWAT, the companies, the government, the quality regulators, and customers have developed. In other regulated sectors, customer bills have declined in real terms since privatization. In water they have increased substantially as a consequence of companies having to achieve higher quality standards for drinking water and environmental discharges.

The statutory framework established in 1989 within the UK as part of the arrangements for privatizing the water and sewerage and the water-service companies is focused through the role of the director. This is a statutory office reporting directly to Parliament and subject to the scrutiny of Parliament through select committees. The director is appointed by the secretaries of state for the environment and for Wales to carry out a range of statutory duties that were set out in the Water Act of 1989 and now in the Water Industry Act of 1991.

The director heads a non ministerial government department, OFWAT, which supports the director in carrying out the statutory duties. To help with the customer protection duty the director appoints statutory customer service committees (CSCs) to investigate complaints against the water companies and to advise. The director has appointed ten such regional committees of around fifteen members. The director also appoints CSC chairs following consultation with the secretary of state (conventionally the president of the Board of Trade and Welsh secretary). Once appointed they also hold statutory offices. They report to the director, who has also created, with the agreement of ministers, a non-statutory OFWAT National Customer Council (ONCC) comprising the director, plus the ten regional CSC chairs. ONCC has the role of advising the director on national issues to do with the protection of the interests of water customers.

The overriding objective that the director has for himself or herself, OFWAT, and the CSCs is to increase value for money for the services provided to customers of the water service companies. The main statutory duties may be summarized as follows:

- To ensure that companies carry out and can finance their functions
- To protect customers interests
- To promote economy and efficiency
- To facilitate competition

The duties as set out in the legislation cover a wider range of functions, including the determination of some disputes between companies and their customers. However, there are key duties in the interactive process between economic and environmental regulation.

There is a further relevant duty on the director created by the Environment Act of 1995. This is to ensure that water-service companies promote the efficient use of water by their customers (OFWAT 1996d). It is also worth noting that the Environment Agency, which was created by the same legislation, has a duty to have regard to costs and benefits in exercising its powers. This was not a statutory duty of the National Rivers Authority (NRA), one of the predecessors of the Environment Agency.

Regime II

This regime is concerned with the regulation of the water environment and of the quality of drinking water. These functions are undertaken quite separately by the Environment Agency and the Drinking Water Inspectorate (DWI). The nature of their activities is somewhat different in both scale and scope.

The Environment Agency was established in 1995 from the former NRA, Her Majesty's Inspectorate of Pollution, and local authority waste-disposal departments. It regulates the disposal of all forms of waste to land, water, and air. In addition, the agency licenses all water abstractions, including those for public water supply. It charges licence fees to cover the costs of administering licences. The concept of incentive regulation has been applied. However, there is scope for the development of an incentive-based approach to environmental regulation through such pricing mechanisms as tradeable permits for both abstractions and discharges.

In contrast, the DWI was created under the Water Act of 1989 as part of the Department of the Environment. The chief drinking water inspector has certain statutory duties undertaken directly for the secretaries of state for the environment and for Wales. These duties include the power to prosecute companies for breaches of their statutory duty to supply potable water. The specific task of the DWI is to monitor the quality-control systems in place within the water companies to ensure they can comply with the drinking water regulations. The DWI also collects compliance statistics and acts as a focus for information, discussion, and action within the Department of the Environment on issues of drinking water quality, such as derogations to permit non-compliance with the EC Drinking Water Directive (EC 1980). This case study concentrates on the interaction between the economic regulator and the environmental quality regulator. The parallel interaction with the DWI has similar characteristics, but may be seen more as part of Regime III in view of the institutional arrangements within which it operates.

The Environment Agency has been established by statute as a non-governmental organization with its chair and members appointed by the secretaries of state for the environment and Wales. There are some executive members of the board of the agency. This structure ensures proper accountability for and executive control of the development of policies to meet the statutory duties of the agency and their implementation. In addition to its regulatory functions, the agency has significant operational duties for land drainage, rivers management, and coastal protection. It has been constituted, as was the NRA, to include statutory regional advisory committees, which have a significant impact on the regulatory behaviour of the agency. Considerable management effort is required by the centre in order to achieve consistency in the application of policy across the regions.

The interaction between economic and environmental regulation was changed significantly as a result of the Environment Act. Much of the discussion on this chapter relates to the NRA. As the main institution absorbed by the agency it formed the template and provided the vast majority of its staff. However, the NRA had a narrower remit and somewhat different duties than the Environment Agency. Nonetheless, institutionally and organizationally the NRA and the Environment Agency have similar structures. The powers and duties are vested in the non-governmental organizations (the authority and now the agency). The relationship between the board of the organizations and the executive is similar to that of a business organization with a board of directors.

Regime III

Government, ministerial, and departmental roles in the regulatory framework are naturally pivotal. Parliament set up the framework. DWI is part of the departmental organizations, and ministers appoint and approve key regulatory staff and departmental responsibilities. Officials, accordingly, have a close working relationship with regulators and with European institutions. Ministers and departments also have working relationships with other government departments. The Department of Trade and Industry figures prominently in this context in view of its involvement in customer representation and competition issues.

There is no formal coordination through an interdepartmental committee system. Most issues are handled on a bilateral basis with an occasional need for an informal interdepartmental process. However, government departments have established mechanisms for communicating individually with the water companies, and collectively through their trade associations. The regulators favour direct contact with individual companies who hold appointment licences. All these mechanisms form part of the wider Regime III and play an important role in the interaction between economic and environmental regulation.

The growth in European competence increasingly dominates the setting of water and environmental standards. The principal preoccupation of the UK government is to apply EC directives to the UK by legislative or administrative means. In general, EC directives are couched in terms that give member states some flexibility in their implementation both as to how far and how fast it proceeds. The process established for the 1994 review of water price limits and for taking decisions on implementation of new water and environmental quality obligations created mechanisms that are also discussed in the second part of this chapter. They might form the basis for taking similar decisions at future price reviews.

Regime IV

The international dimension to environmental regulation is an interesting one. In the explanation of Regime III it has already been noted that departments work closely with their counterparts in the European institutions. The initiative on environmental issues has moved firmly to Europe. The EC already has in place many of the mechanisms and the role within the European Treaty to set quality standards and, increasingly, to monitor compliance with them. It is not obvious, however, that the approach adopted in general and in particular is the most cost-efficient or effective.

The detailed process within Europe is lengthy, cumbersome, and complex. It is also closed and opaque to all but those intimately involved (Weale 1996). This contrasts starkly with the open and transparent processes that are the hallmarks of UK regulation involving a large number of interested parties and institutions. Those involved include the EU Commission through the Directorate General IX, the European Parliament and its committee structure, member states, professional and industrial groupings, pressure groups and a range of lobbyists often working behind the scenes to influence outcomes. In addition to the Directorate General XI, the new Directorate General XXIV for consumer affairs is becoming interested in environmental issues.

A major weakness apparent in the European process is the scant regard that it appears to have for a cost-benefit approach and for the impact on the bills of water customers. It is not possible here to explain the detailed process within Europe for deciding on environmental priorities and quality standards. Suffice it to say that once standards and deadlines for compliance have been set by the EC, member states have to fall in line.

Although the European process is slow to adapt to a new environment where customer views are properly taken into account, there is a role that customers of the UK water companies can play in Europe. This is being increasingly established by ONCC. The role is one of linking with other European consumer bodies to influence the pace and direction of EC legislation in an attempt to ensure that new obligations are adopted at a rate customers can afford. This mechanism is, at this stage, an imperfect one. However, the lessons learned in England and Wales between 1990 and 1994 suggest that this mechanism could be developed and formalized to the advantage of the European process.

In the past the influence of single-issue pressure groups, such as the environmental lobby, brought only one perspective to the establishment of new standards. Wider customer influence would help to ensure that costs and benefits are properly considered before decisions are taken to set higher standards and deadlines established for achieving them.

While the mechanisms are at this stage less able to be developed than those within the EC, international agreements to improve the environment, such as the initiatives put in hand following the Rio Earth Summit, also form part of Regime IV. The World Bank is supporting 137 projects in 62 countries through loans amounting to $10 billion. Proper regulatory arrangements will help to ensure that these funds are used effectively. The World Bank increasingly appears to want to see clear and firm economic regulation in place in a host country as a precursor to funding environmental improvements.

Relationships among Regimes: The Cost of Quality Case Study

With the four regulatory regimes set out, it is now possible to discuss the interaction of the regimes in the case of environmental quality regulation. This is done through a case study on the 'Cost of Quality' debate. Initiated by the director general of water services, the debate demonstrated how these regimes could work together, even in the absence of a legal basis for doing so (OFWAT 1992).

The Position in 1990–2

When the water and sewerage companies were privatized in the winter of 1989, price limits were agreed to that would increase average water bills by some 25 per cent above inflation by 1994–5. In 1991–2 additional environmental quality obligations were beginning to emerge in the form of new or enhanced quality standards imposed by the EC through new or revised directives (European Community 1991) and as a result of government ministers committing the UK

FIGURE 12.1 Average household water and sewerage bills

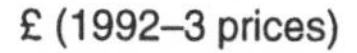

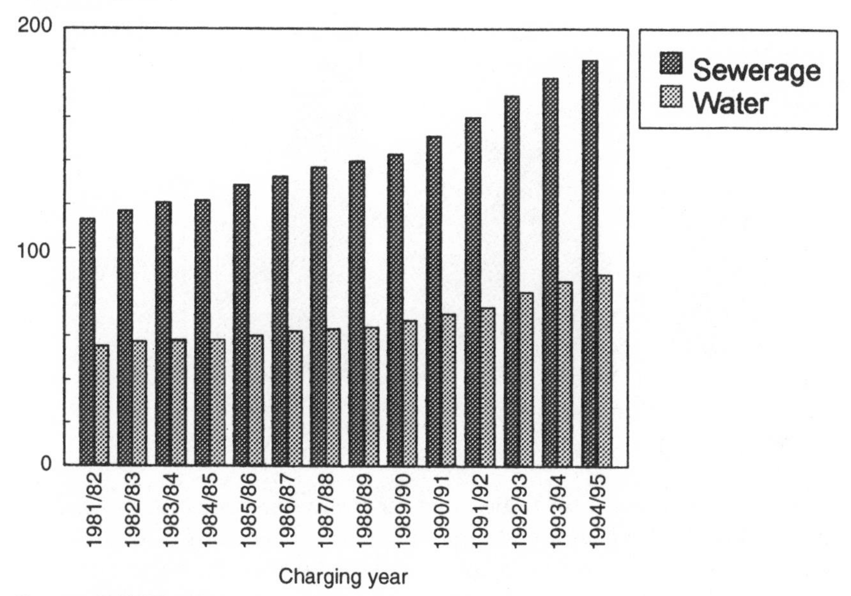

Source: OFWAT 1992.

to stop disposal of sewage sludge in the North Sea. It was thought that the costs of these obligations would be quietly passed through to customers in the form of higher bills. The director did not see things in the same light.

The Cost of Quality

By 1992 it was forecast that the average household sewerage bill in England and Wales would be £185 by 1994–5 (Figure 12.1). This would amount to about 1 per cent of average household income. Average bills in some companies were forecast to be about £285 (Figure 12.2). For some low-income customers in high-charge companies, household water and sewerage bills would amount to around 10 per cent of income. Affordability was clearly becoming a major issue. For instance, in Devon and Cornwall the need to improve discharges of effluent into the sea and to clean up the beaches would drive up average South West Water bills to double those of the lowest charging company. The Cost of Quality issue was fast becoming the most significant one for the privatized companies.

FIGURE 12.2 Variation in 1994–5 average household water and sewerage bills in different companies

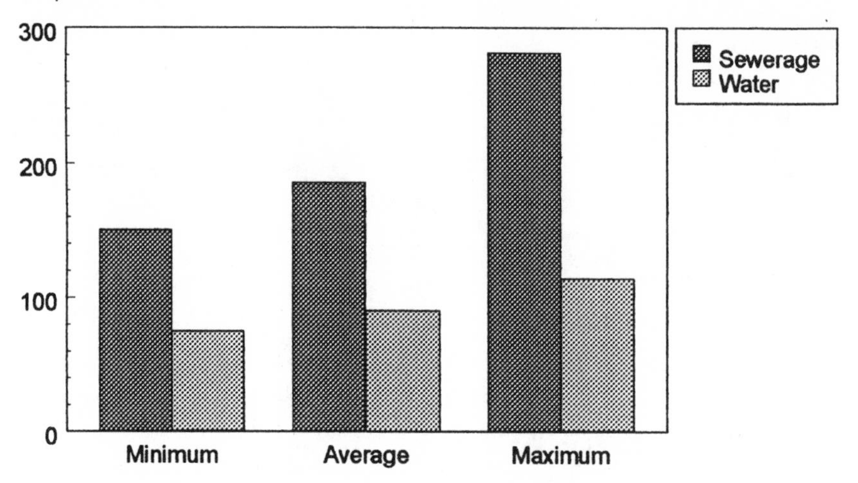

Source: OFWAT 1992.

The director was alerted to the need for a new approach that avoided the imposition of further quality obligations at a rate customers could not afford. He initiated a major public debate on the Cost of Quality issue in August 1992 with a strategic assessment of the prospects for future water bills, which set out graphically the challenges for customers, for government, for regulators, and for the companies on the basis of a number of assumptions built into two broad scenarios called 'Progress Maintained' and 'Pure and Green.' The first reflects a continuation of current programs and the implementation of new firm obligations. The second adds a number of possible new quality improvements, though by no means all that might have been expected. The scenarios had a common base representing the quality improvements assumed at the time initial price limits were set by government in 1989.

The report arising from the Cost of Quality exercise highlighted the need for decisions, and it indicated that the director was discussing the issues set out with the government, the environmental regulators, and the companies. It emphasized the fact that the number of complaints about increases in water charges was growing, and of disconnections increasing because bills were not being paid. The report also invited comments from customers directly and from the ten CSCs, so that there could be proper customer involvement in ensuring the right balance between price and quality.

Predictably there was an immediate response from environmental pressure groups. For instance, the Friends of the Earth published their own document

TABLE 12.1 Possible implications for average household water and sewerage bills (£)

	1994–5	1999–2000	2004–5
Progress maintained – lower			
Water	90	100	115
Sewerage	95	115	130
Total	185	215	245
Progress maintained – upper			
Water	90	105	120
Sewerage	95	125	170
Total	185	230	290
Pure and green			
Water	90	120	165
Sewerage	95	135	180
Total	185	255	345

Source: OFWAT, 1992.

on the Cost of Quality called *The Price of Pollution* – an environmentalist perspective on the debate over environmental standards. In it, the Friends of the Earth accused OFWAT of being in serious danger of misleading water customers. It drew attention to the need for government to consider its social policy and to the problem of valuing some environmental components, and included a reminder about the need for standards to reflect the 'precautionary principle.'

The debate on Cost of Quality was very firmly on the agenda in the summer of 1992. It was to continue for almost a year and a half, and lead to the creation of a workable interactive process between economic and environmental regulation with the objective of achieving affordable quality improvements. At times, the public perception was that there was deep acrimony between the director and the chair of the NRA, and that the interaction between Regime I and Regime II was not working productively. There is little doubt, however, that the robust public exchanges played a part in clarifying the need to establish a workable process.

The Political Perspective

The issues raised in the Cost of Quality process made it clear that further work was required to provide a basis for the companies strategic business plans (SBPs) required by the regulator and incorporating the licence need for an asset management plan. The water and sewerage companies had to submit these to the director in March 1994 to provide the information needed for resetting price limits at the end of July 1994. It was recognized that companies needed guidance on the application of standards and on the timetable for achieving them. In the autumn of 1992 the Department of the Environment (DOE) took the lead in setting up a quadripartite group involving the economic and quality regulators and the companies. The group was charged with the job of agreeing on the guidelines that would be used by companies in compiling their SBPs. The guidelines, attempted to identify and clarify both existing and potential obligations by interpreting EC directives such that the water companies were clear about how far and how fast those obligations should be adopted.

The first edition of the guidelines covering both drinking water and sewerage services, was issued by the respective quality regulators in March 1993 and formed the basis for the costings in a second OFWAT report, *Paying for Quality: The Political Perspective* (OFWAT 1993a). In the report, the director made it clear that his purpose was to seek from the secretaries of state for the environment and for Wales a clear perspective on new obligations and their implementation as a basis for setting revised price limits. He confirmed that when those obligations had been established he had a legal duty to ensure that the companies could finance them. He was looking for clarity and stability.

The assessment in this important publication, in which all the figures had been independently examined by engineering consultants with a duty of care to the director, showed that water bills would continue to rise quickly in real terms. Across England and Wales as a whole they could add £54 to average household bills over the five years from 1995 and a further £23 in the following five years (Table 12.2). The director concluded that he did not believe that customers generally would regard that level of increase as affordable. He invited the perspective of the secretaries of state for the environment and for Wales on the issues raised in it. Before going on to consider the response from the ministers, it is worthwhile pausing to reflect on what had actually happened to allow the political perspective to be produced.

First, while it was too late to influence the timetable and the standards in the EC directives, it was clearly possible to interpret directives in ways that could have a greater or a lesser impact on water bills. Second, it was important that the regulatory regimes interacted in a way that, although not statutorily defined, was nevertheless managed to a tight timetable. The interaction needed to produce outcomes, which would pave the way for decisions from ministers. They could take into account both the obligations and their impact, and balance cost and quality in a political process that tried to ensure quality could continue to improve but at an affordable rate. It was also important to change the perception

TABLE 12.2 Possible increases in current national average household water and sewerage bills: New quality improvements (1993–4 prices in £)

	5 years to 1999–2000			5 years to 2004–5		
	Water	Sewerage	Total	Water	Sewerage	Total
1994–5 bill	90	100	190	90	100	190
Existing obligations	5	31	36	9	37	46
Possible additions	15	39	54	27	50	77

Source: OFWAT 1993a.

that the statutory arrangements prevented proper interaction between the two regimes and hindered acceptable outcomes.

The quadripartite process that had ministerial backing comprised two levels of activity: a high-level group on which all parties were represented, and a working level. The working-level group produced information for the high-level group following work done to cost quality-improvement initiatives company by company with regional NRA and DWI involvement and under the scrutiny of OFWAT. This process, or a development of it, needs to continue for the next periodic review in 1999. In short, an effective informal mechanism was created through which three of the four regimes plus the regulated companies could interact. It also showed that sensible outcomes can be achieved by administrative rather than statutory means.

The same broad scenarios of 'Progress Maintained' and 'Pure and Green' were considered, and the expenditure programs were translated into bills, making some assumed adjustments for efficiency. The results showed that existing obligations could add £36 to average household bills by the year 2000, with possible additions under the Pure and Green scenario adding a further £54. The range in average bills for different companies would tend to increase. Some customers, such as single pensioners on income support, could be paying as much as 9.3 per cent of their income by 1994–5; 12.9 per cent by 1999–2000, and 14 per cent by 2004–5, depending on where they lived.

The Quality Framework

The political perspective had set out the options for government in an unambiguous way. The economic regulator allied to customer representatives had converted costs provided by companies against guidelines set out by quality regulators. The ball was firmly in the court of regime III. Ministers advised by DOE participants in the quadripartite process now needed to take decisions.

TABLE 12.3 Average water and sewerage bills as a percentage of household income for some people on income support (existing obligations plus possible additions)

Household type	National average bill as % of income			Range of average bills (lowest–highest) as % of income		
	1994–5	1999–2000	2004–5	1994–5	1990–2000	2004–5
Single parent on IS (with children under 11)	4.1	5.2	5.7	3.3–6.4	4.1–8.9	4.8–9.7
Single pensioner on IS	5.9	7.5	8.3	4.8–9.3	5.9–12.9	6.9–14.0

Source: OFWAT 1993a.

Those decisions came in the shape of an open memorandum from the secretaries of state for the environment and Wales to the director called *Water Charges: The Quality Framework* (DOE 1993). Essentially the memorandum set out the responsibility of government, companies, quality regulators, and the economic regulator to ensure that costs, particularly investment costs, were no higher than they needed to be to meet statutory requirements, and that proposals should be as cost effective as possible. The memorandum set out very clearly what all parties should do to achieve those broad objectives. Although it has no legally binding force the memorandum represents an important policy innovation as a way to reaching and implementing agreement. It involved commitments from each party.

The secretaries of state pledged:

- To seek derogations from the European Commission where appropriate
- To ensure that new directives pay proper regard to subsidiarity and are subject to cost-benefit assessment
- To require the Environment Agency to take the economic costs of proposals into account
- To try to modify implementation of the Urban Waste Water Treatment Directive

The memorandum required the quality regulators to:

- Demand no more than current regulations require
- Not to try to proceed too quickly with discretionary improvements
- Avoid excessive regulatory caution in achieving new standards
- Pay due regard to the economic cost of proposals

The director, as the economic regulator, should:

- Consider cost of capital in setting price limits (OFWAT 1993b)
- Consider the scope for further relaxation of financial ratios
- Ensure investment costs are no higher than necessary
- Ensure that only cost-effective solutions are financed
- Not anticipate future tightening of standards
- Re-examine capital expenditure programs over the period 1990–5 to ensure that any double counting is avoided

Finally the memorandum said that the companies should:

- Manage their investment programs at the lowest appropriate cost
- Use cost-effective solutions by employing technical innovation and seeking reasonable rather than absolute certainty of meeting the quality regulators' requirements
- Review discretionary expenditure allowed for in the 1989 asset management plans.

This was clearly a great step forward in achieving affordable quality improvements through proper interaction between the regulatory regimes. The way that the quadripartite arrangements operated demonstrates forcibly that it is possible with the goodwill and resolve of participants to achieve sensible outcomes even from the most pessimistic scenarios. Indeed, deep pessimism might significantly contribute to clear thinking and lead to a creative process with satisfactory outcomes.

Regime IV and its interaction with the first three regimes is more problematic. It is also arguably more important for that interaction to be satisfactory than the quadripartite process. In the case of the EC, it is regime IV that sets the standards and therefore drives the need for interaction between the other regimes, a point we return to below.

However, in the case of a wider international regime there is a much less clear process by which it can influence standards and achieve improvements. For instance, in the case of the Rio Earth Summit, progress can only be maintained by the goodwill of contributors to the summit working towards the achievement of targets rather than by enforceable standards set by international agreement. Achievement of targets is, then, in the hands of national governments subject to pressures from the international community. It is not likely that quadripartite-like mechanisms will emerge at the international level in the foreseeable future. In fact, even in Europe, where they could be established, there is no apparent willingness to contemplate such arrangements.

It is worth mentioning at this point that in the case of drinking water, the World Health Organization (WHO) has and continues to do important work in generating upward pressure to improve the quality of drinking water throughout the world. There are, however, no pressures on WHO to carry out cost-benefit work before coming to conclusions about drinking water standards. For instance, epidemiological studies take time and effort, and it can be difficult to draw conclusions from them. However, they can provide important information to help with taking decisions on emotive matters (such as appropriate lead standards) that arise from time to time on water quality. The experience of reconciling environmental and affordability criteria indicate that the work of bodies such as the WHO might be more highly valued by those who need to take informed judgments and balance higher quality against affordability if it was supported by that kind of cost-benefit work.

Monitoring Compliance

The interaction between the four regimes continued to operate through the determination of water price limits that were published on 28 July 1994 (OFWAT 1994). The work helped to clarify guidance on specific issues and specific projects as decisions were taken about financing the work that water companies planned to carry out. A particularly difficult case was the definition of esturial waters. Under the Urban Waste Water Treatment Directive a higher quality effluent was required for an effluent discharged to an estuary. This required more complex and expensive treatment than a discharge to non-esturial water. It was, therefore, important to have clear decisions about the boundary between esturial and non-esturial water. Taking this decision involved all four regimes prior to price limits being set. Subsequently, the decision has been challenged through the courts and reconsideration of initial decisions will be required in order to comply with the ruling of the court.

Aside from such issues, the Cost of Quality debate has been a great success in ensuring proper consideration of key factors by the appropriate people in order for price limits to be determined.

Following the acceptance of the price limits determined by the director, water companies embarked on programs of work to achieve compliance with standards by the due dates. They are subject to penalties for non-compliance through prosecution by what is now the Environment Agency or the DWI. But, just as interaction between regimes was needed in advance of setting price limits, ongoing interaction is needed to monitor the progress of companies towards meeting new quality obligations. The director has a duty to ensure that companies fulfil their functions, one of which is to comply with legally set quality standards. The director relies on the quality regulators supplying information on the performance of companies in meeting their legal obligations.

In May 1995 OFWAT published a consultation document on *Information for Regulation*. In it the director reiterated the intention announced when setting price limits in July 1994 to focus on monitoring the performance of companies on their outputs in delivering service quality and in balancing supply and demand. Performance on quality has two parts: the supply of water and sewerage services to current quality requirements, and progress towards meeting the quality enhancements required. The consultation report indicated that the Environment Agency and the DWI would supply information to OFWAT concerning compliance with both current and new standards. That information would identify where companies might not be making adequate progress towards the achievement of future standards.

The paper also identified where the director thought that information should be published and where it might remain confidential. While customers need to be able to judge for themselves that their interests are being protected, the director did not believe that all information should automatically be available to the public. He believed that would lead to problems for companies that have to raise finance in competitive markets and buy inputs, especially capital equipment, as cheaply as possible. In short, too much published information could be counter-productive to the incentive regulatory process. Competition, even comparative competition, often works best when competitors work independently of each other. Competitive leapfrogging is a powerful process.

During 1995 and 1996 the basis of a joint regulatory approach between the economic regulator and the quality regulators was established (OFWAT 1996c). The quality regulators provide most of the information OFWAT requires on the performance of companies in meeting standards. In August 1995 the director wrote to companies setting out the principles he would use when determining whether the companies have demonstrated the outputs assumed when price limits were set and the financial consequences of non-achievement.

After discussion with the quality regulators, OFWAT confirmed to the companies the nature and extent of the outputs expected from them and that were financed in the price limits set in July 1994. In the case of large projects or those that will extend over a long time period, OFWAT has also established procedures for companies to report progress. Companies must be able to demonstrate that key milestones towards the completion of projects have been achieved by certain dates (OFWAT 1996e). Progress in meeting these key milestones will be confirmed by the independent reporters who have a duty of care to the regulator. These reporters are appointed by the companies under the terms of their licences to report to the director on the information they supply annually and for a periodic review of price limits.

The ensuing regulatory action has two stages. The first stage is the publication of comparative information. As part of the joint regulatory approach between the quality regulators and the economic regulator, the quality regulators therefore contributed for the first time to the 1994–5 *Report on Levels of Service* that was published in the autumn of 1995. The performance of companies in achieving the required standards for drinking water quality and for environmental improvements was included alongside the director's service assessments. Table 12.4 indicates environmental performance. These interesting numbers show extensive variations. This is of less significance in the short term than the way that they change over time. The change should reflect the ongoing levels of investment aimed at improving environmental quality.

The second stage is what the director has called active performance monitoring. On the basis of the comparative information, consideration is given whether the performance of some companies needs more detailed investigations. In the autumn of 1995 the director initiated investigations into the performance of North West Water, South West Water, and Yorkshire Water on the basis of the information provided in the companies' returns for the year ending March 1995. Table 12.5 shows the output performance of South West Water compared with other water and sewerage companies. Following completion of the investigation, South West Water undertook corrective action to meet compliance dates. The director said that he intended to take account of the present delays when setting price limits at the next periodic review, or at an interim determination if one were to take place before the next review. These details were published in an OFWAT press release in April 1996.

More significant regulatory action was taken in the case of Yorkshire Water, which had fallen much further short in fulfilling its obligations (OFWAT 1996b). The director agreed to licence amendments with Yorkshire Water, one of which was to the effect that price limits would be reduced compared with those set in July 1994 to return in aggregate some £40 million to customers by the year 2000. The full conclusions from the OFWAT inquiry were published by OFWAT in June 1996.

This feature of regulatory action in respect of poor performance is now likely to be an annual process in cases where the annual competitive assessment high-

TABLE 12.4 Sewage treatment: Industry performance in 1994–5

Company	Equivalent population served by sewage treatment works (millions)		% equivalent population served by STWs in breach of their consent[2]	Equivalent population served by unsatisfactory sea outfalls[1] (millions)	Successful prosecutions[2]	Pollution incidents reported[2]		Unsatisfactory combined sewer overflows as a percentage of total[1]
	Resident	Peak holiday				Categories 1, 2	1, 2, 3	
Anglian	6.2	6.5	5	0.5	2	68	251	19
Dŵr Cymru (Welsh)	2.1	2.3	16	0.9	2	336	545	52
North West	9.8	10.1	9	1.9	11	235	740	43
Northumbrian	2.6	2.6	1	0.3	1	14	132	6
Severn Trent	10.5	10.5	3	n/a	3	238	510	16
South West	1.6	1.8	30	0.4	1	44	381	23
Southern	4.3	4.7	1	0.5	1	12	266	59
Thames	14.0	14.0	11	n/a	3	38	179	17
Wessex	2.8	3.1	33	0.1	1	46	163	30
Yorkshire	7.6	7.7	28	0.2	5	135	542	34

Notes: Equivalent population relates both to the population served and the non-domestic load on the sewage treatment service. Pollution incident categories 1, 2, and 3 are defined in the NRA report Water Quality Series No. 25, *Water pollution incidents in England and Wales – 1994*. In broad terms categories 1, 2, and 3 correspond to major, significant, and minor incidents respectively. Pollution incident data presented for Anglian, North West, Severn Trent, Thames, and Dŵr Cymru (Welsh) are for the calendar year 1994.

1 July 1995 return to the director general by the companies.

2 NRA's regions report to OFWAT June 1995.

TABLE 12.5 Output Performance of South West Water (SWT) compared with other water and sewerage companies (WaSCs)

		SWT Performance	WaSCs Average/Rate	Rank of SWT	Best WaSC
Water supply	Properties likely to experience low pressure in 1994–5	0.74%	0.64%	8	0.11%
Levels of service	Pressure problems solved since 31 March 1992 per 10,000 connections	1.2	5.8	10	12.7
	Properties affected by supply interruptions over 12 hours	0.82%	0.30%	9	0.03%
	Annual average of properties affected by 12-hour supply interruptions over 3 years	0.38%	0.33%	7	0.05%
Sewerage service	Properties at risk of frequent flooding	0.084%	0.071%	7	0.01%
Levels of service	DG5 problems solved by company action less deterioration since 31 March 1992 per 10,000 customers	0.8	2.0	6	5.5
	Properties flooded due to blockages, collapses, and pumping failures in 1994–5	0.010%	0.017%	4	0.008%
	Annual average of connected properties flooded due to blockages, collapses, and pumping failures over three years	0.010%	0.020%	2	0.005%
Customer service	Billing queries replied to in 10 days	91.44%	95.9%	10	99.9%
	Written complaints replied to in 10 days	96.20%	96.8%	9	99.6%
	Rate of disconnection 1994–5 per 10,000 billed customers	5	3	9	<1
Environmental performance	Category 1 and 2 pollution incidents reported 1994–5 per million equivalent population (resident)	28	19	9	3
	Equivalent population served by sewage treatment works in breach of their consent (excluding non sanitary and upper tier failures)	27%	3%	10	<1%
	Unsatisfactory combined sewer overflows of the total	23%	31%	5	6%
Water quality	Water Quality Index value for 1994	711	731	9	767
	Improvement in Water Quality Index value between 1990 and 1994	12%	4.9%	2	21%
Leakage	Estimated total leakage in 1/prop/hr 1994–5	10.8	11.5	5	6.8

Note: Rank – 1 = best; 10 = worst   Source: OFWAT 1995.

lights the need for a more detailed exploration of issues. These assessments may arise when the regulator is not satisfied that a company is performing adequately or when there appears to be a major departure from assumptions or judgments made at the last periodic review.

Conclusions and Future Developments

The third part of this chapter looks ahead from the Cost of Quality case study. Developments are already taking place in a number of areas that can be traced directly back to the interactions established through the Cost of Quality debate. A number of these developments have to do with the interaction between regime IV and the first three regimes.

OFWAT participates in advisory groups organized by the DOE on European proposals to change or introduce legislation affecting the water and sewerage companies, but it does not deal directly with the European Commission. These proposals include the revision of the Bathing Water Directive, the Drinking Water Directive, the proposed directive on the ecological quality of water, and the Urban Waste Water Treatment Directive. Some of these changes will be grouped under the proposed European framework directive on water resources (EC 1997). OFWAT has encouraged estimates to be made of the cost of implementing any proposed new standards. In particular, it has sought the costing of various options. For example, there may be a number of ways of dealing with the introduction of a new lead standard of 10 micrograms per litre for drinking water at customers' taps to replace the current standard of 50 micrograms per litre. If the interpretation of this standard requires the replacement of all remaining lead communication pipes in the fifteen years from the year 2000, the cost in 1996 prices could be £2 billion for England and Wales. This would add about £1.50 to customers' bills by the year 2005 and a further £3.80 over the next ten years. Another option would be to replace lead communication pipes only when samples taken at the tap show high lead levels. This would place a far lower burden on customers bills.

Within Europe the drafting and legislative machinery is currently in action on these proposals. Many groups are lobbying, including those concerned with environmental matters and public health, interested business groups, and governments of member states. Each constituency has its own objectives. Most of these are clear, but all tend to exert upward pressure on standards and on bills, without any responsibility for the consequences. The most effective groups are those that are persistent, single-minded, and armed with supportive, if partial and incomplete, but irrefutable and often emotive information.

A government does not wish to be viewed as being less concerned about public health than other member states. For their part, water companies sometimes see themselves as environmental contractors. Higher quality means growth in their business, both in carrying out the work and in higher bills to pay for it. There is only one constituent group looking at the implications for bills of higher quality standards and that is those who are going to have to pay. There are no subsidies in England and Wales, and customers of the water and sewerage companies have to pay the full cost of the provision of the water supply and sewerage service in their areas. The introduction of even higher quality standards will be felt directly by them.

ONCC is actively concerned about the impact of proposed and future quality initiatives both in Europe and at the national level (OFWAT 1996a). The council is concerned that within the EC legislative framework the interest of customers is not being properly taken into account at an appropriate level of importance. It is therefore working hard to influence the decisions taken through EC machinery. Over the last few years it has been developing a network of contacts within member states where it has been able to identify organized and legitimate bodies that could represent the interests of water customers in individual member states to Brussels. ONCC has also discussed Cost of Quality issues with various parts of the EC machine. It has now set up a small European working group of ONCC members and has engaged the services of a consultant based in Brussels to work on its behalf. It now seems that it is accepted in Brussels that water consumers have a legitimate interest, not least because they will meet the costs that must be taken into account in developing water policy and proposals for new or revised Directives. The Directorate General XI, the environment directorate, has been hearing the costs and benefit message from ONCC for some time, but it now seems that the affordability of proposals will increasingly be questioned by the Economic and Social Committee, the Environment Committee, and perhaps even by DG XXIV, the directorate covering consumer protection. The problem remains, however, that ONCC seems to be a lone voice within Europe, and that the water consumers' voice is not being heard from other member states. The Scottish Water and Sewerage Customers Council, a new body, is now associating itself with ONCC in sending these messages to Europe. The European consumer representation and protection movement is a fledgling movement, while water customers in Europe are not organized at all. Business customers are adequately organized, but tend to pursue other agendas aimed at levelling the playing fields of Europe rather than the playing fields of the world.

ONCC continues to battle on. Support from Regime III, is crucial to its success in having issues of affordability and willingness to pay considered at an early stage in the standard-setting process. For instance, ONCC has recently issued a briefing note for members of the European Parliament Committee on Environment, Public Health, and Consumer Protection on key issues for water consumers. Individual CSC chairs are encouraged to write to members of the European Parliament within their regions. ONCC has also contacted all MEPs on the Environment Committee to make them aware of the ONCC position on affordability. The briefing note makes clear that ONCC is not opposed to higher standards, but that it seeks to achieve a balance between environmental public health and consumer interests. It also suggests that proposals for higher standards ought to be based on sound science and a proper examination of costs and benefits.

The approach of ONCC appears now, after a few years work, to be bearing fruit. The Environment Public Health and Consumer Affairs section of the Economic and Social Committee has, in its advice on the Water Resource Framework Directive, reflected a number of points from ONCC of particular relevance to the protection of customers interests (Byatt 1996). These include highlighting the need to achieve an economic balance between supply and demand; the protection of existing resources by improved conservation policies; and sensible water charges and better education of customers. The need for particular stress on 'the polluter pays' principle has been endorsed, as has the need to ensure that cost-benefit analysis of water related legislation is effective in order to establish priorities and affordable programs. It is recognized that the cumulative effects of EU policies need to be taken into account. ONCC is now turning its attention to influencing the European Parliament Environment Committee as it considers the commission's communication on water policy.

There is clearly some way to go in Europe in further developing the interaction between regime I and regime IV (Weale 1996). As European institutions such as the European Environment Agency develop both in experience and scope of operation, there will be a need to review and revise the way interaction takes place. The nature and need for interaction continues to change shape as time goes by.

There is a lot of scope for developing customer networks within Europe. When economic regulation becomes established in member states as part of the institutional framework to control privatization, then every possible opportunity will be taken to encourage links between economic regulators and customer representatives with the intention of linking customer representation across member states in the fullness of time. The European water industry has a powerful voice, one that is already linked through 'Eureau.' It is possible, if ONCC retains interest and sticks to its objective, that water customers throughout EC member states could have a powerful voice in the interactive process that determines environmental priorities, standards, and pace of achievement within the EC. The process would be more balanced and therefore likely to secure more balanced outcomes that take into account the whole spectrum of implications in reaching decisions. The four regimes would then be interacting efficiently within the sphere of economic and environmental regulation.

REFERENCES

Byatt, Ian. 1996. 'The Impact of E.C. Directives on Water Customers in England and Wales.' *Journal of European Public Policy* 3, no. 4:665–74.

Department of the Environment. 1993. *Water Charges: The Quality Framework*. London: Department of the Environment and the Welsh Office.

European Community (EC). 1980. *Council Directive Relating to the Quality of Water Intended for Human Consumption*. Official Journal of the European Communities, L229/11.

– 1991. *Council Directive concerning Urban Waste Water Treatment*. Official Journal of the European Communities, L135/40.

– 1997. *Commission Proposal for a Council Directive Establishing a Framework for Community Action in the Field of Water Policy*. Brussels: European Commission.

Maloney, W., and J.J. Richardson. 1996. *Managing Policy Change in Britain: The Politics of Water*. Edinburgh: Edinburgh University Press.

Office of Water Services (OFWAT). 1992. *The Cost of Quality: A Strategic Assessment of the Prospects for the Future of Water Bills*. Birmingham: OFWAT.

– 1993a. *Paying for Quality: The Political Perspective*. Birmingham: OFWAT.

– 1993b. *Setting Price Limits for Water and Sewerage Services: The Framework and Approach to the 1994 Periodic Review*. Birmingham: OFWAT.

– 1994. *Future Charges for Water and Sewerage Services: The Outcome of the Periodic Review*. Birmingham: OFWAT.

– 1995. *Information for Regulation*. Birmingham: OFWAT.

– 1996a. *Annual Report*. Birmingham: OFWAT.

– 1996b. *Report on Conclusions from OFWAT's Inquiry into the Performance of Yorkshire Water Services Ltd.* Birmingham: OFWAT.

– 1996c. *Report on Levels of Service for the Water Industry in England and Wales*. Birmingham: OFWAT.

– 1996d. *Report on Tariff Structures and Charges*. Birmingham: OFWAT.

– 1996b. *Report on the Financial Performance and Capital Investment of the Water Companies in England and Wales*. Birmingham: OFWAT.

O'Neill, D., and Peter Vass. 1996. *Incentive Regulation: A Theoretical and Historical Review*. London: Centre for the Study of Regulated Industries.

Weale, Albert. 1996. 'Environmental Rules and Rule-Making in the European Union.' *Journal of European Public Policy* 3, no. 4:594–11.

13

North American Environmental Regulation

GEORGE HOBERG

While they have broad similarities in policy approaches, the regimes for environmental regulation in Canada and the United States are significantly different.[1] The root of these differences lies in the larger macro-political systems in which each country's regime is embedded. The U.S. constitutional system of separation of powers and of checks and balances has spawned a highly distinctive regulatory regime that is exceptionally formal, open, adversarial, and legalistic. In contrast, the Canadian Westminster parliamentary system has fostered a more informal and cooperative approach to regulation. While both countries are federations, Canada's is significantly more decentralized, a phenomenon that is clearly reflected in the environmental policy regimes.

The U.S. regime emerged as a relatively stable entity in the early 1970s, and it has proven remarkably resistant to challenges both by political opponents of environmental regulation and by advocates of alternative, less legalistic modes of policy making. Canada experienced some significant changes in regulatory processes in the late 1980s and the early 1990s. Some of these changes have moved the Canadian system closer to the American model, but constraints arising from the macro-political system have limited the extent of convergence.

After an analysis of the basic structures of the two countries' regulatory regimes and the efforts at reform in regulatory process, the chapter turns to an analysis of three significant political trends challenging the regimes. First, political opposition to costly regulations has promoted innovation and experimentation with less coercive instruments for pursuing environmental objectives. Second, the persistent fiscal crisis in both countries has resulted in funding cutbacks and institutional devolution that may threaten the regulatory capacities of government. Third, internationalization, both of the economy and of environmental problems, gives rise to challenges to the policy sovereignty of each country's domestic regime.

Evolution of the Environmental Issue: Persistent Support, and Waves of Salience

To understand the development of the environmental policy process in the two countries, it is important to understand the evolution of the environment as a political phenomenon (Hoberg 1993a; Harrison 1996; Doern and Conway 1994). The environmental issue has gone through similar distinct phases in Canada and the United States, largely as a response to fluctuations in the business cycle. The first major wave of environmentalism emerged in the late 1960s, peaking with the first Earth Day in the spring of 1970. The first wave also led to a dramatic rise in the number and resources of environmental groups in both countries. In the United States, the Natural Resources Defense Council, the Environmental Defense Fund, and the Friends of the Earth were all formed in the late 1960s and early 1970s, and the older conservation groups, such as the Sierra Club and the National Audubon Society, acquired new members and adopted a more activist approach to pressuring the government (Mitchell 1979; Ingram and Mann 1989). In Canada, Pollution Probe and the Society Promoting Environmental Conservation (SPEC) were formed in 1969, the Canadian Environmental Law Association was founded in 1970, and Greenpeace got its start in 1971 (Macdonald 1990, 96–9).

As the post-war economic boom came to an end in the early 1970s, however, environmental issues in North America declined in salience. While support for environmental protection among the public continued, the problem ceased to be viewed as a major political priority. By 1987 a second wave of environmentalism began forming and the salience of environmental issues surged, culminating with the second Earth Day in the spring of 1990. This second wave peaked shortly thereafter, and the environmental issue again dropped in salience as a result of economic anxieties in the two countries.

Although there has been no systematic comparative analysis of the organized environmental movements in the two countries, it is clear that they share two key features. Environmental groups in both countries do not match the resources that are available to their business opponents. In addition, the movement is fragmented and diverse, lacking central associations to concentrate pressure on governments (Wilson 1992).

The surge in environmental and other public interest groups that occurred around 1970 caught the business community in both Canada and the United States off guard. The lobbying apparatus of business had atrophied after years of cooperative relations with the government, resulting in a loss of control of both the public agenda and actual policy outcomes (Vogel 1989). American business responded to the increase in government regulation with a massive strengthening of its political capacities. It intensified its lobbying activities by expanding representation in Washington, emulating the successful political tactics of its opponents, and developing coalitions with its natural allies. Lobbying efforts were increasingly coordinated by new or enlarged high-level associations. The National Association of Manufacturing and the Chamber of Commerce were revamped, and a new elite organization, the Business Roundtable, was created to represent the broader interests of the business community. Business also launched an offensive in the ideological and intellectual spheres. Aided by the widespread sharpened public sensitivity to economic concerns resulting from the economic woes of the mid-1970s, the corporate counter-offensive restored some of the political clout of the business community (Edsall 1984; Vogel 1989).

While the Canadian public-interest movement was not as formidable as its American counterpart, the business community also felt threatened by the lack of adequate representation of its interests. Paralleling the changes south of the border, Canadian business began to take government relations more seriously (Stanbury 1986, chap. 5). In addition, a new association was formed, the Business Council on National Issues, modelled on the Business Roundtable, 'to defend corporations against an increasing barrage of criticism from the public and from a growing level of government regulation and intervention' (Brooks and Stritch 1991, 211; Langille 1987).

Pluralist Legalism in the United States

In the United States the first wave of environmentalism around 1970 was met with profound changes in the American regulatory regime (Hoberg 1992; Harris and Milkis 1989). First, regulatory authority over the environment was dramatically expanded and centralized at the federal level. An array of new federal statutes was enacted,[2] and a new federal agency, the Environmental Protection Agency (EPA), was created to carry out these ambitious new programs. Prior to 1970, environmental regulation was largely performed by state and local governments. The centralization of this new regulatory authority at the federal level was particularly important because it eliminated competition between states or localities as a source of leverage for industry (Elliott, Ackerman, and Millian 1985).

Second, these new laws did not merely create more government authority over environmental matters, they also dramatically changed the form of that authority. Traditionally, when Congress enacted new laws it did so by delegating vast amounts of authority to the executive branch. These new environmental laws were written with specific goals and deadlines designed to circumscribe the discretion of administrators. The National Environmental Policy Act, for instance, required administrators to perform environmental impact assessments before they proceeded with any major federal activities. The Clean Air Act, perhaps the most extreme version of these so-called 'action-forcing statutes,' required that automobile emissions be reduced by 90 per cent within five years. Congress thus began to play a far more active role in controlling regulatory agencies and, as a result, determining environmental policies (Ackerman and Hassler 1981; Melnick 1983).

Third, courts became far more active in challenging administrative decisions. The judicial activism that began in the areas of civil rights and social policy in the 1950s was extended to the regulatory policy arena in the late 1960s (Stewart 1975). In the United States it is commonplace to refer to the relationship between regulatory authorities and the courts as a 'partnership' (e.g., Melnick 1985). Through changes in the doctrine of standing, citizen groups were given an access to courts that they were previously denied. The specific goals and timetables in the new statutes, by creating non-discretionary duties on behalf of administrators, gave these groups a 'cause of action' to take to court. As a result, the new regime transformed the relationship between citizens and the administrative state as well as between Congress and the executive branch.

These changes in relations between citizens, Congress, courts, and the administrative state reflected the emergence of a new doctrine of 'pluralist legalism.' This new doctrine consisted of both a set of formal institutional relations and a guiding public philosophy. The notion of business capture of regulatory agencies had become commonplace, and the perceived solution was to restrict agency discretion through more specific statutory mandates and to expand the representation of non-industry groups through the use of formal, legalistic procedures, monitored by the courts (McCann 1986; Harris and Milkis 1989). This new doctrine signalled a marked departure from the 'interest group liberalism' Lowi has used (1979) to describe the American policy process.

These changes have endured into the late 1990s. The regime weathered the storm of the early 1980s, when the Reagan administration sought to revert to the business-dominated system of the New Deal regime that existed prior to 1970. The Reagan administration seriously underestimated the power of environmentalists in Congress, the courts, state governments, and public opinion, and by mid-1983 abandoned its effort to undermine pluralist legalism (Hoberg 1992; Harris and Milkis 1989).

In the wake of the 1994 Congressional elections, producing the first Republican majorities in both houses in forty years, a new assault was launched on the pluralist regime. Centred in the House of Representatives, opponents of environmental regulation sought to de-fund environmental agencies and to restrict or eliminate federal regulatory authority in a number of areas. As a result of counter-mobilization by environmental groups and of opposition in the Senate and the White House, the efforts to scale back regulatory legislation were defeated. In both of these cases, Republicans mistook electoral victories for a mandate to weaken environmental regulations, and were defeated by the persistent reservoir of political support for the environment.

Bargaining in Canada

In Canada the first wave of environmentalism was not met with any comparable change in regulatory regime. Canadian governments did indeed respond with new policies and new institutions. At the federal level, the 26th Parliament (1968–72), enacted nine new environmental statutes, including the Clean Air Act and the Canada Water Act, and amended to the Fisheries Act. A new federal department, Environment Canada, was created in 1971. Provincial governments also responded with a wave of new statutes, agencies, and regulations. Ontario passed its Environmental Protection Act in 1971, and Quebec its Environmental Quality Act in 1972 (Woodrow 1980; Dwivedi 1974; Macdonald 1990, chap. 9). The Canadian Council of Resource Ministers was expanded to include the environment portfolio in 1971, and was renamed the Canadian Council of Resource and Environment Ministers.

But in sharp contrast to the United States, the Canadian political system adapted to the new pressures without any major changes in structure or process. New bureaucracies were created and new policies enacted, but the governing arrangements for environmental policy marked no significant departure from either past patterns or the prevailing patterns in other policy domains. Environmental policy was not centralized to the same extent as it was in the United States. Provincial governments continued to be the dominant players in air and water pollution control (Harrison 1994; Lucas 1989). Policy making continued to be dominated by bipartite bargaining conducted through closed, cooperative negotiations between government and industry. According to Andrew Thompson, 'bargaining is the essence of the environmental regulatory process as it is practised in Canada' (Thompson 1980, 33; Schrecker 1984; Hoberg 1993a).

For the most part, environmentalists were excluded from this bargaining because they lacked the organizational sophistication and political clout to inspire officials to invite them into the process, and the legal or procedural rights to pry the doors open. The ruling norm at the time was that environmental interests were to be represented in the policy process, not by private interest groups as in the pluralist model, but by the relevant government agency headed by the minister. To the extent that environmental interests were to be balanced against other societal concerns, this occurred behind closed doors, either in Cabinet or in the bureaucracy depending on the political sensitivity of the issue.

While a surge in public interest in the environment forced the Canadian government into some response, the rapid decline in salience of the issue in the early 1970s and the limited clout of environmental groups meant that restrained, relatively symbolic responses were sufficient to maintain legitimacy for the system. As time went on, however, challenges to this system and its supporting norms escalated, and pressures for reform forced more fundamental institutional changes.

Recent Trends

Regulatory Process

While the Canadian political system successfully coped with the first wave of environmentalism without significant changes in form, the second wave of environmentalism has posed a greater threat to the system's adaptive capacity. The renewed salience of environmental issues challenged the legitimacy of the dominant regulatory regime (Howlett 1990; Doern and Conway 1994; Doern 1995). The system's ability to provide adequate levels of environmental protection was called into question, and much of the blame fell on the regulatory style itself. After a decade and a half of experience, the idea that the state could adequately represent environmental interests was contested, and it now appeared to many to be a cloak concealing a system dominated by business interests.

Two patterns of institutional response emerged. First, Canada moved to expand traditional bargaining processes to include representatives of environmental interests and others (such as labour, consumers, and so on) in what are referred to as 'multi-stakeholder' consultations. As governments began to feel more pressure to produce new environmental policies, multi-stakeholder forums became a standard operating procedure of the policy process. This new regime of 'multipartite bargaining' represents a departure from Canadian tradition. The traditional bipartite bargaining of the old style has been replaced by an expanded bargaining process that includes environmentalists and other groups. Significantly, the public philosophy underlying the policy process has also changed. The state is no longer trusted to represent environmental interests on its own – this task has devolved to organized environmental groups (Hoberg 1993a).

The second response to the loss of legitimacy of the bipartite bargaining of the Canadian past has been to borrow the strategy from environmentalists south of the border and to rely on the courts to pressure governments to change policy. Legalism emerged in Canadian environmental policy in disputes over environmental impact assessment. In 1989, in response to legal action by environmentalists, courts intervened in several controversies involving the construction of dams, forcing the federal government to perform impact assessments. While standard fare in the United States, these judicial decisions were unprecedented in Canada, and sent shock waves through the environmental policy community. In a series of decisions the Federal Court of Canada responded to requests by environmental groups to block the construction of dams because the federal government did not comply with the Environmental Assessment Review Process (EARP) guidelines order. These decisions transformed the guidelines order into a binding legal requirement, and demonstrated the courts' willingness to force the government to comply with the order. After a period of considerable legal turmoil, the Supreme Court issued a landmark ruling on the issue in January 1992, upholding most of the Appeal Court decision in the Oldman Dam case. The Supreme Court agreed with the lower court interpretation that the EARP guidelines were binding, and it also agreed with the expansive interpretation of federal authority over the provinces. While the Supreme Court did not go as far as some of the earlier decisions, it still provided a solid endorsement of legalism in Canadian impact assessment.

As a result of the uncertainty generated by these court cases, as well as strong public pressures for more rigorous environmental assessments, the federal government tabled legislation in June 1990 to incorporate environmental assessment into a statute through the Canadian Environmental Assessment Act. While originally an attempt by the government to remove the non-discretionary duties the courts have read into the Guidelines Order (Schrecker 1991), the act was later amended to restore a number of non-discretionary duties. The bill passed the House of Commons in March 1992, but was not proclaimed until October 1994.

Efforts to judicialize Canadian environmental policy go beyond impact assessments. In British Columbia the Sierra Legal Defence Fund has launched a concerted effort to use the courts to reform the province's forest practices. Thus far, however, its successes have been limited (Hoberg 1993b). A potentially more dramatic introduction of legalism was suggested by Ontario's commitment to the enactment of an 'environmental bill of rights,' when the New Democratic Party came to power in 1990. Proposals introduced by NDP members while in opposition and urged by environmental lawyers within the Canadian Bar Association would have produced a legalistic framework similar to that south of the border (Muldoon 1988). After a protracted period of consultation and negotiation, however, the Environmental Bill of Rights that ultimately passed in Ontario did not go very far down the road to legalism. It did produce more formal regulatory procedures, similar to notice and comment rule-making in the United States, but it did virtually nothing to impose substantive duties on the government or grant substantive rights to environmentalists, significantly limiting any likely increase in the role of the courts (Estrin and Swaigen 1993, chap. 25; Canadian Institute for Environmental Law and Policy 1995).

While there has been some Canadian movement towards the U.S. model, there has also been some U.S. movement towards the Canadian model. When U.S. institutions underwent their transformation around 1970, the system went directly from one of bipartite bargaining – what Americans refer to as the New Deal policy regime – to pluralist legalism. But in recent years a new form of cooperative pluralism has been struggling to find its place in U.S. regulatory procedures (Administrative Conference of the United States 1990; Fiorino 1988, 1990). 'Regulatory negotiation' is based on the idea that cooperative discussions among relevant stakeholders produces better policy outcomes than the bewilderingly complex process of adversarial legalism. In 1983 EPA established its Regulatory Negotiation Project with great promise – it seemed like an idea whose time had come. By spring 1994, however, regulatory negotiation had only had a marginal impact on EPA's operations. The agency has completed only ten negotiations, about one per year, a disappointing rate, especially considering that the agency typically promulgates around one hundred major regulations every year. The limited success of the program thus far raises grave questions about the prospects for moving away from the adversarial, legalistic nature of U.S. environmental policy making.

The combination of regulatory negotiation in the United States and creeping legalism in Canada may raise the prospect of some institutional convergence between the two countries, but it seems unlikely that the profound differences between them will be significantly reduced. Indeed, a survey of court cases in the two countries up through 1989 (albeit before the judicialization of impact assessments in Canada) found little evidence of convergence in judicial roles in environmental policy in the two countries (Howlett 1994). There are significant macro-political obstacles to substantial departures from each country's dominant regulatory style. Regulatory styles are embedded in distinct national systems of political institutions and culture (Kelman 1981; Brickman, Jasanoff, and Ilgen 1985), making significant changes in regulatory style extremely difficult without simultaneous changes in the macro-political system.

In the United States, institutional fragmentation and a culture of distrust militate against the emergence of cooperative bargaining. Environmental groups are sceptical of regulatory negotiations because in many ways it is antithetical to how they have traditionally operated. Congress is also suspicious, in part because it is concerned that it will be more difficult to monitor what the agency is doing, threatening the existing system of accountability to Congress that is provided by the formalistic notice and comment process. In addition, many members of Congress associate cooperative procedures with the efforts – abandoned long ago – of the early Reagan administration to deregulate the environment through private industry–agency meetings.

Surprisingly, even parts of the executive branch are leery. The cost-conscious Office of Management and Budget is concerned both with the loss of control involved in delegating policy making to negotiating groups, but more importantly that the agreements reached by the participants may have little to do with maximizing net benefits for society. Congress and the White House both share authority over EPA, but neither one trusts the regulatory agency, and they certainly don't trust each other. This competition for power over agency outcomes forces the regulatory process into an open, formalistic, and adversarial mode that is antithetical to the operation of cooperative bargaining.

In Canada, institutional structures militate against legalism. Legalism relies on restricting the autonomy of the executive, whether through specific statutes or a more general environmental right. In the American separation of powers system, Congress does not trust the executive, and therefore writes highly specific statutes. In a parliamentary system like Canada's, the legislature and executive are fused. This fact – along with the presence of extremely tight party discipline – means that there are few institutional incentives to restrict regulatory discretion (Hoberg 1993a). It is this difference in the specificity of regulatory statutes that provides the principal explanation for the different roles of the courts in environmental policy in the two countries (Howlett 1994).

Thus, there are still substantial differences in Canadian and U.S. policy-making institutions and processes, in terms of both the degree of legalism and in the nature of fragmentation. Legalism is far more pervasive in the United States, producing a more open, formal, and adversarial system in which the autonomy of regulators is carefully restricted by Congressional statutes, interest-group demands, and court decisions. In Canada, environmental policy making is more informal and cooperative, and regulators enjoy substantial autonomy. The introduction of multi-stakeholder consultations has made it more open than before, but has not resulted in a profound transformation of the regime. The second wave of environmentalism, combined with the shift towards a less deferential political culture, has placed considerable stress on the Canadian regime, but it has adapted with relatively modest changes.

Regulatory Instruments

One of the most significant trends in environmental policy is the effort to move beyond the conventional 'command and control' regulation that historically has dominated environmental regulation (Doern 1990). Reform efforts have focused on three types of alternatives: market-based incentives, information provision, and voluntary approaches. Since the dawn of the modern era of environmental regulation in the late 1960s, economists have been criticizing regulators for adopting an overly coercive and blunt approach to controlling environmental degradation. Despite decades of cajoling, however, policy makers have been remarkably resistant to embracing more market-oriented incentives such as marketable permits and pollution taxes.

There are some significant recent exceptions. The most important program to date is the provision for emission trading in the acid-rain provisions of the 1990 Clean Air Act amendments. The first significant market-based program in Canada is the one established to implement the Montreal Protocol on stratospheric ozone. But these programs are the exception to the rule – regulation is unquestionably the dominant approach to environmental policy in both countries. Acknowledging the reality that coercive regulations are likely to be a permanent reality in the United States, the Clinton administration has targeted its reform efforts at increasing the flexibility granted to industries in complying with regulatory standards. Project XL is designed to grant to industries, in exchange for commitments to reduce overall pollution and involve local resident, waivers from some of the more complex and burdensome regulatory requirements.

Another alternative approach is requiring the disclosure of information about pullutants rather than explicitly regulating the pollutants. This 'right to know' approach originated with the 1986 amendments to the U.S. 'Superfund' law. The law requires firms using or producing specified toxic chemicals to provide both EPA and state and local governments with information about the chemicals, including the quantities on site and, most importantly, their release into the environment. Any citizen has access to this information. Canada put a similar program into place in 1994. As anticipated, many firms have responded to the disclosure requirements by reducing emissions of hazardous chemicals. The EPA estimates that its program led to a 43 per cent decrease in emissions from 1988 to 1993 (Press and Mazmanian 1996).

While Canada has lagged behind the United States introducing right-to-know laws, it is ahead on eco-labelling. The Canadian federal government has a program to certify products as environmentally friendly by granting them a special seal. No such program exists in the United States. In addition, Canada was the first nation in the world to adopt an 'ozone watch,' which provides daily readings of ultraviolet radiation levels as part of weather forecasts. The United States has yet to adopt such a program.

The third major thrust of instrument reform is relying on voluntary approaches and persuasion, with a particular focus on pollution prevention. The EPA in the United States has introduced several programs to promote energy efficiency, and it has made a major effort to get polluters to reduce voluntarily toxic emissions. The EPA so-called 33/50 program challenged industries to reduce toxic emissions by 33 per cent by 1992 and 50 per cent by 1995. Over 1,300 companies participated, leading to reductions in toxic emissions without any new regulations (Press and Mazmanian 1996). Canada has adopted a similar program called Accelerated Reductions/Elimination of Toxics (ARET).

Experimentation with these new policy instruments is a potentially promising development in environmental policy because they create the possibility of substantial environmental benefits with low marginal costs. However, environmentalists remain highly sceptical of these alternatives, because they see them either as covert efforts to water down environmental controls or as governmental surrender to industry refusals to tolerate additional costly regulations. There is some basis for concern about the potential efficacy of the information provision and voluntary programs. In order to result in substantial environmental benefits, they rely on industry incentives to respond. Businesses are unlikely to voluntarily incur additional costs if they see a benefit in terms of either market advantage or the avoidance of more coercive government regulations. Thus their success depends on continued public interest and support for, and knowledge of, efforts to reduce emissions. They also depend on governments being able to make a realistic threat that the failure to take voluntary action will result in compulsory action. With de-funding and the weakening of regulatory capacity and will discussed below, the influence of this threat may be declining.

De-funding and Decentralization

Both Canada and the United States are witnessing two other trends with significant implications for regulatory regimes: persistent fiscal crises resulting in powerful pressures to reduce government spending, and pressures to decentralize regulatory authority away from the federal government. While the two countries share comparable fiscal pressures, the pressures for decentralization are much stronger in Canada.

Supporters of environmental policy in the United States have been relatively successful at thwarting efforts to weaken regulatory authority contained in statutes both in the early Reagan years and during the recent Republican Revolution in the 104th Congress (1995–6). However, the budgetary resources available to environmental agencies have not fared as well. EPA's operating budget was cut by 19 per cent (in constant dollars) between 1980 and 1985.

After recovering to its pre-Reagan levels in constant dollars in the early 1990s, it was cut by 7.5 per cent in real terms in 1995 and 1996 (Vig and Kraft 1996, app. 3). These cuts occurred despite expanding regulatory responsibilities.

In Canada, the much-touted Green Plan, introduced as a $3 billion five-year plan, promised a significant expansion of federal spending on the environment. However, the federal government never came close to its promised spending levels, and the Green Plan was quietly terminated in early 1995 with only $847 million (28 per cent) of its original commitment spent (Canadian Press 1995). Projected spending levels for Environment Canada in 1997–8 are no higher than they were in 1984–5 (Toner 1996). Ontario, Canada's largest province and historically its most environmentally innovative and progressive, has experienced massive funding cutbacks in its environmemtal programs. Between the 1994–5 and the 1996–7 budget years, the Ministry of Environment and Energy was cut by 37 per cent and the Ministry of Natural Resources by 22 per cent (Canadian Institute for Environmental Law and Policy 1996). Meanwhile, the Canadian Council of Ministers of the Environment, the intergovernmental bureaucracy, has experienced a recent 45 per cent budget cut.[3] These budgetary cutbacks in both countries are significant because they undermine the capacity of the regulatory regime in each country.

Decentralization is another significant trend in environmental regulatory regimes. Both Canada and the United States are federal countries, but the U.S. system is significantly more centralized. Since 1970 the U.S. federal government has taken the leadership in environmental protection and dramatically expanded its authority vis-à-vis the states. Federal regulations directly control a broad range of polluting activities, and for a number of other activities the federal government sets uniform national standards and requires the states to comply with them. In Canada the federal government has played a less significant role, providing support in terms of research and supporting the development of national guidelines based on agreement among the provinces. Very few federal regulatory standards exist, and for those that do enforcement has been delegated to the provinces (Harrison 1996; Doern and Conway 1994).

Both countries have experienced pressures to decentralize regulations. In the United States efforts by Republicans to relax environmental standards in the early 1980s and mid-1990s were accompanied by efforts to transfer regulatory authority to the states. While there have been some marginal changes, the overwhelming dominant federal role has been maintained.

In Canada efforts to reduce the already minor federal role are making greater headway. In the late 1980s and early 1990s, during the second wave of environmental enthusiasm, the trend seemed to be in the opposite direction. With the introduction of the Canadian Environmental Protection Act and the Canadian

Environmental Assessment Act, the federal government seemed intent on expanding its jurisdiction. However, efforts to accommodate provincial opposition undermined any significant centralizing effect of these initiatives (Harrison 1996). More recently, in November 1996, the provinces and the federal government agreed to a major initiative to harmonize environmental standards. The agreement rationalizes federal and provincial roles in areas of duplication and overlap, allowing considerable administrative cost savings. But it also has the effect of further devolving environmental jurisdiction to the provinces. For that reason it has raised the ire of environmentalists who are concerned that without a strong federal role in setting uniform standards, environmental protection will be weakened (Mittlestaedt 1996).

International Pressures

To date the dominant force behind environmental policy has unquestionably been domestic pressure. Recently, however, pressures from the international arena have increased. Four types of international factors influence environmental policy, and they all tend to promote convergence. They are: (1) the escalating importance of global environmental problems and the increased attempts at international collaboration to address the problems; (2) economic integration, including formal trade agreements such as the Canada–U.S. Free Trade Agreement (FTA), the North American Free Trade Agreement (NAFTA), and the General Agreement on Trade and Tariffs (GATT); (3) the cross-national transfer of ideas; and (4) cross-border lobbying. These developments affect both the United States and Canada, but the vulnerability to external forces is much greater in Canada because of its smaller size and more open economy. In addition, Canada faces the unique problem of being overwhelmingly dependent on the United States (Hoberg 1997).[4]

International pressures are, of course, not new to Canadian and U.S. environmental policy. The International Joint Commission was established to address shared environmental concerns in 1909, and the Migratory Birds Convention was forged to protect natural habitats in 1917. The most successful case of bilateral action between the two countries is the Great Lakes Water Quality Agreement, signed in 1972. While it was much slower in coming, collaboration over transboundary air pollution has always been somewhat successful. After over a decade of stubborn refusal, the United States finally entered into an agreement with Canada in 1991 after amendments to the U.S. Clean Air Act were passed by Congress and signed into law in 1990 (Doern and Conway 1994; Munton and Castle 1992).

In the late 1980s and early 1990s mounting concern for global climate change and threats to biodiversity elevated international issues to the forefront of the environmental agenda. Agreement on the Montreal Protocol of 1987 to reduce ozone depleting substances represented a significant collaborative achievement. Much less progress has occurred on the issue of global warming that has higher stakes, and neither Canada nor the United States has taken an aggressive role in promoting action. The highly visible United Nations Conference on Environment and Development in 1992 did much to elevate the profile of global environmental issues on the international agenda, but the progress on concrete measures was disappointing (Haas, Levy, and Parson 1992).

The increasing importance of global environmental problems is not the only international issue putting pressure on domestic environmental policy. Economic globalization also has potentially profound implications, although the direction of its impact is not yet clear (Vogel 1996). First, pressures towards harmonization of standards may occur as a result of the costs that environmental regulations impose on firms competing in international markets. In the case of 'process standards,' that control the way products are produced (such as effluent controls on a chemical plant), they may cause firms to suffer a competitive disadvantage if their costs for complying with environmental regulations exceed those of competitors. Firms in such a situation are likely to lobby their governments to reduce regulatory burdens, creating the potential for a 'race to the bottom,' in which each nation attempts to create a competitive advantage for its firms by weakening environmental standards. Empirical studies show little evidence of such an effect, largely because environmental costs are relatively small compared to other factors. According to a U.S. government study, 'compliance costs are not a major share of total costs for any industry, and are only one of many factors determining competitive advantage' (Office of Technology Assessment 1994). Nonetheless, fears about the impact of environmental controls on competitiveness have been an important political phenomenon in recent years.

In the case of 'product standards' that control the characteristics of the product itself (such as limits on the quantity of a particular chemical contained in a product), firms have an interest in uniform regulations across nations so they can take advantage of the economies involved in producing the same product for a larger market. In this case, however, it is more likely that firms will target their lobbying at international bodies rather than domestic governments.

Second, trade agreements may encourage the harmonization of environmental standards, and open countries' environmental policies to challenge by competitors on the grounds that they provide unfair subsidies or are a non-tariff barrier to trade (Esty 1994). Many environmentalists in Canada were highly critical of the Canada–U.S. FTA because they feared it would lead to a weakening of Canadian environmental standards (Shrybman 1993); many American environmentalists expressed similar fears about NAFTA (Audley 1993).

Nothing in the three major international trade agreements explicitly requires harmonization of environmental standards. In fact, they all recognize the right of countries to have different standards. The environmental side-agreement to NAFTA explicitly addresses the issue, but even it focuses on the enforcement of each country's own laws and contains no requirements that those laws be changed.[5] There are some measures which are designed to *encourage* harmonization. NAFTA's sections on Sanitary and Phytosanitary Standards and on Standards-Related Measures contain provisions that encourage the adoption of international standards, but the measures are intended to promote upward harmonization. Parties are urged to 'pursue equivalence' and use international standards, but 'without reducing the level of protection for the environment.' Countries are explicitly allowed to exceed international standards. It is true that if trading partners believe that standards exceeding the international norm are a barrier to trade, they can challenge the standard under the agreement's dispute settlement measures, but the complaining party bears the burden of proof in demonstrating that the standard is not based on 'scientific principles' (Charnovitz 1993).

These international trade agreements may constrain environmental policy in four ways. First, the principle of national treatment explicitly allows countries to adopt their own regulatory rules, but also requires that the same rules apply to domestically produced and imported products. Second, policies that distort trade are subject to challenge or retaliation by competitors. Policies aimed at conservation and environmental protection are exempted from these challenges under Article xx of GATT, but whether or not the environmental justifications are legitimate is a matter of interpretation and subject to the dispute resolution process (Esty 1994). Third, the ability of countries to use trade measures, such as import bans, on products produced according to environmentally damaging processes is limited.[6] Finally, the NAFTA side-agreement on the environment may make it more difficult for a country to engage in routine non-compliance with its own environmental standards, although the procedural hoops that a country must go through to impose sanctions on a country that fails to enforce its own laws are quite daunting (Charnovitz 1994).

Another potential force for convergence is emulation, where one country adopts another country's policy innovations (Bennett 1991). In North American environmental policy, this phenomenon is pervasive, and it is virtually unidirectional from the United States to Canada (Hoberg 1991). Emulation usually occurs through one of two primary modes. The first is elite driven, when officials or policy specialists evaluating policy alternatives are attracted to the U.S.

experience. Officials may learn about U.S. policies through the media, specialized publications, or participation in transnational policy communities. In many cases, formal meetings are scheduled between government officials in the two countries to share information and discuss common concerns.

The second mode of emulation is activist driven, when political activists use the existence of an American program or standard to support their argument for policy change in Canada. In this case, activists try to 'shame' the government into acting, with the logic that 'if it is good enough for them, it is good enough for us.' This dynamic is facilitated by the penetration of the U.S. mass media into Canada. When an issue of importance emerges in the United States, it is often picked up by Canadian policy activists or the media, forcing the government to respond.

The emulation dynamic goes beyond the bilateral influence of the United States on Canada. Indeed, much of the strategy of nascent international institutions relies less on making international rules that are binding on nation states and more on publicizing comparative information about the environmental policy performance of different nations. Although the Rio Conference in June 1992 did not yield much in the way of substantive agreements, it did set in motion an institutional process whereby national governments would submit reports to a new Commission on Sustainable Development (Haas, Levy, and Parson 1992). Similarly, NAFTA requires reports to the new Commission for Environmental Cooperation. These reporting requirements create the possibility that exposing the performance of national governments may 'shame' laggards into improvements.

The fourth and final international influence on environmental policy is cross-border lobbying. Interest groups from one country increasingly engage in efforts to lobby the government of another country. Cross-border lobbying has occurred in several areas of environmental policy in North America. The northward flow of lobbying is reflected in efforts by U.S. environmentalists to block further hydroelectric developments in northern Quebec and to promote wilderness preservation in British Columbia, the southward flow in efforts by Canadian environmentalists to get Congress to adopt acid-rain controls in the 1980s and by Canadian industry to overturn EPA's ban on asbestos.

All four of these international factors increase the extent of external influences on domestic regulatory regimes. But it is important not to overstate the importance of the internationalization of environmental policy making. National governments still dominate policy making even in the case of global or bilateral issues. In the case of acid rain, for instance, Canada was probably not irrelevant to U.S. decision making, but the 1991 air quality accord between the two countries merely sanctioned the outcomes of a ten-year-long domestic struggle within the United States. The Great Lakes agreement has had more influence, but there is still divergence in regulatory standards and enforcement across the border in the region, and the administrative and regulatory capacities of the International Joint Commission pale in comparison to those of the national and the state and provincial governments in the region.

Economic integration poses a potentially significant threat to domestic sovereignty, but it has limits as well. While this concern underlaid much of the opposition to international trade agreements among Canadian environmentalists, it has not been much of a problem for Canadian policy makers, largely because the environmental regulations of Canada's dominant trading partner, the United States, are at least as stringent as those in Canada (Hoberg 1997).

While strong U.S. standards have mitigated the downward pressures on Canadian policy, economic integration can actually pull environmental controls up rather than merely pushing them down. For instance, the Canadian forest products industry is being forced into more environmentally 'friendly' practices as a result of market pressures from consumers outside the country. American states and municipalities have required newspapers to contain a certain percentage of recycled fibres, forcing Canadian exporters to increase their capacity to supply recycled newsprint. Demands from European governments and consumers for chlorine-free paper products and more environmentally sensitive forest practices have encouraged the industry to adopt expensive controls to reduce emissions of dioxins and furans and the province of British Columbia to overhaul its regulatory regime. Understanding these implications of globalization, Greenpeace and other Canadian environmental groups have been lobbying European governments with the goal of achieving environmental progress in Canada through global market pressures.

Being a small state does restrict the flexibility of Canadian regulators. For instance, when multinational chemical companies attempt to introduce a new pesticide, they typically apply for registration in the United States first because of its large market size. If the product receives approval there, the large market allows relatively rapid recovery of product development and approval costs. Only after getting approval in the United States do manufacturers then seek approval in smaller countries such as Canada. This situation constrains Canadian regulators in that the more 'independent' they choose to be from the United States – for example, by requiring additional tests under Canadian field conditions – the more they drive up the costs of registering the product in Canada, potentially discouraging some manufacturers from applying. There are strong incentives simply to adopt the U.S. decision, especially because growers frequently place pressure on regulators to approve products in use in the United States so they do not suffer a competitive disadvantage (Hoberg 1991). From an environmental perspective, this small state problem would be a much greater concern if the U.S. record on regulating pesticide products was not as strong as it is (Hoberg 1997).

Conclusions

The United States and Canada share commitments to liberal democracy, but their macro-political systems are quite distinct. The two countries also share a commitment to environmental preservation, but their regulatory regimes are still significantly different, in large measure because they are embedded in two distinct macro-political systems. The legalistic U.S. environmental policy regime emerged in the early 1970s, and it has been relatively stable since then. In Canada the emergence of the environment as a political phenomenon has not been accompanied by the same dramatic regime transformation. Canada's regime is still based on decentralization towards the provinces and a policy style centred on the minister. The major change is that the cooperative bargaining style of policy making has been expanded to include a broader range of interests, making the process somewhat more pluralistic.

Both countries have experienced profound pressures for change in recent years – opposition to traditional forms of regulation, budget scarcity, decentralization, and internationalization – and regulatory regimes have begun the awkward task of adapting to these changes. Several of these changes represent promising developments in environmental policy, but they are also potentially significant threats to regulatory capacity that might undermine the pursuit of sustainable development. The increased attention to alternative regulatory instruments offers the promise of achieving additional environmental benefits at reduced marginal costs. But it also threatens to undermine the support for coercive measures that are essential to imposing costs on powerful interests when it is necessary to protect the environment.

Decentralization promises to tap lower levels of government as 'laboratories of democracy,' producing innovation and experimentation that enhance prospects for sustainable development, at the same time as it allows for greater flexibility in policies and administration to respond to local concerns. However, decentralization also threatens to place subnational units in competition with one another for investment and jobs, leading to an unhealthy 'race to the bottom' dynamic that dampens the ability of political units at all levels to pursue environmental objectives. Internationalization promises a new era of collaboration to address international and global environmental problems that are beyond the jurisdiction of any one country to address effectively. But internationalization also creates the potential for still another race to the bottom, not between states or provinces, but between nations. And both greater exposure to the global economy and multilateral legal commitments undermine the policy sovereignty of domestic regulatory regimes. Budget scarcity is the one pervasive pressure that cuts only one way: it undermines the will and capacity of governments to pursue sustainable development.

The challenge for policy makers is to maximize the opportunities created by these forces while minimizing the risks they pose. After analysing the structures and dynamics of the policy regimes of both countries, it appears that Canada is significantly more vulnerable to these risks. The U.S. regime seems relatively formidable in the face of the challenges. Even though it has experienced the anxieties of internationalization, its size and global influence make it far less vulnerable than Canada. In addition, the U.S. constitutional structure makes policy change so difficult that opponents of retrenchment are empowered.

As a small, relatively open economy, Canada is far more vulnerable to internationalization. Canada's political system makes policy change strikingly easy when policy is controlled at one level of government. Parties whose percentage of popular support is in the low forties can readily gain workable governing majorities and change policy abruptly. With the dynamic of fluctuating salience of environmental issues, environmental policy is highly vulnerable to retrenchment. Canadian policy is less easily changed when it gets mixed up in intergovernmental conflicts. However, as a result of a combination of fiscal pressures and the need to manage the separatist threat from Quebec, in the mid-1990s environment issues find themselves in the vanguard of the new wave of Canadian decentralization. Undoubtedly the elimination of duplication and overlap will create some efficiencies. Nonetheless, there is strong basis for concern that reducing the federal environmental role and devolving greater responsibility to cash-strapped provinces will further undermine regulatory will and capacity in Canada.

NOTES

1 Research for this chapter was funded by the Social Sciences and Humanities Research Council of Canada. Parts of this chapter rely extensively on Hoberg (1997).
2 These included the National Environmental Policy Act (1969), Clean Air Act (1970), Federal Water Pollution Control Act (1972), Federal Insecticide, Fungicide, and Rodenticide Act (1972), and the Endangered Species Act (1973).
3 Personal communication with Charlotte Hilton, Director of Administration and Finance, Canadian Council of Ministers of the Environment, December, 1996.
4 For other analyses that emphasize the internationalization of Canadian environmental policy, see Hoberg (1991), Toner and Conway (1996), and Howlett (1996).

5 A prominent expert on trade and the environment denounces this provision as 'retrogressive': 'An international obligation based on each government's own standard is the weakest conceivable form of international agreement ... [T]he three governments resorted to an atavistic, uninspiring approach aimed at the wrong target' (Charnovitz 1994, 22).

6 In a landmark 1991 case, a GATT dispute resolution panel ruled that the United States could not impose a ban on tuna imported from Mexico because of fishing practices that threatened dolphins (Esty 1994, 27–32).

REFERENCES

Ackerman, Bruce, and William Hassler. 1981. *Clean Coal/Dirty Air*. New Haven: Yale University Press.

Administrative Conference of the United States. 1990. *Negotiated Rulemaking Sourcebook*. Washington: Government Printing Office.

Audley, John. 1993. 'Why Environmentalists Are Angry about the North American Free Trade Agreement.' In *Trade and the Environment*, edited by Durwood Zaehlke, Paul Orbuch, and Robert Housman. Washington, DC: Island Press.

Bennett, Colin. 1991. 'How States Utilize Foreign Evidence.' *Journal of Public Policy* 11:31–54.

Brickman, Ronald, Sheila Jasanoff, and Thomas Ilgen. 1985. *Controlling Chemicals*. Ithaca: Cornell University Press.

Brooks, Stephen, and Andrew Stritch. 1991. *Business and Government in Canada*. Scarborough, Ont.: Prentice-Hall Canada.

Canadian Institute for Environmental Law and Policy. 1995. *Achieving the Holy Grail? A Legal and Political Analysis of Ontario's Environmental Bill of Rights*. Toronto: Canadian Institute for Environmental Law and Policy.

– 1996. *Ontario's Environment and the 'Common Sense Revolution.'* Toronto: Canadian Institute for Environmental Law and Policy.

Canadian Press. 1995. 'Canada's Green Plan Strikes Out.' *Vancouver Sun*, 20 April A4.

Charnovitz, Steve. 1993. 'NAFTA: An Analysis of Its Environmental Provisions.' *Environment Law Reporter* 23:10067–73.

– 1994. 'The NAFTA Side Agreement and Its Implications for Environmental Cooperation, Trade Policy, and American Treatymaking.' *Temple International and Comparative Law Journal* 8:257–314.

Doern, Bruce, ed. 1990. *Getting it Green*. Toronto: C.D. Howe Institute.

– 1995. 'Sectoral Green Politics and Environmental Regulation in the Canadian Pulp and Paper Industry.' *Environmental Politics* 4, no. 2:219–43.

Doern, Bruce, and Tom Conway. 1994. *The Greening of Canada*. Toronto: University of Toronto Press.

Dwivedi, O.P. 1974. 'Canadian Governmental Response to Environmental Concern.' In *Protecting the Environment*, edited by O.P. Dwivedi. Vancouver: Copp Clark.

Edsall, Thomas. 1984. *The New Politics of Inequality*. New York: Norton.

Elliott, E. Donald, Bruce Ackerman, and John Millian. 1985. 'Toward a Theory of Statutory Evolution: The Federalization of Environmental Law.' *Journal of Law, Economics, and Organization* 1:313–40.

Estrin, David, and John Swaigen. 1993. *Environment on Trial*. 3rd ed. Toronto: Edmond Montgomery Publications Limited.

Esty, Daniel C. 1994. *Greening the GATT: Trade, Environment, and the Future*. Washington: Institute for International Economics.

Fiorino, Daniel. 1988. 'Regulatory Negotiation as a Policy Process.' *Public Administration Review* 48:764–72.

– 1990. 'Dimensions of Negotiated Rule-Making: Practical Constraints and Theoretical Implications.' In *Conflict Resolution and Public Policy*, edited by Miriam K. Mills. New York: Greenwood Press.

Haas, Peter, Marc Levy, and Edward Parson. 1992. 'Appraising the Earth Summit: How Should We Judge UNCED's Success?' *Environment* 34:6–11, 26–33.

Harris, Richard, and Sidney Milkis. 1989. *The Politics of Regulatory Change*. New York: Oxford University Press.

Harrison, Kathryn. 1994. 'Prospects for Intergovernmental Harmonization in Environmental Policy.' In *Canada: The State of the Federation 1994*, edited by Douglas Brown and Janet Hiebert. Kingston, Ont.: Institute of Intergovernmental Relations.

– 1996. *Passing the Buck: Federalism and Canadian Environmental Policy*. Vancouver: UBC Press.

Hoberg, George. 1991. 'Sleeping with an Elephant: The American Influence on Canadian Environmental Regulation.' *Journal of Public Policy* 11:107–31.

– 1992. *Pluralism by Design: Environmental Policy and the American Regulatory State*. New York: Praeger.

– 1993a. 'Environmental Policy: Alternative Styles.' In *Governing Canada: State Institutions and Public Policy*, edited Michael Atkinson. Toronto: HBJ-Holt.

– 1993b. 'Regulating Forestry: Comparing Institutions and Policies in British Columbia and the American Pacific Northwest.' Forest Economics and Policy Analysis Unit, University of British Columbia, Working Paper 185, May.

– 1997. 'Governing the Environment: Comparing Canada and the United States.' In *Degrees of Freedom: Canada and the United States in a Changing World*, edited by Keith Banting, George Hoberg, and Richard Simeon. Kingston and Montreal: McGill-Queen's University Press.

Howlett, Michael. 1990. 'The Round Table Experience: Representation and Legitimacy in Canadian Environmental Policy-Making.' *Queen's Quarterly* 97:580–601.

– 1994. 'The Judicialization of Canadian Environmental Policy, 1980–1990: A Test of the Canada–United States Convergence Thesis.' *Canadian Journal of Political Science* 17:99–128.

Ingram, Helen, and Dean Mann. 1989. 'Interest Groups and Environmental Policy.' In *Environmental Politics and Policy: Theories and Evidence*, edited by James P. Lester. Durham, N.C.: Duke University Press.

Kelman, Steven. 1981. *Regulating America, Regulating Sweden*. Cambridge: MIT Press.

Langille, David. 1987. 'The Business Council on National Issues and the Canadian State.' *Studies in Political Economy* 24:41–85.

Lowi, Theodore. 1979. *The End of Liberalism*. New York: Norton.

Lucas, Alastair. 1989. 'The New Environmental Law.' In *Canada: State of the Federation 1989*. Kingston, Ont.: Queen's University, Institute of Intergovernmental Relations.

Macdonald, Doug. 1990. *The Politics of Pollution*. Toronto: McClelland and Stewart.

McCann, Michael. 1986. *Taking Reform Seriously*. Ithaca: Cornell University Press.

Melnick, R. Shep. 1983. *Regulation and the Courts*. Washington: Brookings Institution.

– 1985. 'The Politics of Partnership.' *Public Administration Review* 45:653–60.

Mitchell, Robert Cameron. 1979. 'National Environmental Lobbies and the Apparent Illogic of Collective Action.' In *Collective Decision Making*, edited by Clifford Russell. Baltimore: Johns Hopkins University Press.

Mittelstaedt, Martin. 1996. 'Ministers Reach Pollution Accord.' *Globe and Mail*. 21 November, A4.

Muldoon, Paul. 1988. 'The Fight for an Environmental Bill of Rights.' *Alternatives* 15:33–9.

Munton, Don, and Geoffrey Castle. 1992. 'Air, Water, and Political Fire: Building a North American Environmental Regime.' In *Canadian Foreign Policy and International Economic Regimes*, edited by A. Claire Cutler and Mark W. Zacher. Vancouver: UBC Press.

Office of Technology Assessment. 1994. *Industry, Technology, and the Environment: Competitive Challenges and Business Opportunities*. Washington: Government Printing Office.

Press, Daniel, and Daniel Mazmanian. 1996. 'The Greening of Industry: Achievement and Potential.' *Environmental Policy in the 1990s,* edited by Norman Vig and Michael Kraft. 3rd ed. Washington: CQ Press.

Schrecker, Ted. 1984. *The Political Economy of Environmental Hazards*. Ottawa: Law Reform Commission.

– 1991. 'The Canadian Environmental Assessment Act: Tremulous Step Forward to Retreat into Smoke and Mirrors?' *Canadian Environmental Law Reports* 5 (March): 192–246.

Shrybman, Steven. 1993. 'Trading Away the Environment.' In *The Political Economy of*

North American Free Trade, edited by Richard Grinspun and Maxwell Cameron. Montreal and Kingston: McGill-Queen's University Press.

Stanbury, W.T. 1986. *Business–Government Relations in Canada*. Toronto: Methuen.

Stewart, Richard. 1975. 'The Reformation of American Administrative Law.' *Harvard Law Review* 88:1667–813.

Thompson, Andrew. 1980. *Environmental Regulation in Canada*. A study prepared for the Economic Council of Canada by the Westwater Research Centre, University of British Columbia.

Toner, Glen. 1996. 'Environment Canada's Continuing Roller Coaster Ride.' In *How Ottawa Spends 1996–7: Life under the Knife*, edited by Gene Swimmer. Ottawa: Carleton University Press.

Toner, Glen, and Tom Conway. 1996. 'Environmental Policy.' *Border Crossings: The Internationalization of Canadian Public Policy*, edited by G. Bruce Doern, Leslie Pal, and Brian Tomlin. Toronto: Oxford University Press.

Vig, Norman, and Michael Kraft, eds. 1996. *Environmental Policy in the 1990s*. 3rd ed. Washington: CQ Press.

Vogel, David. 1989. *Fluctuating Fortunes: The Political Power of Business in America*. New York: Basic Books.

– 1996. 'International Trade and Environmental Regulation.' *Environmental Policy in the 1990s*, edited by Norman Vig and Michael Kraft. 3rd ed. Washington: CQ Press.

Wilson, Jeremy. 1992. 'Green Lobbies: Pressure Groups and Environmental Policy.' In *Canadian Environmental Policy*, edited by Robert Boardman. Toronto: Oxford University Press.

Woodrow, R. Brian. 1980. 'Resources and Environmental Policy-making at the National Level: The Search for Focus.' In O.P. Dwivedi, *Resources and the Environment: Policy Perspectives for Canada*. Toronto: McClelland and Stewart.

14

The Office of Telecommunications: A New Competition Authority?

COSMO GRAHAM

Telecommunications is today one of the most dynamic industries in the UK, and one that has changed dramatically over a comparatively short space of time.[1] When British Telecommunications (BT) was privatized in 1984 it was by far the dominant player in the industry. There was only one competitor, Mercury Communications, whose business was in its infancy, and cable companies and mobile telephony were just beginning. By 1996 there were 17 licensed fixed-link operators, 107 cable companies that could provide phone services and many of which do, 2 cellular mobile telephone networks, and 2 non-cellular mobile telephone networks, as well as Vodafone and Cellnet's digital networks (Kennedy 1996, 18). In the process, BT's market share has dropped significantly, particularly in the business sector, and there is substantial competition on price, especially over international calls and even local calls and line rental. In addition, technological changes, notably the onset of digital systems, have meant that the boundaries between the telecommunications, broadcasting, and computer markets have become increasingly blurred, and this looks set to continue. Finally, BT as a company has global ambitions, best evidenced by its proposal to merge with the second largest American long distance carrier, MCI. The purpose of this chapter is to examine at a general level the policy challenges that this environment throws up for the existing regulatory system in the UK, and to explore the options for reform.

As the industry has changed from monopoly to duopoly, and then to a competitive market, so the thrust of regulatory policy has been to move away from a focus on price-control issues towards regulation of a competitive market, which means, among other things, ensuring that the market is a competitive one and that there is no abuse of economic power. This fundamental transformation of a regulator into a competition authority does raise a number of broad questions. First, there is the issue of the allocation of functions: to what extent do we need sectoral regulators as opposed to a general competition authority? Second, given that there are a number of social issues, such as content regulation and universal service, what is the appropriate division of functions between the regulators? The difficulty of resolving this issue is increased by the growing convergence between markets, which have traditionally been regulated independently, and the increasing importance of European Community law, which adds another dimension to the appropriate allocation of functions to institutions. Finally, overlaying the issue of allocation of functions is the problem of ensuring the accountability of institutions for the policies they undertake. This is in part a question of the clear specification of regulatory tasks, but also involves wider issues touching on more general constitutional questions.

The chapter is organized as follows: there is a brief introduction discussing the issues that various disciplinary approaches would highlight in relation to regulation, followed by brief discussions of the purpose of regulation in telecommunications, the current institutional structure, and a short history of the development of regulation. I then examine a selection of policy areas: the growth of competition, universal service, convergence, and the role of the EC in order to identify and analyse possible future developments.

Theories of Regulation

To talk about theories of regulation is somewhat misleading, not least because there are widely differing views on what constitutes the object of study (see Daintith 1989, and Majone 1990, 1–2, for some discussion of this issue). It is more accurate to refer to different disciplinary traditions that study regulation and offer differing, and sometimes competing, insights into the object of study. First and foremost are perhaps the contributions of the economists. For our purposes, their most interesting argument is that the problems raised by monopoly enterprises are best dealt with by increasing competition rather than regulation, which is only a second-best policy alternative. This was most famously put by Professor Littlechild, who argued, in the context of regulating BT's prices, that 'competition is indisputably the most effective means – perhaps ultimately the *only* effective means – of protecting consumers against monopoly power. Regulation is essentially a means of preventing the worst excesses of monopoly; it is not a substitute for competition. It is a means of "holding the fort" until competition arrives' (Littlechild 1983, par. 4.11, emphasis in original). One of the central questions for this essay will be whether, in telecommunications, the cavalry has arrived and the regulatory fort can be abandoned. To anticipate, it will be argued that the regulatory task is wider than Professor Littlechild is prepared to accept, and thus it would be premature to abandon specific, sectoral regulation.

The second insight comes mainly from political science or policy analysis, and it is that the specific institutional arrangements adopted in any one area matter; they are worthy of analysis and may have an effect on policy outcomes (although certain economists also make this point, for example, Vickers and Yarrow 1988, and Kay and Vickers 1990). In the context of telecommunications, Thatcher (1992) has argued that institutionalist analyses fail to give enough weight to technological and economic developments, but that, although this point should not be forgotten, particular institutional arrangements can affect the voice of various interest groups and may make policy outcomes easier or more difficult. The first point can be illustrated by the declining influence of the unions in public utilities after privatization, although this may also be due to economic factors, and the second by the belief at the EC level that regulatory and commercial operations need to be institutionally separated in order to encourage the growth of the internal market and competition.

This institutional concern relates to the concerns of legal analysis, or more narrowly the concerns of public lawyers in regard to the accountability of institutions, their decision making, and the principles upon which such decisions are taken. Although independent regulatory institutions are becoming increasingly commonplace in industrialized societies, they raise difficult issues of accountability because they combine legislative, executive, and judicial functions in one body, and this causes some unease. In the United States the problem is addressed through freedom of information legislation, legal structuring of administrative procedures, and a prominent role for judicial review. The idea of a regulatory body combining these three functions looks even more anomalous in the UK, as one of the master principles of the constitution is the accountability of ministers to Parliament. The telecommunications regulator in the United Kingdom, the Office of Telecommunications (OFTEL), has not, therefore, explicitly been given legislative or judicial functions. As we shall see, however, it has had to develop these roles within the interstices of its legislative mandate and, because OFTEL is independent in certain ways from the minister, this raises problems of accountability and legitimacy. One question is whether or not the changes that are envisaged would improve accountability of decision making, especially bearing in mind that with the increasing interest of the European Commission in this area, the level of decision making may change.

Finally, we should consider the issue of principles for decision making. The lawyers' concern is to have a clear set of rules or principles, on the basis of which decisions are made, and this ties in with a concern of the economists. Economists conventionally distinguish economic from social regulation (for example, Foster 1992, and Ogus 1994, 4–5), the former dealing in the main with natural monopoly industries and the need to provide a substitute for competition in these, while the latter is more broadly focused on market failures and externalities, although both are susceptible to principled economic analysis. What I want to suggest at this point is that there is another social aspect to regulation, namely the issue of universal service. The question here is to what extent individuals should have a right of access to a certain level of service. There has been long-standing concern with universal service in telecommunications, although the meaning has shifted quite radically (Mueller 1993), an issue that has been sharpened by the convergence of markets and the promise of an 'information superhighway' that may create information haves and have-nots.

Regulating Telecommunications in the UK: Purposes and Institutions

The origins of OFTEL are contained in the records of the Department of Trade and Industry (DTI), and, until they are opened up, the debates surrounding its origins must remain obscure. Privatization of BT did not necessarily imply the creation of an independent regulatory agency, as this job could have remained with the department. Given that one of the political objectives of the privatization was to distance government from the operations of BT and that apparently the experience of the period between liberalization (1981) and privatization was that 'BT was capable of overwhelming civil servants with lengthy technical arguments, that civil servants were not trained for the detailed regulation necessary' (Hills 1986, 97), therefore a body in addition to the Office of Fair Trading (OFT) was needed. This second point does not entirely square with Foster's suggestion (1992, 125) that the job was offered initially to the director general of fair trading, who declined to take it on, or with the fact that most of the original staff of OFTEL were on secondment from DTI. This suggests that the main idea, confirmed by Foster, was to distance government ministers from the day-to-day operation of the regulatory system although, as we shall see, important powers are retained in their hands.

As regards the purposes of regulation, this was one area where, compared to subsequent privatizations, somewhat more information is in the public domain. The key document is Professor Littlechild's report to DTI, which focused on the regulation of BT's profitability; that is, it was concerned primarily with finding a means of regulating BT's prices that would protect consumers against BT's market power. A secondary object of his investigation was to find as non-discretionary a scheme as possible, as he felt that it would make the institutions less vulnerable to 'regulatory capture.' The result was the famous RPI-X price control, and the purpose of regulation, as expressed in this paper, can be said to be economic regulation, with a strong bias to encouraging competition. This point was glossed in the parliamentary debates by the relevant ministers, who referred to regulation with a 'light rein' or a 'light touch,'[2] although it is not clear what this phrase meant, and, it has been said, 'to a large degree the sale itself diverted attention from many of the issues of regulation' (Hills 1986: 130)

Close study of the legislation (the Telecommunications Act of 1984) reveals a more complicated picture than seems to have been envisaged by Professor Littlechild, or indeed the various ministerial sponsors of the bill. The act provides for a director general of telecommunications (DGT), appointed by the minister, who is to head the Office of Telecommunications. The DGT is independent in the sense that the minister cannot give him or her specific directions except, first, in limited circumstances relating to national security and international relations and second, a power to give general directions indicating the considerations that the DGT should have particular regard to when either reviewing telecommunications matters or carrying out any of his or her functions (sections 47(2) and 94). The secretary of state also has specific powers, notably to issue licences for telecommunications systems and to prevent references to the Monopolies and Mergers Commission (MMC) (sections 7 and 13(5)).

The basic scheme is that telecommunications operators are granted licences, and it is the role of the DGT to monitor and enforce the licence conditions. If the DGT wishes to amend a licence there are only two routes: first by agreement with the company, subject to certain limited procedural requirements, or, if no agreement can be reached, through a reference to the MMC (sections 12–15). The DGT also has powers to enforce the licence conditions that can be exercised when it appears to the DGT that a telecommunications operator is contravening, or has contravened and is likely again to contravene, that condition of the licence. The aim of such orders is to procure compliance with the licence conditions, not to levy fines or compensate people who have been damaged by breach of the order (section 16). In addition, there are various procedural requirements, including some limited access to the courts (sections 17–18). Neither the enforcement powers nor the powers to amend licences by reference to the MMC are particularly easy to use. An MMC reference is likely to be a time-consuming process, using up scarce resources for the regulator, and the MMC may not agree with the regulator's views.

In addition to these enforcement powers, the DGT is given concurrent powers with the director general of fair trading as regards the investigations of monopoly situations and anti-competitive practices in relation to telecommunications matters (section 50). The director general of fair trading may also ask the DGT to exercise certain powers relating to consumer protection that exist under the Fair Trading Act. It should be noticed that BT's original licence contained no general prohibition on anti-competitive practices, simply a prohibition on undue discrimination and a variety of specific restraints on its activities in the market.

These are some of the most important basic powers of the DGT. What then, are his or her duties? These are set out in Section 3 of the 1984 Act which is reproduced for ease of reference (Box 14.1).

There are a number of points to notice in this section. First, the duties of the DGT are not solely to do with economic regulation. Indeed, unlike some later legislation the duty to promote competition is not even a primary duty but is subject to the duties to ensure that all reasonable demand for telecommunications services are satisfied and that service providers can finance the provision of those services. This leads to a second point, which is that it can be argued, contrary to Professor Littlechild's expectations, that the legislation requires the DGT to balance social and economic objectives (see Prosser 1994 for details of this). Third, as well as standard social obligations, for example to take into account the interests of the elderly and disabled, there are also a variety of what look like, on the face of them, industrial policy objectives such as the encouragement to major users of telecommunications services whose places of business are outside the UK to establish places of business in the UK. Finally, these duties pull in different directions, and there is some tension between them. In conclusion, what has been created is not a non-discretionary system, but one that asks the DGT to balance various duties and to make judgments about policy objectives.

The History of Telecommunications Regulation

The period from 1984 to 1991 was dominated by four issues: the duopoly policy and its review, the first review of BT's price control, the controversy over BT's quality of service, and OFTEL's successful attempt to rid itself of responsibility for regulating content. The first review of BT's price control was notable for both a toughening of the X factor, from 3 to 4.5, and an extension of price controls to cover, among other things, line rental. The duopoly policy arose from the government's initial decision to license only one fixed-link competitor to BT, namely Mercury, for seven years from 1983 in order to give Mercury time to instal and consolidate its national network and BT time to adjust to competition. After reviewing this policy it was decided to end the duopoly policy and to consider on its merits any application for a licence to offer telecommunications services over fixed links in the UK. In addition, the government took the necessary decisions to allow cable companies to offer their own voice telephony services, but it continued the prohibition on BT conveying entertainment services in its own right for the next ten years and in providing entertain-

BOX 14.1 Excerpt from Telecommunications Act, 1984

Section 3
(1) The Secretary of State and the Director shall each have a duty to exercise [his] functions ... in the manner which he considers is best calculated
(a) to secure that there are provided throughout the United Kingdom, save in so far as the provision thereof is impracticable or not reasonably practicable, such telecommunications services as satisfy all reasonable demands for them including, in particular, emergency services, public call box services, directory information services, maritime services and services in rural areas, and
(b) without prejudice to the generality of paragraph (a) above, to secure that any person by whom any such services fall to be provided is able to finance the provision of those services.
(2) Subject to subsection (1) above, the Secretary of State and the Director shall each have a duty to exercise [his] functions ... in the manner which he considers is best calculated –
(a) to promote the interests of consumers, purchasers and other users in the United Kingdom (including, in particular, those who are disabled or of pensionable age)
(b) to maintain and promote effective competition between persons engaged in commercial activities connected with telecommunications in the United Kingdom;
(c) to promote efficiency and economy on the part of such persons;
(d) to promote research into and the development and use of new techniques by such persons;
(e) to encourage major users of telecommunications services whose place of business are outside the United Kingdom to establish places of business in the United Kingdom;
(f) to promote the provision of international transit services by persons providing telecommunications services in the United Kingdom;
(g) to enable persons providing telecommunications service in the United Kingdom to compete effectively in the provision of such services outside the United Kingdom;
(h) to enable persons producing telecommunications apparatus in the United Kingdom to compete effectively in the supply of such apparatus both in and outside the United Kingdom.

ment services for a period greater than ten years. The government also allowed the resale of services, both domestically and internationally, thus going some way to introducing the recommendations of the Beesley Report of 1981.

Although the change in the duopoly policy has had the most far-reaching effect on the telecommunications industry, it is worth mentioning, albeit briefly, two other regulatory issues. In 1987 it became apparent that there were a number of concerns about the quality of service offered by BT, an issue that was exacerbated by an engineers' strike at the time. OFTEL, however, had no statutory powers to deal with this issue of the quality of service, and neither were there any licence conditions relating to the quality of service. OFTEL had to organize its own quality of service surveys and threaten to include this issue in the review of BT's price control before BT began to publish its own indicators of the quality of service (generally, see Scott 1993). The gap in the statutory powers has now been filled by amendments to the Telecommunications Act, contained in the Competition and Service (Utilities) Act of 1992. The second issue related to the control of the content of premium-rate telephone services and, in particular, chatlines. The control of chatlines was the occasion of the first ever reference to the MMC, which promptly disagreed with the DGT's analysis of the problem, and of perhaps the first judicial review case against OFTEL that was settled at the door of the court by OFTEL accepting that it had acted unlawfully. OFTEL's reaction has been to encourage a system of self-regulation, based in part on the contracts that service providers have with BT, which is administered by an industry-funded body, the Independent Committee for the Supervision of Telephone Information Services (ICSTIS). This episode indicates that OFTEL saw its core mandate as being economic regulation, and it illustrates the very difficult regulatory problems that can arise in the sphere of content regulation.

From 1991 to 1996 we can see the implications of the abandoning of the duopoly policy and some of the related policy decisions that are developing. One of the major points of debate during this time was the issue of interconnection, that is, the terms on which BT's competitors could be given access to BT's system and vice versa. An additional problem arose because of a cap on BT's prices for line rental, which meant that BT was able to argue that the costs of access to BT's network were higher than the revenues BT derived from line rental. This was referred to as the 'access deficit,' and a decision was taken that, when competitors to BT used the BT network for calls, they were obliged to make a contribution to BT to compensate it for the revenue it had lost by not carrying that call, the so-called Access Deficit Contribution (ADC). The interconnection system that evolved was highly complicated, depended on the DGT's discretion, and was the subject of much controversy, resulting in Mercury taking a court case against the DGT that eventually was decided in Mercury's favour in the House of Lords (Mercury Communications v Director General of Telecommunications, [1996] 1 All ER 575; for comment see McHarg 1995). This need to settle the general issue of interconnection seems to have been one of the driving forces behind a burst of activity by OFTEL in 1995, when it issued a stream of consultation papers discussing the future shape of regulation. Four main issues are of interest: OFTEL's response to the growth of competition in telecommunications, the debate over universal service, the issue of convergence in communications markets, and the role, actual or potential, played by the EC in telecommunications regulation, although this latter is not touched upon in the OFTEL papers.

The Growth of Competition and the Regulatory Response

Although there are many statements about how competitive the telecommunications industry has become, the evidence that is publicly available seems somewhat more ambiguous. Tables 14.1 to 14.4, from different sources, give a breakdown of market shares.

The figures in these tables are not strictly comparable, but they give a good indication of trends in telephony and market shares over recent years. A couple of points are evident. First, BT is still overwhelmingly dominant in the market for local and residential calls and clearly dominant in the market for national calls. Second, competition has affected BT most severely in two areas, business and international calls, but even here BT still retains a market share of at least 70 per cent, although it is reported that BT has lost significantly more business custom in certain markets, for example the City of London. Recent analysis (Kennedy 1996) also suggests that competitors to BT, are able to offer more attractive price and service combinations than BT which raises the question as to whether or not BT's market share will decline over time or whether there are barriers to entry into the market?

When OFTEL surveyed telecommunications operators on their views as to likely trends in competition, the overall opinion was that the trends identified above would continue. OFTEL summarized it thus: 'Most operators saw the continued development of competition across the range of markets through to 2001 with the largest increases being experienced in the business sector and in urban areas. There was general agreement that competition for access and inland calls would increase although few operators envisaged that, by the year 2001, these markets ... would be fully competitive by then' (OFTEL 1995c, par. 3.51). What this evidence suggests is that BT will still be the dominant operator in the local and residential call markets by the year 2001.[3] In support of this is Kennedy's analysis (1996, 20–2) that there are consumer-switching costs, and that these may explain the low level of penetration of BT's competitors. Now, although OFTEL has dealt with some of the factors preventing penetration, such as the issue of number portability, it is right to be cautious about the extent to which competitors can make inroads into BT's market. If that is correct, then the assumption that the 1996 price control round will be the last time that a price control is imposed on BT may be incorrect. This is not to suggest that OFTEL's strategy is fundamentally flawed, rather it is to make the point that reports of its early demise (see, for example, OFTEL 1996, par. 2.12: 'the retail

TABLE 14.1 Market share by type of call and customer in 1992–3 (in percentages)

	Telephone operators		
Type of call	BT	Mercury	Kingston and others
Local calls	96.1	3.3	0.6
National calls	89.1	10.0	0.9
International calls	77.6	21.2	0.6
Business calls	82.2	17.6	0.3
Residential calls	96.9	2.4	0.2
All calls	89.3	10.0	0.8

Source: Kennedy 1996, 14.

TABLE 14.2 Market share by type of call and customer in 1993–4 (in percentages)

	Telephone operators		
Type of call	BT	Mercury	Kingston and others
Local calls	95.3	3.6	1.2
National calls	86.0	12.5	1.5
International calls	73.4	23.9	2.6
Business calls	79.1	19.7	1.2
Residential calls	94.6	4.2	1.1
All calls	86.8	11.6	1.6

Source: Kennedy 1996, 14.

price control arrangements proposed here will be the last'; Wright 1996) are perhaps exaggerated.

OFTEL's response to the changes in the environment is contained in a number of documents (most importantly, see OFTEL 1994, 1995a, 1995b, 1995c, 1995d, 1995e, and 1996). OFTEL finally proposed that there should be a formal price cap covering those services that were currently controlled, but applied to the residential market only. In addition, the formal price cap would be applied using only the revenues and calling patterns of the first 80 per cent of residential customers by bill size. X in this cap will be 4.5 per cent, which OFTEL argues is equivalent to 7–8.5 per cent on the old basis, because BT has less opportunity to re-balance the tariff basket. To protect small businesses, OFTEL is requiring BT to offer a control package, which is broadly similar to the residential control. The effect of this move is that there will be no price controls in the business market. In addition, OFTEL also proposed that a new licence condition should

TABLE 14.3 Market share for fixed-link telephony: Retail call revenues in 1994–5 (in percentages)

	Telephone operators		
Type of call	BT	Mercury	Kingston and others
Local and national calls	88.8	8.6	2.6
Outgoing international calls	70.0	24.5	5.5
Value added and other systems business calls	88.8	9.36	1.9

Source OFTEL 1995c, 23.

TABLE 14.4 Market shares of international and national business and residential calls in 1994–5 (in percentages)

	Telephone operators			
Type of call	BT	Mercury	Cable operators	Others
International				
Business	53	23	2	22
Residential	81	9	8	1
National long-distance				
Business	73	19	2	6
Residential	90	6	4	—

Source: Trade and Industry Select Committee 1997.

be inserted into BT's licence and the licences of all significant operators, which would prohibit abuse of a dominant position and agreements that distorted competition. Once this was in place, many of the detailed conditions in BT's licence would be deleted. Finally, as regards interconnection charging arrangements, OFTEL proposed an annual determination of charges, with a system of network controls for those services that were not competitive, using baskets of interconnections services, each subject to the charge cap formula of RPI-X. The full details of this have not been worked out at the time of writing.

These radical proposals are an interconnected package and mark a large step, at least in OFTEL's eyes, away from being a 'detailed, prescriptive monopoly regulator towards being a fair trading authority' (OFTEL 1996, par. 2.6; see also Wright 1996, 96). There is no doubt that the imposition of the fair trading condition is a radical change, in terms of both regulatory and competition policy, in the UK, and it is one that was bitterly resisted by BT, to the point of bringing an unsuccessful judicial review action against the DGT. To understand just how radical requires a brief description of competition policy as it currently stands in the UK. The current system is unusual in that it does not impose any outright prohibitions of whatever sort on anti-competitive behaviour.[4] Instead, the UK system relies on the investigation of particular situations by the administrative authorities, primarily the OFT, with a view to seeing whether or not any situation is against the 'public interest' (section 84, Fair Trading Act of 1973). If a situation is discovered to be against the public interest, then, typically, informal undertakings are negotiated between the authorities and the firms concerned to remedy the situation. Only on rare occasions are the formal powers to make delegated legislation resorted to. Thus competition law aims to fix the situation for the future, rather than penalize firms for their past conduct, and this is emphasized by the state of the law, which does not allow private actions for damages, except in very limited circumstances, by competitors or consumers against firms that offend against competition law, unlike the situation in the United States or under EC law. At the same time as being subject to this, 'domestic' form of competition law, firms are also subject to EC competition law,[5] which does prohibit certain anti-competitive practices and does allow for firms to be punished for past behaviour, either through decisions of the European Commission or through private actions taken by competitors and consumers.[6] There has been trenchant criticism of the UK's competition law for being insufficiently pro-competitive and inconsistent with EC law, and there have been proposals for its reform to bring it more into line with the EC, law which first surfaced in 1988 and reached the stage of a draft bill in 1996, although this was not proceeded with in the parliamentary session 1996–7.

The long delay in introducing any reforms to competition law in the UK and the heavy criticism of OFTEL's existing powers to deal with competition matters, plus the urgency of the matter in the new environment, apparently convinced OFTEL that it should act in advance of any legislative changes (OFTEL 1996, par. 3.14). OFTEL's condition (see Box 14.2) prevents a licensee from doing anything that has the object or effect of preventing, restricting, or distorting competition in relation to commercial activities connected with telecommunications, and this can constitute the abuse of a dominant position or the making of an agreement or the carrying on of any concerted practice with another firm that has the object or effect of preventing, restricting, or distorting competition. The question of whether or not such an act is in breach of the condition is a question for the DGT, who must take into account relevant decisions and rules of EC competition law and relevant decisions of the OFT and the MMC. If the DGT feels that there has been a breach of the prohibition, then he or she can issue an initial determination; the licensee then has twenty-eight days to request

BOX 14.2 The Fair-Trading Condition

18A. 1 The Licensee shall not do any thing, whether by act or omission, which has or is intended to have or is likely to have the effect of preventing, restricting or distorting competition in relation to any commercial activity connected with telecommunications, where such act or omission is done in the course of, as a result of or in connection with, providing telecommunication services, or any particular description of telecommunication service, or running a telecommunication system.

For the purpose of this Condition such an act or omission may take the form of:

(a) any abuse by the Licensee, either alone or with other undertakings, of a dominant position enjoyed by the Licensee's Group within the United Kingdom or a substantial part of it. Such abuse may, in particular, consist in: directly or indirectly imposing unfair purchase or selling prices or other unfair trading conditions; limiting production, markets or technical development to the prejudice of consumers; applying dissimilar conditions to equivalent transactions with other parties, thereby placing them at a conpetitive disadvantage; making the conclusion of contracts subject to acceptance by the other parties of supplementary obligations which, by their nature or according to commercial usage, have no connection with the subject of such contracts;

(b) the making of any agreement, the compliance with any decision of any association of undertakings or the carrying on of any concerted practice with any other undertaking which has the object or effect of preventing, restricting or distorting competition within the United Kingdom.

the DGT to make a final determination, although the DGT can move to a final determination of his or her own accord. Only if the licensee continues to breach a final order may private parties seek damages against it.

We can see from this description that the changes still retain the prospective character of UK competition law. We should also note that similar problems have also been found with existing competition law as it applies to the deregulated bus industry (Transport Select Committee 1995) and that the vast majority of those consulted, with the exception of BT, supported this change. This suggests that OFTEL was right to pursue the path it chose and to create such a condition. The more interesting question, however, is what it means for a regulator to become a competition authority?

A New Competition Authority?

This opens up the question of what it means to be a competition authority, or, to put it another way, what is the purpose of competition policy? There is no one answer to this question. In the country with the longest history of competition policy, the United States, the goals of policy have fluctuated since its inception at the turn of the century from an activist 'anti–big business approach' to a more relaxed approach founded on 'Chicago school' economic analysis (see Freyer 1992 for an overall summary). Policy in the UK has also fluctuated, but it has been notably pragmatic, and it was only in 1984, and then only in the context of mergers, that a statement by the secretary of state for trade and industry placed competition concerns, as exhibited through economic analysis, on centre stage as a general rule. As regards EC competition law, there are a range of objectives, one of which has been the creation of a single market, which has meant that the competition authorities of the EC have been less tolerant of vertical restrictions than domestic authorities have been.

To what extent are such considerations applicable to a body like OFTEL, concerned with a single sector and one that has clear objectives for its own activities (see OFTEL 1995d, 12, for these)? There are, perhaps, two central difficulties. The first is that in attempting to encourage a competitive telecommunications market, especially in pursuing the idea of competing networks, OFTEL is adopting a policy that looks close to one favouring small- and medium-sized enterprises over BT. This would not be inconsistent with the European competition model that it has adopted, but there have been severe criticisms, on economic efficiency grounds, of such an approach in general. This is related to the question of OFTEL's non-economic objectives, something that becomes a large issue in the debate on convergence. Thus, for example, in the debate on the educational uses of the information superhighway one of the major barriers identified has been the cost of telecommunications use by schools (House of Lords 1996, par. 4.73). One way around this would be to provide a subsidized service to the schools, something BT has offered to the Labour Party in return for the lifting of the restrictions on its providing entertainment services. How would such an approach square with OFTEL's competition goals, given that this would clearly represent a preferential subsidy to a class of consumers not justified by the economics of the situation? The issue is currently being examined by an OFTEL working party, which is looking for a 'voluntary' approach to the issue.

The second issue may be a more theoretical one. We have seen that OFTEL has adopted a fair-trading condition based on EC law, which is, in turn, based on German competition law. It has been argued (Gerber 1994) that German competition law was conceived of as part of a broader political and economic project, namely the creation of an economic constitution, one that supported a transaction-based economy (market economy may also be a reasonable rendering of this term) and limited the scope for governmental intervention. Gerber argues (1994, 57) that the view of the intellectual authors of this system was that competition law was necessary as part of the system and that it would be of little value if it stood alone. What OFTEL has done is to create an island of competition law within the unprincipled UK regime. The question for the future is whether such an island can be maintained effectively. Although there are plans for the reform of competition law in the UK, it has taken eight years for a draft bill to appear, and it is not clear what the future prospects for reform of competition policy are. At the same time, there is increasing convergence of markets in the telecommunications and broadcasting sectors, which increases the incentive for governments to intervene for any number of non-economic reasons. It could be very difficult to be an effective competition authority in those circumstances. For example, if the argument is accepted that the country needs BT as a national champion, then the temptation is to give it the benefit of the doubt in relation to domestic competition decisions, as has been the case with British Airways in the past (for example, Souter 1995, 45–6; for the British Airways example, see Baldwin 1990).

A third issue for the future should be mentioned. If OFTEL is moving towards being a competition authority and away from economic regulation, why shouldn't its competition responsibilities be given to OFT so that there are consistent competition policies across the country in the different industrial sectors? The alternative model is to have a number of different sectoral competition regulators. Indeed, this is the conclusion drawn by the House of Lords select committee at the end of its inquiry into the information superhighway (House of Lords 1996, par. 5.40). Their conclusion, however, is not that OFTEL should be abolished, but that it, or an enlarged version, should retain responsibility for issues of content regulation, something that OFTEL has been very unenthusiastic about.

The fair-trading provision thus raises a number of difficult questions. If OFTEL has become a competition authority, what does this mean? If, in the medium term, UK competition policy is brought closer into line with European competition law, will there still be a role for OFTEL's competition functions? Some of the answers to these questions will be dependent on what the market looks like, and this is the next issue to examine.

Convergence

Traditionally the telephone and broadcasting markets have been seen as separate, one dealing in personal voice communication, the other in impersonal, one-way broadcasts of sound and images, and in the UK, although not the

United States, they were subject to different regulatory regimes. The last ten to fifteen years have seen the rise of a third market, mass computer networks that allow individuals to communicate, not usually using voice, and to have access to large amounts of information – text, images, or sound. The distinctions between these markets are breaking down because of the increasing use of digital technology, which opens up the possibility of, for example, interactive links between a broadcast and a viewer or the provision of a variety of services through the telephone system, such as video-on-demand.

This development has raised a multitude of policy questions, primarily focused on the fear of a country being left behind in the new 'Information Age' and on considering what the appropriate strategies should be to ensure that the country gains the maximum benefit. There is not the space to consider these questions in any detail here (for discussion in the UK, see Trade and Industry Select Committee 1994; House of Lords 1996). Here I focus on the effect that these developments will have on the regulatory structures, or rather the potential avenues that might be taken.

The current situation in relation to broadcasting regulation is that the independent television sector is regulated by the Independent Television Commission (ITC), which is responsible for the franchising process as well as content regulation, the latter also overseen by the Broadcasting Standards Council. The public sector is the preserve of the British Broadcasting Corporation (BBC), which is still technically a nationalized industry, and therefore regulated, in theory, by the Department of National Heritage, although in practice it regulates itself and is also subject to the Broadcasting Standards Council in relation to content. Cable companies are regulated by OFTEL in relation to economic matters and the ITC in relation to content. Computer networks, or the Internet, has no sector-specific regulator, although there have been moves to get the service providers to organize themselves and to engage in self-regulation.

The obvious question is, if these markets are converging and if they converge to the point where they are indistinguishable, what is the point in having all these different regulatory institutions? Regulation would be carried out more efficiently if there was only regulator called, for example, the Office of Communications (a conclusion drawn notably by Souter 1995, 43; House of Lords 1996, par. 5.46, suggests the same conclusion as regards content regulation). At the moment, an artificial separation is being maintained through the decision in 1991 to prohibit BT and Mercury from conveying entertainment services in their own right for the next ten years and from providing national entertainment services for a period greater than ten years. The conveyance prohibition will be reconsidered in 1998 if, after review by the DGT, the latter advises that removing the restriction would be likely to promote more effective competition in telecommunications. The provisions prohibition will only be *reviewed* after ten years, on the advice of the DGT that a change of policy would lead to more effective competition in telecommunications. Not surprisingly, these prohibitions, which were not supported by a majority of the consultees at the time, have been heavily criticized by BT and the other telecommunications operators affected, and the Trade and Industry Select Committee recommended in 1994 and 1997 that the policy should be changed, something that the government rejected in its response in 1994. The House of Lords select committee has also recommended that the review of both prohibitions should be completed by 1998, commenting that 'the attempt to go against the powerful trend towards convergence of the telecommunications and broadcasting industries is unlikely to succeed in the long term, and in the short term is preventing BT from developing its role in service provision. The US already enjoys a dominant position in this industry; one effect of the UK's current regulatory policy is to assist its global competitors' (House of Lords 1996, par. 5.27).

Convergence has already caused one difficult regulatory problem, namely the allocation of responsibility for the regulation of conditional access systems for digital television. There was some debate about whether OFTEL or the ITC was the most appropriate body, which was ultimately resolved in favour of OFTEL, although there will still need to be coordination between the two regulatory bodies. Before returning to that issue, it is worth discussing what principles might inform regulation of the information superhighway. These are set out in detail in an OFTEL consultative document (1995b), and reflect its general interpretation of its remit. What is evident from this document is that OFTEL wishes to concentrate its efforts on the regulation of dominant distribution systems with the aim of ensuring open access for service providers, direct commercial relationships between service providers and commercial customers, appropriate separation between network distribution and service provision, and the use of technical standards that will allow open access, as well as, in certain circumstances, controls on pricing (see OFTEL 1995a, para. 5.2.5 and 5.3.9, for more detail). It is reasonably clear that OFTEL does not want to be involved in consumer protection issues, unless they overlap with the development of competition through, for example, bundling together the provision of a service with the costs of the telecommunications service (OFTEL 1995a, para. 5.6.1–12), and it is notably unenthusiastic about regulating the content of service provision (OFTEL 1995a, para. 4.5.7–12). In other words, OFTEL sees itself as essentially regulating for competition, in line with its approach to telecommunications regulation in general.

This brings us back to the future of OFTEL when the existing markets have converged. One analysis (put clearly in Souter 1995) argues that regulation should be sectoral, that it should mirror the industrial structure that it regulates and seeks to regulate in the future. On this analysis, 'all regulatory functions concerning the digital transmission of information ... should be brought together in a single regulatory authority for communications' (Souter 1995, 43). The role of the integrated regulator, in this scenario, is in part to regulate a competitive market and to apply general competition law or similar principles. The other part of the regulator's job is to carry out public-service functions which seems to mean mainly universal service obligations. By contrast the House of Lords select committee, although accepting the scenario of a competitive market, reached somewhat different conclusions. It thought that if regulatory policy was no more than competition policy, then there was no point in having a sectoral economic regulator and that this function should be left with the ordinary competition authorities. On the other hand, on an issue that Souter does not address, the committee felt that there would be a need for the regulation of the content of such services, leaving aside the question of the practicability of such regulation for the moment, as well as the carrying out of certain public-service functions.

The select committee's approach explicitly reminds us that the question of institutional structures cannot be approached in isolation from the issue of regulatory purpose. What their proposals seek to do is to separate out the competition issues from the social issues, and to leave the former with a general competition authority and the social issues also with a specific authority. This can be seen as similar to the distinction between economic and social regulation that is made by economists and, insofar as such an institutional structure allows clarity in regard to the economic costs of certain social obligations, would be supported by economic analysts. Souter's proposal is also tied into a view about the purposes of regulation, although this is perhaps more clearly expressed in an earlier, more general piece (Souter 1994). In this piece he makes it clear that in his opinion one of the major failings of the current institutional arrangements 'is the absence of any strategic policy' (ibid., 32), by which he means an industrial policy. There is thus a logic in keeping all the powers, economic and social, within a single sectoral regulator as there will be a need to balance and coordinate the various instruments of policy, depending on what are the objectives of the government of the day.

There is perhaps a third possibility for regulatory evolution, which involves extending the logic of the select committee's report somewhat. If we suppose a competitive market, then there is no role for economic regulation, simply a role for competition law, although it is arguable that interconnection may require continuing regulation additional to competition law. What about social obligations, meaning universal service and content regulation? Most economists would argue that the appropriate mechanism for providing universal service is through subsidies provided by the benefits system rather than through the regulatory system, as this makes the cost of these obligations clearer and, since they cannot be justified on economic analysis, they need to be decided through political means. Alternatively, OFTEL has recently argued (1997, chap. 6) that such obligations should be provided exclusively by BT, as the cost is no greater than the reputational gain to BT. Either argument would do away with half of the agency's rationale. What about content regulation? The argument here is that it is impracticable, given the technology, to regulate content beyond the normal criminal and civil law, such as libel and incitement to racial hatred. There are also arguments of principle about how much regulation there should be of what anyone sees in their own home. However, the market will provide control mechanisms, either in the form of filters that will prevent access from any individual's terminal to services they consider 'undesirable,' or by the creation of 'walled gardens,' that is, by eliminating access to sites other than those suitable for children or for educational purposes. In this scenario, specialized regulation disappears entirely and all that is left is general competition law and the general laws of criminal and civil liability, adapted to deal with the new technology.

Universal Service

Universal service is a slippery term that has changed its meaning over the years (see Mueller 1993 for discussion in a U.S. context). In the UK there was little debate over universal service until OFTEL's intervention, and universal service obligations have been hidden away in the Telecommunications Act and in the conditions of BT's licence. It was really only when OFTEL approached the issue of regulating a competitive telecommunications market and the need for a new regime to replace ADCs that the issue of universal service had to be addressed, as funding for it was tied up, in part, with ADCs. OFTEL's initial definition (1994, 42) brings out the essential issues:

Geographic accessibility
Basic telephony service should be available to all who reasonably request it, regardless of where they live.

Access should be affordable
Basic telephony service should be reasonably available for consumers who have difficulty in paying the standard price.

Access should be equitable
Reasonable measures should be put in place to give customers with special needs or disabilities access to basic services.

What we can see from this definition is that universal service is comprised of a set of social obligations that should be placed on the telecommunications industry. Underlying this seems to be a conception of telecommunications services as a set of social and economic rights of citizens, although it has never been stated as such by OFTEL, and, as we shall see, OFTEL's most recent arguments are more economically centred.

Having identified the issue, OFTEL then undertook further work on the definition of universal service, the cost to telecommunications operators of these obligations, and the mechanism by which the obligations should be funded. Perhaps the most surprising finding of its investigation into the costs of universal service obligations for BT was that it was actually comparatively small; gross costs were estimated in region of £60 to £90 million, and net costs, after account had been taken of the benefits, within the range of zero to £40 million (OFTEL 1995e, 27). This discovery seems to have taken much of the heat out of the issue and has allowed OFTEL to expand the class of those eligible for universal service benefits. Indeed, at the end of its most recent review, OFTEL concludes that, after taking into account the benefits BT has derived from being the universal service provider, it remains unproved that there is a current net cost involved in the provision of universal service.

OFTEL now states (1997) that there is no need to establish a funding mechanism for universal service, although this may change in the future. The original general definition was 'affordable access to basic telecommunication services for all those reasonably requesting it regardless of where they live' (OFTEL 1995e, 11). The level of service would depend on the customer call or group under consideration, and there would be geographic averaging of tariffs applied to all levels of services. As well as discussing what sort of regulatory action was necessary to provide for those who found telecommunications services difficult to afford and for those with disabilities, OFTEL also argued that schools should be a class of customer eligible to receive an enhanced level of basic service, although this is now subject to discussion by a working party outside the universal service debate.

In all this the most interesting development is OFTEL's argument that there is an economic basis for universal service (OFTEL 1995e, 5–6). The general argument is that there are a number of genuine economic benefits from the use of telecommunications services that are difficult to capture in the price charged, and that therefore it is worth providing the service at below cost. The first example is that the greater the size of the network the more the benefit to the network subscribers. The second is that telecommunications may provide a substitute for transport and thereby cut down on pollution. There are also social benefits in terms of access to a telephone in cases of emergency, such as illness and crime. Third, if public services are increasingly delivered over the telecommunications networks, it makes delivery more efficient if the maximum possible number of people are hooked up to the network. Finally, as regards education the quality and scope of the service can be substantially enhanced through electronic communications and digital technology.

The first and second of these arguments are fairly conventional in economic terms, although the second is the externality argument reversed, as externalities are often conceived of as problems. The arguments about public service, and especially that about education, seem to be of a rather different kind altogether. Although it is probably possible to quantify the efficiency savings from having someone on the network as opposed to having to deal with them via paper transactions, this does not seem possible in relation to schools and educational establishments. The educational issue seems to be a matter where there is a general consensus that accepts it as a desirable policy initiative rather than something with a clear economic justification. The interesting question is, with the growing convergence of markets, will there be other areas like this? To take a possible example, should women at risk of violence from estranged partners be a class eligible for enhanced provision of services, in this instance free mobile phones? The merit of OFTEL's approach is that it provides a framework for debating questions such as these, but it seems to me that the issues are not going to disappear in the same way that, arguably, economic regulation is going to. The implication for regulatory policy is that the social side of OFTEL's remit will remain in place for some time to come. At the same time as OFTEL has been working on the notion of universal service, there has been a parallel debate going on at the EC level (Commission of the European Communities 1993). In fact, OFTEL's proposals are consistent with those proposed at the EC level, but it is to the issue of telecommunications regulation at the EC level that we now turn.

Telecommunications Regulation and the EC

The basic objective of the EC telecommunications policy in 1997 is to move to a liberalized environment for the provision of telecommunications services within a year. The idea is to create regulators in the various member states, independent of the telecommunications companies, to have competition both in the services market and between infrastructures, and to open access across networks and universal service obligations. When described like this, the proposed regime seems to be following developments at the UK level and would not, in itself, have any impact on regulatory policies in the UK, although the general European approach to regulation, being more formal and legalistic, is likely to have some impact.

The more difficult question is whether or not such a policy will entail the development of an EC telecommunications regulatory authority. There are a number of considerations here (generally, see Commission 1996). It is not clear what the role of such an authority would be. It would not be an economic regulator, and, insofar at it was enforcing competition rules or pursuing non-implementation of directives, it would appear to duplicate the commission's role. In addition, the creation of an independent regulatory authority within the EC's institutional structure would be a radical step, as the debate over the creation of a European cartel office illustrates, and would require a treaty amendment. Where such a body might be useful is at an international level, in conducting negotiations with other regulatory authorities, notably those in the United States.

There are, in any event, already existing 'regulators' of telecommunications at the European level, the most important of which is the commission in the exercise of its competition law powers derived from Articles 85, 86, and 90 and from the Merger Regulation. It is clear that activities within one member state can have sufficient effect on interstate trade to fall within the commission's powers under competition law, and so in this sense the issue of dual jurisdictions already arises.

Conclusions

What then is the future for the regulatory system in telecommunications? Assuming for the moment that price control regulation will become less of a central issue, there are five continuing issues that can be identified: access regulation (i.e., access to networks by competitors), the application of competition rules, universal service, issues of social policy, and content regulation. The positions of the various commentators are summarized in Table 14.5. This is, of course, a simplified schema, but it illustrates the current range of options. The first point to notice is what is *not* being recommended. There is no one in the current debate who is suggesting that we should return to a position where the department, headed by a politically accountable minister, is responsible for the regulation of telecommunications. There may be differing views about the extent to which ministers ought to intervene or about what their role might be, but it seems to be accepted that some form of agency, separate from government, should be in place to undertake the regulatory task, however this is conceived. The second point to notice is that there is substantial agreement that content regulation should be done by an authority separate from the economic or competition regulator, in other words that there should be two regulatory authorities in the telecommunications area. The third point is that, with the

TABLE 14.5 Synopsis of reform positions on telecommunications issues and policies

	Issues and policies				
	Access regulation	Competition law	Universal service	Social policy	Content regulation
Current position	OFTEL	OFTEL/ OFT	OFTEL	?	ICSTIS
House of Lords	OFT	OFT	New content regulator	New content regulator	Content regulator
Souter	OFCOM	OFCOM	OFCOM	OFCOM/ Minister	Content regulator
European Policy Forum	OFCOM	OFCOM	Minister	Minister	Content regulator
Rightist	OFT	OFT	Universal service authority	Minister	Self-regulation

exception of Souter's suggestions, there is also a general view that issues of universal service and social policy should be dealt with separately from economic regulation and, probably, content regulation, although the House of Lords select committee seems to dissent here. In one sense, this range of suggestions is a response to the accountability problem identified earlier in the chapter. One way of dealing with the accountability problem in a British context is to separate out the functions of the various bodies. This will make it more difficult for them to discuss and compromise issues behind closed doors, and it will be more likely that there will be a debate in the public domain, as happened, for example, between the Office of Water Services and the National Rivers Authority over the issue of the quality of the water supplied to customers. This is only a partial solution because there is also an argument that with a number of bodies with overlapping responsibilities, accountability is more likely to be jeopardized because it is not clear who, if anyone, has responsibility for particular policies. This problem will in the future have an increasingly regional dimension as the EC becomes more involved in the regulation of telecommunications issues, especially after 1998, and this will add another layer of complexity to the decision-making process.

What, however, about the issue of regulatory policies, which is just as important as any institutional changes? The thrust of most of the policies is that the object of regulation should be regulating for competition, that is, regulation that is geared towards ensuring competitive markets exist and that they operate properly. Even within itself, such a policy has tensions, as in one, admittedly crude, interpretation the success of the policy is measured by the number of competitors and licences issued while in another view it is the contestability of the market that counts. In this view, it would not matter that there are only a few infrastructure or indeed service providers as long as there was an opportunity for market entry, which would discipline their behaviour. There is also a tension between competition policy and social and industrial policy. It is quite common to argue that industries need national, or European, champions; although this argument is not currently very fashionable in Britain, it has had some influence in the operation of EC competition policy. In addition, with the convergence of communications systems, it is likely that politicians will have non-economic policy objectives for the telecommunications industry that will have to be balanced against the competition law objectives.

This leads to some final thoughts. Regulatory policy in relation to telecommunications is the clearest example of where competition might take over from regulation. More accurately, it should be said that the instruments of regulation are changing, away from economic regulation and price control and towards regulating for competition. This change will not, however, resolve pervasive problems about the discretion of regulatory authorities, coordination between them, and the balance of regulatory policies. In the British context we are seeing the development of a more open regulatory system, the result in no small measure of OFTEL's efforts, but also, I think, a system that will gradually become more legalistic and less discretionary. This can be seen in an obvious form in the EC's insistence on proper procedures for licensing telecommunications operators (Hunt 1997), but also in OFTEL's adoption of a fair-trading provision in BT's licence. A pure prohibition approach, as in EC law, implies a clear set of rules and, most importantly, a clear set of procedural protections. Although there is some argument about whether or not commission procedures meet the standards set down by the European Convention on Human Rights (see Kerse 1993, chap. 8, for references), these procedures are notably more legalistic than the ones mooted by OFTEL. There will be increasing tension between a more legalistic approach, driven in part from European obligations, and the British tradition of discretionary policy intervention, especially from ministerial level. The resolution of this in the long run is not simply a matter of regulatory policy, but depends on there being fundamental changes in the constitutional structure of Britain.

NOTES

1 My thanks for their helpful comments to Tony Prosser, Colin Scott. and Stephen Trotter. All errors are my own responsibility.

2 Although, as Curwen (1986, 250) points out, some of the references to 'light reins' came before the Littlechild Report and were interpreted as meaning a similar system to American rate of return regulation.
3 A conclusion also reached by the Trade and Industry Select Committee (1997, para. 15)
4 This phrase is used here in a non-technical sense to cover cartels, concerted practices, abuse of dominant position, etc.
5 This is true if their activities affect interstate trade.
6 In principle it is accepted that such a remedy is available in the UK, but there are a number of technical difficulties with obtaining it.

REFERENCES

Baldwin, R. 1990. 'Privatisation and Regulation: The Case of British Airways.' In *Privatization and Deregulation in Canada and Britain*, edited by J.J. Richardson. Montreal: Institute for Research on Public Policy.

Commission of the European Communities. 1993. *Developing Universal Service for Telecommunications in a Competitive Environment*. COM (93) 543 final, 15 November.

– 1996. *The Institutional Framework for the Regulation of Telecommunicaions and the Application of EC Competition Rules*. Luxembourg: Office for Official Publications.

Curwen, P. 1986. *Public Enterprise*. Brighton: Wheatsheaf.

Daintith, T. 1989. 'A Regulatory Space Agency?' *Oxford Journal of Legal Studies* 9:534–46.

Foster, C. 1992. *Privatization, Public Ownership and the Regulation of Natural Monopoly*. Oxford: Blackwell.

Freyer, T. 1992. *Regulating Big Business: Antitrust in Great Britain and America 1880–1990*. Cambridge: Cambridge University Press.

Gerber, D. 1994. 'Constitutionalizing the Economy: German Neo-liberalism, Competition Law and the "New" Europe.' *American Journal of Comparative Law* 42:25–84.

Hills, J. 1986. *Deregulating Telecoms*. London: Frances Pinter.

House of Lords, Select Committee on Science and Technology. 1996. *Information Society: Agenda for Action in the UK*. Session 1995–6. HL 77. London: HMSO.

Hunt, A. 1997. 'Regulation of Telecommunications: The developing E.U. Regulatory Framework and Its Impact in the United Kingdom.' *European Public Law* 3:93–115.

Kay, J. and J. Vickers. 1990. 'Regulatory Reform: An Appraisal.' In *Deregulation or Re-regulation*, edited by G. Majone. London: Pinter.

Kennedy, D. 1996. *Liberalisation of the British Telecommunications Industry*. Regulatory Brief 8. Centre for the Study of Regulated Industries: London.

Kerse, C.S. 1993. *EC Antitrust Procedure*. 3rd edition. London: Sweet and Maxwell.

Littlechild, S. 1983. *Regulation of British Telecommunication's Profitability.* London: HMSO.

Majone, G., ed. 1990. *Deregulation or Re-regulation?* London: Pinter.

McHarg, A. 1995. 'Regulation as a Private Law Function?' *Public Law* 23:539–50.

Mueller, M. 1993. 'Universal Service in Telephone History: A Reconstruction.' *Telecommunications Policy* 17:352–69.

Office of Telecommunications (OFTEL). 1994. *A Framework for Effective Competition.* London: OFTEL.

– 1995a. *Beyond the Telephone, the Television and the PC.* London: OFTEL, August.

– 1995b. *Effective Competition: A Framework for Action.* London: OFTEL, July.

– 1995c. *Fair Trading in Telecommunications.* London: OFTEL, December.

– 1995d. *Pricing of Telecommunications Services from 1997.* London: OFTEL, December.

– 1995e. *Universal Telecommunications Services 1997.* London: OFTEL.

– 1996. *Pricing of Telecommunications Services from 1997.* London: OFTEL.

– 1997. *Universal Telecommunications Services.* London: OFTEL.

Ogus, A. 1994. *Regulation.* Oxford: Oxford University Press.

Prosser, T. 1994. 'Privatization, Regulation and Public Services.' *Juridical Review* 3–17.

Scott, C. 1993. 'Regulating the Liberalised Telecommunications Sector.' *International Journal of Regulatory Law and Practice* 1, no. 2:185–92.

Souter, D. 1994. 'A Stakeholder Approach to Regulation.' In *Regulating Our Utilities*, edited by D. Corry. London: Institute of Public Policy Research.

– 1995. 'Regulating Telecommunications.' In *Regulating in the Public Interest: Looking to the Future*, edited by D. Corry. London: Institute of Public Policy Research.

Thatcher, M. 1992. 'Telecommunications in Britain and France: The Impact of National Institutions.' *Communications and Strategies* 6:35–61.

Trade and Industry Select Committee. 1994. *Optical Fibre Networks.* Session 1993–4. House of Commons, London: HMSO.

– 1997. *Telecommunications Regulation.* Session 1996–7. House of Commons, 285. London: HMSO.

Transport Select Committee. 1995. *Consequences of Bus Deregulation.* Session 1995–6. House of Commons, 54, vols. 1–3. London: HMSO.

Vickers, J., and G. Yarrow. 1988. *Privatization.* Boston: MIT Press.

Wright, J. 1996. 'Telecommunications 1995/6.' In *Regulatory Review 1996*, edited by P. Vass. London: Centre for the Study of Regulated Industries.

15

The Canadian Radio-television and Telecommunications Commission: Transformation in the 1990s

G. BRUCE DOERN

The Canadian Radio-television and Telecommunications Commission (CRTC) is one of the most important of Canada's federal regulatory bodies, but it is remarkable how little analysis there is of the CRTC as a regulatory institution per se. Books on its predecessor bodies and its early years are a valuable base (Peers 1969; Stewart and Hull 1994), and there are other articles that deal with selected aspects of the CRTC or of telecommunications and broadcasting policy more generally (Tardi 1981; Scott 1990; Conklin 1991; Schultz 1983, 1994; Globerman, Stanbury, and Wilson 1995; Raboy 1995a; 1995b). However, a somewhat more holistic institutional look has been missing. Obviously, the analysis below cannot cover every aspect of the CRTC's mandate or institutional relations, but it does seek reasonable breadth through the five-point framework set out below.

The analysis focuses on changes in the 1990s or, broadly, in the last decade, during which it is not inappropriate to say that the CRTC has been regulating 'on the run.' Some time ago Richard Schultz metaphorically referred to telecommunications regulation by the CRTC as a 'Maginot Line,' the image being one of a stationary behemoth with others running around it (Schultz 1983). This was coined at a time when technological change in the telecommunications field was beginning but had not yet reached its current almost convulsive pace. In the last decade the CRTC has been regulating 'on the run,' but in ways that can arguably never be fast enough. The 1990s in particular have seen the competitive globalizing transformation of converging computing and telecommunications technologies. These developments have produced myriad new telecommunications products and firms, not to mention the information highway, and have placed the CRTC in the midst of a maelstrom of change (Canada 1995; Crandall and Waverman 1995; Drake 1995).

At the same time, as Chapter 6 has shown, it is possible to say that the CRTC has not changed as much as two of Canada's other national regulators, the National Energy Board (NEB) and the National Transportation Agency (NTA), in that it still possesses an array of functions, staff, and resources that these other regulators have now shed. Nor has it changed to the extent that the technologies seem to imply or that some of its critics have suggested, and that is simply to have gotten out of the way and let the new markets flourish. Yet the CRTC has nevertheless been transformed.

To do justice to an analysis that argues that the CRTC has been transformed as an institution but has also resisted some aspects of the pace of change felt or expected by others, we need a regulatory institutional framework for analysis that deals with both old and newer attributes of regulatory institutions. Accordingly, this chapter looks at the CRTC in relation to five such features, the first two of which can be considered traditional, and the next three of more recent vintage, though none was never fully absent from earlier periods. The five institutional features are: (1) the contemporary nature of an independent regulator in relation to ministers, regulated interests, and the public, as well as multi-member commissions and other issues in the choice of specific modes of regulation that centre on representation; (2) the characteristics of quasi-judicial, adjudicative, and quasi-political regulatory functions and decision processes; (3) changing views of regulatory compliance, enforcement, and reforms centred on flexible regulation; (4) the changing relations between horizontal- or business-framework regulators (e.g., competition and intellectual property) and sectoral regulators such as the CRTC; and (5) the internationalization of regulation through both new or incremental international and regional regimes, such as the General Agreement on Tariffs and Trade (GATT) and the North American Free Trade Agreement (NAFTA), and the effects of globalization on regulated industries. These institutional features will be described more fully below, but together they raise new and old concerns about how the CRTC is structured and controlled, how representative regulatory decision making is or should be, and how relations and conflicts among regulators are managed so as to promote both economic efficiency and democratic values. Institutional design issues also centre on fiscal restraints and severe budget cutbacks, as well as on the often radical changes that accompany the use of modern computerized telecommunications in regulation and related service delivery activities.

The structure of the chapter follows from the tasks at hand. First, we put the basic nature of the CRTC and its mandate in a brief historical context. The next five sections deal in turn with each of the five institutional features, and in the process more is revealed about changes and political dynamics in the CRTC. Each section begins by sketching out the core issue involved in that feature, and then discusses it in relation to the CRTC of the 1990s. Conclusions then follow.

The CRTC and Its Mandate in a Brief Historical Context

The initial federal regulator on the broadcast side was the Board of Broadcast Governors (BBG). The BBG was a more independent regulator than had been the previous CBC-dominated system of public-service broadcasting management. The BBG, however, still adhered strongly to many of the earlier central concepts, such as the basic notion of a single system (Peers 1969; Stewart and Hull 1994), which were based on a fear of American cultural domination, first in radio and then in television. Stated more positively, the regulatory system was rooted in a desire to ensure Canadian content and values in broadcasting. Relative to its predecessor system, the BBG was itself a deregulatory step in that it recognized the legitmacy of a private broadcasting system.

The CRTC was established in 1968 with an initial mandate that was focused on broadcasting, but it was clearly a child of the television age, where there was the need to regulate the cable-television industry as well as direct broadcasting. It did not acquire a telecommunications regulatory role until 1976, when the regulation of the telephone sector was transferred to it from the Canadian Transport Commission. If both cultural nationalism and defensive expansionism were central to broadcasting, they were less obvious imperatives on the telephone side, at least until the recent formation of the information highway where Canadian content is again a concern.

Telephone service in Canada (as in the United States) was built on a policy-regulatory mix that had five crucial features (Schultz 1994; Crandall and Waverman 1995). First, it rested on a monopoly provision with provincially based telephone companies (mainly private, except in the three Prairie provinces). This included provincial regulation and some federal-provincial dispute over jurisdiction, which the courts resolved in the federal government's favour only in the last decade. Second, it centred on a regime of rate-of-return regulation. Third, it was established with a view to providing 'end-to-end' service or 'system integrity.' Fourth, universal service was a goal that was largely achieved, so much so that Canada has one of the most 'wired' economies and societies in the world. Fifth, affordability of service was important and was largely linked, as was universal service, to the extensive practice of cross-subsidization, especially between long-distance and local users.

In the early 1990s the CRTC still functioned in two regulatory solitudes, one in broadcasting and the other one based on telephones. Indeed, the regulatory realms of broadcasting and telecommunications came under the provisions of two different statutes (Canada 1995). Much of this was to change, first gradually in the later 1980s, and then almost convulsively in the 1990s as new technologies brought convergence and a rate of change that no regulator could keep up with. But before profiling the nature of these competitive and deregulatory changes, we need a brief description of the CRTC's overall mandate.

The CRTC is an independent agency operating at arms length from government and reporting to Parliament through the minister of Canadian heritage. The objectives of the CRTC are to 'regulate and supervise all aspects of the Canadian broadcasting system' with a view to implementing the broadcasting policy set out in the Broadcasting Act, and to 'regulate rates and other aspects of telecommunications in Canada' so as to implement the policy set out in the Telecommunications Act (CRTC 1995b) and so as to 'balance the interests of consumers, the creative community, and distribution industries' (CRTC 1995b).

With respect to television, the CRTC's mandate is to ensure that Canadians have a diversity of high quality programming to choose from, that Canadian programs have a chance to be made, and that the programming meets established Canadian standards (regarding issues such as violence, advertising aimed at children, and gender portrayal). Regulations specify that all Canadian television stations must broadcast at least 60 per cent Canadian content over the course of a day, and at least 50 per cent in evening hours. Such regulations have been an important stimulus to Canadian creative producers and remain cushioned by NAFTA protections, which exempt the cultural sector from the provisions of free trade. Without such rules, the underlying economics of television would undoubtedly result in Canadian television stations simply buying cheaper off-the-shelf U.S. programs. The regulation of radio, which is of course the older medium of broadcasting, has similar principles of regulation regarding content and these are centred on a 30 per cent rule, but they also involve concerns about ensuring that communities hear a diversity of voices and views. In addition, the CRTC has had to manage the issue of preventing joint ownership of FM and AM stations in a single market.

The regulation of cable television has resulted in Canada being one of the most extensively cabled societies among Western countries. The CTRC regulatory regime involves rate regulation for regional and urban monopolies so as to ensure that the cost of service remains affordable, that Canadian, including local, programming, is encouraged, and that reasonable choice is available to subscribers. More recently, specialty services and pay-TV have also been both encouraged and regulated.

With respect to telephone service, the CRTC regulates both local and some long-distance rates (e.g., Stentor but not Unitel rates). Again the regulatory goal has been to promote universally available, high quality, and affordable telecommunications services. More will be said later about the obvious movement towards the promotion of competition in the converging worlds of telecommunications and broadcasting. However, it remains the case that even in such a competitive context the CRTC is in the midst of having to determine what fair and reasonable rates should be among various classes of users of telecommunications services. The CRTC also presents itself as a place where consumers can complain if they are dissatisfied with the responses of the direct service provider.

The CRTC actively advertises itself as a public-interest oriented agency. Its brochures are headed 'The CRTC: For Communication in the Public Interest.' This is also manifest in the CRTC's pride over its public-hearings process. Public hearings are held for new station licences, for rate increase applications, and on emerging issues that need a public airing and debate, such as violence in television. Some of these hearings are themselves broadcast on cable television (at the discretion of the cable channel).

The CRTC has also differed from such other regulators as the NEB and NTA in that it has not shrunk as an organization, or at least not as much or in a uniform direction. The staff on its broadcast side has been reduced, but its telecommunications staff has increased. Moreover, in 1968 the CRTC consisted of five full-time commission members and ten part-time members. The former made all the decisions, while the latter, who did not have a vote, supplied a regional presence in the hearings. In 1976, when the telephone element was added to the agency, the CRTC's full-time membership increased from five to nine. The part-time commissioners were only involved, as before, on broadcasting matters. In 1991 the CRTC, as it eased its way into the competitive realities of the new telecommunications technologies, became a commission with thirteen full-time members and six additional part-time commissioners. The full-time commissioners came from across the country, typically seven in Ottawa and six in regional offices. A more explicit form of regional representation was sought from this system, but to many members of the staff of the agency the measures weakened the cohesiveness of the operation as a whole. In addition, part-time members now have a vote on broadcasting licensing matters, and these decisions are now being taken at the level of panels in the CRTC's internal decision-making system. Previously, decisions on licences could not be decided at the panel level but had to be decided by the full commission. The part-time members also have a vote on policy matters at the level of the commission itself.

As mentioned, the CRTC has had to absorb staff cuts on its broadcasting side in recent years, some of them a result of pressures on government spending because of the deficit. These cuts have also brought on initiatives to deregulate. For example, the Canadian-content rules for radio were initially quite detailed, but have recently been kept to a few simple basics, thus reducing monitoring. In part, this reduction was seen simply as a sensible step, but they were also undertaken because the radio sector was a mature, even a saturated, market, with many stations in financial difficulty. Television licences have simpler provisions as well and, in addition, are now for seven rather than five years' duration. Combined with the fact that CRTC commissioners are now appointed for five instead of seven years, the odds are greatly increased that a commissioner will not deal with a licensee more than once.

While these milder deregulation pressures have undoubtedly penetrated the CRTC's world, it is clearly the technological revolution that is shaking it towards a pro-competitive position. The core technological change is undoubtedly the increased capacities and flexibility that have been made available by the switch from analogue to digitalized signals that is ultimately allowing both the broadcasting and cable industries and the telephone industry to get into each other's businesses.

At one level, a response to the convulsive changes would simply be for the CRTC to get out of the way and let them happen (Crandall and Waverman 1995). Space does not allow a full account here of the changes, which range from particular services such as direct-to-home TV to numerous Internet, speciality telephone and video-on-demand services. Suffice to say at this stage that neither the micro- nor the macro-politics of regulation allows the CRTC to vacate the field. The micro-political economic realities essentially turn on the relative sizes of the cable industry, on the one hand, and of the telecommunications industry on the other. The latter includes the far bigger enterprises, with the field led by Bell Canada and the Stentor group of companies. The cable companies are smaller, and they fear that they will lose out, in part because they must invest heavily in new fibre-optic trunk lines. Thus, the key lies in the transition provisions and the question of the ownership of firms. There is a general recognition that competition will occur, but there is no agreement on when or at what speed.

At the macro-political level there is also a sense of both speed and caution. This is because the international regulatory and competitive aspects of convergence are also moving at different rates (Lee 1996; U.S. Information Insfrastucture Task Force 1995). Canada resisted some early U.S. deregulatory pressures in the mid- and late 1980s, partly out of simple caution but also out of a concern to ensure that its own very good telecommunications industries were in a state of readiness to compete. By the 1990s, especially with the more open trade-in-services provisions of the GATT agreement, the pressure to deregulate and allow competition had greatly increased (Brawley and Schultz 1996).

In the midst of the imperatives of competition and convergence, this time on a global information highway, the CRTC's instincts to deregulate economically are complemented by an inherent tendency to increase regulation socially. The reference to social regulation is still to Canadian content, but the meaning of content is broader. Thus, the information on the Internet and in various telecommunications modes and products increases concerns about privacy, hate literature, copyright, and other issues. The CRTC does not have jurisdiction over most of these areas, but it does become a lightening rod for many of them, precisely because it holds public hearings on related matters within its jurisdiction.

With the context of this evolving mandate and related institutional history made clearer, we can now turn to a closer look at the five institutional issues in relation to the CRTC. Each institutional issue is examined in turn, along with the necessary more detailed information on the CRTC's situation.

The Independence Issue and Representation

Independence and representation have always been linked in the politics of establishing and changing the CRTC and other regulators (Economic Council of Canada 1979, 1981; Doern 1978; Johnson 1991). Independence has involved the immediate corollary question, Independence from whom? The CRTC is a micro-sector of governance that is intended to be broadly but not totally independent from, first, elected ministers, second, political corruption that may otherwise arise in relations between business and politicians, and third, Parliament and the regular bureaucracy, partly on the same grounds of avoiding political corruption, but often so that special expertise can be brought to bear and thus yield technically competent and objective (i.e., non-political) decisions (Willis 1941; Stanbury and Thompson 1982; Thomas and Zajcew 1993).

Virtually in the same institutional context, however, regulatory commissions such as the CRTC are immediately 're-politicized,' precisely because concerns about alternative or complementary representational values and mechanisms arise as a result of the way they were designed. Representation on the CRTC or in its proceedings arise in several ways: from regions or provinces; from interest groups; from within the commission as a whole as an expression of the public interest; and through the interests of the government in ensuring that cross-governmental policy coherence is possible (Raboy 1995a, 1995b)

A closer look at the CRTC on the basis of these multi-layered aspects of the independence/representation question suggests immediately that there is no absolute independence and that there are many grounds on which independence may be partially claimed or justified. In the discussion that follows, the analysis deals primarily with the representational aspects, in part because other aspects of independence turn on other issues that are discussed as a whole, including the one of quasi-judicial roles.

One can begin with the representational role of the chair of the CRTC. This issue is often not directly thought of in the terms of representation, but there are reasons for doing so. The first point to note is that all of the chairs have come from the broadcasting side of the business. There has been no 'telecommunications' chair. Pierre Juneau, Harry Boyle, John Meisel, André Bureau, Keith Spicer, and Françoise Bertrand were all appointed with a firm eye on the culturally sensitive broadcasting sector. There may well be arguments that the time for a telecommunications person has come, in part because this is where the technological innovations are mostly coming from, and indeed because many of the social aspects of telecommunications regulation will be related to the Internet and computer modes (Canada 1995; Drake 1995). On the other hand, because the firms on the telecommunications side are so much larger, it may be argued that the chair should in some symbolic sense be a counterweight to them.

On a more informal basis, however, the telecommunications side does secure representation. A division of labour arose during the Spicer years, in that R.L. Sherman, and, later, David Colville, became a deputy chair. Sherman, for example, led a CRTC federal-provincial task force on long-distance competition that paved the way for competition.

The representational nature of the commission itself has changed in other ways. In its earlier days, when broadcasting predominated and when there was a concern for a 'single system,' a sense of coherence was mirrored in, or reinforced by, a small commission with mainly full-time, Ottawa-based commissioners, complemented by a modest number of part-time regional representatives with limited roles. As the mandate broadened (the addition of the telecommunications sector) and the nature of the two separate industries broadened, the structure of the representation also broadened. The Conservative government of Prime Minister Brian Mulroney established, as we have seen, a larger commission, with greater regional representation and powers, and this occurred at a time when the industry was itself awash with technological change and new specialized services. In the view of some, the quality of the appointees has diminished, in that there is less attention paid to expertise and more to politically sympathetic persons who are interested more in local concerns than the system as a system.

Interacting with this formal system of representation was an interest-group structure that, at first glance seems to have been remarkably stable from the 1960s to the present. The Canadian Association of Broadcasters (CAB), the Canadian Cable Television Association (CCTA), and the Stentor group of companies (under various names) were the dominant business interest groups that interacted closely with the members and staff of the CRTC. A broader cluster of 'social-cultural' interests had less cohesive representation but was nonethless a strong presence in the psyche of the CRTC. These interests included consumer groups, variously styled friends of public broadcasting, and, more recently, anti-poverty and social-welfare groups concerned about issues such as the charges for local calls.

In fact, however, the late 1990s reality of the CRTC's interest-group structure is that the interests are no longer readily captured by such umbrella groups. The convergence issue and the burgeoning and division of telecommunications markets and products has produced numerous more particular and more competitive 'interests' rather than just interest groups. The large, heretofore monopoly suppliers are being 'watched' not only by the CRTC but also, even more vigilantly, by smaller competitive firms. Consumer and social groups are similarly more diverse, and they range across a local, regional, and national spectrum. Consumer groups in particular are more diverse among businesses that are themselves users and consumers. They increasingly treat telecommunications services 'like oil,' in that they do not care where it comes from as long as the price is right and quality and reliability are assured.

The representation of this more diverse set of interests on the CRTC presents a real dilemma for its redesign. It is less and less possible to have all such diverse groups *on* the CRTC. Indeed, it may be necessary for the CRTC to become a smaller, more cohesive body, with a full-time commissioner, so that it can keep its eye on the crucial issues ahead. On the other hand, there is so much concern, mixed with enthusiasm, about the information highway and related communications technologies that a broadly based arena of discussion and hearings is arguably even more essential for the widening set of interests that seek representation *before* the CRTC. And conducting innovative public hearings is what the CRTC is especially good at.

But this leaves open the issues of whether a 'public interest' is discoverable and possible in such a fast-changing field and whether an appointed collective commission (regardless of shape or size) can claim to represent it. The role of elected ministers and governments invariably enters the debate here as well. One line of argument is simply: if some kind of public-interest rationale is claimed, then the tasks should be handed to elected ministers to carry out in both a policy and administrative sense and with traditional parliamentary accountability put into operation. Clearly, many areas of Canadian regulation are handled in precisely this manner, and, as Chapter 6 has shown, the previously mentioned energy and transportation sector changes exemplified the Cabinet's desire to claw back powers over policy. An opposite line of argument is that competitive markets are emerging in the converging telecommunications sector, and that 'the public interest' resides in getting the CRTC out of the way so that participants in the market can make their own arrangements and purchases, subject only to the general rules of competition and other business framework laws that are not administered by the CRTC (see more below).

Last, but not least, in this array of representation choices and debates is the role of the Cabinet and elected ministers. As we have seen, the Cabinet can issue policy directives to the CRTC, and there are also provisions for appeals to Cabinet on limited grounds. This approach is intended to ensure that the Cabinet is not deciding on single cases or licences and that the CRTC is left to make these decisions independently, objectively, and without partisan political considerations. However, before discussing what arrangements at this level might make sense for a future CRTC, we need to deal more explicitly with the mix of functions played by the CRTC, including the current state of the quasi-judicial function.

The Quasi-judicial and Adjudicative Functions and the Mix of Functions

The CRTC is more than a regulatory agency in that it goes beyond just making rules on the basis of a statute. It carries out a range of functions. Typically, the issue of independence centres on whether, and to what extent, the regulator carries out adjudicative and quasi-judicial functions or both. As a Law Reform Commission study pointed out, adjudicative functions 'can occur when conflicts arise between two parties but the existing courts are not seen as a suitable forum for their resolution' (Law Reform Commission of Canada 1982, 13). Independent regulatory commissions and other types of administrative tribunals are said to have advantages as adjudicators in that they can relax the rules of evidence and need not be bound by their previous decisions. But agencies that carry out such functions are often seen by the courts as being 'quasi-judicial,' and 'so it is the administrative agency as adjudicator which has been most often subject to judicial review' (Law Reform Commission of Canada 1982, 14). Quasi-judicial features are said to arise, for example, if principles of natural justice are involved, and there is thus a duty to hear both sides of a dispute.

Legal scholars point out that the 'delineations between these various functions are often far from precise' (Ratushny 1987, 4). In fact, Ratushny characterizes adjudicative functions as decisions that 'involve the application of specific criteria to individuals' (Ratushny 1987, 4). This latter view could make many areas of ordinary administration into adjudicative activity.

The CRTC is partly a quasi-judicial body in the sense that it may be called on to carry out the principles of natural justice. But it is much less involved than in the past in adjudicative activities, if these are seen to be disputes between two private parties. For the most part it is engaged in granting licences to applicants based on the criteria in the law and in regulations. The CRTC is also involved in policy reviews to establish new conditions for licences. But in recent years there have not been many new licences granted, and thus, increasingly, the CRTC is engaged in ensuring that existing licensees are complying with the terms of their grants. Even the renewal of licences is presumed to be virtually automatic in that there is a legal presumption that they are renewable unless there is clear evidence of non-compliance.

It is likely that the CRTC cannot be considered an adjudicative agency in any overall sense, but considerations here must go deeper into its changing environment. First, it is important to note that legal issues for the CRTC have grown in importance. This growth is due to two factors: first, a greater willingness of parties to take, or threaten, legal action, especially smaller firms challenging the large telecommunications companies, and second, the impact of the Charter of Rights and Freedoms and the need for the CRTC to 'Charter-proof' everything it does. This applies in particular to challenges to possible new regulations, where the right to 'freedom of expression' may be being limited, such as in areas of advertising.

This increase in legal and rights-oriented parameters goes beyond individual cases to the making of the regulations and rules themselves. However, we must still be careful in how we label the continuum of functions actually involved because they could be partly quasi-judicial, adjudicative, or administrative.

Another factor in these assessments of change is the central fact that technology and convergence are themselves reducing the extent and nature of the monopoly or 'utility' aspect of the industry, and hence of the fundamental allocative task of the regulator in matters of entry. There are still some aspects of the traditional broadcasting spectrum where regulation by a public utility is technically needed. But on an overall basis, this is less and less true. At the same time, there are issues of transition, as convergence occurs and as firms, interest groups, and the government struggle with how the new competitive era is to be managed.

For the purposes of this section, the CRTC's mix of de facto functions must then be extended to a consideration of another cluster of its activities, its quasi-political functions, and its inquiry, study, and advisory functions. The CRTC's quasi-political functions refers not to politics as partisan activity, but rather to the areas in which the CRTC takes on roles in resolving or simply debating issues where the different values of interests must be aired and discussed. Convergence is certainly one such issue. It involves politics with a very big 'P.' The relative power and the future roles and profitability of the cable and telecommunications companies are politics and business of a high order, and the CRTC is one arena in which they are being played out. But it is clearly not the only arena or even the main one, in that this is the stuff of the politics of Cabinet, Canada–

U.S. relations, federal-provincial relations, and Industry Canada and Heritage Canada departmental and ministerial politics. Because of its focus on the CRTC, this chapter deals only with the influences of the dual or divided assignment of telecommunications policy between Industry Canada and Canadian Heritage, as decided in the 1993 reorganization of the government of Canada (Doern 1996). The CRTC reports to the minister of Canadian heritage, and the heritage minister has policy jurisdiction over the cable companies. Industry Canada has jurisdiction over the telephone and telecommunications sector. Thus there is a further and quite deliberate institutionalized tension built into the CRTC's environment for policy and quasi-political activities.

Partly for these reasons, the convergence issue was handed to the CRTC for hearings and study, and the agency promptly carried out an extensive and very public review (CRTC 1995a). These are competences that the CRTC has built up with considerable skill over the years and that are likely to be needed in the future. This is because issues such as violence, pornography, privacy, hate literature, and the like will raise difficult problems that will need an appropriate expert forum for debate and careful independent public consideration.

Regulatory Compliance, Enforcement, and Service Delivery

In the current era of reinvented government, compliance activity is often distinguished from enforcement (Sparrow 1994; Grabosky 1995). This separation in the words is intended to show that the task of getting various actors to 'behave as intended' under regulation involves a complex array of soft instruments and activities by government and others. These activities range from education and information to incentives and codes, and then, finally, to direct enforcement. The CRTC has never had its own 'regulatory police force.' Its rulings and decisions are enforced ultimately by the courts, and it has always had to pay reasonable attention to having good compliance approaches. In the 1990s, however, both budget cuts and government-wide policies for ensuring better service delivery have resulted in a somewhat different focus on compliance.

First, there has been a considerable simplification by the CRTC of the monitoring and information process needed to ensure that licence holders comply with Canadian-content rules in both radio and television. There is also a simplified rate-regulation process for the cable sector. Prior to the early 1990s these aspects of implementation were 'micro-managed' to the considerable consternation of the industry. On the telecommunications side, the rate-of-return approach to regulation is being replaced by a pricing-capping system that is more flexible and incentive-based (Bauer, Trebing, and Wilsey 1995; Crandall and Waverman 1995).

A greater focus on compliance in the CRTC also arose out of the fact that new licences were not being granted, and hence a greater part of the CRTC's work was on routine compliance reviews. The nature of licence-based monitoring and compliance can be seen by a brief account of the mix of activities involved when the problem of non-performance by a licence holder arises.

One of the charges made against many forms of broadcast licencing is that a licensee is allowed to promise a lot when applying for a licence but almost always delivers little or a lot less once in possession of it. However, a licence is in fact a promise to perform, and the CRTC's compliance processes provide for various kinds and stages of intervention in the licence as conditions for obtaining it. Where performance is suspect, the CRTC can engage in such steps as informal contact, formal correspondence, public criticism and notice (which, among other things, may make a licensee's bankers take notice), calling the licensee to a formal hearing, issuing a mandatory order that is registered with the Federal Court of Canada and thus becomes a court order, prosecution, and the use of very short renewal periods rather than the usual seven-year licences. The ultimate act of revoking a licence is a very rare occurence, and, as mentioned earlier, the legal basis of a licence as determined in court cases is that licensees have a right to expect renewal. Other devices that could be used but have never been contemplated in CRTC circles is to auction licences (as occurred in the UK for private ITV network licences). This opens up the possibility that a licensee would lose the licence to a higher or better bidder.

When seen in the context of the above potential stages, compliance consists in fact of an array of activities, but under the recent service-oriented managerial ethos of the federal government it is also seen as a service activity. Accordingly, the CRTC is being encouraged to see all its activities in terms of service and client satisfaction rather than of the harder-edged traditions of regulatory enforcement or even of the earlier compliance approaches.

In the above example, clients are seen largely as licensees. But compliance of the broadened kind described above also extends to the mass and intermediate consumers and users of the newly converging and fast developing services of the firms being regulated. The fierce January 1995 consumer rebellion against the cable companies for the way they were selling their compulsory package of new channels is but a precursor of the new realities of consumer politics. In short, there will be a host of potential compliance issues in which the CRTC will find itself in the important but vague business of being a grievance handler for consumers, or a quasi-consumer ombudsman, as well as a regulator. Clearly most consumers should direct their complaints to the licence holder delivering the service, but the CRTC has a willing or unwilling interest in the nature and pattern of these grievances. These grievances often deal with issues in which the CRTC has a regulatory mandate, such as those dealing with violence and gender, but they may also lead to the consideration a whole new array of consumer social issues, as the convergence process results in yet unknown technological and social effects.

Framework Competition versus Sectoral Regulators

The CRTC is best seen historically as a sectoral regulator in the sense that it was regulating two sectors of industry, broadcasting and telephones. Overlaying all industrial sectors, in principle at least, are horizontal or framework regulators such as competition law, whose general purpose is to promote competition and to prevent anti-competitive behaviour like monopoly or predatory pricing.

For most of its history, the CRTC and the firms it regulated were essentially sheltered from the direct operation of federal competition regulation (Doern 1995). The main connection between the two sets of regulators came in the Competition Act under sections 125 and 126. As Chapter 9 has shown, these provisions authorize the director of investigation and research (who heads the Bureau of Competition Policy) to make representations to, and call evidence before, federal and provincial (the latter by invitation) boards, commissions, or other tribunals. The minister of industry may also direct the director to make such representations. Over the years, but particularly in the late 1980s and early 1990s, the competition regulator did appear before the CRTC to press for a faster movement towards competition, but in the role of advocate and not a regulator as such.

The analysis in Chapter 9 of this book analysed these interventions and concluded that they exerted a steady pro-competition pressure on the CRTC. It also showed how the CRTC has been increasingly practising the doctrine of regulatory forbearance, whereby a regulator chooses, or is required by law, not to regulate, or forbears from regulating, in situations where the market situation indicates that effective competition exists (Colville 1996).

Since these developments concerning the CRTC are examined in Chapter 9, it is useful to see the interplay between the regimes in another way, namely through a particular example, the case study of Fundy Cable. Fundy Cable, the dominant cable television company in the province of New Brunswick, decided in the early 1990s to compete in the converged telecommunications market with the far larger province-owned New Brunswick Telephone Company (NBtel), which had a virtual monopoly in the traditional telephone market (Fundy Cable 1996). It immediately began drawing attention to what it regarded as NBtel's abuse of its dominant position, especially over convergence-related support structures. Fundy Cable believed that NBtel's actions contravened both the Competition and the Telecommunications acts.

Following unsuccessful direct approaches to NBtel, Fundy Cable tried the two available regulatory venues. Some initial frustrations at using the CRTC led it, through the New Brunswick Cable Television Association, to lodge a complaint with the director of investigation and research under the Competition Act (Fundy Cable 1996, attachment I). The director basically supported the complaint, and in the wake of NBtel's timely and positive behind-the-scenes response to resolving the concerns, did not proceed to the full legal range of the processes that could be used. While this step took a few months, it appeared to give a fairly speedy positive response.

A few months later, however, Fundy Cable, was back at the CRTC, arguing that the complaint to the director of investigation and research had only resolved the matter 'in principle' because, in the view of Fundy Cable, NBtel was continuing to abuse in various ways its dominant position (Fundy Cable 1996, 8). Fundy Cable filed an application to have the CRTC resolve a broad range of alleged NBtel inter-corporate and pricing transactions with its affiliates.

While a case such as that of Fundy Cable must be examined in much greater detail than is possible here, it does show the willingness of firms to use various regulatory arenas, and hence to take their own private actions. At the same time, the process is time-consuming and potentially uncertain. The competition regulator's decision was supportive in the Fundy Cable example, but appears to have not had the full immediate expected impact. The telecommunications regulator allows a broad range of approaches, but it is also bound by different procedural requirements that we have not explored fully but that slowed matters in this case.

In the 1990s it can thus be seen that three things have clearly changed in the telecommunications-competition nexus. First, convergence has produced competition and created firms that are testing the boundaries of colliding sectoral and competition, regulatory law and practice more aggressively. Second, the CRTC is promoting competition, but not as fast as might be wished. Some interests, and the CRTC itself, see the need for 'fair competition.' Third, competition regulators are pushing, not just on their own but also because of the impetus of liberalized trade law, for competition law to have fewer exceptions – in other words for the law to become more truly framework and horizontal in nature.

At present the CRTC's legal jurisdiction over competition in the broadcasting and telecommunications sector is dominant, but pressure is leading towards a doctrine that would see increased primacy of the Competition Act over sectoral regulatory law.

The Internationalization of Regulation and the CRTC

International influences have in one sense always been crucial to the CRTC. The very existence of the CRTC (as was the case with its predecessor bodies) is the result in part of the need to fend off the onslaught of the U.S. cultural broadcasting influence and to create room for Canadian values, culture, and life to be fully reflected in radio and television programming. In the technical realm, telecommunications and broadcasting have always been bound to the International Telcommunications Union located in Geneva (Lee 1996). Outside of these two areas, however, Canada and the United States largely respected and did not challenge the traditional monopoly regulatory systems each had separately constructed, Canada around the CRTC, and the United States around the Federal Communications Commission (Geller 1995).

In the 1990s, however, the internationalization of regulation has escalated in several important ways, driven by the direct and indirect effects of globalization (Brawley and Schultz 1996; Janisch 1987). The changes have influenced the convergence process and the explosion of new products and services. However, in terms of institutional change, there are two developments that are especially crucial for the CRTC and its working environment.

First, a telecommunications law passed recently in the United States deregulates massively the converged sector by allowing competitor among local telephone companies, long-distance carriers, cable-television operators, and even electric utilities (Bureau of National Affairs 1996). Its deregulatory reach extends to a relaxation of ownership restrictions. Equally, however, the legislation increases social regulation in such areas as indecent sexual material and transmission of material to children (Bureau of National Affairs 1996).

These changes in the United States promise to spill over the border, as did those in the early 1990s, not only through their impact on the CRTC, but, more importantly, through changes underway in U.S. firms and in Canadian-American and other global alliances and mergers (Drake 1995). The CRTC's difficulties over the direct-to-home television licencing issue is a telling reflection of how fast things can move and how fiercely firms are prepared to fight (through, around, and over the figurative 'dead bodies' of regulators) to get their foot in the door (Policy Review Panel 1995).

The second international development is that telecommunications policy is now a field shared by international trade regulators and international trade institutions (Hoekman and Kostecki 1995; Trebilcock and Howse 1995). The trade in services agreement that is part of the Uruguay Round agreement of the GATT brings telecommunications services partly into the realm of the settlement provisions for trade rules and trade disputes. Not only must the CRTC and other federal departments be aware of the new obligations and rules, the changes also mean that the number of players within the government of Canada that have a say in telecommunications policy have been expanded considerably. Changing international arrangements in the telecommunications field will also clearly not wait until the next round of GATT–World Trade Organization (WTO) negotiations begins. At the time of writing, important negotiations involving a subset of sixty-eight WTO member nations had concluded an agreement to liberalize telecommunications markets and hence break up key features of national monopolies (*Financial Times*, 17 February 1997, 1).

This broadening of the telecommunications policy community began in the Canada–U.S. free-trade negotiations of the mid- and late 1980s, and has become more entrenched since the deal struck by the Uruguay Round. The telecommunications policy function within Industry Canada has also resulted in a more internationalized emphasis, largely because the mandate of Industry Canada has become more oriented to international competitiveness than it was for most of the 1980s (Doern 1996). In addition, Heritage Canada also has an important national policy role.

Conclusions

The CRTC is a significant and visible national regulatory institution in Canada. It is being transformed as a regulatory institution, but it has not been pared back as much as some other federal regulators, nor have the changes gone as far or as fast as the revolution in telecommunications would lead one to expect. The five institutional features that have been examined each convey some of the reasons for change, but they also show how institutional directions and trade-offs for the CRTC do not all pull in the direction of deregulation and contraction.

The issue of independence and representation is likely to pull the CRTC in two directions. First, precisely because of the tighter interplay among sectoral, competition, and international regulation, the federal Cabinet is likely to want to ensure that overall policy and perceived public-interest issues are increasingly in the hands of elected ministers. This would follow recent similar developments elsewhere, particularly in the transportation sector. Second, at the same time, the complex issues surrounding the convergence of the information highway and of telecommunications are undoubtedly going to need appropriate policy review and consultation through the arenas of hearings and other forms of direct democracy, including electronic democracy. This suggests the continuing need for a wider quasi-advisory role for the CRTC, given that it is skilled in these tasks. But this assignment in turn raises practical concerns about the membership of the commission. It would appear that the increased use in the last decade of part-time commissioners is counterproductive because it has made the CRTC a less coherent body precisely when concerted full-time consideration of convergence and of the social impact of that convergence is required, if only to allow the proper conduct of public advisory hearings and discussion. At the same time, the convergence issues also require ever broader sets of interests to become involved, and to do so mainly *at* the hearings of the CRTC rather than *on* the CRTC itself.

When these concerns are linked to the issue of quasi-judicial and adjudicative functions and from these to the overall mix of CRTC functions, the conclusion is that the CRTC has a reduced adjudicative role and that it has become much more an administrative and compliance body, a trend that appears likely to continue. On the other hand, the complex nature of the information and telecommunication services produced by competing, though still partially regulated, firms is likely to propel the CRTC (or some form of substitute institution) into a role involving greater market mediation or even in the nature of an ombudsman.

The full mix of functions of the CRTC will still involve some important forms of independence in its structure and powers in order to carry out continuing rule-making functions. However, the responsibilities may tilt, as a whole, towards a greater array of activities concerning the delivery of services and in compliance and mediation than is the case presently.

With regard to the CRTC's relationships with horizontal regulators, there is little doubt that the pressure will, and should be, for competition law to take precedence over sectoral regulatory law. At a minimum these relationships must be clarified and made more transparent. Moreover, this transparency must apply in both directions; in other words, reforms to competition law also have to occur given that, as the Fundy Cable case partly showed, its institutions are not always amenable to speedy and effective decision making and may not have the necessary expertise in the fast-changing telecommunications field. The CRTC's relationships to horizontal regulators will also not be confined to competition regulators. Intellectual property and privacy regulators will also loom large.

Last, but hardly least, there are the issues inherent in the internationalization of telecommunications regulation. The impact on the CRTC is mixed and undoubtedly fast-moving and potentially contradictory. First, global competitive forces are such that new telecommunications products and services emerge almost every day. In the face of so many developments, the wise regulator or government will not even attempt to regulate because it will always be years behind in getting rules in place. Hence its legitimacy and credibility will deteriorate rapidly.

Second, the internationalization of telecommunications regulation has meant that telecommunications policy making is shared among a far larger number of players than a decade ago, and the trend will continue. Along with cultural policy makers, foreign policy, industry, and trade ministers and officials are now also intricately involved. This is a further reason why the policy function is coveted so much more by the Cabinet than it might have been twenty years ago when fewer ministers could legitimately claim a role in telecommunications policy formation.

But internationalization, including the compelling realities of the 1996 U.S. Telecommunications Act, will also produce concerns among Canadian economic and social interest groups that the telecommunications policy-hearing process needs a greater CRTC-like presence. This is because domestic interest groups may rightly fear that national policy makers are paying more attention to their foreign counterparts than to their own citizens. Accordingly, they may demand that international negotiations be preceded by ever more transparent and democratic hearing and consultative processes in the development of national positions on convergence and telecommunications policy.

It is in this context that it must be reiterated that the CRTC is more than just a vertical sectoral regulator. Its jurisdiction over Canadian content rules in broadcasting and de facto universal telephone service (with crucial social considerations such as free local calls) has meant that the CRTC is itself a social regulator. The latter is also horizontal and embraces a range of cultural, redistributive, and other goals that stretch beyond the 'vertical' boundaries of the industry. These regulatory reaches are likely to increase as privacy, intellectual property, and other concerns emerge and extend across the converged telecommunications sectors as well as across borders.

What all of the above means for the CRTC is not totally clear. Other regulatory bodies already exist for matters of privacy and intellectual property. And there are unresolved technical issues about *how* to regulate and *if* one should regulate the entire sweep of the information highway. These realms could be a source of new roles for the CRTC or, alternatively, could send other regulators into campaigns for carving up the CRTC.

The five institutional issues all suggest that the CRTC will have to become a different more focused institution, still central to the broadcasting and telecommunications policy and to the service-delivery process, but joined by many players in a fast-changing and increasingly quasi-regulatory competitive realm.

REFERENCES

Bauer, Johannes M., H.M. Trebing, and Michelle F. Wilsey. 1995. 'An Analysis and Assessment of Price Caps and Incentive Regulation in Telecommunications.' Paper prepared for the Canadian Radio-television and Telecommunications Commission, Ottawa, December.

Brawley, D., and Richard Schultz. 1996. 'The Internationalization of Telecommunications Policy.' In *Border Crossings: The Internationalization of Canadian Public Policy*, edited by Bruce Doern, Les Pal, and Brian Tomlin. Toronto: Oxford University Press of Canada.

Bureau of National Affairs. 1996. *Antitrust and Trade Regulation Report*, vol. 70, no. 1748, 8 February. (See Telecommunications Reform Bill, 102, 122–79.)

Canada. 1995. *Connection, Community, Content: The Challenge of the Information Highway*. Ottawa: Minister of Supply and Services.

Canadian Radio-television and Telecommunications Commission. 1995a. *Competition and Culture on Canada's Information Highway: Managing the Realities of Transition*. Ottawa: Public Works and Government Services Canada.

– 1995b. *Synopsis*. Ottawa: CRTC.

Colville, David. 1996. 'The Changing Role of the CRTC.' Paper presented to the Globe and Mail Insight Conference, Toronto, 30 January.

Conklin, David B. 1991. 'The Broadcasting Act and the Changing Pathology of Cabinet Appeals.' *Media and Communications Law Review* 2:297–333.

Crandall, R.W., and L. Waverman. 1995. *Talk is Cheap: The Promise of Regulatory Reform in North American Telecommunications*. Washington: The Brookings Institution.

Doern, G. Bruce, ed. 1978. *The Regulatory Process in Canada*. Toronto: Macmillan of Canada.

– 1995. *Fairer Play: Canadian Competition Policy Institutions in a Global Market*. Toronto: C.D. Howe Institute.

– 1996. 'Looking for the Core: Industry Canada and Program Review.' In *How Ottawa Spends, 1996–97: Life Under the Knife*, edited by Gene Swimmer. Ottawa: Carleton University Press 1996, Chap. 2.

Drake, W.J., ed. 1995. *The New Information Infrastructure: Strategies for U.S. Policy*. New York: Twentieth Century Fund Press.

Economic Council of Canada. 1979. *Responsible Regulation*. Ottawa: Economic Council of Canada.

– 1981. *Reforming Regulation*. Ottawa: Economic Council of Canada.

Fundy Cable. 1996. 'Part VII Application Concerning the Inter-Corporate and Pricing Transactions of the New Brunswick Telephone Company Limited and its Affiliates.' Submitted to the Canadian Radio-television and Telecommunications Commission, 17 May.

Geller, Henry. 1995. 'Reforming the U.S. Telecommunications Policymaking Process.' In *The New Information Infrastructure: Strategies for U.S. Policy*, edited by William J. Drake. 115–36. New York: Twentieth Century Fund Press.

Globerman, S., W.T. Stanbury, and T.A. Wilson, eds. 1995. *The Future of Telecommunications Policy in Canada.* Toronto: Institute for Policy Analysis.

Grabosky, Peter N. 1995 'Using Non-Governmental Resources to Foster Regulatory Compliance.' *Governance* 8, no. 4 (October): 527–50.

Hoekman, Bernard, and M. Kostecki. 1995. *The Political Economy of the World Trading System: From GATT to WTO.* Oxford: Oxford University Press.

Janisch, H.N. 1987. 'Telecommunications and the Canada–U.S. Free Trade Agreement.' *Telecommunications Policy* 13, no. 2.

Johnson, David. 1991. 'Regulatory Agencies and Accountability: An Ontario Perspective.' *Canadian Public Administration* 34, no. 3: 417–34.

Law Reform Commission of Canada. 1982. *Parliament and Administrative Agencies.* Ottawa: Law Reform Commission of Canada.

Lee, Kelly. 1996. *Global Telecommunications Regulation: A Political Economy Perspective.* London: Pinter.

Monteiro, Joseph. 1993. *Interventions by the Bureau of Competition Policy.* Ottawa: Bureau of Competition Policy, Industry Canada, September.

Peers, Frank W. 1969. *The Politics of Canadian Broadcasting, 1920–1951.* Toronto: University of Toronto Press.

Policy Review Panel. 1995. *Direct-to-Home Satellite Broadcasting: Report of the Policy Review Panel.* Ottawa: Industry Canada.

Raboy, Marc. 1995a. Influencing Public Policy on Canadian Broadcasting. *Canadian Public Administration*, 38, no. 3, 411–32.

– 1995b. 'The Role of Public Consultation in Shaping the Canadian Broadcasting System.' *Canadian Journal of Political Science* 28, no. 3, 455–78.

Ratushny, Ed. 1987. 'What Are Administrative Tribunals? The Pursuit of Uniformity in Diversity.' *Canadian Public Administration* 30, no. 1:1–13.

Schultz, Richard. 1983. 'Regulation as Maginot Line: Confronting the Technological Revolution in Telecommunications.' *Canadian Public Administration* 26, no. 2 (Summer):203–18.

– 1994. 'Regulation and Telecommunications Reform: Exploring the Alternatives.' In *International Review of Comparative Public Policy: International Perspectives on Telecommunications Policy*, edited by R. Stevenson, et al. London: Jai Press.

Scott, Sheridan. 1990. 'The New Broadcasting Act: An Analysis.' *Media and Communications Law Review* 1:25–58.

Sparrow, Malcolm K. 1994. *Imposing Duties: Government's Changing Approach to Compliance.* London: Praeger, Chap 1.

Stanbury, W.T., and Fred Thompson. eds. 1982. *Regulatory Reform in Canada.* Montreal: Institute for Research on Public Policy.

Stewart, Andrew, and William Hull. 1994. *Canadian Television Policy and the Board of Broadcast Governors 1958–1968.* Edmonton: University of Alberta Press.

Tardi, Gregory. 1981. 'The Appointment of Federal Regulatory Commissioners: A Case Study of the CRTC.' *Canadian Public Administration* 24, no. 4:587–95.

Thomas, Paul, and Orest W. Zajcew. 1993. 'Structural Heretics: Crown Corporations and Regulatory Agencies.' In *Governing Canada: Institutions and Public Policy*, edited by Michael Atkinson, 115–48. Toronto: Harcourt Brace Jovanovich.

Trebilcock, Michael, and Robert Howse. 1995. *The Regulation of International Trade*. London: Routledge.

U.S. Information Infrastructure Task Force. 1995. *Intellectual Property and the National Information Infrastructure*. Washington: Department of Commerce.

Willis, John. 1941. *Canadian Boards at Work*. Toronto: Macmillan.

16

Conclusions

STEPHEN WILKS AND G. BRUCE DOERN

This is a book about regulatory institutions, one to set alongside those that deal with the theories of economic regulation and of legal form. In our introductory chapter we focused on four ways in which we believe this collection advances regulatory institutional analysis. First, we made the case for a much broader conceptual definition of regulation if it is to accommodate comparative analysis in a more complete way. Second, we argued the need to examine regulatory institutional change in the context of an interplay among four regulatory regimes: sectoral, framework, the regime for managing regulation within the state, and international. Third, we have shown the need for a broadened conception of regulatory interests and of reform ideas. And finally, we have examined the need for closer inter-regime analysis to understand particular kinds of regulatory change.

The purpose of this final chapter is to offer a concluding discussion of the broad context of comparative regulatory change and of some other themes that are less thoroughly explored in the opening chapter. These include such institutional issues as the independence and autonomy of regulators, regulatory implementation, economic governance, and comparative 'paths to reform.'

Comparative Regulatory Change

These studies, which take a broad historical sweep, underline an historic transformation that has strong elements of transatlantic convergence. Put simply, the United States and Canada have always been 'regulatory states,' and the UK is becoming one. Or, more correctly, the UK is rediscovering its origins as a regulatory state.

A regulatory state is defined by its relationship to the private sector. It is a state in which the public authorities provide a legal and administrative framework within which public needs are met by the organizations and individuals of civil society. This framework is built on a philosophy of public authority that is embedded in political culture and constitutional arrangements. It recognizes the market as a natural way to meet needs, but it also recognizes the importance of individual and collective action through groups and voluntary organizations. In the UK the transition from an interventionist welfare state to an enabling regulatory state is the story of the Thatcher revolution. In dismantling the mixed economy and in prioritizing the market, the Conservatives moved the British polity much closer to the North American model, but they also changed political culture and expectations in a way that has allowed Tony Blair and New Labour to consolidate that shift rather than to challenge it.

In fact, we would argue that the regulatory state is also to be found as a distinctive variant in Germany and Japan and in the emergent governance of the European Union. But these states are characterized by a far higher level of suspicion of the market, a greater interpenetration of the state and civil society, and regulatory systems that stress the joint pursuit of public goals in a more distinctively 'corporatist' system. We would therefore recognize the common cultural legacy of 'Anglo-Saxon' states, which give particular prominence to market solutions, to citizen independence, and to the autonomy of the groups and companies that make up civil society. This common legacy has a particular resonance in the field of utility regulation.

The antecedents of virtually all utility regulation are with the regulation of railways. The first consideration of regulatory options came within a decade of the introduction of commercial services, in the British Parliament of the 1830s. Gladstone's Railways Act of 1844 was the model for the U.S. Interstate Commerce Act of 1887, and the British debate had a direct influence on American and Canadian thinking. The contemporary convergence of regimes thus has deep historical roots. And while it would be far-fetched to compare the current UK regulatory system with the 'nightwatchman state' of Victorian Britain, some of the attitudes and the institutions do show a familiar pattern. There are elements of institutional continuity at work. Just as Thatcherism owed some of its success to an appeal to traditional British values and a traditional respect for the market, so too regulatory initiatives benefit from historical precedent, as Hogwood's chapter in this volume illustrates.

Just as we see a very broad convergence in the nature of the regulatory state with a major shift in the UK, so also we see a broad convergence in the objectives of regulation, this time with a shift in the United States and Canada towards more efficiency-oriented and competition-oriented regulatory goals. Peters in his chapter discusses this in his review of the deregulatory imperatives of U.S. policy since President Carter, but we would emphasize the relevance of his argument to economic regulation, where the public-interest, market-restricting regulation of the New Deal has been overturned by a deregulation drive towards economic efficiency. This emphasis on creating competition, on compliance cost, on cost-benefit analysis, and on the influence of economic ideas when designing regulation shows strong similarities with the British experience. Peters remarks that 'a coterie of free-market economists now tends to dominate thinking within the major regulatory agencies.' This parallels the British experience and is underlined by the rapidly growing interest in the United States in incentive regulation. Schultz and Doern emphasize the way in which Canadian regulation in the 1930s was actually designed to suppress competition, but they go on to review a more contemporary cross-border influence of American economic liberalism. In Canada this influence from the United States provoked the deregulatory initiatives of the Mulroney government in the mid-1980s, but in a different form. In addition to attempting to impose economic priorities on agencies, the Canadian response was to cut the agencies down to size and to reassert federal Cabinet control over the policy-making function (Doern et al. 1998).

The main areas of convergence are seen in the field of economic regulation. We have given less emphasis to the growth in social and environmental regulation, which in the United States has grown to such extensive proportions that Sunstein has talked of a 'rights revolution.' He describes an extraordinary growth in legal entitlements based on legislation passed during the 1960s and 1970s that constitute virtually the American equivalent of a welfare state. He suggests that the growth of this national regulatory state 'has renovated the original constitutional framework and the system of government under which the nation operated for most of its history' (Sunstein 1990, 13). It is less plausible to suggest that either Canada or the UK has converged towards this extensive and legalistic expansion of private rights. Indeed, the chapters by Hoberg and Booker present environmental regulation in Canada and the UK as far less activist than in the United States. But this contrast between economic and social regulation may help explain one of the apparent contradictions between the earlier chapters of the book. While Peters describes the institutionalization of deregulation in the United States, Francis talks of 'resurgent regulation.' Peters concentrates on the economic side, while Francis puts more emphasis on social regulatory areas where 'there remains broad levels of popular support and deep commitment on the part of specific constituencies to particular regulatory regimes.' Thus the importance of competition. In the economic field a common commitment to competition as a way of supplementing or even supplanting regulation is evident in regulation in the United States, Canada, and the United Kingdom. In this field it is the UK that is making the running.

There is one final area of common ground on both sides of the Atlantic. Notwithstanding Peters's emphasis on deregulation, it does appear that regulation has not declined on a net overall basis. There is sectoral deregulation but expanded framework and international regulation. The idea of a regulatory state must encompass all of its component regimes. It is therefore a concept flexible enough to permit change in the intensity, the form, and even the objectives of regulation, but it recognizes that regulation is a constant and that it is part of the constitutional settlement. In Chapter 1 we defined regulation both in broad constitutional terms and in specific policy instrument terms. As a policy instrument, regulation is, as Hill points out, a tool of government to be used as an alternative to taxation or spending. Just as taxing and spending are inevitable aspects of modern government, so is regulation. The basic legal framework, which allows transactions to take place and markets to operate, is provided by regulation. 'It was in this spirit that President Roosevelt ... suggested that "We must lay hold of the fact that the laws of economics are not made by nature. They are made by human beings"' (Sunstein 1990, 20). The challenge is not to eliminate regulation but to improve its workings.

In constitutional terms, regulation becomes a principle of government and we share Graham's view that the growth of regulation poses fundamental questions for the British constitution. Ayres and Braithwaite (1992) present an eloquent case for the argument that regulation should be seen not simply as a technical issue but also as a democratic process in which communities can participate. Their advocacy of republican communitarianism is presented in a book that is significantly subtitled *Transcending the Deregulation Debate* in which they deal with various avenues towards flexible, performance-related regulation. In a similar vein Sunstein regards regulation not only as inevitable but as preferable to other political principles. His vigorous defence of regulation argues that 'the modern regulatory system is superior not only to more collectivist alternatives but also to its common law predecessor' (Sunstein 1990, 228). Furthermore, he is insistent that regulation should be seen as a process of republican participation that is much wider than the market-failures approach of traditional neoclassical economics or the private-interest approach of capture theorists. He launches a strong attack on rent-seeking approaches, since 'the notion of rent-seeking rejects as unproductive nearly all of the basic workings of politics. It treats citizenship itself as evil ... [T]o collapse all political behavior into the category of objectionable rent-seeking is grotesquely to devalue the activities of citizenship' (Sunstein 1990, 71). This rather anticipates our final comments, but we note a general trend in regulatory debates away from ideas of deregulation or even regulatory reform towards the 'management' of regulation, which treats regulation as a component part of a system of governance. This trend has been taken furthest in the United States where the centralized management of regulation through the Office of Management and Budget (OMB) has been a distinguishing feature of recent presidencies. It has also been developed considerably in Canada through the Treasury Board, as reviewed in Hills' chapter, but it is underdeveloped in the UK where, as revealed by the chapters by Hogwood, Locke, and others, a regulatory system has grown up piecemeal and has received very little strategic examination (for exploration of this curiosity see Hood and Scott 1996).

Beyond these very general regulatory trends, we do not see any inevitable pressure for full regulatory convergence between Britain and North America. Our position, stated elsewhere, is that national institutional endowments possess distinctive interlinked features and considerable inertia (see Wilks 1996; also Berger and Dore 1996). This position finds confirmation in the chapters presented above. They indicate considerable cross-fertilization between the United States and Canada (chapters by Schultz and Doern and by Hoberg) but much less between North America and the UK. Most of the national and sectoral chapters tell nationally specific stories that show an awareness of foreign practice (such as Vass's chapter) but only modest substantive foreign influence. Clearly there are common pressures at work, including a transatlantic ideology of liberalism, a common experience of radical expenditure cuts, and a breakdown of market barriers, based on explosive technological change (see Francis on banking and telecommunications, and Doern and Graham on telecommunications). Similarly, several authors mention internationalization (Regime IV) and the possibilities of a regulatory 'race to the bottom' in areas such as the environment, but always as a smaller element in overall regulatory change.

The chapter that deals most directly with cross-national policy borrowing is Hill's chapter on regulatory learning. She argues that the North American experience 'offers a basis for regulatory learning in the UK,' and in so doing she parallels an argument that Majone (1996) has made about the potential for the European Union to learn from the United States. Her productive discussion emphasizes the richness of the American experience and literature, but she is also sensitive to the very different political systems and institutional complexes. Thus she tends to point to a potential for learning rather than enumerating a schedule of examples. This is a potential that we should stress. Hill emphasizes the underdeveloped nature of the British regulatory literature (a point echoed by Hogwood) and the 'hidden' nature of British regulatory activity. This is a powerful reproach to British administrators and political scientists that finds expression in Hogwood's review of the bemusingly hit-and-miss nature of British regulatory design. He observes that British political parties have 'no coherent philosophy of the appropriate form for different types of regulation' (although the issue is debated; see Hutton 1996, 292, and publications by the right-leaning Institute of Economic Affairs or the left-leaning Institute for Public Policy Research). But among academic studies it is notable that some of the best regulatory texts are by socio-legal specialists (Ayres and Braithwaite 1992; Baldwin 1996; Ogus 1994), with few authors following in the footsteps of Hancher and Moran (1989) to undertake interpretations based in political science.

In the light of these sceptical comments about the forces making for full regulatory convergence, examples of some de facto convergence in several aspects of the three national regimes are in evidence. There is considerable convergence in the emphasis given to competition and in the resort to novel means of implementation that exploit the autonomy of the corporation. More strikingly, there is convergence in the use of independent agencies. While Canada has reduced the influence of her independent agencies, the independent commissions of the United States have retained their position (the abolition of the ICC to the contrary notwithstanding). Meanwhile, the UK has created a range of new and powerful independent regulators that have transformed the face of the regulatory state. The contagion is even spreading to Europe, where independent agencies have been strongly advocated and some agencies – although far from independent – have been created (Majone 1997; Shapiro 1997).

In the following section, the varying versions of the idea of the independence of regulators are explored, together with two other themes dealing with regulatory implementation and regulation as economic governance.

Institutional Reform Issues: Independence, Implementation, and Economic Governance

It follows from our commitment in this volume to an institutional approach that we expect the evolution of reform in the three political systems to be dominated by institutional factors that mediate economic prescriptions and legal ideals. The 'regimes' we analyse in Chapter 2 and the institutional approaches reviewed by Peters in Chapter 3 attest to regulatory systems that are the outcome of complex historical agreements and that are embedded in a set of political and administrative arrangements. In identifying the context in which reform takes place we have therefore to identify the dynamic elements within these regimes.

Among the several forces at work we pick out three influential issues and factors that have been emphasized in earlier chapters. They are, first, the nature of the regulatory agencies and the leadership and biases embodied in the idea of 'independent' regulation; second, the implementation of regulation and the tensions generated when implementation measures appear too expensive, too inflexible, ineffective, or sometimes actually counter-productive. The third force is the holistic concept of regulation as a mode of market governance in which several stakeholders are affected and the focus of regulation moves beyond specific targets or behavioural changes to encompass market structure.

Independent Regulation

The most striking similarity between the United States, the United Kingdom, and Canada is the resort to independent regulators, particularly for sectoral or Regime I regulation. The nature and extent of independence is a crucial dynamic in our analysis, since it identifies the autonomy of the institution. Independent regulators have the potential to develop their institutional identity, which takes the form of a separate organization, distinctive legal powers, separate procedures, a dedicated staff, and, above all, 'ideas' in the form of a technical perspective and an organizational culture. Peters stresses the importance of ideas in defining a regulatory regime (see also Harris and Milkis 1996, 25, 29) but the development of distinctive ideas is enhanced by a separate institutional history. Some regulatory agencies have a long and proud history of independence, such as the Federal Trade Commission (FTC) in the United States, the British Monopolies and Mergers Commission (which will be fifty years old in 1999), or the Canadian Radio-television Commission (CRTC) (see Chapter 15 by Doern). American independent regulatory commissions combine executive, legislative, and quasi-judicial powers, and have been termed a 'fourth branch' of government. One would not go so far with their British equivalents, but already in their short history the British regulatory offices have developed their own individual styles that reflect also the personalities of the regulators. One can contrast the aloof and intellectual style of the Office of Electricity Regulation (OFFER) with the more down-to-earth and confrontational style of the Office of Gas Supply. Even prosaic factors such as geography underline independence, which OFFER flaunts from its head office in Birmingham. The Canadian National Energy Board is also making a statement through its location in Calgary (and proximity to the oil and gas industry).

The independence of American regulatory agencies such as the FTC or the Environmental Protection Agency (EPA) reflects their incorporation into an institutional system that has protected their mandates against attempts at deregulation. In their study of these two agencies, Harris and Milkis chart the relative failure of Reagan's deregulatory efforts, which they attribute to the power of the public lobby (see also the chapters by Francis and by Hoberg) and to the way in which the agencies had become part of the sub-government networks that provide political protection, but also to the legitimacy that had grown up around their missions. They remark that 'regulatory programmes have become difficult to challenge because they have become part of *a new understanding of rights,*' and they go on to argue: 'The character of bureaucracy and of American political institutions combines with the prevailing public philosophy to generate a great deal of systemic inertia. Changing a regulatory regime in the face of these inertial pressures is formidable indeed' (Harris and Milkis 1996, 44, 49, emphasis in original). In the United States the role of Congress and especially of the courts has been paramount in providing autonomy from deregulatory presidents. But even in the UK the regulatory agencies have established a degree of acceptance and legitimacy that has caused reformers to hesitate. As Vass argues in his chapter, Labour Party proposals for radical reform of the regulatory offices were gradually watered down until they became only marginal in effect. Of course, this argument can be overstated. Institutional autonomy is not an absolute, as the New Labour government's radical redesign of financial regulation demonstrates. Their plans for the new super Securities and Investments Board (*Financial Times*, 21 May 1997) represented a major political initiative, but they also invited comparison with the Securities and Exchange Commission (SEC) in the United States. A regulatory agency such as the SEC illustrates the staying power of independent regulation, which – to take the extreme case – is also manifest in the power of independent central banks.

Agency autonomy can therefore be very extensive, but it is subject to very real political limits. This is the lesson of the analysis by Schultz and Doern in Chapter 5 of the way in which the Canadian 'governments in miniature' were dismantled by the federal government. But what are the arguments for autonomy? In the Canadian case, Schultz and Doern outline how the regulatory agencies captured the policy-making and planning process so that they pre-empted the public-policy role of government. This is what provoked the political reaction. A more typical justification for independence is not in terms of policy making but in terms of a combination of technical skill and the appearance of political impartiality, so that regulatory agencies can provide a neutral and predictable long-term framework in which markets can operate. This justification comes back to the basic rationale of the regulatory state, which is the need to create and structure markets as the means to fulfil public needs. This is certainly clear in the history of the UK regulatory agencies, which were entrusted with the creation of markets following privatization. It is also nicely summed up in the U.S. context by the New Deal supporter Justice William O. Douglas, who said of regulatory agencies: 'They have become more and more the *outposts of capitalism*: they have been given increasingly larger patrol duties, lest capitalism by its own greed, avarice or myopia destroy itself' (cited in Bernstein 1955,

251, emphasis added). A quote applicable to the United States in the 1930s applies aptly to UK utility regulation in the 1990s. Regulation of the market is too important to be left to politicians and it is not to be entrusted to companies. But regulatory independence is relative, and is constrained by the complexity of the apparatus of regulatory institutions and by the market itself. In this respect the U.S. and Canadian institutions are undoubtedly more constrained than their British equivalents, in part as a result of the systems of federalism as well as executive government.

In fact, the strict agency independence of regulation may be, as has often been recognized, something of a misnomer. It may be more accurate to talk of an independent political arena or, like Hogwood, to conceive of the 'interdependence' of several actors in an area of sectoral politics in which the agency is a lead player but a player who often will simply declare a result rather than dictate it. Thus the analysis of U.S. agency independence undertaken by Peters, Francis, and Hoberg throws light on the subtleties of the system. Some U.S. agencies are structured as formal statutorily independent commissions (such as the FTC and state public utility commissions), while others are the equivalents of departments of state (such as the EPA). But all the agencies are controlled by Congress and the courts to an extent unheard of in Canada or the UK. Each agency is responsible to at least four Congressional committees, to the procedural requirements of the Administrative Procedures Act, and to an extraordinary level of legal challenge through private actions. The 'independence' of the agencies is thus seen as independence from the president, not from the political system at large. But even this independence is limited. Presidents change agency leaders. They appoint new commissioners and they can change the chairs of the commissions. The real purpose of agency independence and of the design of the independent regulatory commissions was to protect regulation from party politics.

Looking back at the origins of the U.S. commissions throws new light on the British debate about single-person regulators versus regulatory commissions. Shapiro argues that the Progressives of the late nineteenth century, who created the independent regulatory commissions, would have preferred single-person agency heads. Thus, 'they did not favour the commission form of administrative organization,' but 'in the American political system of the day a single executive would necessarily mean either a Democrat or a Republican controlled agency' (Shapiro 1997, 279). This detracts somewhat from the idea that the British single-person regulator is somehow departing from the U.S. ideal. The British regulator may find his or her job unduly personalized, but, since the UK does not have a 'spoils system,' he or she is a non-party political figure. Thus the arguments that persuaded U.S. reformers to employ multi-member commissions do not apply in the British case. This reasoning rather supports the status quo, in which single-person regulators hold statutory authority as individual office holders, and are able to act with decisiveness, consistency, and transparency. This is a difficult and demanding role, and it puts great emphasis on the character and competence of utility regulators and how they are selected. Vass remarks that they come from similar backgrounds and are appointed by ministers without the U.S. apparatus of review and hearings. Once appointed, however, they have a five-year guaranteed tenure of office, and no regulator has yet been removed, which gives them substantial political discretion.

Despite our institutional bias, we accept one ubiquitous 'law' of regulatory studies, which is that 'people matter.' Indeed, our view of institutions is that they influence and structure policy, but they do not determine it. Similarly, we accept that institutions evolve and change. They do so in ways that are conditioned by their cultures and histories, and in this process regulators will be shaped by their institutions but will, in turn, impart new directions and ideas. The current British utility regulators have had a huge impact on their institutions, since they are among the first appointees and have established the utility offices according to their own preferences. It is remarkable, as Hogwood relates, that they received very little specific guidance from ministers as to regulatory methods, procedures, and expectations. Even their multiple objectives had to be operationalized. Thus Sir Bryan Carsberg, the first Office of Telecommunications (OFTEL) director general, has had a disproportionate influence as the very first utility regulator. To take one example, in his invaluable study Foster talks of the meetings held with the industry, and observes that: 'It was Carsberg's need and achievement to convert such meetings at which everyone still sat at similar chairs on the same level around an ordinary civil service table exchanging views and consensus-seeking into a quasi-judicial process or fair hearing which was subtly, but powerfully, different. (It was not a coincidence that he had experienced American regulation at first hand.)' (Foster 1992, 276). Similarly, the contributions of Ian Byatt at the Office of Water Services (OFWAT) and Stephen Littlechild at OFFER will provide benchmarks for those offices. The extensive discretion of these British regulators becomes clear when they are compared to U.S. regulators – heavily constrained by bureaucratic networks, Congress, and the courts – or to Canadian regulators working as a commission. Doern's review of the most powerful Canadian commission, the CRTC, in Chapter 15, reveals a body currently composed of thirteen commissioners plus six part-time members. The Canadian tradition has been for commissioners to undertake a 'representative' role, so that external pressures and compromizes are reproduced in the complex internal politics of the cnstitution. The discretion of the commission thus faces internal limits, and the chair has nothing like the decisive authority enjoyed by his British counterparts.

We can end this section with some comments on the uses of independence. Regulatory discretion has been extensively studied and widely criticized by economists – who wish to apply rule-based economic principles – and by lawyers – who prefer legal certainty, formal precedent, and procedures that allow judicial review. Discretion is, however, in practice unavoidable. It is fundamental to successful regulation, and is becoming more and more widespread and accepted in processes of flexible implementation and compliance. Our authors all explore discretion in various ways. Booker implicitly stresses Byatt's discretion over the Cost of Quality debate, and Vass argues, in effect, that regulators have systematically interpreted their regulatory brief to give priority to consumer interests, even where these were not pre-eminent in the legislation. As regards consumers, Locke is less satisfied, and American observers have argued that consumers have been excluded from the British regulatory process (Stelzer 1996, 191). Perceptively, Locke also argues that the prominence and ostensible independence of the regulators has been exploited by ministers to avoid responsibility. Thus British regulators have used their discretion, but have done so judiciously and with an awareness of contemporary constraints. Those constraints have been posed by ministers, the public, and the financial markets. Wilks emphasizes the opaque nature of the relationship between the regulator and the sponsoring minister. In practice, ministers and their officials monitor regulators closely; they have regular discussions and, while there is no provision for them to instruct, it would be quite within the British administrative tradition for regulators to act – as the traditional phrase has it – 'in the mind of the minister.' Astute regulators will respond to ministerial preferences, a process particularly noticeable after the May 1997 general election, when regulators appointed by the Conservatives appointed regulators began to adapt to the views of their New Labour sponsors. Equally, the regulators are responsive to public opinion, and are actually very vulnerable to strident media campaigns, thanks to their visibility. But Wilks also suggests that the financial implications of regulatory decisions and the power of financial interests in the British political economy makes regulators unhealthily responsive to the financial markets.

The Implementation of Regulation

In Chapter 4 Hogwood notes the irony that privatization in Britain has produced more, and more salient, government intervention in industry than the previous policy of nationalization. The regulation that followed from privatization has resulted in a greater degree of transparency in the process of intervention and in a greater degree of clarity in regulatory goals. In North America, regulators have been grappling with the problems of implementation for over one hundred years and, as Hill emphasizes, their experience provides a rich store of material on which British regulators can draw. In Britain and North America the goals of economic regulation have shifted with the neo-liberal agenda to stress efficiency, value for money, and the creation of competition within the regulated industries. The question is how to combine these welfare enhancing goals with the traditional public-interest goals, such as access, universal service, protection of vulnerable consumers, regional development, policy planning, and federal cohesion, as well as newer public-interest goals such as environmental protection and international competitiveness. The debate has shifted from questions of Why regulate? to How to regulate? and here North America provides a sumptuous laboratory.

As noted by Hill, the subject of 'the management of regulation' was developed in North America in the 1980s. The movement can be dated to the creation in 1981 by President Reagan of the Office of Information and Regulatory Affairs within the OMB, which Peters calls 'a regulatory KGB.' Under the Clinton administration, the emphasis was shifted by Executive Order 12866 in 1993 towards reinventing government themes and towards cost-effective implementation. Pildes and Sunstein (1995, 96), in exploring the background to the order, remark on the widespread failure of 'command and control' regulation, and they point out that 'The current system of public regulation is extraordinarily inefficient' (see also Chapter 8 by Hill). This has prompted a search for new means of regulation, which Hill begins to explore in her review of 'regulatory flexibility' and her discussion of negotiated and performance-related regulation in Canada. Various forms of, and options for, new and more flexible regulation are raised in the earlier chapters. As Hill also remarks, the resort to novel modes of implementation has been reinforced in North America by ubiquitous expenditure cutbacks, which Hoberg rather pessimistically considers will have a damaging effect on environmental regulation as they push implementation down from the federal to the provincial level.

The ideal for regulatory implementation is often said to be uncoerced compliance. If those being regulated cheerfully comply, then the whole implementing apparatus can be dismantled. Compliance can be pursued by the creation of strict rules policed by the courts, or by persuasion and administrative negotiation. Crudely, the former can be termed 'command and control' and is more typical of the adversarial and legalistic U.S. system. The latter can be termed 'negotiated regulation' and is more typical of the British tradition. The huge gulf between U.S. and British implementation arises from the importance of law, judicial activism, and private litigation in the United States compared with their almost complete absence in Britain. Canada sits, perhaps uncomfortably, halfway across this spectrum, and in the environmental field legalism from the late 1980s, as Hoberg notes, 'sent shock waves' through the Canadian community of environmental regulators. British policy makers were very careful to avoid U.S.-style legalism. There are no formal provisions for judicial accountability in the British regulatory system beyond the standard legislative duties and the normal requirements of judicial review – which in Britain is extremely weak. This shying-away from the law seems appropriate, since the general tendency in new forms of regulatory implementation is to pursue methods of negotiation, flexibility, or self-regulation.

Compliance rests on a respect for the legitimacy of the regulatory statutes, agencies, and procedures, and on reciprocal trust between regulators and the regulated (Wilks 1996). Various mechanisms are available to increase trust and understanding, including hearings in the United States and consultation in the UK. Priority is also increasingly being given to transparency and to the availability of appropriate information provided on a consistent basis. As Doern remarks in Chapter 2, information asymmetry is conventionally regarded as providing a powerful advantage for regulated companies, but information can also be used to encourage compliance. Companies can be required to release stipulated information to regulators, employees, consumers, and the public at large, thus allowing wider participation in the regulatory process. This is especially valuable where performance can be compared among equivalent competitors, which provides a basis for 'yardstick regulation.' Information is widely available in the United States and fuels private litigation. In the UK, information is more closely guarded, with perhaps excessive importance given to the observation of commercial confidentiality. All the same, some extremely telling statistics are available, as analysed in Booker's chapter on the performance of the water companies. The groups best able to utilize information are the statutory consumer bodies attached to each regulatory office. They undoubtedly lobby internally and have an effect, but of course they are to a large degree 'captured' by the regulator. Doern observes the contrast between the well-developed consumer movement in the UK and the consumer groups analysed by Locke, as against the collapse of the consumer movement in North America. As Doern points out, however, North America may have transcended the need for consumer organizations, which have been replaced by well-informed individual consumers, litigants, and public lobbies.

The same principle of using abstract, impersonal forces to induce compliance applies to market forces as well as to information. The development of 'incentive regulation' in the UK is nicely described by Vass, who goes into some of the details of the way in which the RPI-X formula has been designed. Some common technical procedures have been developed, but Vass also presents an appeal for a better understanding of the principle of incentive regulation that amounts, in his interpretation, to an effective way of creating and sharing profits. British-style incentive regulation has attracted wide attention in North America. It has been adopted in Canadian telecommunications price control as of May 1997 and is resulting in a reappraisal of rate-of-return regulation in the United States. In practice, of course, RPI-X and rate-of-return calculations have similarities, and the latter calculations are used to set X, but the regulatory philosophy and the idea of periodic reviews also distinguish the British system. A third approach to enhancing compliance can be seen in the increased recourse to negotiated regulation and to self-regulation. In a sense, all regulation is negotiated. This is widely accepted in the literature reviewed by Doern and Wilks in Chapter 1, and Wilks maintains in Chapter 6 that negotiation was explicitly recognized in the RPI-X formula. But, as Vass, Booker, and Hill all show, negotiation is now more easily accepted as a normal and productive part of the regulatory process, rather than as a rather suspect and concealed reality. Negotiated regulation directs attention to the regulatory partners, which for most regulation, and certainly for utility regulation, means private-sector companies.

There is no doubt that industrial or company self-regulation is one of the prime areas for administrative reform. There are many cross currents at work, so that, on the one hand, we see extensive formal regulation of previously self-regulated industries – a prime example being the British financial services industry described by Hogwood – and on the other an increase in self-regulation in telecommunications, in the environmental field (although Hoberg is very sceptical about voluntary compliance here), and in the UK water industry. Indeed, Booker mentions the intriguing idea of an 'independent reporter' employed by water companies to report back to OFWAT on the effectiveness of self-regulation. Budgetary pressures also lead to increased self-regulation, which takes many forms, including regulation by trade associations, through codes of conduct, by cross-industry agreements, by individual companies, and by compliance departments within companies. Such self-regulation can be voluntary or 'enforced,' it can be indicative or statutory, or it can be legally enforceable by private action or simply enforced by moral suasion. Wilks analyses the relationship between companies and regulators, and suggests that there are so many pressures and incentives for companies to break the regulatory bargain that they are not to be trusted. He suggests that a greater emphasis should be placed on stakeholder involvement and on reform of corporate governance.

The logic of Wilks's argument in Chapter 6, and of those of Doern in Chapter 2 and Peters in Chapter 3, is that in comparing regimes we should be comparing the relationship between regulators and regulated, and that we should be comparing the regimes as a whole, including companies and other market actors. Since regulation is essentially about structuring private-sector activity, it makes sense to examine it as a form of economic governance, and in the third part of this section we pursue that approach.

Regulation and Economic Governance

An implicit theme in all of the chapters on economic regulation is the importance of competition as a supplement to, or substitute for, regulation. This arises from the paradigm shift in economic regulation, which, in the 1930s, was posited on a suspicion of competition and was designed as 'public interest' regulation, but which, in the 1980s, became based on a suspicion of government and was designed as 'regulated competition.' This shift from perceptions of market failure to perceptions of government failure gave rise in the UK to privatization and regulation, and in the United States and Canada to deregulation and the management of regulation within the state.

This reconceptualization of regulation as a means by which competition can be created, encouraged, or exploited in a market setting directs attention to regulation as a form of 'economic governance,' in which markets are constituted and coordinated through the regulatory framework. This expands the focus of regulation beyond the concern with policies, organizations, and intragovernmental relations (which is the prime focus of many of our chapters) to a concern with the whole market and the range of actors within it. These actors include the consumers analysed by Locke, the businesses dealt with by Wilks, and the lobby groups discussed by Francis and Hoberg. It also emphasizes a further 'law' of regulatory studies, which is that 'market structure is the single most important influence on regulatory performance.'

Market structure changes according to many factors. In earlier chapters authors have emphasized internationalization, technological development, mergers, and new categories of consumers. The chapters on telecommunications by Doern and by Graham recount the fundamental way in which new competitive possibilities created by technology have altered the regulatory equation. Suddenly the majority of telecommunications activities no longer have natural monopoly characteristics, and the UK telecommunications regulator can contemplate a shift to applying horizontal, generic competition law (see Graham in Chapter 14). But market structure also changes in response to regulation. The British experiment in electricity regulation comprises a determined and persistent attempt to create a competitive market. Such attempts are fraught with uncertainties and perverse outcomes. Nonetheless, every regulatory statute and regulatory agency has profound effects on the market. Indeed, that is their purpose. As Vietor (1994, 310) observes, 'by viewing regulation primarily as a market-structuring process, we can see that each regulatory policy or program has a host of consequences that are often unanticipated and frequently undesirable.' From this perspective we would therefore advance a plea for economic regulation to be considered not simply as a government output or a policy instrument, but as the governing arrangements for some defined sector of the market.

To understand regulation and its effects it is therefore necessary to review the responses of multiple market actors to regulatory constraints, and to analyse the dynamic process thus set in motion. This is the perspective pursued by Wilks in Chapter 6, in which he examines the reciprocal relationship between regulators and their prime regulatory targets – the companies. He argues that reform of the companies is as important as reform of regulatory arrangements, and therefore puts forward the case for company-law reform in Britain to improve the corporate governance of utilities. In making this argument he also taps into linkages with a wider debate on various kinds of capitalist systems and the way in which companies in different countries treat their 'stakeholders.' This is very much a current debate in the UK, and one that is linked to the victory of New Labour in the 1997 election and its program to reform British capitalism. For our purposes, we should draw attention to the differences between U.S., Canadian, and British companies. Companies in the United States are fiercely free enterprize in rhetoric, but have learned to live with regulation and to accept a share of social responsibility – reinforced by vocal lobbyists and a critical public. Canadian companies work within a tradition of public enterprize and economic redistribution that grows out of the perennial tension with the United States and the imperatives of binding together a huge and economically diverse nation (Hardin 1974, 300). British companies, argues Wilks, are systemically irresponsible and have still to develop the more responsible attitudes that would contribute to a constructive regulatory partnership. Our point is that comparison of regulatory regimes must recognize that the national settings in which regimes are embedded include important variations in the key economic actors – the companies.

Paths to Reform

The final part of our account is to convey the twin ideas that regulatory reform is ubiquitous in our three subject countries, and that reform is progressing along distinctive national paths. In the language of institutional analysis, reform can be said to be 'path dependent.'

Nowhere in our chapters do we find complete satisfaction with current arrangements. The spectrum stretches from the support that Vass expresses for the British system of utility regulation to the discontent with which Hoberg regards Canadian environmental regulation. The chapters convey a process of continuing change and re-examination, driven by the conventional considerations of efficiency, equity, and accountability, but also by the volatile conditions that we associate with the last quarter of the twentieth century – technological change, globalization, expanded markets, aggressive business strategies, and, of course, the creation and adaptation of the regulatory state. It is a curiosity that the magnitude of regulatory change has released a 'gale of creative destruction' that can be compared with the market forces Schumpeter so vividly described. Revolutionary change in the U.S. airline industry, in British financial services, and in the British energy industries has been created by regulatory change, which in turn has been fostered by governments under slogans such as 'deregulation' and Reagan's 'regulatory relief.' We prefer the term 'regulatory reform,' which is less normative and which conveys the reality of continuing regulation. The term 'regulatory management' is also attractive in conveying the idea that regulation has become a systematic concern of public policy and constitutional principle.

What, then, of the direction of change? Our theme and assumption has been that there is much to be learned by comparing the change in regulatory institutions in Canada, the United States, and the United Kingdom. But while regulation has been affected by foreign examples, we actually find few cases of direct or mechanical policy borrowing. The world of regulators is sophisticated in Britain and North America. Those who design regulation have access to competent technical advice, and they have a refined understanding of what will be accepted by the markets and will find political support. The transmission mechanisms that appear to convey regulatory ideas to developing countries and the states of Eastern Europe include private consultants, aid agencies, and the World Bank. These mechanisms do not feature in transatlantic exchange. Foreign examples are extremely important in generating new ideas, in offering practical examples of how alternative arrangements work, and in providing confidence and legitimacy for reform proposals. These processes are undoubtedly helped by a common language, a common cultural inheritance, and a regular exchange of academics, officials, and ministers between countries that also include Australia and New Zealand. Thus ideas about independent regulation, the promotion of competition, price control formulas, consumer participation and self-regulation provide a common discourse, but it is one that generates quite variable institutional configurations in the three countries.

If foreign examples have had only a limited impact on regulatory design, then what elements do provide a path to reform? Hogwood reviews the range of available explanations in the British case. While he admits the existence of identifiable patterns, he sees no consistent logic and opts for 'ad hoc additionality' in regulatory innovation. In a comparative context, we stress again the idea of 'path dependency,' which has been explored since the mid-1960s. It is a basic concept in the approach to the analysis of political and economic change that is normally termed 'new institutionalist' (or 'historical institutionalism,' as Peters describes it in Chapter 3). Path dependency recognizes the weight of history and the inertia embedded in contemporary institutional arrangements. It suggests that when change is undertaken, the repertoire of alternatives is composed of historical experiences and incremental variations on existing arrangements that are politically acceptable and economically rational. In his extended review of path dependence, for instance, North stresses the transaction costs involved in adopting radical new economic arrangements (North 1990, 96), a lesson amply confirmed in Eastern Europe where old behaviours and old organizational forms die hard (Stark 1994). Path dependence is not deterministic. At each point of choice, several alternatives are available, but the weight of political bargaining, institutional inertia, and cultural legacies – not least those enshrined in law – will tend to sustain a nationally specific path. This enhances the possibilities for prediction. North concludes that 'although the specific short-run paths are unforeseeable, the overall direction in the long run is both more predictable and more difficult to reverse' (North 1990, 104). Major discontinuities in regulatory change do occur, but if anything they reinforce the general expectation of continuity. And in any case discontinuities are often relative. For example, the creation of OFTEL, reviewed by Hogwood and by Graham, was conditioned by the nature of British ministerial responsibility, the autonomy of the big company to be regulated (British Telecom), and the availability of the Office of Fair Trading as a model of independent regulation. Moreover, the whole process of regulatory design, which has had such far-reaching implications, was undertaken by pragmatic officials, under acute time pressure, and with a limited legislative brief. They produced an ingenious solution, but it was one that was very 'British' and was sensitively attuned to British administrative practices. Indeed, one could almost argue that the creation of the enlightened, independent regulator – a select and enlightened individual (to paraphrase Foster 1992, 286) – harks back to the pre-modern English gentleman magistrate. So too, in the American and Canadian settings, the analyses advanced by Schultz and Doern, Peters, and Francis stress the continuities and the perpetuation of distinctive regulatory priorities and national traditions.

We therefore maintain that regulatory reform in the countries we have studied follows a distinctive national path, and that the 'regulatory state' and its component regimes are an expression of the peculiar histories of each nation state. We also maintain that there is a greater degree of cross-fertilization between countries that is beginning to exhibit an involuntary dimension. Regulatory change is beginning to be imposed on states by international agreement (particularly the influence of the EU on the UK) and by the imperatives of international competitiveness. Both of these forces are still marginal compared to national determinants, but will become much more important over the next decade. National paths will be challenged by international dynamics, and this means that both practitioners and academics must become more systematically aware of foreign practices. This is where we hope that this book has made a contribution. As Graham points out, regulatory theories are discipline-specific. It is difficult for economists to adapt formal models to varying national political and organizational arrangements, but it comes naturally to political scientists. Where economists tend to be 'state neutral' in their analyses, political scientists are 'state specific.' We certainly do not have the last word on contemporary regulatory studies in this volume, but we trust that this area of comparative political economy will expand rapidly so that regulatory design can be undertaken with a fuller analysis of domestic options and international pressures.

REFERENCES

Ayres, I., and J. Braithwaite. 1992. *Responsive Regulation: Transcending the Deregulation Debate*. Oxford: Oxford University Press.

Baldwin, R. 1995. *Rules and Government*. Oxford: Clarendon.

Berger, S., and R. Dore, eds. 1996. *National Diversity and Global Capitalism*. Ithaca: Cornell University Press.

Bernstein, M. 1955. *Regulation by Independent Commission*. Princeton: Princeton University Press.

Doern, G. Bruce, Margaret M. Hill, Michael J. Prince, and Richard J. Schultz, eds. 1998. *Changing the Rules: Canadian Regulatory Regimes and Institutions*. Toronto: University of Toronto Press.

Foster, C.D. 1992. *Privatization, Public Ownership and the Regulation of Natural Monopoly*. Oxford: Blackwell.

Hancher, L., and Moran, M. 1989. *Capitalism, Culture and Economic Regulation*. Oxford: Clarendon.

Hardin, H. 1974. *A Nation Unaware: The Canadian Economic Culture*. Vancouver: J.J. Douglas.

Harris, R., and S. Milkis. 1996. *The Politics of Regulatory Change: A Tale of Two Agencies*. 2nd ed. Oxford: Oxford University Press.

Hood, C., and C. Scott. 1996. 'Bureaucratic Regulation and New Public Management in the United Kingdom: Mirror Image Developments.' *Journal of Law and Society* 23, no. 3 (September):321–45.

Hutton, W. 1996. *The State We're In*. London: Vintage.

Majone, G., ed. 1996. *Regulating Europe*. London: Routledge.

– 1997. 'The New European Agencies: Regulation by Information.' *Journal of European Public Policy* 4, no. 2 (June): 262–75.

North, D. 1990. *Institutions, Institutional Change and Economic Performance*. Cambridge: Cambridge University Press.

Ogus, A. 1994. *Regulation: Legal Form and Economic Theory*. Oxford: Clarendon.

Pildes, R., and C. Sunstein. 1995. 'Reinventing the Regulatory State.' *University of Chicago Law Review* 62, no. 1 (winter):1–129.

Shapiro, M. 1997. 'The Problems of Independent Agencies in the United States and the European Union.' *Journal of European Public Policy* 4, no. 2 (June): 276–91.

Stark, D. 1994. 'Path Dependence and Privatisation Strategies in East-Central Europe.' In *Changing Political Economies: Privatization in Post-Communist and Reforming Communist States*, edited by V. Milor, 115–46. London: Lynne Rienner.

Stelzer, I. 1996. 'Lessons for UK Regulation from the US Experience,' In *Regulating Utilities: A Time for Change?*, edited by M. Beesley. London: IEA.

Sunstein, C. 1990. *After the Rights Revolution: Reconceiving the Regulatory State*. Cambridge, Mass.: Harvard University Press.

Vietor, R. 1994. *Contrived Competition: Regulation and Deregulation in America*. Cambridge, Mass.: Harvard University Press.

Wilks, S. 1996. 'Regulatory Compliance and Capitalist Diversity in Europe.' *Journal of European Public Policy* 3, no. 4 (December):536–59.

Contributors

Alan Booker is deputy director general of the Office of Water Services (OFWAT) in the UK. A civil engineer by profession, he was for several years the chief executive of the East Worcestershire Water Company. He has written and spoken widely in the UK and Europe about water and related environmental regulation. He has taken a particular interest in bringing together the offices of the sectoral utility regulators in the UK to discuss common issues and approaches.

G. Bruce Doern is a professor in the School of Public Administration, Carleton University, and holds a joint chair in public policy in the Politics Department, University of Exeter. His recent books include *Comparative Competition Policy* (1995, co-edited with Stephen Wilks), *Border Crossings: The Internationalization of Canadian Public Policy* (1996, co-edited with Brian Tomlin and Leslie Pal), and *The Greening of Canada* (1994, co-authored with Tom Conway).

John Francis is a professor in the Department of Political Science at the University of Utah. He is the author of *The Politics of Regulation* (1993).

Cosmo Graham is the H.K. Bevan professor of law at the University of Hull. He is the co-author (with Tony Prosser) of *Privatising Public Enterprises: Constitutions, the State and Regulation in Comparative Perspective* (1991) and the author of *Consumer Representation and Privatised Utilities* (1996). He is also co-editor of the journal *Utilities Law Review.*

Margaret M. Hill is a visting professor in the School of Public Administration, Carleton University, and was formerly a lecturer in comparative public policy and public administration at the Politics Department, University of Exeter. She is the author of *Changing the Rules: Canadian Regulatory Regimes and Institutions* (1998, co-edited with G. Bruce Doern, M. Prince, and R. Schultz), as well as several articles and reports on comparative and Canadian regulation. She has also worked as a consultant and adviser to several federal departments and regulatory bodies in Canada, and is currently a senior policy adviser at Environment Canada.

George Hoberg is a professor in the Department of Political Science, University of British Columbia. He is the author of *Pluralism by Design; Environmental Policy and the American Regulatory State* (1993) and *Risk, Science and Politics* (1994, with Kathryn Harrison), as well as numerous journal articles on social regulation.

Brian W. Hogwood is a professor in the Department of Government at the University of Strathclyde. He is the author of *Trends in British Public Policy* (1990), *From Crisis to Complacency? Shaping Public Policy in Britain* (1987), and *The Pathology of Public Policy* (1985, with Guy Peters).

Stephen Locke is a consultant with Anderson Consulting in London. A former director of policy for the Consumers Association in the UK, he has written extensively on consumer issues and regulatory policy in several regulatory sectors. He has also been an expert witness before several parliamentary and other committees concerned with regulatory and consumer matters.

B. Guy Peters is the Maurice Falk professor of American government in the Department of Political Science, University of Pittsburgh, and is a co-editor of the policy journal *Governance*. He is the author of *Governance in a Changing Environment* (1995, co-edited with Donald Savoie), *The Future of Governing* (1996), *The Politics of Taxation: A Comparative Perspective* (1991), and *The Politics of Bureaucracy* (1988).

Richard Schultz is a professor of political science at McGill University and formerly director of the Centre for the Study of Regulated Industries at McGill. He is the author of *Changing the Rules: Canadian Regulatory Regimes and Institutions* (1998, co-edited with G. Bruce Doern, M. Hill, and M. Prince), *Economic Regulation and the Federal System* (1985, with Alan Alexandroff), and *Federalism, Bureaucracy and Public Policy* (1980).

Peter Vass is a senior lecturer at the School of Management, University of Bath. He is also the research director of the Centre for the Study of Regulated

Industries. He is the author of *Incentive Regulation: A Theoretical and Historical Review* (1996, with D. O'Neill) and *Regulating the Utilities: Accountability and Process* (1994, editor). He served as a special adviser in 1996 to the House of Commons Trade and Industry Committee in its inquiry into energy regulation.

Stephen Wilks is a professor of politics at the University of Exeter. He is the author of *Comparative Competition Policy: National Institutions in a Global Market* (1995, co-edited with G. Bruce Doern), *The Office of Fair Trading in Administrative Context* (1994), *Comparative Government-Industry Relations* (1987, with Maurice Wright), and *The Promotion and Regulation of Industry in Japan* (1991, with Maurice Wright).